The Irish Brigades, 1685–2006

The Heroic Dead of Ireland have every right to the homage of the living: for they proved in some of the heaviest fighting of the World War that the unconquerable spirit of the Irish race – the spirit that has placed them among the world's greatest soldiers – still lives and is stronger than it ever was. I had occasions to put to the test the valour of the Irishmen serving in France, and, whether they were Irishmen from the North or the South, or from one party or another, they did not fail me.

MARSHAL FOCH
speaking at the Armistice Day Commemoration in Paris
9 November 1928

The Irish Brigades, 1685–2006

A gazetteer of Irish military service, past and present

DAVID MURPHY

FOUR COURTS PRESS

Set in 10 on 12 point Ehrhardt for
FOUR COURTS PRESS LTD
7 Malpas Street, Dublin 8, Ireland
e-mail: info@fourcourtspress.ie
http://www.fourcourtspress.ie
and in North America by
FOUR COURTS PRESS
c/o ISBS, 920 N.E. 58th Avenue, Suite 300, Portland, OR 97213.

© The Military Heritage of Ireland Trust, 2007

ISBN 978–1–84682–080–9

A catalogue record for this title
is available from the British Library.

All rights reserved. No part of this publication may be reproduced,
stored in or introduced into a retrieval system, or transmitted, in any
form or by any means (electronic, mechanical, photocopying, recording
or otherwise), without the prior written permission of both the
copyright owner and the publisher of this book.

Printed in England
by MPG Books, Bodmin, Cornwall.

Contents

LIST OF ILLUSTRATIONS	xi
FOREWORD	xiii
ACKNOWLEDGMENTS	xv
INTRODUCTION	xvii
NOTES ON FORMATIONS AND ON RANKING SYSTEMS	xxiii

1 THE STUART ARMY ESTABLISHMENT, 1689–97   1
   Campaigns of James II   1
   The exiled Stuart army in France   6

2 IRISH SOLDIERS IN AUSTRIAN SERVICE, 1689–1918   8
   The regiments   8

3 IRISH REGIMENTS IN FRENCH SERVICE, 1685–1871   10
   The Regiment of Walsh, 1662–1791   12
   The Regiment of Bulkeley, 1683–1775 (Regiment of Mountcashel/
      Regiment of Lee)   15
   The Regiment of Clare, 1689–1775   17
   The Regiment of Dillon, 1690–1791   20
   The Regiment of Berwick, 1698–1791   23
   The Regiment of Galmoy, 1698–1715   25
   The Regiment of Fitzjames, 1698–1762 (originally the
      Regiment of Sheldon)   27
   The Regiment of Lally, 1744–66   28
   Quebec Company, 1756–7   30
   Irish Bourbon regiments in the British service, 1794–8   30
      1st Regiment of the Irish Brigade: Régiment de le Duc de Fitzjames   31
      2nd Regiment of the Irish Brigade: Régiment de le
         Comte de Walsh-Serrant   31
      3rd Regiment of the Irish Brigade: Régiment de Dillon   32
      4th Regiment of the Irish Brigade: Régiment de le Comte O'Connell   32
      5th Regiment of the Irish Brigade: Régiment de le
         Vicomte de Walsh-Serrant   33
      6th Regiment of the Irish Brigade   33
   Légion Irlandaise, 1803–15   33
   La Compagnie Irlandaise, 1870–1   38
   The Franco-Irish Ambulance, 1870–1   39

4 IRISH REGIMENTS IN SPANISH SERVICE, 1709–1939   41

The 'Wild Geese' regiments, 1709–1818   41
- The Irlanda Regiment, 1699–1818   42
- The Ultonia Regiment, 1709–1818   44
- The Hibernia Regiment, 1709–1818   47

Irish regiments in the British Legion in the Carlist War, 1835–8   51
Irish volunteers in the Spanish Civil War, 1936–9   53
- XV Bandera, Legión Extranjera (pro-Nationalist Irish brigade)   53
- 16th British Battalion, XV International Brigade (Republican army)   54

5 IRISH REGIMENTS IN ITALIAN SERVICE, 1702–1862   57

The Irish Bodyguard of the Duke of Parma, 1702–33   57
Regimento Infanteria del Rey (previously the Regiment of Limerick)   60
The St Patrick's Battalion, 1860 and the St Patrick's Company, 1860–2   62

6 IRISH REGIMENTS IN NORTH AND SOUTH AMERICA   65

The Volunteers of Ireland or Loyal Volunteers of Ireland (later, the 105th (King's Irish) Regiment of Foot, 1777–84   66
Irish troops in the army of Simón Bolívar, 1817–21   67
The Irish regiment in Brazil, 1826–8   68
San Patricio Battalion, 1846–8   69
Irish regiments in the Union army, 1861–5   70
- 69th New York Volunteer Infantry Regiment, 1849–2006   72
  - 69th New York State Militia   72
  - 69th New York Volunteer Infantry   73
  - 69th New York National Guard Artillery Regiment, serving as infantry (182nd New York Infantry Regiment, Corcoran Legion)   74
- 7th Missouri Volunteer Infantry Regiment, 1861–4: 'The Irish Seventh'   78
- 9th Massachusetts Volunteer Infantry Regiment, 1861–4   79
- 23rd Illinois Volunteer Infantry Regiment, 1861–5 ('Mulligan's Irish Brigade')   80
- 63rd New York Volunteer Infantry Regiment, 1861–5   81
- 88th New York Volunteer Infantry Regiment, 1861–5   82
- The Irish Dragoons, 1861–5   83
- 9th Connecticut Infantry, 1861–5   84
- 28th Massachusetts Infantry, 1861–5   85
- 37th New York Volunteer Infantry Regiment, 1861–3, 'The Irish Rifles'   86
- 69th Pennsylvania Volunteer Infantry Regiment, 1861–5   87
- 116th Pennsylvania Volunteer Infantry Regiment, 1862–5   88
- 30th Missouri Volunteer Infantry Regiment, 1862–5   89
- 17th Wisconsin Infantry Regiment, 1862–5 ('Wisconsin Irish Brigade')   90
- Corcoran's Irish Legion, 1862–5   91

Irish units in the army of the Confederate States of America, 1861–5   94
- 6th Louisiana Volunteers   95
- 10th Tennessee Infantry Regiment (Irish) Confederate States Volunteers   96

Contents

A list of Irish units in the army of the Confederate States of America	98
The Fenians in America	104

7 IRISH REGIMENTS IN THE BRITISH ARMY, 1685–2006 — 105

Larger Irish formations in the British army, 1899–2006	106
The 18th Royal Irish Regiment, 1684–1922	109
4th Royal Irish Dragoon Guards, 1685–1922	116
6th Inniskilling Dragoons	120
27th (Inniskilling) Regiment of Foot (later the Royal Inniskilling Fusiliers, 1689–1968	128
5th Royal Irish Lancers, 1689–1922	139
8th King's Royal Irish Hussars, 1693–2006	144
The Royal Irish Artillery, 1755–1801	159
18th King's Irish Hussars, 1759–1821	163
The Royal Irish Rifles, later the Royal Ulster Rifles	166
83rd Regiment of Foot	166
86th Regiment of Foot	168
The Royal Irish Fusiliers (Princess Victoria's)	175
87th Regiment of Foot	176
89th Regiment of Foot	177
Princess Victoria's (Royal Irish Fusiliers)	179
The Connaught Rangers	184
88th Regiment of Foot	185
94th Regiment of Foot	187
The Royal Dublin Fusiliers, 1881–1922	191
The Madras Europeans, later the 102nd Regiment of Foot (Royal Madras Fusiliers) and from 1881 the 1st Battalion, Royal Dublin Fusiliers	191
The Bombay Europeans, later the 103rd Regiment of Foot (Royal Bombay Fusiliers) and from 1881 the 2nd Battalion, Royal Dublin Fusiliers in 1881	193
The Royal Munster Fusiliers, 1881–1922	199
101st Regiment of Foot (Royal Bengal Fusiliers), later the 1st Battalion, Royal Munster Fusiliers	199
104th Regiment of Foot (Bengal Fusiliers), later the 2nd Battalion, Royal Munster Fusiliers	201
The Prince of Wales's Leinster Regiment (Royal Canadians), 1881–1922	205
100th Foot or Prince of Wales's Royal Canadian Regiment, later the 1st Battalion of the Prince of Wales's Leinster Regiment (Royal Canadians)	206
109th Bombay Infantry, later the 2nd Battalion of the Prince of Wales's Leinster Regiment (Royal Canadians)	207
The Prince of Wales's Leinster Regiment (Royal Canadians)	208
The London Irish Rifles, 1860–2006	213

64th Lancashire (Liverpool Irish) Rifle Volunteers Corps, later the 8th
(Irish) Battalion, the King's (Liverpool) Regiment, 'The Liverpool Irish',
1860–2006   216
The Imperial Yeomanry, 1900–2   219
The Irish Guards, 1900–2006   220
The South Irish Horse, 1902–22   226
The North Irish Horse, 1902–2006   228
The Tyneside Irish Brigade, 1914–18   231
Reserve Cavalry Regiments, 1914–18   232
The Royal Irish Rangers, 1968–92   234
The Ulster Defence Regiment, 1970–92   235
The Royal Irish Regiment, 1992–2006   236
Reserve, Militia and Volunteer units, 1744–2006 (British Army)   238
    The Fencible Regiments, 1756–1803   238
    The Volunteers, 1744–93   239
Regiments of the Irish Militia   244
The Territorial Army of Northern Ireland   250

8   SOUTH AFRICAN IRISH REGIMENTS, 1885–2006   252
The South African Irish Regiment   252
Irish Commandos in the 2nd Anglo-Boer War, 1899–1902   255
1st Irish Transvaal Brigade   255
2nd Irish Transvaal Brigade   257

9   NEW SOUTH WALES IRISH RIFLES, 1896–1930   259

10   CANADIAN IRISH REGIMENTS, 1859–2006   261
The Irish Canadian Rangers, 1914–18   261
The Canadian Irish Fusiliers, 1913–45   262
The Irish Regiment of Canada, 1915–2006   263

11   THE IRISH DEFENCE FORCES   266
Irish Volunteer forces in Dublin, April 1916   267
National Army Organization, July 1923   274
Defence Forces Organization, 1926   276
Defence Forces Organization on 1 December 1940   280
Defence Forces Organization on 31 December 1944   282
Defence Forces Organization on 31 December 1970   284
Defence Forces Organization, 2004   285
Irish United Missions, 1958–2006   287
    Organisation de Nations Unies au Congo   287
    UN Forces in Cyprus   288
    UNIFIL: United Nations Interim Force in Lebanon, 1978
      to the present   289
Army reserves in the Irish Defence Forces, 1923–2006   293

Local Defence Forces Organization	295
FCA establishment, 1970	299
Pre-2005 FCA establishment	301
Establishment of the Reserve Defence Forces	301
ARCHIVES	303
MUSEUMS	304
SELECT BIBLIOGRAPHY	305
ADDENDUM	311

Illustrations

appear between pp 104 and 105, and 200 and 201

1. A private and officer of the Regiment of Dillon, c.1724.
2. A trooper of the cavalry Regiment of Fitzjames, c.1740.
3. A private in the Irish company of Quebec, 1756.
4. Contemporary illustration of an officer and private of Napoleon's Irish Legion.
5. A voluntary hospital during the Franco-Prussian War.
6. Uniforms and colours of the Spanish regiments of Irlanda and Hibernia, c.1740.
7. Uniforms of the Spanish regiments of Ultonia, Irlanda and Hibernia after 1802.
8. An 1802 illustration of the regiment of Hibernia.
9. The British Legion in action during the First Carlist War of 1833–40.
10. Count Maximilian Ulysses Browne (d.1757), an Irish officer in the Austrian service.
11. A grenadier of the 18th Royal Irish Regiment at Namur, 1695.
12. Sergeant Masterson of the 87th Foot capturing the French eagle at Barrosa, 1811.
13. An officer of the Inniskilling Dragoons, c.1825.
14. Troopers of the 8th King's Royal Irish Hussars in the Crimea, 1854.
15. Uniforms of the 86th Foot during the Indian Mutiny, 1857.
16. The colours of the 89th Foot in 1866.
17. A Simkin illustration of 1897 showing uniforms of the Irish regiments.
18. The landings from the *River Clyde* at Gallipoli in 1915.
19. V-Beach at Galliploi, as seen from the *River Clyde*.
20. The Tyneside Irish going over the top at the Somme 1916.
21. Men of the 1st Bn Royal Irish Regiment in Palestine in 1917.
22. The Liverpool Irish entering Lille at the end of WWI.
23. Disbandment parade of the Irish regiments at Winsdor in June 1922.
24. Lord Gort and General Georges inspect the 2nd Bn Royal Inniskilling Fusiliers in France in 1940.
25. Stuart tanks of the 8th King's Royal Irish Hussars in Egypt, 1941.
26. Riflemen of 2nd Bn Royal Ulster Rifles, Normandy, June 1944.
27. The pipe bands of the 38th (Irish) Brigade, Rome, June 1944.
28. Uniforms of the 69th New York National Guard, 1853.
29. Recruiting for the 'Irish Zouaves', 1862.

30 The colour of the 69th New York Volunteers.
31 Captain (later Brigadier-General) Thomas Francis Meagher, 1861.
32 A private of the 69th New York National Guard, 1861.
33 The battle of Fredericksburg, 1862.
34 Major-General Patrick R. Cleburne, Confederate States Army.
35 Confederate guerrilla fighters firing on Mississippi paddle steamers.
36 A soldier of the Fenian 1870 raiding force into Canada.
37 Officers and men of the Hibernian Rifles, 1913.
38 Boer forces firing on British troops during the 2nd Anglo-Boer War, 1899–1902.
39 Officers of the South African Irish Regiment, North Africa, 1941.
40 Pipers of the Irish Regiment of Canada entering Ravenna, 1944.
41 The Cork company of the Irish Volunteers, 1914.
42 Mayo flying column during the War of Independence, 1919–21.
43 Colour Party of the National Army at Griffith Barracks, 1922.
44 Troopers of the Mounted Escort or 'Blue Hussars'.
45 Pre-war photograph of men of the 2nd Infantry Battalion.
46 Parade of troops in Cork during the Emergency.
47 Light anti-aircraft battery at Cobh during the Emergency.
48 Irish troops boarding a plane at Baldonnel aerodrome bound for the Congo.
49 Irish troops of the UNICYP force in Cyprus being inspected.
50 Recruiting for the Pearse Battalion of the FCA at Trinity College, 1960s.
51 Members of 73rd Battalion UNIFIL.
52 An Irish mobile patrol in Somalia, part of the UNOSOM II mission.
53 Members of the Irish army on patrol in East Timor.
54 Irish troops prevent civil disorder while serving with KFOR in Kosovo.
55 Irish UNMIL troops on long range patrol in Liberia.
56 Women members of the Reserve Defence Forces on an artillery potential officers course
57 Members of the Army Ranger Wing on exercise.
58 President Mary McAleese reviews a RDF guard of honour during the Easter commemorations, 2007.

Foreword

For years I have found that sorting out something as apparently straightforward as the location of individual Irish military formations, even for the pretty well-recorded Irish units in the British Army, is both time-consuming and frustrating. Now David Murphy has provided us with a handy single volume providing from the late seventeenth century to the present day not only the location (in Ireland and abroad) of an extraordinary number of organised Irish military formations, but also details of their organisation, deployment, commanding officers, and much else.

The Irish Brigades was commissioned by the Military Heritage of Ireland Trust who are to be warmly congratulated on the fine result of their sponsorship. David Murphy's book now joins Brian Hanley's *A Guide to Irish Military Heritage* (Dublin, 2004) – another Military Heritage of Ireland Trust venture – as essential additions to the library of anyone interested in the military history of Ireland and the Irish across the world.

This book is an extremely useful reference work which also celebrates the wide range and diversity of Irish military service over the past 350 years or so, from the 'Wild Geese' regiments in the French and Spanish service, to the Irish regiment in Brazil in the 1820s, the 1st garrison battalion of the Royal Munster Fusiliers in the Veneto of north-east Italy in 1917–18 and the 55,000 tours of duty which soldiers from the contemporary Irish Defence Forces have completed on United Nations' missions in the Congo, Cyprus, Lebanon and other places. Where else, too, could one readily discover that in the 1860s the 102nd Madras Fusiliers, later the 1st Royal Dublin Fusiliers, had a Bengal tiger named Plassey as a mascot and, perhaps more conventionally (and certainly less hazardously), that the Irish Regiment of Canada's mascot during the Second World War was an Irish wolfhound named Captain Kilkenny?

KEITH JEFFERY
Queen's University Belfast
June 2007

Since the seventeenth century, hundreds of thousands of Irishmen have served in numerous different armies across the world in the name of various causes. During the period covered by this study, Irish soldiers fought in every major war and have campaigned all over the world. This gazetteer is dedicated to the memory of all those who served, fought and died, regardless of which army they served in. It is also dedicated to the memory of their wives and families who, until the 1900s, often shared in the hardships of campaign life, but have since largely disappeared from the pages of history books.

Acknowledgments

In compiling this gazetteer, I have incurred debts of gratitude to numerous people. Considering the large scope of the project, and the limited time and resources available to complete it, the information and assistance given by many people were invaluable to me. Firstly, I would like to thank all those associated with the Military Heritage of Ireland Trust, not only for commissioning me to produce this gazetteer but also for the assistance they gave me while working on it. I would like to thank Professor Eunan O'Halpin of Trinity College Dublin.

My thanks go to Commandant Victor Laing and all the staff at the Military Archives is Dublin. I would also like to thank all the staff of the Infantry School at the Curragh, especially Colonel Don O'Keeffe, Commandant Harry O'Connor and Commandant Gareth Prendergast. I am especially thankful to Commandant Prendergast for allowing me to reproduce some of the photographs in this volume.

At the National Museum of Ireland, I would like to thank Lábhras Joye and Siobhan Pierce who, despite the fact that they were busy preparing a major new military exhibition, were always available with information and support.

The fact that so many primary sources on Irish military history are held in overseas archives proved a major problem. This was overcome to a large degree by the assistance given by both scholars and soldiers from abroad. In France, I would like to thank all the staff at the Service Historique de la Défense at Vincennes. My special thanks are due to Dr Nathalie Genet-Rouffiac for her practical help and also her vast knowledge on the Irish regiments in the French service. The assistance of Monsieur Michel Grimeaux, mayor of Graye-sur-Mer in Normandy, and Xavier Paturel of the Juno Beach Museum, is gratefully acknowledged. In England, I would like to thank Lieutenant-Colonel Bullock-Webster and Mr Dominic Kearney of the Irish Guards. At the Imperial War Museum, the assistance of Sarah Martin and Yvonne Oliver was invaluable. I am particularly indebted to Dr Alicia Laspra-Rodríquez of Oviedo University and General Ramos Oliver of the Spanish Army for information on the later histories of the Irish regiments in Spanish service.

Even further afield, I would like to acknowledge the help of Colonel Abel Esterhuyse and Commander Thean Potgieter of the South African Military Academy and also Colonel Eddie Watson of the South African Irish Regiment. In America, the help of Professor Gregory Hospodor and his insights on Irish units in the Confederacy, were most valuable. I am also indebted to Dr Caroline Rerucha for her advice on Irish units in the American Civil War. Colonel James Tierney of the 69th New York Regiment is deserving of a huge debt of gratitude for providing further information and insight on this most famous Irish regiment. In Canada, my thanks go to Dr Bill Rawlings and Dr Adam Lynde for their help in dealing with Irish-Canadian units.

Numerous other people, on hearing of this project, supplied information and support. My thanks go Aisling Dunne of the Irish Architectural Archive, Catherine Ivers of the US Embassy in Dublin, Dr Anthony McCormack of the Irish History Online Project, Martin Windrow of Osprey Publishing and Mike McNally. I would like to formally acknowledge Ms Mary Bryan for giving me access to the MA thesis of her late sister, Ms Patricia Ann O'Sullivan's, on the duke of Parma's bodyguard.

Many people helped with illustrative material for this gazetteer and I would like to especially thank Billy Galligan of *An Cosantóir* and Seán Ó Brógáin. I owe a special debt of thanks to René Chartrand in Canada for supplying further illustrations. His help in the final stages of this work was much appreciated. Finally, I would like to thank Donna J. Neary for allowing the use of her splendid painting 'Do Your Duty Boys' for the cover of this gazetteer. This evocative work, which depicts one of the most famous episodes in Irish military history, makes a most fitting cover illustration for this gazetteer.

Introduction

What is a regiment? Viewed in straightforward terms it is an administrative unit in an army and the term can be applied to infantry, cavalry and artillery units. A regiment is further subdivided into smaller units such as battalions, companies, troops, batteries and platoons, depending on the branch of service that the regiment belongs to. A basic definition, therefore, would be that it is a military unit that is bigger than a battalion but smaller than a brigade.

Taking the infantry model as an example, on a simple organizational level a regiment represents the administrative family of a battalion or, depending on the historical period, a number of battalions. In 1692, the Irish Regiment of Dillon in the French service consisted of three battalions with a paper establishment of 1,950 men. By 1762 the Regiment of Dillon had been reduced to just one battalion, with an establishment of 675 men. During the First World War, the Royal Irish Rifles was expanded and eventually included twenty-one battalions. Therefore, while the number of battalions and men serving within a regiment may vary, the parent regiment represents the administrative unit to which they all belong. At the same time, the smaller sub-units of a regiment can be deployed independently and in different theatres during the same war or campaign. The simplest way of viewing regimental organization is to view battalions as tactical units and regiments as the parent administrative units.

The date of 1685 was chosen as a start date for this gazetteer as the accession of James II to the throne of England saw the beginning of a new phase of military activity. Many Irish regiments were raised either for James II's service or in the cause of his opponent, William III, and they survived in various services after the end of the Jacobite Wars. For the sake of continuity therefore, 1685 presented itself as a logical start date for any study of Irish regiments. It should be noted, however, that there were Irish regiments in various armies before 1685 and these included the French, Spanish and Austrian services. There is a growing literature on these earlier Irish regiments.

This study is intended to be a gazetteer of all the Irish regiments that have been founded since 1685 and its intention is to outline the history of all major Irish regiments and larger formations. During the course of the last 350 years Irishmen have served in the armies of various European and world powers. In many cases, these men travelled as individuals and then joined various regiments in their adoptive countries. In doing so, they disappear from the record in the context of this study and it should be remembered that while there were numerous Irish regiments serving throughout the world, the majority of Irishmen served in regiments that were not designated as being Irish. This is especially true in the case of the British army. By the mid-nineteenth century, somewhere between 35 and 40 per cent of the British army was composed of Irishmen and the majority of these served in regiments that were not classified as being Irish. In a similar vein, there were large numbers of Irishmen serving in the American army during the nineteenth century but the regiments in which they served were not classed as being Irish.

For example, 128 Irish-born soldiers were serving with the 7th Cavalry at the time of the Little Big Horn campaign in 1876. Yet despite this large Irish contingent and even a regimental tune introduced by an Irish officer, the 7th Cavalry cannot in any way be classed as an Irish regiment, not only because other nationalities were present in large numbers, but also because it was never designated as such.

In the context of this gazetteer, therefore, it has been necessary to concentrate on regiments that were raised in Ireland and regiments that had an Irish designation in their title. To extend the scope of this study to include regiments that had large numbers of Irish soldiers would involve including the majority of the regiments of the British army. Also, during the period of the First World War many regiments raised in Canada and Australia would have had large numbers of Irish emigrants in their ranks but they were never classed as being Irish regiments.

The compiling of this work presented a number of practical problems. Firstly, there is the problem of sources. Due to the fact that the majority of Irish soldiers served outside of Ireland, most of the major archives on Irish regimental history are located outside of Ireland. The primary sources relevant to this work are held in archives in Washington, Richmond, Château Vincennes, London, Madrid, Rome, Johannesburg and numerous other archives across the world.

Secondly, in terms of printed sources, it would be true to say that most regimental histories have been written by people associated with the actual regiment. As the majority of Irish regiments have long since been disbanded, there is a definite lack of modern published secondary sources. The occasional articles that have appeared in military history journals, while useful, are far from being comprehensive. This lack of secondary sources has, however, been partly remedied by a number of new regimental studies, which would seem to indicate that the study of Irish regimental history is once again being viewed as a legitimate field of scholarly interest.

A third and perhaps more serious problem has been the uneven nature of the printed sources. In some cases these have provided comprehensive information. In other cases they provided little of historical value being composed of largely anecdotal material.

The most serious problems in relation to compiling this gazetteer arose in relation to the post-1922 Irish Army. With respect to sources, the new National Army of the Irish Free State never developed the practice of maintaining battalion diaries or publishing official army gazettes on an ongoing basis. As a result, while one might perhaps know that a certain battalion existed during the Irish Civil War or the Emergency period, its movements are difficult to follow. To trace these movements would entail spending a considerable period researching command movement orders and unfortunately this time was not available when compiling this gazetteer.

Introduction

A further problem arises in the case of the Irish Army due to the fact that it does not have a regimental system. Since 1922, many battalions have been raised, disbanded and then later their designations were re-used. This makes it impossible to establish any concept of regimental lineage and has created a highly confusing history of unit formation, disbandment, re-formation, designation and re-designation. In many ways, it is not the question of formation and disbandment of units that has created this problem. It is the re-use of the battalion designations that creates confusion as in no case did the army promote the idea that the subsequent battalions were successor units to the original Civil War battalions.

This does not mean, however, that soldiers serving in the Irish Defence Forces have not tried to foster and observe their own traditions. The majority of Irish soldiers have shown great pride in their numbered battalions and most servicemen and women today would have some awareness of their unit's earlier history. It would also be true to say that Irish soldiers display justifiable pride in their unit's involvement with the United Nations missions. While the personnel for all Irish UN battalions have been drawn from numerous different units, those who have served on UN duty have retained a sense of collective unit identity long after their mission has ended and their UN battalion has been disbanded. In a similar vein, the parent units that have provided personnel for UN battalions are profoundly aware of the contribution that they have made to peacekeeping missions and of the losses they have suffered during this overseas service.

The research for this gazetteer has shown that, during the period in question, there were several broad types of Irish regiments. These included exiled Wild Geese regiments, regiments in the British Army and East India Company and also regiments raised among the emigrant communities of America, Canada, Australia and South Africa. Occasionally specific political causes resulted in new Irish units being formed and we can see examples of this in the battalion raised to serve in the Papal service in 1860 and also the Irish units that served in the Spanish Civil War, on both sides. Finally, from 1922 we can see the creation of a new army in Ireland itself, which has developed in various stages and, since the 1950s, played an important part in UN missions.

These regiments are organized within this gazetteer on a country by country basis, the earliest formed regiment being the first in each section. It is hoped that this will make the gazetteer more user friendly. It was initially planned to organize the gazetteer on a chronological basis but this would have been incredibly confusing for the reader as new Irish regiments were constantly being formed and in the service of different countries.

When compiling the entries for this gazetteer, an effort was made to provide as much information as possible for each regiment. The primary aim was to create brief but accurate histories of each regiment and that these would provide information on each unit's formation and its major battles and campaigns. In some cases extra information has been included on topics such as regimental colonels, music and mascots. A list of sources is given at the end of the gazetteer and this will allow the reader to source more extensive histories of most of the regiments covered.

The length of the regimental entries was, however, dictated by the availability of sources. While some regiments have quite long entries, others have very brief ones due to the fact that there is little published on them and also that the archive material relating to them is held somewhere abroad. Therefore, where certain regiments have been covered in short entries, this does not reflect any bias on the part of the author or the Military Heritage of Ireland Trust. It merely reflects the difficulties of obtaining source material.

In some cases the total lack of sources has meant that certain regiments were not included in this gazetteer. For example, it is known that the Ancient Order of Hibernians in America began organizing volunteer companies of Hibernian Rifles from around 1900. The almost total absence of sources on these units has resulted in them not being included in this gazetteer. It can only hoped that such omissions will be remedied in later editions in light of further research.

The main focus of this gazetteer is on the actual Irish regiments, rather than the individual soldiers who served in them. As a result, this gazetteer does not focus on individuals such as the many distinguished Irish soldiers who served in Russia and Austria. For those seeking biographical information on individual soldiers, see Brian Hanley's *A guide to Irish military heritage* (Four Courts Press, Dublin, 2004) as a guide to researching service records. This publication, which was also a project of the Military Heritage of Ireland Trust, provides information on how to source information on ex-servicemen and women.

During the compiling of this gazetteer, it became increasingly obvious that numerous subjects connected with the Irish regiments would benefit from further research. Subjects such as Irish volunteer units in antebellum America, the Irish in the Venetian service and the Irish regiments in Spain could all benefit from further research. The service of Irish UN missions would make a interesting topic for research as would several other subjects that are touched upon within this gazetteer. It can only be hoped that some of these subjects will be addressed in the years to come by a new generation of scholars. Due to the dispersed nature of the sources, the perennial problem of research funding is a major one when it comes to carrying out such research. For the few organizations that fund Irish historical research, Irish military history is low on the list of priorities. When writing on the Wild Geese regiments, the Marquess McSwiney called for greater levels of government funding and coordination with academic institutions to:

> Give our scholars and students all the encouragement necessary to enable them to collect and publish in the course of time the huge mass of materials of Irish interest which lie unexplored in the archives of France, Spain, Austria, Italy etc.

Further scholarship would indicate that we can now add to McSwiney's list of countries and include archives in America (both state and national) and also sources in Mexico, South America, South Africa, among other countries. Yet the hoped for coordination and funding has not come and it should be pointed out that the Marquess McSwiney published the above comment in a journal in 1927!

In recent years, there have been many positive developments in this field of study with both scholars and the general public showing an increasing amount of interest in Ireland's military history. The newly opened military exhibition at the National Museum of Ireland, Collins Barracks, is a further acknowledgment of the importance of the military tradition in Irish history. In the introduction to the seminal *A military history of Ireland*, Thomas Bartlett and Keith Jeffery commented that:

> It may not in fact be so surprising if, on examination, an Irish military tradition turns out to be central to the Irish historical experience, and a key element in modern Irish identity.

Currently there is divided opinion once again on the importance of regimental tradition. In 2005, the British Army amalgamated, and effectively destroyed, many of its most historic regiments to create 'super regiments' such as the Royal Regiment of Scotland. It is ironic that the army that fostered the regimental tradition so assiduously over the centuries should do this, especially as British soldiers had recently returned to some of the army's former battlegrounds in Afghanistan and Iraq. This is typical or the increasing tendency to view military units in a utilitarian fashion.

Conversely, other countries continue to foster a regimental tradition, considering it vital for both the morale and performance of their troops. France still maintains a traditional system, simply considering it essential to military life that each regiment should have some form of lineage, tradition and insignia. When regiments are newly raised, they are assigned the lineage or identity of a former disbanded regiment. It is due to this system that the 92ᵉ Regiment of the French army was assigned the linage of the Regiment of Walsh on its creation.

The history of the regiments contained in this gazetteer show that the military aspect of Ireland's history was significant indeed. The Irish regiments played a major role all military campaigns after 1685 and the within their respective histories we can follow the development of the regimental system itself. In modern times, the Irish soldier has continued this tradition of service. As the nature of soldiering has changed, Irish servicemen and women have continued to play an important role in UN peacekeeping duties, on occasion returning to regions where their ancestors campaigned with other armies. The regimental histories outlined in this gazetteer represent a summarized account of a huge Irish military tradition but hopefully they will lead to further research on this important aspect of Ireland's history.

Notes on formations and on ranking systems

A NOTE ON FORMATIONS

The battalions of regiments operate within a larger army structure. In recent times it has become more common to assign support units to a battalion to allow it to operate independently as a Battle Group. The historical practice was to group battalions into larger formations such as brigades and divisions. The large army formations are outlined below in decreasing order of size.

Army Group A large land force formation composed of two or more armies. This is a rare grouping of large units and is used only in tactical deployments and is not a permanently established formation. It will consist of units of all the fighting arms (infantry, artillery and cavalry/armour) and also support arms (medical services, signals and military police etc.). During WWII some army groups consisted of over 600,000 men. An Army Group is commanded by a Field-Marshal or General.

Army In an administrative sense, this term can be taken to include a country's entire armed forces. For example, one could refer to the 'Irish Army'. In tactical terms, it is a land force formation consisting of at least one corps. This would be made up of units of all arms. During WWII some armies were composed of over 150,000 men. This formation is commanded by a Field-Marshal or General.

Corps This is an army formation of two or more divisions. This would include infantry, cavalry and artillery and also support units. This unit would be commanded by a General or Lieutenant-General. During the Arnhem campaign in 1944, the British XXX Corps consisted of around 100,000 men.

Division A formation of two to three brigades. It would consist of 15,000 to 18,000 men and would normally be commanded by a Major-General.

Brigade A formation of two to three battalions, usually of infantry and with supporting cavalry/armour, artillery and other services. It is commanded by a Brigadier-General, although Colonels can sometimes be given command of a brigade. It consists of 3,000 to 4,000 men.

Regiment A largely administrative unit. A regiment is a the largest, permanently established, unit of infantry, cavalry/armour or artillery. This is further sub-divided into Battalions, which serve as the operational units of the regiment. Each battalion is normally commanded by a lieutenant-colonel. A battalion consists of around 500 men.

Company (Squadron, Battery) A unit of around 120 men which is further subdivided into two or three platoons. The Squadron or Battery would be the company-sized unit in the cavalry or artillery. It is commanded by a major/commandant or a captain.

Platoon (Troop) A unit of around 30–40 men, commanded by a lieutenant or 2nd lieutenant. Each platoon is further divided into Sections of around 10 men, each commanded by an NCO.

Since WWII, new formations have developed within armies such as the Brigade Group and the Battle Group. These formations are designed to act independently and usually consist of combined infantry, armour and artillery units. The Brigade Group would consist of usually three infantry battalions but with a larger contingent of support troops in order to allow it to operate with greater independence.

The Battle Group is usually built around a single infantry battalion but with supporting units of armour and artillery to allow it to operate independently on operations that require less than a brigade. The last Irish battle group to see action was the Royal Irish Regiment Battle Group in Iraq.

A NOTE ON RANKING SYSTEMS

The system of ranks within armies has changed greatly over the centuries and some ranks have all but disappeared. This is especially true of ranks associated with the mounted arms and these would have included ranks such as Rough Rider and Farrier. At the same time, different armies developed their own ranking systems and these often included ranks not found in other armies. The French army, for example, maintains the NCO rank of caporal-chef or chief corporal, a rank unique to the French army. The ranking system below represents the modern conventional ranking system and is arranged here in descending order of seniority.

Officers
- Field-Marshal
- General
- Lieutenant-General
- Major-General
- Brigadier-General
- Colonel
- Lieutenant-Colonel
- Major/Commandant
- Captain
- Lieutenant
- 2nd Lieutenant

Warrant officers
- Regimental Sergeant Major
- Regimental Quartermaster Sergeant Major

Non-commissioned officers
- Company Sergeant
- Company Quartermaster Sergeant
- Sergeant
- Corporal
- Lance-Corporal

Enlisted men
The traditional enlisted ranks are Private, Gunner, Trooper or Sapper.

CHAPTER I

The Stuart army establishment, 1689–97

CAMPAIGNS OF JAMES II

The main reason for the large number of Irish military exiles that populated Continental armies during the seventeenth and eighteenth centuries was the 'Glorious Revolution' of 1688 that deposed the Catholic James II; replacing him with the Protestant William of Orange who, with James' daughter Mary, would later rule Britain as William III.

James II sought the support of Louis XIV of France and decided to try to regain his throne by beginning his military campaign in Ireland. On his arrival in Ireland, James II found that some regiments of the old Irish establishment had remained loyal and were available to serve him. These included:

>Three regiments of horse – Tyrconnell's, Russell's and Galway's
>One regiment of dragoons
>Five regiments of infantry – the Foot Guards, MacCarthy's, Clancarty's, Newcomen's and Mountjoy's.

After a massive expansion and reorganization of the Stuart army, this establishment was expanded to include many more. John Dalton listed the following regiments in his *King James' Irish army list*:

>1st Troop Royal Horse Guards, commanded by Henry, Lord Viscount Dover
>2nd Troop Royal Horse Guards, commanded by the Duke of Berwick
>A troop of mounted grenadiers attached to the Horse Guards, commanded by Colonel Butler.

Regiments of horse
Earl of Tyrconnell's Regiment
Lord Galmoy's Regiment
Colonel Patrick Sarsfield's Regiment
Lord Abercorn's Regiment

Colonel Henry Luttrell's Regiment
Colonel Hugh Sutherland's Regiment
Colonel John Parker's Regiment
Colonel Nicholas Purcell's Regiment

Regiments of dragoons
Lord Dongan's Regiment
Sir Neill O'Neill's Regiment

Colonel Robert Clifford's Regiment
Colonel Francis Carroll's Regiment

Lord Clare's Regiment
Colonel Simon Luttrell's Regiment

Brigadier Thomas Maxwell's Regiment

Regiments of foot
The King's Regiment or Foot Guards (2 battalions)
Colonel John Hamilton's Regiment
Colonel Henry Fitzjames's Regiment or the Lord Grand Prior's Regiment
Lord Mountcashel's Regiment
Lord Clancarthy's Regiment
Lord Clanricarde's Regiment
The Earl of Antrim's Regiment
The Earl of Tyrone's Regiment
Colonel Richard Nugent's Regiment
Lord Gormanston's Regiment
Colonel Henry Dillon's Regiment
Lord Galway's Regiment
Lord Bellew's Regiment
Lord Kenmare's Regiment
Lord Slane's Regiment
Colonel Cormuck O'Neill's Regiment
Colonel Charles Cavanagh's Regiment
Colonel Thomas Butler's Regiment
Colonel John Fitzgerald's Regiment
Lord Louth's Regiment
Lord Killmallock's Regiment
Sir Maurice Eustace's Regiment
The Earl of Westmeath's Regiment
Major-General Boisseleau's Regiment
Lord Bophin's Regiment
Colonel Oliver O'Gara's Regiment

Colonel John Grace's Regiment
Colonel Edward Butler's Regiment
Colonel Art McMahon's Regiment
Colonel Charles Moore's Regiment
Colonel Dudley Bagnell's Regiment
Colonel Gordon O'Neill's Regiment
Colonel Nicholas Browne's Regiment
Sir Michael Creagh's Regiment
Sir Heward Oxburgh's Regiment
Colonel Dominick Browne's Regiment
Colonel Owen MacCarties' Regiment
Colonel John Barrett's Regiment
Colonel Charles O'Brien's (O'Brien's) Regiment
Colonel Daniel O'Donovan's Regiment
Lord Iveagh's Regiment
Colonel Roger McElligott's Regiment
Colonel Edmund O'Reilly's Regiment
Colonel Cuconaught MacGuire's Regiment
Colonel Walter Bourke's Regiment
Colonel Felix O'Neill's Regiment
Colonel Hugh McMahon's Regiment
Colonel Denis McGillicuddy's Regiment
Colonel James Purcell's Regiment
Lord Hunsdon's Regiment
Colonel Richard Butler's Regiment
Lord Clare's Regiment

There were also 12 'independent' troops of horse and companies of infantry.

In some cases the colonels of these regiments were changed and later in the war they were known by another name. Many of the infantry regiments never reached full strength and were afterwards disbanded, their personnel being transferred into other regiments. Several regiments were disbanded almost immediately after being raised, due to the shortage of recruits.

Dalton lists these regiments as:

Lord Castleconnel's Regiment
Colonel Roger O'Conor's Regiment

Colonel Bryan McDermott's Regiment
Colonel James Talbot's Regiment

The Stuart army establishment, 1689–97

Sir Charles Geoghegan's Regiment
Colonel Manus O'Donnel's Regiment
Colonel James Roth's Regiment
Colonel Roger Cahane's
  (or O'Cahan's) Regiment
Colonel Christopher Kelly's Regiment
Colonel Ulick Bourke's Regiment
Sir Edmund Scott's Regiment
Colonel Myles Kelly's Regiment
Colonel John Browne's Regiment
Colonel James Butler's Regiment
Colonel Edward Nugent's Regiment

There remains a level of confusion here as some of these regiments that Dalton stated were disbanded early in the campaign, appear on the lists of regiments at later reviews of the army. For example, both Roth's and O'Cahan's regiments are listed as being present at a review of 9 August 1691.

Therefore, there would appear to have been many changes in the Stuart army establishment over this period and the details of later reviews provide information on the composition of the army during this period.

A review of the Stuart army of October 1689 listed the following regiments:

Regiments of Infantry (numbering 15,761 all ranks)
Foot Guards
Lord Antrim's Regiment
Colonel Dudley Bagnal's Regiment
Lord Bellew's Regiment
Major-General Boisseleau's Regiment
Lord Clancarty's Regiment
Lord Clanricarde's Regiment
Colonel Comack O'Neill's Regiment
Sir Michael Creagh's Regiment
Colonel Henry Dillon's Regiment
Colonel Edward Butler's Regiment
Sir Maurice Eustace's Regiment
Lord Galway's Regiment
Lord Gormanston's Regiment
Colonel John Grace's
Lord Grand Prior's Regiment
  (Fitzjames's)
Colonel John Hamilton's Regiment
Lord Kenmare's Regiment
Lord Kilmallock's Regiment
Macarthy Mor's
Lord Mountcashel's Regiment
Colonel Richard Nugent's Regiment
Lord Oxburgh's Regiment
Colonel Richard Butler's Regiment
Lord Slane's Regiment
Colonel Thomas Butler's Regiment

Regiments of horse/cavalry (numbering 1,953 all ranks)
Life Guards
Lord Tyrconnell's Regiment
Lord Galmoy's Regiment
Colonel Patrick Sarsfield's Regiment
Colonel John Parker's Regiment
Lord Abercorn's Regiment
Colonel Henry Luttrell's Regiment
Colonel Nicholas Purcell's

Regiments of dragoons (numbering 1,513 all ranks)
Lord Dongan's Regiment
Colonel Simon Luttrell's Regiment
Colonel Purcell's Regiment
Colonel Cotter's Regiment
Colonel Robert Clifford's Regiment

Jacobite order of battle at the Boyne, taken from the Cookstown review of 24 June 1690:

Regiments of infantry
Foot Guards
Lord Antrim's Regiment
Lord Bellew's Regiment
Colonel Gordon O'Neill's Regiment
Lord Louth's Regiment
Lord Grand Prior's Regiment
 (Fitzjames's)
Colonel John Grace's Regiment
Colonel Art McMahon's Regiment
Colonel Hugh McMahon's Regiment
Colonel John Hamilton's Regiment
Lord Westmeath's Regiment
Sir Michael Creagh's Regiment
Colonel Roger MacElligott's Regiment

Colonel Charles O'Bryan's
 (O'Brien's) Regiment
Major-General Boisseleau's Regiment
Colonel Dudley Bagnal's Regiment
Colonel Dudley Bagnal's Regiment
Lord Tyrone's Regiment
Lord Slane's Regiment
Colonel Henry Dillon's Regiment
Lord Clanrickarde's Regiment
Lord Galway's Regiment
Colonel Walter Bourke's Regiment
Lord Gormanston's Regiment
Colonel Richard Nugent's Regiment

Regiments of horse
Life Guards
Lord Tyrconnell's Regiment
Lord Galmoy's Regiment
Colonel Hugh Sutherland's Regiment

Colonel John Parker's Regiment
Colonel Patrick Sarsfield's Regiment
Lord Abercorn's Regiment

Regiments of dragoons
Brigadier Thomas Maxwell's Regiment
Sir Niall O'Neill's Regiment
Lord Dongan's Regiment

Lord Clare's Regiment
Colonel Robert Clifford's
Colonel Francis Carroll's

There were also a number of French regiments in James II's army. They included the regiments of Famechon, Forez, La Marche, Mérode, Tournaisis and Zurlauben, which together numbered over 7,000 men.

The Jacobite army as reviewed on 9 August 1691 (After the battle of Aughrim)

Regiments of infantry
Foot Guards
Colonel John Grace's Regiment
Colonel Charles Moore's Regiment
Colonel Edward Butler's Regiment
Colonel Michael Burke's Regiment
Lord Bophin's Regiment

Colonel Nicholas Fitzgerald's Regiment
Lord Louth's Regiment
Lord Iveagh's Regiment
Colonel James Talbot's Regiment
Colonel John Hamilton's Regiment
Colonel Maurice Eustace's Regiment

The Stuart army establishment, 1689–97

Colonel Murphy's Regiment
Colonel Richard Nugent's Regiment
Colonel Cormack O'Neill's Regiment
Colonel Moore Power's Regiment
Colonel Art MacMahon's Regiment
Lord Galway's Regiment
Lord Oxburgh's Regiment
Colonel Felix O'Neill's Regiment
Lord Slane's Regiment
Colonel James Roth's Regiment
Colonel Edmund Fitzgerald's Regiment
Colonel Alexander Maguire's Regiment
Lord Kenmare's Regiment
Lord Bellew's Regiment
Colonel Hugh McMahon's Regiment
Lord Antrim's Regiment
Colonel Gordon O'Neill's
Lord Killmallock's Regiment
Colonel Charles O'Brien's Regiment
Lord Westmeath's Regiment
Merrion's Regiment
Colonel Richard Nugent's Regiment
Colonel Edmund O'Reilly's Regiment

Regiments of horse
Squadron of Life Guards commanded by Colonel Sarsfield
Squadron of Life Guards commanded by the Duke of Berwick
Lord Tyrconnel's Regiment
Lord Galmoy's Regiment
Lord Abercorn's Regiment
Colonel Nicholas Purcell's Regiment
Colonel Hugh Sutherland's Regiment
Colonel Henry Luttrell's Regiment

Regiments of dragoons
Colonel Neill O'Neill's Regiment
Brigadier Maxwell's Regiment
Colonel Simon Luttrell's Regiment
Colonel Clifford's Regiment
Colonel Francis Carroll's Regiment

Garrison in Limerick and surrounding areas
Lord Kinsale's Regiment
Colonel Roger O'Cahan's Regiment
Prince of Wales's Regiment
Colonel Con O'Connor's Regiment
Colonel Richard Eustace's Regiment
Colonel Mahony's Regiment
Colonel Wilson's Regiment
Captain Charles Moore's independent company
Sir Michael Creagh's Regiment
Colonel Donovan's Regiment
Colonel Brian O'Neill's Regiment
Colonel Francis O'Toole's Regiment
Colonel Brian MacDermott's Regiment
Colonel Patrick Burke's Regiment

Galway Garrison (arrive at Limerick, August 1691)
Lord Clanrickarde's Regiment
Lord Bophin's Regiment
Colonel Oliver O'Gara's Regiment
Colonel Walter Burke's Regiment
Colonel Henry Dillon's Regiment
Colonel Edmund Reilly's Regiment
Colonel Doherty's Regiment
Colonel Brian Mac Art O'Neill's Regiment
Lord Enniskillen's Regiment
Colonel Dominic Browne's Regiment

THE EXILED STUART ARMY IN FRANCE

After the Jacobite defeat at Aughrim, many Irish officers and men began to leave Ireland and travel to France. This process accelerated after the signing of the Treaty of Limerick and these exile soldiers were formed into a new Stuart army in France. This exiled army was initially organized as follows:

Two troops of Horse Guards
The Kings' Regiment of Horse
The Queen's Regiment of Horse
The King's Regiment of Dismounted Dragoons
The Queen's Regiment of Dismounted Dragoons
The King's Royal Irish Regiment of Foot Guards
The Queen's Regiment of Infantry

The Infantry Regiment of the Marine
The Infantry Regiment of Limerick
The Infantry Regiment of Charlemont
The Infantry Regiment of Dublin
The Infantry Regiment of Athlone
The Infantry Regiment of Clancarty
The Infantry Regiment of Galmoy
The Infantry Regiment of Bourke
The Horse Regiment of Sheldon
Three independent companies

This army was reformed and somewhat reduced in size, many of the surplus soldiers joining the Irish regiments in the French service while the Regiment of Bourke entered the Neapolitan service. The exile Stuart army in France, after the 1692 reorganization and amalgamations, was formed as follows:

Two troops of Horse Guards
The Kings' Regiment of Horse
The Queen's Regiment of Horse
The King's Regiment of Dismounted Dragoons
The Queen's Regiment of Dismounted Dragoons

The King's Royal Irish Regiment of Foot Guards
The Queen's Regiment of Infantry
The Infantry Regiment of the Marine
The Infantry Regiment of Limerick
The Infantry Regiment of Charlemont
The Infantry Regiment of Dublin

This army numbered just over 14,000 officers and men and was initially quartered at St Germain but was later moved to Brittany. It was still technically the army of James II but it served alongside the French army for the remainder of the Nine Years War (also known as the War of the League of Augsburg). It was a sizeable contingent in the French army in a series of campaigns on the Continent and these regiments served in the Low Countries, Spain, on the Rhine and in Savoy. Regiments of the exiled Stuart army were present at the following engagements:

1692   Battle of Steenkirk (The Rhine)
The storming of Dudenhoven (The Rhine)
Defence of Guillestre (Savoy)
Defence of Embrun (Savoy)

1693	Battle of Landen (Netherlands)
	Battle of Neerwinden (Netherlands)
	Battle of Marsaglia (Orbassan, Savoy)
1694	Battle of the Ter River (Spain)
	Siege and capture of Palamos (Spain)
	Capture of Gerona (Spain)
	Capture of Castelfollit (Spain)
	La Perouse Valley campaign (Savoy)
1695	Campaign against the Vaudois guerrillas (Savoy)
1696	Battle of Hostarich (Spain)
	Siege of Valenza (Savoy)
1697	Siege of Barcelona

At the end of the Nine Years War, the terms of the Treaty of Ryswick (1697) stipulated that the army of James II be disbanded. While these regiments were disbanded in 1698 and the conditions of the treaty were technically met, a number of different devices were used to ensure that Irish soldiers from these regiments continued in French service.

> The King's and Queen's Regiments of Horse were disbanded but were reorganized into the Regiment of Sheldon. This regiment would later be renamed as the Regiment of Fitzjames.

> The Regiment of Athlone, the King's Dismounted Dragoons and the men of the independent companies were reorganized into the Regiment of Berwick.

> The Royal Irish Regiment of Foot Guards were disbanded on the 28th February 1698. The next day they reformed as the Regiment of Dorrington. This regiment would later be renamed as the Regiment of Walsh.

Many of the officers and men from the other disbanded regiments joined the Irish regiments in the French service and brought these units up to strength. Many Irish soldiers, however, found themselves unemployed after this disbandment. In the decades that followed, Irish officers and men would continue to serve in the French service while others served in the army of Spain, the army of the Holy Roman Emperor (later the Austrian Imperial Service) and also in the service of Italian princes. The primary cause of this Irish military diaspora was the defeat of the Stuart army in Ireland.

CHAPTER 2

Irish soldiers in Austrian service, 1689–1918

The history of Irish soldiers in the Imperial Austrian service was a long and distinguished one. The first Irish soldiers to serve in the Imperial army left Ireland in the 1600s and they were followed by subsequent waves of émigré Irish officers. There were still men from Irish families serving in the Austrian army and navy in the late 1800s, while the last of this 'Wild Geese' tradition saw service in WWI. They included officers such as Field-Marshal Count Maximilian Ulysses Browne (1706–57), Colonel Baron John O'Brien of Thomond (1775–1830) and Linienschiffsleutenant Gottfried Freiherr Von Banfield (d.1986). The experience of the Irish officer class in the Imperial service was an unqualified success and many achieved high rank in the army and navy or were appointed to senior positions in the Imperial administration. As this gazetteer is devoted to outlining regimental histories, the experiences of these officers falls outside its remit. These Irish officers have become the subject of a growing literature, however, and have been the focus of museum exhibitions in Dublin and Vienna.

The history of actual Irish regiments in the Austrian Imperial service was much less successful. While some Irish regiments were raised after 1689 for the Imperial service, their histories were brief and undistinguished. During the late 1630s, recruiting officers from the Imperial service were stationed in Ireland and the men they recruited would seem to have performed well. The regiments raised after 1689 were not successful and they were formed due to an agreement between William III and the Emperor Leopold I.

THE REGIMENTS

1689   The first Irish regiment for the Imperial service was raised in early 1689. Referred to as the 'Irish Regiment of Foot', it numbered around 1,800 men and included soldiers raised in Ireland and also Irish soldiers who had been imprisoned on the Isle of Wight after James II fled from England. The regiment arrived in Hamburg, whereupon many deserted. It would seem that they did not wish to fight for a Catholic king who had failed to support James II. By June 1689, only 930 men of this regiment remained. It was intended to deploy them against the Turkish army in Hungary and consequently they were marched eastwards through Silesia and Moravia to join the blockading forces at Grosswaradin. En route they plundered Bratislava in September. In 1690, the regiment was broken up and its companies were distributed among other Imperial regiments serving in Hungary.

1692   A second Irish regiment was raised in this year from among Irish Jacobite prisoners who had surrendered at Limerick in 1691. This force was 2,200 strong and was commanded by Georg von Hessen-Dermstadt, who kept it in strict control. It was landed at Hamburg but by August 1692 had lost 800 men due to illness. While based in winter quarters there was a series of violent disputes with members of other Imperial regiments and the regiment was disbanded in 1693, its companies again being distributed among other regiments.

1702   An Irish battalion was raised at Mirandola in Italy from among Irish deserters who had left the French service. Its original commanding officer was Lt.-Col. Franz Matthias MacDonnell. It was composed of four companies but would appear to have had difficulty finding further recruits and it was disbanded before 1705.

1710   A final attempt was made to raise an Irish regiment by Count Christopher Taaffe. Due to nervousness on the part of the British administration at the idea of recruiting large numbers of Irish Catholics, the scheme was never given proper government backing and was abandoned.

CHAPTER 3

Irish regiments in French service, 1685–1871

The tradition of Irish regiments in the French service dates back to the early seventeenth century. The Service Historique de la Défense at Chateau Vincennes lists over twenty Irish regiments that served in the French army between 1615 and 1657. These included the Regiment of Rodrigo (raised in 1615) the Regiment of Wall (1640), the Regiment of York (1652) and the Regiment of Dillon (1653). These earlier Irish regiments in the French service fall outside the remit of this gazetteer but they would make a fascinating subject for further research.

In the period 1685 to 1871, there were essentially four main phases of Irish military involvement in the French service. They were as follows:

The 'Wild Geese' Regiments, 1688–1791
These included the original contingent that went to France as part of Mountcashel's Brigade and also the Irish regiments that went to France following the end of the Jacobite War in Ireland.

The regiments of the Royalist Irish Legion, 1794–8
These were recruited on the Irish establishment and were technically part of the British army. However, some former royalist officers served in them and, given French regimental titles, they were raised as part of the campaign to restore the French monarchy. The later Regiment of Dillon, raised for the British service in 1795, also falls within this category.

Napoleon's Irish Legion, 1803–15
This formation represented a later phase of Irish political and military migration. It was officered by many ex-United Irishmen who had fled to Revolutionary France following the failed rebellion of 1798.

The Compagnie Irlandaise and the Franco-Irish Ambulance in the Franco-Prussian War

While the histories of the Irish units in both Napoleon's army and the Franco-Prussian War are straightforward, the histories of the earlier Irish regiments are quite complex.

In 1689 Lord Mountcashel brought a contingent of 5,000 Irish troops to France to replace the regiments that Louis XIV had sent to Ireland. These troops were initially formed into five regiments but they were later reorganized into an Irish Brigade of three regiments.

Regiment of Mountcashel (later re-titled as the Regiment of Bulkeley)
Regiment of O'Brien (later re-titled as the Regiment of Clare)
Regiment of Dillon
Regiment of Butler
Regiment of Fielding

The regiments of Butler and Fielding were disbanded in 1690 and their personnel was absorbed into the remaining three regiments. Each of the surviving regiments had three battalions each.

At the end of the Jacobite War in Ireland, the remnants of James II's army went to France where they formed an exiled Stuart army. Technically these were Stuart rather than French regiments. Nevertheless they represented a significant source of experienced troops for Louis XIV and these regiments campaigned alongside the French army in the later phase of the Nine Years War. Under the terms of the Peace of Ryswick (1697), these Stuart regiments were disbanded in 1698. (The organization of these Stuart regiments both before and after the Treaty of Ryswick is dealt with in a separate section.) In 1701, the Irish Brigade in the French service consisted of:

Regiment of Mountcashel (later Bulkeley)
Regiment of O'Brien (later Clare)
Regiment of Dillon
Regiment of Dorrington (later Walsh)
Regiment of Berwick
Regiment of Galmoy, disbanded in 1715
Regiment of Bourke, transferred to Spanish service in 1715 and re-named as the Irlanda Regiment (see separate entry in Spanish section)
Albemarle's Regiment of Horse (later O'Donnell), disbanded in 1715
Sheldon's Regiment of Horse (later Fitzjames)

In 1715 some of these regiments were disbanded as part of the army reductions that followed the end of the War of the Spanish Succession in 1714. In 1744, a further Irish regiment was formed as the Regiment of Lally but this was disbanded in 1762 along with the Regiment of Fitzjames. A decline in the number of Irish recruits made a further series of disbandments necessary in 1775 and the regiments of Clare and Bulkeley were disbanded, their personnel being absorbed by the remaining three Irish regiments – the regiments of Dillon, Berwick and Walsh.

Therefore, the tradition of the Wild Geese regiments in the French army developed in a number of phases between 1689 and 1775. During the course of the eighteenth century, these regiments saw service in every major war and were present at the majority of significant battles and sieges. In the course of these campaigns they saw service not only in Europe but also in America, the West Indies, India and Africa. The Irish regiments in the French service were also brigaded together to form an 'Irish Brigade'. This larger formation of Irish regiments was recognized as being among the best troops in the army of the Bourbons and it would play a significant role at a number of battles, most particularly at Fontenoy in 1745. While the sources for some of the earlier regiments remain poor, the following entries cover the histories of the most important units.

THE REGIMENT OF WALSH, 1662–1791

Formation

This regiment was originally raised by Charles II in 1662 as the Royal Irish Regiment of Foot Guards, its first colonel being James Butler, 1st Duke of Ormonde and Viceroy of Ireland. It traced its lineage back to a battalion of Irish Guards raised in 1642, which was disbanded after the battle of Naseby in 1645.

Until its re-designation in 1791 as the 92^e Regiment d'Infanterie de Ligne, it saw almost continuous service. It also took the family name of successive colonel-proprietors and would later be designated as the Regiment of Dorrington, the Regiment of Rothe, the Regiment of Roscommon and the Regiment of Walsh. It is under this last title that the regiment is best known.

Operational history

1662   The regiment was raised as the **King's Royal Irish Regiment of Foot Guards**.

Jacobite War/the Nine Years War, 1688–1697

1689   It was present at the siege of Derry.
1690   The regiment was engaged at the battle of the Boyne.
1691   It fought at the battle of Aughrim.
1692   It formed part of the Stuart army in France.
1693   It was present at the capture of Huy, the battle of Linden and the capture of Charleroi.
1694   The regiment was attached to the army of Flanders.
1695   It was present at the siege of Brussels.
1696   The regiment was attached to the army of Flanders.
1698   By an order of 28 February 1698 the Royal Irish Regiment of Foot Guards was disbanded, as it was one of the Irish regiments designated for disbandment under the terms of the Treaty of Ryswick. It was re-formed the following day under the title of the **Regiment of Dorrington**, taking the name of its colonel-proprietor.

The War of the Spanish Succession, 1701–14

1701   It was attached to the army of Germany.
1703   The regiment was attached to the army of Bavaria and was present at the siege of Kehl, the capture of the Stolhoffen entrenchments and the battles of Munderkingen and 1st Hochstedt and the storming of Kempten.
1704   It took part in the battle of 2nd Hochstedt (Blenheim).

1705	The regiment was attached to the army of the Rhine.
1706	It was attached to the army of Germany.
1718	On the death of Dorrington, the regiment was transferred to the colonelship of Comte Michael de Roth and was renamed the **Regiment of Roth**.

War with Spain, 1719–20

1719	It was attached to the Duke of Berwick's army in Spain and was present at the captures of Fuenterrabia, San Sebastian and Roses.

War of the Polish Succession, 1733–5

1733	The regiment took part in the siege of Kehl and the assault on the entrenchments at Etlingen.
1734	It took part in the siege of Philippsburg and the campaign on the Rhine.

War of the Austrian Succession, 1740–8

1742	It was attached to the army of Flanders.
1743	The regiment was present at the battle of Dettingen but was not engaged.
1744	The regiment took part in the sieges of Menin, Ypres and Furnes.
1745	It was engaged at the battle of Fontenoy and took part in the sieges of Tournai, Oudenarde, Dendermonde and Ath.
1745–6	A detachment of the regiment went to Scotland as part of Prince Charles Edward Stuart's expedition. Many of these were captured at sea, including the regiment's colonel, Charles Edward, Comte de Roth. A further detachment served with the 'Irish Piquets' and was present at the battles of Penrith, Falkirk and Culloden Moor.
1747	The regiment was engaged at the battle of Laffeldt and the siege of Bergen-op-Zoom.
1748	It was present at the siege of Maestricht.

Seven Years War, 1756–63

1759	It was attached to the army of Germany.
1761	The regiment took part in the battle of Marburg.
1766	On the death of the Comte de Roth, Robert Dillon, 9th Earl of Roscommon, succeeded as colonel. The regiment's title was therefore changed to the **Regiment of Roscommon**.
1770	On the death of the Earl of Roscommon, Comte Antoine Joseph Philippe de Walsh-Serrant succeeded as colonel and the regiment's title was changed to the **Regiment of Walsh**.
1775	The regiment was briefly disbanded and reformed as part of the Légion de Dauphiné.
1776	The regiment was restored under the title of the Regiment of Walsh.

American Revolutionary War, 1775–83

1779	A detachment of the regiment was sent to the West Indies, where it served alongside a detachment from the Regiment of Dillon. It took part in the capture of Grenada and the unsuccessful siege of Savannah, Georgia.

In May 1779 a detachment of 137 men under the command of Lieutenant Eugene McCarthy and Lieutenant Edward Stack joined the American ship *Bonhomme Richard*, which was commanded by Captain John Paul Jones. Serving as marines in the Continental Navy, they took part in the action against HMS *Serapis* and HMS *Countess* off Scarborough on 23 September 1779.

1781   While serving as marines with the French fleet, this detachment took part in the capture of St Eustache. The remainder of the regiment served in West Africa and took part in the capture of Senegal.

1788   Dutch officials in the Cape noted the arrival in October of the Regiment of Walsh aboard French ships bound for Mauritius. As the local Dutch officials were alarmed at the arrival of such a large body of French troops, they were only allowed disembark 20 at a time and were not permitted to carry weapons while on shore leave.

The French Revolution and its aftermath

In 1791 the traditional regimental titles were abolished and the regiment was re-designated as the 92ᵉ Regiment d'Infanterie de Ligne.

A party of around 120 officers and NCOs from the Regiment of Walsh who remained loyal to the Bourbon cause joined the remnants of other Irish regiments at Koblenz. These men were incorporated into the royalist 'Brigade Irlandese' of the 'Armée des Princes'. This faction of the regiment was only of company strength and the whole brigade was disbanded in 1792.

In 1794 the regiment was re-formed in Ireland as the Regiment of Le Comte de Walsh-Serrant or the 2nd Regiment of the Irish Brigade in the British service. This regiment contained a number of officers who had served in the original Regiment of Walsh. The regiment was disbanded at Chatham in 1798 and its personnel drafted into other British units. (See separate entry for this regiment).

The 92ᵉ Régiment d'Infanterie de Ligne

This regiment served in the Revolutionary and Napoleonic wars and was disbanded in 1815. In 1855 it was re-formed by re-naming the 17ᵉ Régiment d'Infanterie de Légère as the 92ᵉ Régiment d'Infanterie de Ligne. It remained in service until its disbandment in 1956 but was re-formed as a battalion in 1963.

In 1964 it was re-designated as a full regiment and it continues to serve as part of the French army, based at Clermont-Ferrand. In the French tradition, the modern regiment acts as the guardian of the history and traditions not only of its Napoleonic predecessor but also of the earlier Regiment of Walsh.

In 1998 a detachment of the regiment visited Ireland as part of the bicentennial commemorations of the 1798 Rebellion. They were presented with a replica of the colour of the Regiment of Walsh and this is kept with other relics of the regiment's Irish lineage at the regimental salle de tradition in Clermont-Ferrand. The 92ᵉ Régiment's battle honours include:

Irish regiments in French service, 1685–1871   15

Rivoli 1797, Austerlitz 1805, Iena 1806, Constantine 1837, Ypres 1914, Verdun, 1916–17, La Somme 1916, L'Ourcq 1918, Resistence Auvergne 1944

Colonel Proprietors of the Regiment of Walsh

1662	James Butler, 1st Duke of Ormonde
1685	James Butler, 2nd Duke of Ormonde, deprived of the colonelcy on defecting to the Williamite cause
1689	Colonel (later Lieutenant-General) William Dorrington
1718	Comte Michael de Roth (sometimes spelt 'de Rothe')
1733	Comte Charles Edward de Roth
1766	Robert Dillon, 9th Earl of Roscommon
1770	Comte Antoine Joseph Philippe de Walsh-Serrant
1775	Colonel Arthur Dillon
1788	Comte Charles Antoine Augustin de Walsh-Serrant. He also served as colonel-proprietor of the Régiment de le Comte de Walsh-Serrant in British service (see entry for that regiment).

Regimental Colours

The field of the regimental colour was consisted of a white flag with a red cross. At the centre of the cross was a golden crown surmounted by a lion.

REGIMENT OF BULKELEY, 1683–1775

(Regiment of Mountcashel/Regiment of Lee)

Formation

This regiment owes its origins to a number of independent companies that initially served in Tangiers. In 1683 they were withdrawn from North Africa and re-organized into a single regiment in 1684. Its first colonel was James Butler, later 2nd Duke of Ormond. In 1685 the colonelship of the regiment passed to Justin MacCarthy who was later made Viscount Mountcashel and the regiment was re-named after its new commander. Subsequent colonel-proprietors would later rename it as the Regiment of Lee and the Regiment of Bulkeley.

Operational History

Jacobite Wars/The Nine Years War, 1688–97

1689	The regiment of Mountcashel was heavily engaged at Newtown Butler, where it sustained severe casualties.
1690	It was reinforced with fresh troops and brought to France where it formed part of Mountcashel's Irish Brigade, serving alongside the regiments of Dillon and Clare in Savoy.
1691	The regiment took part in the campaign in Catalonia and was present at the sieges of Urgel, Valencia and Boy and the raising of the siege of Pratz de Mollo.

1693	It was attached to the army in Germany and took part in the sieges of Heidelburg, Wingemburg, Eppenheim and Darmstadt.
1694	Colonel Andrew Lee succeeded in command and the regiment was re-named as the **Regiment of Lee** and served in Italy.
1695	It was attached to the army in Germany and on the Meuse.
1697	The regiment took part in the siege of Ath. After the Peace of Ryswick the regiment was reinforced by men from the disbanded Stuart regiments.

The War of the Spanish Succession, 1701–14

1701	The regiment was attached to the army in Flanders.
1702	It was attached to the army in Germany.
1703	The regiment took part in the campaigns in Bavaria and was present at the sieges of Kehl, Stolhoffen and the battles of Munderkingen and 1st Hochstedt.
1704	It fought in the battles of Schellemberg and 2nd Hochstedt (Blenheim).
1705–7	It was attached to the armies of the Moselle and the Rhine and campaigned in Alsace.
1708	The regiment served in the defence of Lille.
1709	It was attached to the army in Germany.
1712	The regiment was attached to the army in Flanders and was present at the sieges of Douay, Quesnoy and Bonchain.

War of the Polish Succession, 1733–5

1733	The Comte Francois de Bulkeley succeeded as colonel-proprietor of the regiment, which was renamed after him. It was attached to the army on the Rhine, it was present at the siege of Kehl.
1734	It served during the siege of Philippsburg.
1735	The regiment was attached to the army in Flanders.

War of the Austrian Succession, 1740–8

1742	The regiment was attached to the army in Bavaria and campaigned in Bohemia.
1743	It was attached to the army on the Rhine and was present at the battle of Dettingen but was not engaged.
1744	The regiment campaigned in Flanders and took part in the sieges of Menin and Ypres.
1745	Alongside the other regiments of the Irish Brigade, it fought in the battle of Fontenoy.
1745–6	A detachment of the regiment served with the 'Irish Piquets' as part of Prince Charles Edward Stuart's expedition to Scotland. They were present at the battles of Penrith, Falkirk and Culloden Moor.
1747	The regiment fought in the battle of Laffeldt.

Seven Years War, 1756–63

1761	It fought in the battle of Marburg.

Amalgamation, 1775

By 1762, fewer than half the men assigned to the Irish regiments were actually of Irish origin. The lack of Irish recruits was made up with drafts of Dutch, German and French soldiers.

In 1775 the Regiment of Bulkeley was incorporated into the Regiment of Dillon, the new enlarged regiment retaining the title of Regiment of Dillon.

While the regimental traditions were maintained within the Regiment of Dillon, this amalgamation effectively ended the separate history of the Regiment of Bulkeley.

Colonel proprietors

1684	Colonel James Butler, later 2nd Duke of Ormonde
1685	Colonel Justin MacCarthy, later Lord Mountcashel
1694	Colonel, later Maréchal de Camp, Andrew Lee
1704	Colonel Francis Lee
1720	Colonel Andrew Lee took over the colonelcy of the regiment for a second term on the death of his son, Francis Lee, in 1720
1733	Lieutenant-General Comte François de Bulkeley
1754–75	Maréchal de Camp François Henri Comte de Bulkeley

Regimental colours

The field of the regimental colour was divided into four cantons – cantons 1 and 4 were emerald green and cantons 2 and 3 were red. Superimposed on these cantons was the red cross of St George, trimmed in white. In the centre of the cross an Irish harp device, surmounted by a small crown. The inscription on the arms of the cross read 'In Hoc Signo Vinces' (In this sign you will conquer).

In each canton, a large crown in gold and filled in red, the tip of the crown pointing outwards towards the corner of each canton. There was a white cravat on the flagstaff.

The colonel's colour was white with a red cross. All the devices and inscriptions on the regimental colour were repeated on the colonel's colour.

THE REGIMENT OF CLARE, 1689–1775

Formation

This regiment was raised by Daniel O'Brien, 3rd Viscount Clare, in 1689 and was originally titled the Regiment of O'Brien as he had levied the regiment in the name of his eldest son, the Hon. Daniel O'Brien. In 1690 it travelled to France as part of Lord Mountcashel's Irish Brigade. On arriving in France, however, it was felt that the regiment's officers and men were too inexperienced to embark immediately on campaign; 200 Irish veterans who were serving with the German Regiment of Greider were drafted in to provide much-needed experience.

The first colonel of the regiment to see active service, Lieutenant-Colonel Andrew Lee, was also an experienced officer of the Regiment of Greider and in 1704 became colonel of the Regiment of Lee (Mountcashel/Bulkeley).

The regiment was later re-named several times taking the names of different colonel-proprietors.

Operational history

The Nine Years War, 1688–97

1690–4   The regiment was attached to the army of Marshal Catinat and campaigned in Savoy and Piedmont.
1691   The Hon. Daniel O'Brien succeeded as 4th Viscount Clare on the death of his father. The regiment's title changed from the Regiment of O'Brien to the **Regiment of Clare**.
1693   The regiment was present at the battle of Marsaglia.
1696   It was present at the siege of Valenza (Lombardy) and then attached to the army on the Meuse.

The War of the Spanish Succession, 1701–14

1701   The regiment was attached to the army of Germany.
1703   It was heavily engaged at the battle of 1st Hochstedt.
1704   The regiment took part in the battle of 2nd Hochstedt (Blenheim).
1706   It took part in the battle of Ramilles.
1708   It was present at the battle of Oudenarde.
1709   The regiment was engaged at Malplaquet.
1711   It took part in the assault on Arleux.
1712   The regiment was present at the sieges of Douay, Quesnoy and Bouchain.
1713   It was attached to the army of the Rhine and present at the sieges of Landau and Fridburgh.

War of the Polish Succession, 1733–5

1733   The regiment was attached to the army of the Rhine and was present at the siege of Kehl.
1734   It served in the siege of Philippsburg.

War of the Austrian Succession, 1740–8

1742   The regiment took part the defence of Lintz (Austria)
1743   It was attached to the army of the Rhine and present at Dettingen but was not engaged.
1744   The regiment was attached to the army of Flanders and was present at the sieges of Menin and Ypres.
1745   It was engaged at Fontenoy and later present at the siege of Tournai.
1745–6   A detachment of the regiment served with the 'Irish Piquets' as part of Prince Charles Edward Stuart's expedition to Scotland. They were present at the battles of Penrith, Falkirk and Culloden Moor.
1746   The regiment was engaged at the battle of Rocoux.
1747   It was present at the battle of Laffeldt and the siege of Maestricht.

Seven Years War, 1756–63

1760   The regiment was engaged at the battles of Corback and Warburgh.
1761   It was present at the battles of Felingshausen and Marburg.

Amalgamation, 1775
In 1775 the Regiment of Clare was incorporated into the Regiment of Berwick, the new regiment retaining the latter title.

Colonel proprietors
1689   The Hon. Daniel O'Brien, later 4th Viscount Clare
1693   Colonel Andrew Lee
1694   Brigadier-General Richard Talbot, deprived of his command by Louis XIV
1696   Charles O'Brien, 5th Lord Clare, died of wounds received at Ramillies
1706   Charles O'Brien, 6th Lord Clare and 9th Earl of Thomond. This colonel-proprietor was just an infant when he succeeded to the regiment and consequently Major-General Murrough O'Brien commanded until he came of age in 1720.
1761   Charles O'Brien, 7th Viscount Clare. This successor was also an infant and, while the colonelcy was reserved for him, the regiment was commanded by a series of colonels 'en second'. He never succeeded to command the regiment as he died underage in Paris in 1774.

'Colonel-en-Second' of the Regiment of Clare
1689   Lieutenant-Colonel Fitzmauric
1690   Lieutenant-Colonel Andrew Lee; succeeds as colonel-proprietor in 1693. Later colonel of the Regiment of Mountcashel/Lee.
1706–20 Major-General Murrough O'Brien, commanded the regiment as the 'Regiment of O'Brien' during the infancy of Charles, 6th Lord Clare.
1761   Brigadier James Fitzgerald
1763   The Chevalier, later Comte, de Betagh
1770–5 The Chevalier de Meade

Regimental colours
The field of the regimental colour was divided into four cantons – cantons 2 and 3 were yellow; 1 and 4 were red. Superimposed on these cantons was the red cross of St George, trimmed in white. In the centre of the cross an Irish harp device, surmounted by a small crown. The inscription on the arms of the cross read 'In Hoc Signo Vinces' (In this sign you will conquer).

    In each canton, a large crown in gold and filled in red, the tip of the crown pointing outwards towards the corner of each canton. There was a white cravat on the flagstaff. The colonel's colour consisted of a white flag with a red cross. The devices and inscriptions of the regimental colour were repeated on the colonel's colour.

THE REGIMENT OF DILLON, 1690–1791

Formation

In June 1653 an Irish regiment was raised for the French service and took the title of Regiment of Dillon, after its original colonel-proprietor. This regiment was disbanded in February 1664. The later Regiment of Dillon was one of two infantry regiments raised by Theobald, 7th Viscount Dillon of Costello-Gallen for the service of James II. In 1690 it was sent to France as part of Lord Mountcashel's brigade. During the course of the succeeding century, the regiment built up an enviable service record as it served in every major war of the eighteenth century.

Operational history

The Nine Years War, 1688–97

1691   It was attached to the Army of Rousillon and was at the siege of Urgel and the relief of Pratz de Mollo.
1693   It took part in the capture of Roses.
1694   The regiment was present at the captures of Palamos, Girona, Ostalric and Castelfollit.
1695   It took part in a supply relief mission to Ostalric.
1696   The regiment was present at the raising of the siege of Palamos and the defeat of the army of the Prince of Hesse-Darmstadt near Ostalric.
1697   It took part in the capture of Barcelona.

After the Peace of Ryswick in 1697, the regiment was reinforced by Irish troops from the disbanded Stuart regiments.

The War of the Spanish Succession, 1701–14

1701   The regiment was attached to the Army of Italy, commanded by the Duke of Vendôme and fought in the battle Chiari.
1702   It fought at defence of Cremona and the battles of Santa Vittoria and Luzzara.
1703   The regiment was present at the battles of Castelnuovo, Riva and San Sebastian. The regiment then took part in the siege of Asti.
1704   It took part in the sieges of Vercelli and Verue.
1705   It served in the siege of Mirandola, present at the battle of Cassano.
1706   The regiment of Dillon fought in the battles of Calcinato and Castiglione.
1707–10   It was stationed in the vicinity of Briancon and took part in a series of defensive actions against allied invading forces.
1712   The regiment took part in the expedition to Catalonia and the relief of Gerona.
1713   It was attached to the army of the Rhine and was present at the sieges of Kaiserlauten, Verastein, Landau and Friburgh.
1714   The regiment was present at the capture of Barcelona.
1715   The regiment absorbed the personnel from the disbanded Regiment of Galmoy.

War of the Polish Succession, 1733–5

1734   The regiment served during the siege of Philippsburg and the campaign on the Rhine.

War of the Austrian Succession, 1740–8

1743   The Regiment of Dillon was present at the battle of Dettingen but was not engaged.

1745   It was engaged at the battle of Fontenoy.

1745–6   A detachment of the regiment served with the 'Irish Piquets' as part of Prince Charles Edward Stuart's expedition to Scotland. They were present at the battles of Penrith, Falkirk and Culloden Moor.

1747   The regiment fought in the battle of Laffeldt.

Seven Years War, 1756–63

1761   It was present at the battle of Marburg.

American Revolutionary War, 1775–83

1775   The Regiment of Bulkeley was incorporated into the Regiment of Dillon, the regiment retaining the latter regimental title. This amalgamation brought the regiment up to full strength.

1779   The regiment campaigned in the West Indies and took part in the capture of Grenada and the unsuccessful siege of Savannah, Georgia.

1781   While serving as marines with the French fleet, it took part in the capture of St Eustache.

French Revolution and subsequent history

After the outbreak of the French Revolution in 1789, the regiment's battalions were split up and sent to different demi-brigades. In 1791 the traditional regimental titles were abolished and the regiment was re-designated as the 87e Régiment d'Infanterie, effectively destroying the regiment's Irish identity.

A party of around 150 men of the old Regiment of Dillon remained loyal to the monarchy and made its way to Koblenz where it joined the 'Armée des Princes'. This faction of the regiment was only of company strength and the whole brigade was disbanded in 1792.

Captain Jacques O'Moran, who had served with the regiment at Savannah, formed a Dillon Battalion for the French Directory. This battalion served on San Domingo and was captured by the British in 1793. Many of its members then passed into the British service.

In 1793 Colonel the Hon. Henry Dillon raised a new regiment which adopted the old regimental title and served in Haiti until 1796, when it was disbanded. The same officer later raised another Regiment of Dillon and this served as the 3rd regiment of the Irish Brigade in the British service. Some of its officers had served in the Bourbon army. In 1797 it was amalgamated with Viscomte Walsh's regiment in San Domingo and was reduced to cadre in January 1798. It was disbanded later in the same year, its personnel being sent to other British units. (see separate entry on the regiments of this British-raised brigade, often referred to as 'Pitt's Irish Legion').

The final episode in the distinguished history of this regiment began in February 1795 Comte Edouard Dillon, formerly of the French service, raised a new Regiment of Dillon in Northern Italy. Only two of its officers were of Irish descent and the ranks were filled by recruits from Italy and also exiled French royalists. Ultimately, men of twenty-two nationalities served in this regiment which was taken on the British establishment in 1806. It served as a two-battalion regiment, both battalions being 750 men strong. During the course of its history, this regiment served in Corsica (1796), Elba, Portugal (1797), Minorca, Egypt (1801), Malta (1803), Sicily and Spain. It was disbanded at Gibraltar on 24 December 1814. While much of its time was spent on garrison duties, the regiment also saw active service in Egypt and Spain and during the 1801 Egyptian campaign, it fought at several engagements with some distinction. Comte Edouard Dillon served as the regiment's colonel while Lt.-Col. Francis Dillon served as colonel 'en seconde', exercising actual command in the field.

The disbandment of this regiment in 1814 effectively ended the long and distinguished history of the Regiment of Dillon. Founded in 1690, the regiment went through a number of incarnations following the French Revolution as the members of the Dillon family sought a means to keep the regiment alive, either in the French or British service.

The 87ᵉ Régiment d'Infanterie

This regiment served in the Revolutionary wars and was disbanded in 1803. Through a re-naming of the 12ᵉ Régiment d'Infanterie, it was re-formed in 1855 and was not disbanded until 1920, its traditions being maintained by the 51ᵉ Régiment d'Infanterie.

In 1939 it was re-formed as the 87ᵉ Régiment d'Infanterie de Fortresse and was finally disbanded after the fall of France in 1940. The regiment's battle honours included:

> Castiglione, 1796, Rivoli 1797, Dantzig 1807, Freidland 1807; Verdun 1917, Picardie 1918, Mondidier 1918

(These include the battle honours of the re-named 12ᵉ Régiment d'Infanterie)

Colonel proprietors of the Regiment of Dillon

1688	Theobald, 7th Viscount Dillon
1690	Lieutenant-General Comte Arthur de Dillon
1730	Brigadier-General Comte Charles de Dillon
1741	Brigadier-General Comte Henri de Dillon (Lord Henry Dillon, 11th Viscount Dillon in the British peerage).
1744	Colonel, the Chevalier Jacques de Dillon; killed in action while commanding the regiment at Fontenoy
1745	Colonel Comte Edouard de Dillon, mortally wounded at Laffeldt

Irish regiments in French service, 1685–1871

1747   Louis XV allowed Lord Henry Dillon to hold the colonelship of the regiment, despite the fact that Dillon was absent in England. This was on account of there being no natural successor on the death of Comte Edouard Dillon in 1747.

1767   Major-General Count Arthur de Dillon [executed by the revolutionary government in 1794]

1780   Major-General Comte Theobald de Dillon (brutally murdered by soldiers at Lille in 1794)

Regimental colours

The field of the regimental colour was divided into four cantons – cantons 1 and 4 (top left and bottom right) were red while 2 and 3 (top right and bottom left) were black. Superimposed on these cantons was the red cross of St George, trimmed in white. In the centre of the cross an Irish harp device, surmounted by a small crown. The inscription on the arms of the cross read 'In Hoc Signo Vinces' (In this sign you will conquer).

In each canton, a large crown in gold and filled in red, the tip of the crown pointing outwards towards the corner of each canton. There was a white cravat on the flagstaff. One of the original regimental colours survived in the possession of the Dillon family until 1950 when it was presented to the Military History Society of Ireland (the flag is now in the National Museum of Ireland). It measures 5ft 2" by 4ft 8' and is on display at the new military exhibition at the National Museum of Ireland, Collins Barracks. The colonel's colour consisted of a white flag with a red cross. The devices and inscriptions of the regimental colour were repeated on the colonel's colour.

THE REGIMENT OF BERWICK, 1698–1791

Formation

This regiment was founded after the Peace of Ryswick (1697) when a number of the Stuart regiments were disbanded. Its date of inception was 27th February 1698 and its initial drafts came from the disbanded Regiment of Athlone, the King's Dismounted Dragoons and the men of the three independent companies. The colonel-proprietorship was given to James Fitzjames, Duke of Berwick.

Operational history

The War of the Spanish Succession, 1701–14

1702   The regiment was attached to the army of the Duke of Burgundy and campaigned in Flanders.

1703   It was sent to take part in the campaign in Spain and Portugal.

1704   The regiment took part in the prolonged operations around Ciudad Rodrigo.

1705   It took part in the suppression of a Huguenot rebellion in the Languedoc.

1706   The regiment was present at the conclusion of the successful siege of Nice. It then returned to the campaign in Spain and was at the capture of Madrid.

1707 It was present at the battle of Almansa and the siege of Lerida.
1708 It was attached to the army of the Rhine.
1709–12 The regiment was stationed on the French-Piedmont border.
1713 It took part in the relief of Gerona.
1714 The regiment was present at the siege and capture of Barcelona.

War with Spain, 1719–20

During this short campaign, the regiment took part in the sieges of Fuanterrabia, San Sebastian and Urgel.

War of the Polish Succession, 1733–5

1734 The regiment took part in the capture of the fortifications at Etlingen, and was present at the siege of Philippsburg and during the campaign on the Rhine.

War of the Austrian Succession, 1740–8

1743 It was present at the battle of Dettingen but was not engaged.
1745 The regiment took part in the battle of Fontenoy as part of the Irish Brigade.
1745–6 A detachment was captured at sea en route to Scotland while another served with the 'Irish Piquets' as part of Prince Charles Edward Stuart's expedition. They took part in actions at Penrith, Falkirk and Culloden Moor.
1747 The regiment took part in the battle of Laffeldt.

Seven Years War, 1756–63

1759 It was present at the battle of Minden (Corbach)
1761 The regiment fought at the battle of Marburg
1775 The Regiment of Clare was merged with the Regiment of Berwick. This new amalgamated regiment retained the title of **Regiment of Berwick**.

American Revolutionary War, 1775–83

1781 A battalion of the regiment was sent to the West Indies where it took part in the siege of St Christopher.

The French Revolution, 1789

By the time of the French Revolution in 1789, the regiment had essentially lost its Irish identity. While many of the officers were of Irish descent, the majority of the rank and file were Frenchmen by this time. In 1791, the regiment lost its regimental title and was re-designated as the 88ᵉ Régiment de Ligne.

However, a number of officers and men who remained loyal to the royalist cause, made their way to Koblenz where, in 1792, they organized a battalion sized unit in the 'Brigade Irlandese' of the 'Armée des Princes'. This consisted of 220 men from the original regiment and a further 350 that had been recruited in Liège. This battalion was disbanded in the winter of 1792.

In October 1794 a new regiment was raised in Ireland as the Regiment of Le Duc de Fitzjames and this new regiment maintained the traditions and lineage of the Regiment of Berwick. This was the 1st Regiment of the Irish Brigade in the British service, composed of officers loyal to the Bourbon cause. The regiment was disbanded in 1796 due to recruiting difficulties. (see separate entry for this regiment).

The 88ᵉ Régiment de Ligne.
This revolutionary regiment served throughout the Revolutionary and Napoleonic Wars and was disbanded in 1815. In 1855 it was re-constituted following the re-titling of the 13ᵉ Régiment d'Infanterie Légère as the 88ᵉ Régiment d'Infanterie de Ligne.

In 1923 this regiment was disbanded but its traditions were maintained by the 14ᵉ Régiment d'Infanterie. The 88ᵉ Régiment d'Infanterie was re-formed for a final time in 1956 but the regiment was again disbanded in 1957. The battle honours of the 88ᵉ Régiment d'Infanterie included:

Sediman 1798, Austerlitz 1805, Wagram 1809, La Moskowa 1812, Champagne 1915, Verdun 1916

Colonel proprietors of the Regiment of Berwick
1698 Maréchal James Fitzjames, Duke of Berwick (Duc de Fitzjames)
1713 James Francis Stuart Fitzjames, Marquis of Tinmouth and 2nd Duke of Liria y Xercia. He was deprived of the colonelship in 1716 for taking part in James II's expedition to Scotland.
1716 Henry James de Fitzjames, 2ᵉ Duc de Fitzjames
1721 Lord Henri de Fitzjames
1729 Comte Edouard de Fitzjames
1758 Charles de Fitzjames, 3ᵉ Duc de Fitzjames
1783–91 Jean Charles de FitzJames, 4ᵉ Duc de Fitzjames, who also commanded the remains of the regiment in 1792 when it formed part of the Armée des Princes in Koblenz. In 1794, he was appointed as colonel-proprietor of the Régiment de le Duc de Fitzjames in the British service – the 1st Regiment of the Irish Brigade (See later entry on that regiment).

Regimental colours
The regimental colour was a green flag with the red saltire of St Patrick. Superimposed on this was a red cross, trimmed in white. There were no other crowns or devices.

The motto was the same as the Regiment of Dillon: 'In Hoc Signo Vinces' (In this sign you will conquer). The colonel's colour was white colour with a red cross with the regimental motto repeated.

THE REGIMENT OF GALMOY, 1698–1715

Formation
This regiment was formed on 27 February 1698 from the personnel of the disbanded Regiment of Charlemont and the Queen's Regiment of Foot Dragoons. Its founding

colonel was Major-General Pierce Butler, 3rd Viscount Galmoy, who had a distinguished career as a cavalry commander during the war in Ireland and the Nine Years War. This regiment had a short but distinguished history and fought at many major engagements during the War of the Spanish Succession.

Operational history

War of the Spanish Succession, 1701–14

1701   The Regiment of Galmoy joined the French expeditionary force in Italy and fought at the battles of Carpi and Chiari.

1702   It took part in the defence of Cremona and the battles of Santa Vittoria and Luzzara.

1703   The regiment was attached to the army of the Rhine and was present at the engagement at Breisach, the siege of Landau and the battle of Speyerbach.

1704   It joined the army in Italy and took part in the battle of Genivolta.

1705   The Regiment of Galway was engaged at the battles of Cassano and Castiglione.

1706   It took part in the siege of Turin.

1707   The regiment re-joined the army on the Rhine and served throughout the defence of Stollhofen.

1708   The Regiment of Galmoy joined the army in Spain and fought in the battles of Tortosa, Valentia and Alicante.

1709   It joined the army in Flanders and fought in the battle of Malplaquet.

1710   The regiment remained in Flanders.

1712   It took part in the successful sieges of Douai, Le Quesnoy and Bouchain.

1713   Stationed at Roussillon.

1714   The Regiment of Galmoy was present at the siege of Barcelona.

On 30 January 1715, the regiment was disbanded as part of the post-war reductions in the size of the army. Its remaining personnel joined the Regiment of Dillon.

Regimental colours

The first regimental colour, which was used up to 1702, was of an unusual design. It consisted of a white cross which divided the body of the flag into four cantons. Each canton was further divided into nine wavy lines which alternated blue and white. This was very much in the style of the colours of some of the Swiss regiments in French service.

This regimental colour was replaced in 1702 with a more traditional British-style flag. This consisted of a red central cross which divided the flag into four cantons. Cantons 1 and 4 were yellow; cantons 2 and 3 were red. The red central cross was edged blue at cantons 1 and 4 and yellow at cantons 2 and 3. In each canton there was a gold Irish harp with a crown.

At the centre of the cross, a crowned 'JR' device. On the arms of the cross, the motto 'Pro Deo Rege et Patria' in gold letters (For God, King and Country).

The colonel's colour is believed to have been a white flag with the designs of the regimental flag repeated.

THE REGIMENT OF FITZJAMES, 1698–1762
(originally the Regiment of Sheldon)

Formation
This cavalry regiment had a relatively short but extremely distinguished history in the service of France. When James II went into exile in France, he brought two Irish regiments of horse with him; the King's and Queen's regiments of horse. After the Treaty of Ryswick in 1697 these regiments were disbanded and the majority of their personnel formed a new regiment commanded by Major-General Dominick Sheldon; the new regiment being named after him as the 'Regiment of Sheldon'.

Sheldon was an extremely experienced commander who had served in the exiled Charles II and with the armies of Louis XIV. He had served throughout the Jacobite War in Ireland and had then travelled with the first wave of Irish exiles into France. Subsequent colonel proprietors of the regiment re-named the regiment, using their own family name. The regiment was later known as both the Regiment of Nugent and the Regiment of Fitzjames.

Operational history
War of the Spanish Succession, 1701–14
1701 The regiment was attached to the French army in Germany and then it was sent to Italy. During its service in Italy it was present at the battles of Chiari, Mantua and Cremona.

1702 It took part in an engagement with Austrian cavalry at Santa Vittoria and was heavily engaged at Luzzara (August 1702).

1703 The regiment took part in the campaign in Germany, where it fought at the battle of Spire in November 1703.

1704 The regiment was attached to the army of Flanders.

1706 When Sheldon relinquished command the regiment it was re-named as the **Regiment of Nugent**, after its new colonel proprietor, Major-General Christopher Nugent. During a series of campaigns in Flanders it took part in a series of important battles including Ramilles (1706), Oudenarde (1708) and Malplaquet (1709).

1712 The regiment was present at the attack on Denain and the siege of Douay.

1713 It was transferred to the French army in Germany and took part in the sieges of Friburgh and Landau before joining the campaign on the Lower Meuse.

War of the Polish Succession, 1733–5
1733 The Comte Charles de Fitzjames took command of the regiment, changing its name for the final time to the **Regiment of Fitzjames**.

War of the Austrian Succession, 1740–8

1745   The regiment particularly distinguished itself at the battle of Fontenoy where it was brigaded with French cavalry and carried out a series of successful, if costly charges.

1745   A detachment of the regiment was granted leave to travel with Prince Charles Edward Stuart (the Young Pretender) on his expedition to Scotland. Some of these were captured aboard ship and around 130 officers and men landed at Aberdeen in February

1746   At the battle of Culloden in April 1746, the remnant of this detachment formed the prince's bodyguard and charged Lord Keir's Dragoons towards the end of the battle. Colonel Robert O'Shea (also spelt O'Shee), led the prince from the field when the battle was lost. The regiment's losses at Fontenoy and in Scotland almost destroyed it and the next two years were spent recruiting and re-organizing.

Seven Years War, 1756–63

1757   The regiment was engaged at the battle of Rossbach, where it went to the aid of an Austrian cuirassier regiment that was being attacked by Prussian cavalry. Once again it was virtually wiped out and it three years before it was ready to campaign again.

1762   The Regiment of Fitzjames fought its last battle at Wilhelmstal on the frontier of Hesse-Cassel. It took up positions near the village of Grobenstein but was attacked on three sides and overrun. Effectively destroyed for the third time since 1745, the regiment was officially disbanded on 21st December 1762.

Colonel proprietors
1698–1706   Major-General Dominick Sheldon
1706–16   Major-General Christopher Nugent
1716–33   Comte de Nugent
1733–59   Comte Charles de Fitzjames
1759–62   Comte Jean Charles de Fitzjames

Regimental colours
The regimental colour was a yellow square cavalry standard, trimmed with silver. At its centre was the sunburst device of Louis XIV.

THE REGIMENT OF LALLY, 1744–66

Formation
This regiment was the last Irish regiment to be raised in the eighteenth century for the French service and it enjoyed but a brief, but event-filled, history. It was raised

Irish regiments in French service, 1685–1871

in 1744 by Colonel (later General) Thomas Arthur Lally, the son of Brigadier Sir Gerald Lally of Tuam, Co. Galway.

Like his father, he had gained much military experience in the service of France and was allowed raise a new regiment in his family name. The initial recruits for this regiment were either deserters from the British army or new recruits from Ireland. By early 1745 the regiment was ready to take the field and was immediately put into action during the Fontenoy campaign.

Operational history

War of the Austrian Succession, 1740–8

1745   The regiment's first battle was at Fontenoy.

1745–6   A detachment of the regiment captured at sea during the expedition to Scotland. Another detachment reached Scotland and served with the 'Irish Piquets' as part of Prince Charles Edward Stuart's expedition to Scotland. They were present at the battles of Penrith, Falkirk and Culloden Moor.

1747   The regiment was present at the battle of Laffeldt and the siege of Maestricht.

Seven Years War, 1756–63

1757   The regiment was dispatched to India in May of 1757 as part of an expeditionary force commanded by Lieutenant-General Comte Thomas Arthur Lally, who served both as military commander and viceroy of the French possessions in India.

1758   It arrived at Pondicherry, India (April 1758).

1760   The French forces were defeated at Wandiwash by the army of Sir Eyre Coote.

1761   The regiment played a prominent part in the defence of Pondicherry. The survivors of the regiment were taken prisoner when the town capitulated.

Disbandment, 1762

The remnants of the Regiment of Lally returned to France in 1762 and where the regiment was disbanded. In its short career, it had been engaged in several major battles in Europe and in India.

Lally himself became the scapegoat for the French defeat in India and after a term of imprisonment was executed in 1766. By order of Louis XV, he was gagged before he mounted the scaffold so that he could not address the crowd. His son, the Comte et Marquis de Lally Tolendal, successfully petitioned Louis XVI and in 1778 his Lally's name was vindicated.

Colonel proprietors

1744–62   Lieutenant-General Comte Thomas Arthur Lally

Regimental colours

The field of the regimental colour was divided into four cantons – cantons 1 and 4 were royal blue and cantons 2 and 3 were black. Superimposed on these cantons was the red cross of St George, trimmed in white. In the centre of the cross an Irish harp device, surmounted by a small crown. The inscription on the arms of the cross read 'In Hoc Signo Vinces' (In this sign conquer). In each canton, a large crown in gold and filled in red, the tip of the crown pointing outwards towards the corner of each canton. There was a white cravat on the flagstaff.

The colonel's colour consisted of a white flag with a red cross. The devices and inscriptions of the regimental colour were repeated on the colonel's colour.

QUEBEC COMPANY, 1756–7

Very little is known of this short-lived Irish company and it is doubtful that they it ever formed an official unit in the French army. On 14 August 1756, the French army of General Montcalm took Fort Oswego, on the southern shore of Lake Ontario, and captured 1,700 British soldiers and also servants and workmen. These prisoners were shipped to Montreal and then Quebec.

While at Quebec, around 50 Irish soldiers appealed to the governor to be allowed join the French service. This was allowed and these Irish soldiers took a new oath to the French king on 15 June 1757. They were used to work on the fortifications of Quebec and they were later sent to France.

Surviving records show that they were sent to France on 15 September 1757 aboard the *Célébre* which arrived at Brest on 12 November 1757.

They then disappear from the record. It is unclear what later became of them but the logical assumption would be that they were absorbed into the Irish regiments in the French service.

IRISH BOURBON REGIMENTS IN THE BRITISH SERVICE, 1794–8

Formation
After the French revolution and the re-designation of the remaining Irish regiments in the French service, some of the officers and men of these regiments remained loyal to the royalist cause. In 1792 there was an unsuccessful attempt to re-form the Irish regiments as part of the Armée des Princes in Koblenz.

The British government realized that this could prove to be a means of raising new regiments for their war against revolutionary France. They authorized the raising of six new regiments in Ireland that were to recruit Irish Catholics and these would be officered in part by former officers of the Bourbon army. These regiments would in theory serve the French royalist cause and would be part of a wider effort to restore the French monarchy. They were raised for the British service and were placed on the Irish establishment of the army and used French regimental titles. In many contemporary accounts, this brigade of Irish regiments was referred to as 'Pitt's Irish Brigade'.

From its inception this plan attracted much opposition, especially from the Irish Protestant community. It was agreed that these regiments would be raised in Ireland but would then serve abroad. This overseas service was often in notoriously unhealthy stations in the West Indies. Two regiments were disbanded in 1796, due to continued opposition and a failure to attract sufficient recruits, while the others survived until 1797 and 1798. Three of these regiments adopted the lineage of the original Irish regiments in French service and saw themselves as the direct descendents of the regiments of Berwick, Walsh and Dillon. Reference has been made to this in the separate entries for these regiments. The brief history of the six regiments of Britain's Irish Brigade is outlined below.

1st REGIMENT OF THE IRISH BRIGADE

Régiment de le Duc de Fitzjames

1794	Raised in Ireland in October.
1796	Reviewed at New Geneva, Co. Waterford, in September.
	Disbanded due to recruiting difficulties in September 1796.
	Personnel absorbed into the Dillon Regiment, Comte de Walsh-Serrant's Regiment and Vicomte Walsh-Serrant's Regiment.

Colonel
Jacques Charles de Fitzjames, 4th Duc de Fitzjames

Regimental colours
On the king's and regimental colour, a central device of a gold harp surrounded by a wreath. On a crimson ribbon scroll beneath, the inscription '1st Regiment of the Irish Brigade'.

2nd REGIMENT OF THE IRISH BRIGADE

Régiment de le Comte de Walsh-Serrant

1794	The regiment was raised in Ireland in October.
1796	Reviewed at New Geneva, Co. Waterford, in September. Absorbed some of the personnel of the disbanded regiments of the brigade. In November 1796, it boarded ship for the West Indies.
1797	In February, the regiment was based at Martinique before being stationed in Jamaica and San Domingo.
1798	Based at San Domingo. The regiment moved to Jamaica in August. In October 1798 it boarded ship for England and was disbanded at Chatham in November. The regiment's personnel were drafted into other British units.

Colonel
Comte Antoine de Walsh-Serrant

Regimental colours
On king's and regimental colour, a central harp device. A crimson scroll beneath with the inscription '2nd Regiment of the Irish Brigade'.

3rd REGIMENT OF THE IRISH BRIGADE
Régiment de Dillon

1794   Raised in Ireland in October
1796   Reviewed at New Geneva, Co. Waterford, in September.
Absorbs some of the personnel of the disbanded regiments of the brigade. The regiment was sent to West Indies where the regiment served in Jamaica and San Domingo.
1798   In June the regiment embarked at Port au Prince, bound for England. It was disbanded in England on its arrival. The regiment's personnel was drafted into other British units.

Colonel
Colonel the Hon. Henry Dillon

Regimental colours
The same as those of other regiments of the brigade. The crimson scroll on the colours reading '3rd Regiment of the Irish Brigade'.

4th REGIMENT OF THE IRISH BRIGADE
Régiment de le Comte O'Connell

1794   Raised in Ireland in October.
1796   Reviewed at New Geneva, Co. Waterford, in September. The regiment was disbanded shortly afterwards due to recruiting difficulties. Its personnel were absorbed into the regiments of the Comte de Walsh-Serrant, the Viscomte de Walsh-Serrant and the Regiment of Dillon.

Colonel
Comte Daniel Charles O'Connell

Regimental colours
The same as the other regiments of the brigade with the scroll reading '4th Regiment of the Irish Brigade'.

5th REGIMENT OF THE IRISH BRIGADE
Régiment de le Vicomte de Walsh-Serrant

1794   Raised in Ireland in October
1796   Reviewed at New Geneva in September. It then absorbed some of the personnel of the regiments of the brigade that had been disbanded.
           The regiment was sent to the West Indies.
1797   The regiment was stationed at Halifax, Nova Scotia.
           In October the regiment boarded ship for England and was disbanded at Chatham on Christmas Day, 1797. The regiment's personnel were sent to other British units.

Colonel
Comte Thomas de Conway (d.1795)   Vicomte Charles de Walsh-Serrant

Regimental colours
As with the other regiments of this brigade, the scroll reading '5th Regiment of the Irish Brigade'.

6th REGIMENT OF THE IRISH BRIGADE
Régiment de le Comte de Conway

1794   Raised in Ireland in October.
1796   Reviewed at New Geneva, Co. Waterford, in September.
1797   The regiment was stationed at Halifax, Nova Scotia.
1798   Disbanded in England.

Colonel
Comte James Henry de Conway (d.1800)

Regimental colours
As with the other regiments in this brigade, the king's and regimental colour had a central harp device, surrounded with a wreath motif. There was a crimson scroll beneath with the inscription '6th Regiment of the Irish Brigade'.

LÉGION IRLANDAISE, 1803–1815

Formation
At the outbreak of the French Revolution, the remnants of the Irish 'Wild Geese' regiments were still serving in the French army. By this time there were very few Irish

troops still serving in their ranks and although there were still officers of Irish descent, a series of army reforms succeeded in destroying the Irish identity of these regiments.

As early as 1796 the Directory considered raising new Irish regiments for their planned invasion of Ireland. The idea was raised again in 1800 but it was not until 1803 that a new regiment was founded. Following the outbreak of war in 1803, Napoleon issued a consular decree establishing an Irish legion that was to be composed of Irishmen or Frenchmen of Irish descent. The date of this new legion's creation was 31 August 1803 and it was initially established as a single battalion of nine companies and a staff company. It would eventually increase to four battalions with a depot unit. In 1808 it was re-designated as the **Régiment Irlandais** and, in 1811, as the 3ᵉᵐᵉ **Régiment Étranger** (3rd Foreign Regiment). In a final re-designation of 1815, it was re-titled as the 7ᵉᵐᵉ **Régiment Étranger**.

Operational history

1803–6 The legion was raised in Brittany and was based there from late 1803. There was a sufficient number of officers. These were composed of Frenchmen of Irish descent and also political exiles who had fled to France after the 1798 Rebellion. The recruitment of the rank and file proved difficult, however, and the legion took on the character of an 'officers unit'. In late 1804 the legion had 66 officers but only 22 NCOs and privates.

1806 Months of inactivity and the boredom of garrison life in the small town of Quimper resulted in disciplinary problems and also resignations. The situation was so bad by the summer of 1806, that the remaining officers wrote directly to the Emperor requesting that he remedy the situation. As a result of this the legion, by then numbering only 80 men, was sent to the city of Mainz (then Mayence) where it was brought up to establishment.

Some 1,500 Prussian POWs who had opted to enter the French army were assigned to the legion. The majority of these men were Poles but there was also a large number of Irishmen. These Irishmen had been British prisoners following the 1798 Rebellion but they had been sold to Prussia to serve in its army or work as miners.

1807 In February 1807 the legion was sent to Boulogne, before carrying out garrison duty in Antwerp. In September 1807 a detachment of the legion was posted to the Walcheren Island in the Scheldt estuary.

In December 1807 a provisional 2nd Battalion was formed from the legion's surplus personnel.

1808 While the rest of the legion remained bottled up on garrison duty on Walcheren Island throughout 1808, the second provisional battalion was sent to Spain. It was commanded by Captain Louis Lacy and was assigned to Marshal Moncey's corps of observation. Much of this unit's service in Spain was spent on garrison duty. In December 1808, Napoleon issued an imperial decree which re-designated the legion as the **Régiment Irlandais** and gave the provisional battalion official status as the regiment's 2nd Battalion.

1809 On 17 January 1809 the 2nd Battalion provided a guard for Napoleon at Burgos. It remained in Spain for all of 1809 and took part in an anti-guerrilla campaign around Castille and also an expedition into the Asturias. In April 1809 Napoleon issued a further decree which increased the regiment's establishment to four battalions and a depot unit.

The first battalion of the regiment remained at Walcheren Island and formed part of the garrison at Flushing when it was besieged by British land and sea forces in July 1809. The garrison surrendered on 15 August 1809 and the battalion was marched into captivity.

The regiment's new 3rd Battalion was raised in April 1809 and was initially commanded by Battalion Chief Jean François Mahony. Its first recruits were a mixture of Frenchmen and also Irish prisoners of war who were encouraged to join the French army. It was rushed to Antwerp in August in the hope that it could help raise the siege of Flushing. As it arrived too late, it was then sent to Spain. By the time it joined the 2nd Battalion at Burgos in Spain, sickness and desertion had reduced it from 1,500 men to around 350.

In September 1809 the regiment's 4th Battalion was founded at the depot at Landau but recruiting was the new battalion was slow.

1810 In January 1810 the battalions of the regiment were located as follows:

1st Battalion	Prisoners of war
2nd Battalion	15 officers and 700 men at Burgos, Spain
3rd Battalion	12 Officers and 350 men at Burgos, Spain
4th Battalion	Recruiting at Landau
Depot	Landau

Due to recruiting difficulties and also changes in organization the 1st and 4th Battalions were amalgamated in September 1810, effectively creating a full-strength 1st Battalion.

For the 2nd and 3rd Battalions, 1810 was a year of active campaigning in Spain. The 2nd Battalion took part in the night action at Najara in February and was then present at the siege of Astoria. The Irish battalions were later were present at the sieges of Ciudad Rodrigo and Almeida and also took part in the battle of Busaco and the march to the Lines of Torres Vedras. The campaign took a high toll of both battalions and by October 1810 they collectively numbered just 439 men.

1811 In February 1811 the two battalions were amalgamated and a cadre staff of the 3rd Battalion returned to France to begin recruiting. The 2nd Battalion played a prominent role in the rearguard during the march out of Portugal in 1811. By April it was down to 19 officers and 254 men. It was present at the battle of Fuentes de Oñoro in May 1811 but did not come under fire. For the remainder of the year it took part in anti-guerrilla operations.

Under the terms of an Imperial decree of 3 August 1811, the regiment was denationalized and was re-designated as the 3ème **Régiment Étranger**

(3rd Foreign Regiment). It was intended to increase the regiment to five battalions by using Austrian recruits and then use it for the defence of Holland. The 2nd Battalion in Spain was disbanded and its personnel were spread among other units while a cadre staff returned to France.

1812 In early 1812 the three battalions were sent to Holland where they were based at Hertogenbosch before being sent to garrison the island of Goree and the towns of Bergen-op-Zoomand and Willemstadt.

1813 These Irish battalions took no part in the Russian campaign of 1812 but in February 1813 the 1st and 2nd Battalions were sent to join the Grand Army in the east. By this time the regiment had essentially lost its Irish identity. The 1st Battalion had only 65 Irish soldiers while the 2nd Battalion had only nine.

The regiment joined General Lauriston's Vth Corps on the lower Elbe and took part in the second day of the battle of Bautzen (22 May 1813). After the collapse of the armistice in August 1813 the regiment took part in the battle of Löwenberg on 19 August where it suffered serious casualties and was almost overrun. On 21 August they spearheaded a counter-attack across the Bober River and took the strategic Goldberg Hill on 23 August. After the French defeat at the battle of Katzbach on 26 August, the regiment fought a rearguard action to the Bober River where it found itself trapped. Only 10 officers and 30 men managed to swim to the other side but they carried with them the regimental eagle. The remnants of these two battalions returned to Holland where they joined the under-strength 3rd and 4th Battalions to make one effective battalion. The disbandment of other decimated foreign regiments provided an influx of fresh recruits and by December 1813 the regiment could muster 85 officers and 396 men. This battalion was used to garrison Antwerp.

1814 During the allied campaign in Holland the regiment distinguished itself at the battle of Merxem on the outskirts of Antwerp. This battle took place on 13 and 14 January 1814. They then formed the largest component of the garrison of Antwerp when that city was besieged. They held out after Napoleon's abdication and did not surrender until 4 May 1814.

The remnants of this regiment lingered on under the Restoration government which had decided to retain a number of foreign regiments. By September 1814 it numbered just 102 officers and 200 men. The retention of the regiment was confirmed by royal decree in December 1814.

1815 When Napoleon returned from Elba in 1815, the regiment immediately declared for the Emperor. Its royalist commanding officer, Colonel Mahony, was replaced by Major Hugh Ware, a noted Bonapartist and a hero of the Bober River actions.

Napoleon re-designated the regiment as the **7th Foreign Regiment** in May 1815 and decided that the unit should retain its Irish identity. When all non-Irish personnel were distributed to other units, however, the new regiment was no longer strong enough to play an effective role in the 1815 campaign. The aftermath of Waterloo found the regiment blockaded by allied forces in the town of Montreuil before it finally surrendered.

Louis XVIII issued a decree disbanding all of Napoleons' foreign regiments in September 1815. The Irish regiment was disbanded on 29 September 1815. Some of its members joined the Royal Foreign Legion, the forerunner of the modern French Foreign Legion.

Commanding officers
1803–4 Battalion Chef James Bartholomew Blackwell was appointed as the first commanding officer although actual command was exercised by Adjutant-Commandant Bernard MacSheehy.

September 1804–9	Battalion Chef Antoine Petrezzoli
May 1809–November 1811	Colonel Daniel Joseph O'Meara
February 1812–13	Colonel William Lawless
December 1813–1814	Colonel Jean François Mahony
1815	Major Hugh Ware

Regimental colours
The first standard of the Irish Legion was granted in January 1804. It was green with a gold harp in each corner. The obverse had a central tricolour oval with the motto 'Le Premier Consul Aux Irlandois [sic] Unis' (The First Consul to the United Irishmen). The reverse had a central medallion decorated with a green wreath of laurel and oak leaves. The motto on the reverse read 'Liberté des Consciences/ Indépendence de L'Irande (Freedom of Conscience Independence of Ireland).

In December 1804 the legion was granted a new colour and also an Imperial Eagle. It was the first foreign unit to receive an Imperial Eagle. The colour was a green silk banner with a gold fringe and on the obverse the inscription read 'L'Empereur des Francais a la Légion Irlandaise' .On the reverse there was a gold harp with the inscription 'L'Indépendence de L'Irlande'.

There is also some evidence to suggest that a new colour was issued in 1812. The 2nd and 3rd Battalions would also seem to have had their own colours which were green with a harp in the centre. When the remains of the regiment was trapped at Montreuil after the Waterloo campaign, these battalion colours were destroyed to prevent them being taken by the enemy.

When the 1st Battalion was taken prisoner at Flushing in 1809, Colonel William Lawless escaped from the town and carried the regimental eagle to safety. The remnants of the 1st and 2nd Battalions who swam across the Bober River in 1813 carried the eagle with them. After the restoration of the Bourbon monarchy in 1814, the eagle was hidden among regimental stores but was brought out again when Napoleon returned from Elba.

LA COMPAGNIE IRLANDAISE, 1870–1

Formation

This Irish unit was formed in October 1870 by which time France had suffered a series of defeats at Wörth, Spicheren, Mars la Tour and Gravelotte. The Emperor Louis Napoleon and Marshal MacMahon had surrendered at Sedan on 2 September 1870, along with an army of over 100,000 men. Léon Gambetta, the leader of the new republican government, had however proclaimed that France would continue to fight.

In Dublin an ambulance corps had been founded under the auspices of the International Red Cross Society. In early October 1870 a contingent of 250 Irishmen left Dublin, ostensibly to serve in the Irish Ambulance Corps, and they landed at Le Havre on 11 October. (The service of this ambulance unit is noticed separately below.) Less than 100 men were needed to serve with the ambulance unit and the remainder were encouraged by Martin W. Kirwan to form an Irish company, which could serve as infantry in the French army. Kirwan had previously been a lieutenant in the militia and he initially experienced difficulties at Le Havre having this company accepted for service. He marched them to Caen where, after some negotiation, they were accepted into the French army and began their training. Kirwan was commissioned as a captain and two other members of the company who had military experience, F. McAlevey and B. Cotter, were commissioned as lieutenants.

Operational history

1870   The Compagnie Irlandaise was dispatched to Bourges where they were officially attached to the French Foreign Legion. The company's actual designation was as the 8th Company of the 5th Battalion, Régiment Etranger. The 5th Battalion, RE, formed part of the 2nd Brigade, 1st Division of the 15th Army Corps, commanded by General Bourbaki.

During December they were involved in series of marches and countermarches as the Germans threatened Bourges, before forming part of its garrison in January 1871.

1871   After some small skirmishes in the Bourges area, they boarded trains on 7 January 1871 and were sent to Clarval, near the front line, were they rejoined Bourbaki's corps.

Bourbaki was engaged south of Belfort with a Prussian corps commanded by General Von Werder. On the night of 14th to 15th January the Compagnie Irlandaise marched with the reserve division of the 15th Corps towards Montbéliard where they took up a position on the right flank of the French line. During the course of the three-day battle that followed the company was moved about various parts of the battlefield as part of the 5th Battalion, Régiment Etranger. Kiwan later wrote that much of this movement seemed to him to be a total waste of time and energy. During some of the battlefield movements they were exposed to Prussian artillery fire and in the course of the battle lost over 30 men killed and wounded. It should also be noted that this campaign was fought during one of the worst French winters in years.

Bourbaki had meanwhile taken one wing of the army towards the Swiss frontier. Soon a general retreat was ordered and the Compagnie Irlandaise and the other companies of the 5th Battalion RE formed the rearguard, taking part in several engagements during the retreat. On 23 January 1871 they took up positions at the 'Red Farm' at the village of Busy, on the outskirts of Besançon. They remained there until the armistice came into effect in their area on 2 February. The unit was disbanded on 27 March and the surviving members arrived back in Ireland in April 1871. They numbered 55 men, all ranks.

THE FRANCO-IRISH AMBULANCE, 1870–1

Formation
On the outbreak of the Franco-Prussian War groups in Ireland sympathetic to the French cause began seeking ways to be of practical help. Neutrality laws prevented a military unit being raised in Ireland and the Compagnie Irlandaise noted above circumvented these laws due to the fact that they were formed in France. The initial efforts in Ireland were devoted to providing medical assistance. After a series of articles in *The Nation*, a medical assistance committee was formed in Dublin in September 1870. This committee decided to form an 'Franco-Irish Ambulance' and, with the approval of the International Red Cross Committee, a call was made for volunteers in early October.

Within a week around 250 men had volunteered. Many of these men were from Dublin but there were also volunteers from other towns and cities, including a large contingent from Dundalk. On 8 October 1870, 250 men boarded ship for Le Havre but this was too many to serve in the ambulance unit. After their arrival in France, many of these men volunteered to serve in Kirwan's Compangnie Irlandaise. The eventual composition of the Franco-Irish Ambulance was six surgeons, thirty medical students and fifty 'infirmarians'. They had four ambulance wagons and the unit was divided into smaller groups, each commanded by a surgeon. Dr C.P.Baxter, previously a surgeon with the 93rd Sutherland Highlanders, was in command. The Societé de Secours aux Blessés Militaires also assigned a director to the unit. This was originally a Monsieur Duquet and he was later succeeded by a Monsieur Bourse and then a Monsieur Picard.

Operational history
1870   The ambulance unit was immediately put into service and by 15 October 1870 it was treating and evacuating its first wounded at Conches, near Evreux.

On 9 November 1870, it was decided that the ambulance unit was still too large and two surgeons were dispatched to join General Mocquart's Army of the North, taking two ambulance wagons and some of the unit's other staff with them. This sub-unit was present at a number of lesser engagements such as Bonnieres, Courcelles and Elboeuf. This section of the Irish Ambulance, numbering 23 men, was disbanded at Le Havre in January 1871 and returned to Ireland.

The main component of the Franco-Irish Ambulance was attached to the Army of the Loire and was posted to Chateaudun, where it arrived on 12 November 1870. The city had already suffered from a Prussian bombardment and a series of engagements took place in its vicinity. The ambulance took control of twelve buildings in Chateaudun to use as dressing stations. A section of the ambulance remained there until February 1871, treating wounded in their own dressing stations and also sending parties into the field to deal with the aftermath of the battle of Loigny (2 December 1870).

1871   During the final phase of the war, sections of the Irish Ambulance were present at engagements such as Parigné. After the fall of Le Mans on 12 January 1871, the Army of the Loire effectively ceased to exist and the Irish Ambulance proceeded to wind down operations. The unit disbanded and the majority of the volunteers travelled to Le Havre and returned to Ireland. Dr Baxter remained in Chateaudun until the end of February 1871 when he handed the last of his patients over to the civilian authorities.

CHAPTER 4

Irish regiments in Spanish service, 1709–1939

While the Irish regiments in the French service have received a certain amount of historical attention, the history of the Irish regiments in the Spanish service is generally less well-known. The Irish military connection with Spain has been a long one. In 1585 Sir John Stanley took a force of 1,500 Irish troops to Holland in order to serve with Britain's Dutch allies. Once there, however, he accepted a bribe and turned his regiment over to the Spanish.

During the sixteenth century, further Irish regiments were raised for the Spanish service by exiled Irish leaders such as Owen Roe O'Neil and Hugh O'Donnell. The history of these regiments falls outside the remit of this gazetteer but it is interesting to note that the Irish military connection with Spain had such a long history, starting in the sixteenth century and continuing in various phases until the early twentieth century. For the purposes of this gazetteer, the Irish regiments in Spain can be classed in three categories.

- The 'Wild Geese' regiments, 1709–1818
- The Irish regiments in the First Carlist War, 1835–8
- The Irish units in the Spanish Civil War, 1936–9

THE 'WILD GEESE' REGIMENTS, 1709–1818

In the early years of the eighteenth century, as it became increasingly obvious that the House of Stuart was not going to regain the throne of Britain, it was decided to disband several of the Irish regiments in the Stuart and French service. In 1709 it was learned that Philip V of Spain intended to raise Irish regiments and James III opened negotiations with the Spanish authorities. The men of some of James' Irish regiments were released from their contracts and allowed to negotiate a new contract with Philip V.

The last clause of this new contract allowed for these regiments to be disbanded if Irish recruits became scarce and it was this clause that was invoked to allow for the disbandment of these regiments in 1818. In all seven regiments served in the Spanish service during this period although only three were to have long and significant histories. These regiments were:

1. The Irlanda Regiment – founded in 1699, it entered the Spanish service in 1715 and was designated as the senior Irish regiment.

2. The Hibernia Regiment – entered Spanish service in 1709.

3. The Ultonia Regiment – entered Spanish service in 1709.

4. The Limerick Regiment – entered Spanish service in 1709 but was transferred to the Bourbon King of Sicily in 1735.(See separate entry on this regiment in the section on Italian regiments. In the Neapolitan service, this regiment was renamed as the Regimento Infanteria del Rey).

5. The Waterford Regiment – entered Spanish service in 1709 but disbanded in 1734, its personnel being allocated to the other Irish regiments, in particular the Hibernia Regiment.

6. The dragoon regiment of Crofton, disbanded before 1714.

7. The infantry battalion of MacDonnel, disbanded before 1714.

As the histories of the Irlanda, Hibernia and Ultonia regiments were both significant and well-documented, they will be the focus of this section.

From the time they came into the Spanish service they wore their traditional red uniforms but these were replaced in 1794 for white uniforms. In 1802 they received new sky-blue uniforms, each regiment having a different facing colour. The Irish regiments were initially two battalion regiments but, in 1793, they became three battalion regiments. Due to the losses sustained in the Napoleonic wars they were reduced to one battalion regiment in 1812. In 1814 they became three battalion regiments again and this was still officially the case when they were disbanded in 1818, although by this time the number of Irish recruits had dwindled.

THE IRLANDA REGIMENT, 1699–1818

Foundation
This regiment was the most senior Irish regiment in the Spanish service. The Tercio Irlanda traced its lineage back to the regiment raised by Sir Edward Stanley in 1585. This original Tercio Irlanda was disbanded in 1698. The traditions and name of the Tercio Irlanda were kept alive, however, by a new regiment that was raised in 1699 by Colonel Raymound Bourke from the remnants of the of the Queen's Regiment of Foot, which had been disbanded in 1698.

It should be noted that this regiment, named Bourke's Regiment of Foot, was originally part of the exiled Stuart army that campaigned in the French service. During the War of the Spanish Succession it fought under Marshal Catinat in Italy and was with Marshal Dillon at Cremona. The regiment was also present at the battles of Oudenarde, Malplaquet and Denain.

At the end of the war, the French army was reduced in size and it looked as if this regiment would be disbanded. James III secured permission to allow this regiment to enter the Spanish service and negotiated a contract with Philip V. The regiment entered the Spanish service in 1715 and was initially designated as the Principe de

Asturias Regiment. In 1718 it was re-named as the Primera Infanteria Irlandesa (the 1st Irish Regiment), taking seniority over its fellow Irish regiments.

The patron saint of the regiment was St Patrick and its regimental emblem was a blue shield with a gold harp. These distinctions were also used by the Ultonia and Hibernia regiments.

Operational history

War of the Quadruple Alliance, 1718–20

The Irlanda campaigned in Sicily in 1718 and with the other Irish regiments and took part in the storming of Melazzo.

They were involved in desperate last stand at Mount de San Juan before the Spanish forces were ejected from Sicily by the Austrians in 1720.

The 'Spanish War', 1727–9[1]

The regiment took part in the siege of Gibraltar.

North Africa, 1732

The Irlanda took part in the campaign against the Moor and was present at the recapture of the Spanish *presidio* at Oran, which had fallen to the Moors in 1708.

War of the Austrian Succession, 1740–8

1741   The Irlanda took part in the extended campaign in Italy, landing in Tuscany in 1741.

1743   The Irlanda and Hibernia formed part of the army of General Don Juan de Gages and engaged the Austrians at Campo Santo, north of Bologna, on 8 February 1743. It was a bloody and inconclusive battle with both sides later claiming victory. Both of the Irish regiments suffered serious losses, the Irlanda losing 6 officers and 186 men killed.

1744   On the night of 10 August 1744, the Irlanda played a prominent role in the action at Velletri, blocking the Austrian advance into the town and later taking part in a decisive counter-attack alongside the Hibernia.

As a result of this action, the Irish regiments were allowed to use a new motto on their colours – 'In Omnem Terram, exhivit sonos eorum' ('Their sound hath gone forth into all the earth', taken from Psalm 19:4). The regiment was also awarded a regimental soubriquet and became known as 'El Fomoso'.

The Irlanda continued to campaign in Italy until the end of the war in 1748.

North Africa, 1756

The regiment took part in the campaign in North Africa in 1756.

American Revolutionary War, 1777–81

The regiment besieged Gibraltar when Spain declared war on Britain.

---

1 A war of Spain against Britain and France.

North Africa, 1790–2

During the 1790s, the Irlanda again saw service in North Africa and were present at the final Spanish evacuation of Oran in 1792.

French Revolutionary and Napoleonic Wars, 1792–1815

1808 Following the collapse of the Spanish-French alliance, the Irlanda was attached to General Cuesta's army of Estremadura.

1809 It took part in the battle of Talavera before transferring to the army of General Joaquín Blake.

1811 The Irlanda was present at the battle of Albuera and at the siege of Tarifa

1814 At the end of the war the regiment was stationed in Navarre.

1818 Due to the lack of Irish recruits, the regiment was disbanded.

Colonel Proprietors

1715 Coronel Brigadier Don Francisco Wachop (Wauchope)
1718 Coronel Don Reynaldo MacDonnald (MacDonald)
1732 El Conde de Bearheven (Berehaven)
1734 Coronel Don Eduardo Burck (Burke)
1747 Coronel Don Daniel MacDonnald
1756 Coronel Don Reynaldo MacDonnald
1760 Coronel Don Juan Comesford (Comerford)
1768 Coronel Don Vicente Kindelan
1777 Coronel Don Juan MacKenna
1788 Coronel Don Eugenio O'Neylly (O'Neill)
1790 Coronel Don Diego O'Neylly
1794 Coronel Don Félix Jones
1807 Coronel Don Juan José Sardeñ
1808 Coronel Don Juan Nacten (Naughton)
1810 El Conde de Ibeagh
1813 Coronel Don Joaquín Gómez de Menchaca
1815 Coronel Don Antonio Gaspar Blanco
1816 Coronel Don Juilián de Estrada (until disbandment)

THE ULTONIA REGIMENT, 1709–1818

Foundation

The regiment was raised by Colonel Dermott MacAuliffe on 1 November 1709 from the remnants of the Regiment of Galmoy, which had previously served in French service but was now disbanded. The regiment was originally referred to as the 'Regiment of MacAuliffe'.

Irish regiments in Spanish service, 1709-1939

Operational History

War of the Spanish Succession, 1701-14

1710   Alongside the other Irish regiments in the Spanish service and, the regiment campaigned during the War of the Spanish Succession and saw its first major action at the battle of Almenara on 27 July 1710 and later fought its way into Gerona to relieve the besieged garrison. In September 1710 it was part of the besieging forces at Barcelona.

1711   The regiment played a prominent part in the capture of Palma on Mallorca and also in the capture if Ibiza.

War in Sicily, 1718-20

1718   The regiment was renamed as the Ultonia Regiment and was sent to Sicily to take part in the campaign against the Austrians. On 1 August the Ultonia landed on the beach at Loreto and in September it captured Messina.

1719   The Ultonia fought at the battle of Francovilla on 20 June and suffered heavy casualties, among whom was Colonel MacAuliffe, who was mortally wounded. It took part in an heroic last stand at Mount de San Juan and left Sicily at the end of the war in 1720.

The 'Spanish War', 1727-9

The regiment was part of the besieging forces at Gibraltar.

North Africa, 1732

1732   The Ultonia sailed to North Africa in November 1732 to take part in the campaign against the Moorish. After the recapture of Oran they defended it against besieging Moorish forces. They took part in a sally against the Moors forces and when the Spanish column was driven back into Oran, they formed the rearguard.

1734   The Regiment of Waterford was disbanded and its personnel were divided among the other remaining Irish regiments. The Ultonia were brought back up to strength after the disbandment of the Regiment of Waterford, although the majority of the disbanded regiment's personnel joined the Hibernia Regiment.

War of the Austrian Succession, 1740-8

1740   At the outbreak of the War of the Austrian Succession, the regiment was on garrison duty in Oran.

1745   The regiment was moved to Italy where it joined the regiments of Irlanda and Hibernia to form an Irish Brigade. It took part in the siege and capture of Tortona which fell on 4 September 1745. At the end of the war it went into garrison duty in Barcelona. In the aftermath of the battle of Velletri (1744), the Ultonia was also allowed to attach the new Irish Brigade motto to its flag – 'In Omnem Terram, exhivit sonos eorum' ('Their sound hath gone forth into all the earth', Psalm 19:4); despite the fact that they were not present at the battle. They were also given the regimental soubriquet 'El Immortal' and henceforth they were known as 'The Immortals'.

North Africa, 1756

1756   The regiment was back in North Africa campaigning against the Moors.

Spanish-Portuguese War of 1761–3

1762   The Ultonia campaigned in the province of Tras os Montes.

1768   The second battalion of the Ultonia was posted to Mexico City where it remained on garrison duty until 1771.

American Revolutionary War, 1777–81

When Spain declared war on England the Ultonia was present at the siege of Port Mahon on Minorca and captured the San Felipe castle.

French Revolutionary and Napoleonic Wars, 1792–1815

1792–5   The regiment was initially garrisoned at the important arsenal at Ferrol in Galicia. At the battle of Irun, the commanding officer of the Ultonia, Colonel Francis Comerford, was killed as the regiment stormed the Cruz de Busquets battery. During the French counterattack that followed, they played an important part in the rearguard.

1795–1801   The Ultonia was on garrison duty in the Canary Islands. During the Spanish-French alliance they served in the siege of Gibraltar.

1808   The most famous actions of the Ultonia Regiment occurred at the siege of Gerona, after the Spanish alliance with the French had collapsed. The 800 men of the Ultonia were prominent in the defence of the city's walls while also making sallies to drive off the besiegers and to allow supply columns to enter. They formed about 10 per cent of General Alvarez de Castro's command and were tasked with defending the Santa Clara bastion, which the French soon identified as a key position. The Ultonia played a major role in beating off several French assaults. During the 'grand assault' of 19 June 1808, a breach in the city's walls was defended by Sergeant-Major Ricardo MacCarthy and 200 men of the regiment. They later defended two breaches during another attack. When the garrison surrendered due to starvation on 11 December 1808, only 250 men of the regiment remained alive and these were marched away to imprisonment in France. All were later awarded a special medal – the 'Cross of Gerona' – while the depot battalion of the regiment was henceforth referred to as 'Distinguidos de Ultonia'.

1809   The regiment was re-formed by Colonel Peter Sarsfield, who gathered together invalids, members of the regiment who had been detached on garrison duty and also escaped prisoners of war.

1810   The reconstituted Ultonia fought at Vich and a year later were present at the battle of Pla.

1811   The 1st Battalion made up part of the garrison of Tarragona which surrendered in 1811. In August 1811, the 3rd Battalion was captured when the town of Figueras fell to the French.

1812–14   The regiment was rebuilt again by its new commanding officer, Colonel

Vincent McGrath, who was the last Irish-born commander of the Ultonia. After a long campaign against the forces of Marshal Suchet, they were present when he surrendered at Lerida on 14 February 1814.

1814 The Ultonia went into garrison in Barcelona where it was commanded by Colonel Phillipe des Fleurs who had previously commanded the Brussels Regiment. This was the first occasion on which the regiment was commanded by a non-Irish officer and this situation was symptomatic of the difficulties in obtaining Irish recruits.

1818 On 1 June the regiment was disbanded as part of the post-war reduction of the army.

In December 1943, as part of a re-organization of the Spanish army, it was decided that existing regiments would adopt the traditions and lineage of some of the disbanded regiments. Infantry Regiment No. 84 was re-designated with the new title of 'Ultonia No.59' and it was tasked with maintaining the traditions of the disbanded Irish regiment. This arrangement continued until 1986, when the Ultonia No. 59 was disbanded at Gerona, a city long associated with the former Irish regiment.[2]

Colonel proprietors

1709	Coronel Don Demetrio MacAulif
1716	Coronel Don Tadeo MacAulif
1720	Coronel Don Guillermo de Lacy
1726	Coronel Don Juan Sckerlock (Sherlock)
1734	Coronel Don Diego Aylmer
1742	Coronel Don Francisco Comesford (Comerford)
1759	Coronel Don Juan O'Slateri (O'Slattery)
1776	Coronel Don Juan MacKenna
1781	Coronel Don Pedro Tirrell
1791	Coronel Don Miguel Kuaresbroug
1793	Coronel Don Francisco Comesford (Comerford)
1795	Coronel Don Juan Kindelan
1802	Coronel Don Antonio O'Kelly
1808	Coronel Don Enrique O'Donnell
1811	Coronel Don Pedro Sarsfield
1814	Coronel Don Vicente MacGrath
1815	Coronel Don Felipe Fleures (until disbandment)

THE HIBERNIA REGIMENT, 1709–1818

Foundation

The Hibernia regiment was raised on 1 November 1709 by Don Reynaldo MacDonald, who became the regiment's first lieutenant-colonel. He was authorized

---

2 I am indebted to Dr Alicia Laspra-Rodriquez and General Ramos Oliver for this information.

to recruit Irish deserters from English regiments in Spain. Its first colonel was Don Lucas Patino, Marquis of Castelar. The regiment consisted of two battalions of thirteen companies. Each company held fifty men.

The articles of the regiment's foundation stated that all the officers had to be of Irish origin or ancestry. It was hoped that all the rank and file would be Irish but foreign nationals were also admitted and by the time of the regiment's disbandment the number of Irish troops had declined.

Operational history

War of the Spanish Succession, 1701–14

1710   The Hibernia Regiment saw its first action at Zaragosa on 20 August.

1714   It took part in the battles at Brihuega and Villaviciosa and was present at the siege of Barcelona in 1714.

War of the Quadruple Alliance, 1718–20

1718   Philip V was determined to regain ex-Spanish territory in Italy and in 1718 an expeditionary force was sent to Sicily. One battalion of the Hibernia was attached to this and was present at the siege of Palermo.

1719   The regiment fought in the battles of Francavilla and Melazzo. The Irish Brigade made a gallant stand against the Austrians at Mount de San Juan but ultimately the Spanish force was driven from Sicily and Philip sued for peace in 1720.

The 'Spanish War', 1727–9

Both battalions of the Hibernia took part in the unsuccessful siege of Gibraltar in 1727–8 during an outbreak of hostilities between Britain and Spain.

North Africa, 1732

In the campaign against the Moors in Oran in 1732 the regiment met with more success and, following the recapture of Oran, it remained in Oran on garrison duty.

In 1734 the Waterford Regiment was disbanded and the majority of its personnel were incorporated into the Hibernia.

War of the Austrian Succession, 1740–48

1741   The Hibernia joined other Irish regiments in the Spanish service (the Ultonia and the Irlanda) to form an Irish brigade during the campaign in Italy and they landed in Tuscany in 1741.

1743   The regiment suffered serious losses during the inconclusive battle of Campo Santo, losing 18 officers and 189 men killed. By the end of the 1743 campaigning season the regiment had lost at least half of its original contingent.

1744   During the Austrian night attack at Velletri on 11 August, the Irish brigade incurred serious losses again as they delayed the enemy advance. Colonel MacDonald and over forty other officers were among the regiment's casualties. Accounts of the battle later recounted how the dead of the Irish regiments were in heaps at the Nettuno Gate. This was the main point of the

Austrian attack on Velletri as the Austrian general, Lobkowitz, pressed home his advantage in numbers.

Over 6,000 seasoned Imperial troops fell on the Irish and Walloon Guards but as the Austrians prepared to set up siege lines, a counter attack by the defenders caught them off-balance and threw them back.

After the action at Velletri, the Irish regiments received a motto to attach to their flags – 'In Omnem Terram, exhivit sonos eorum' ('Their sound hath gone forth into all the earth', Psalm 19:4). They were also each given a regimental sobriquet. The Hibernia was henceforth referred to as 'La Columna Hibernia' ('The Pillar of Ireland'). The remnants of the Hibernia fought at the successful sieges of Nochera and Tortosa and at the battles of Solana, Fidone and Bortagio.

1748   The regiment remained in Italy until 1748. When returning from the Italian campaign, a party of the Hibernia's second battalion was attacked at sea by Algerian pirates. After a stiff action they were forced to surrender and were imprisoned in Algiers for three years.

North Africa, 1756

The regiment returned to North Africa but the Moors captured Algiers and 170 men of the regiment were imprisoned.

Spanish-Portuguese War, 1761–63

The Hibernia campaigned in Portugal and garrisoned the town of Plaza de Chaves.

1768   The regiment was sent to Mexico City where it formed part of the garrison for several years.

North Africa, 1775

The regiment took part in an another unsuccessful expedition against the Moors of Algiers. After this campaign, they were garrisoned in Barcelona.

American Revolutionary War, 1777–81

1777   The Hibernia took part in the expedition to Brazil where they were present at the capture of the island of Santa Catalina. They later formed part of the attacking forces at Colonia del Sacramento and the island of San Gabriel.

1780   The regiment returned to Spain on the conclusion of this campaign but was dispatched to Havana, Cuba. Spain was allied with France and the American revolutionary government and, attached to the army of Lt-Gen. Don Victorio de Navia, the Hibernia operated against British forces in the West Indies and Florida.

1781   Bad weather prevented a landing at Pensacola Bay in Florida in October.

In April siege operations began against Fort George at Pensacola and nearly 600 men of the regiment took part in this siege, under the command of Lt.-Col. Arturo O'Neil. The siege dragged on until the 29th April 1781 and cost the Hibernia 16 dead and 27 wounded by the time of its successful completion.

An expedition against Jamaica was aborted due to bad weather and the Hibernia then sent detachments on garrison duty in Honduras and in other forts along the 'Mosquito Coast'.

1784   The Hibernia was sent to garrison Saint Augustine in Florida. Here they found themselves trying to combat the operations of the various bandit groups that operated in northern Florida.

North Africa, 1791–2

The regiment returned to Oran but following an unsuccessful campaign, the territory was surrendered to the Moors and they took part in the final Spanish evacuation in 1792.

French Revolutionary and Napoleonic Wars, 1792–1815

1792–3   The Hibernia was enlarged to three battalions and, following the outbreak of war between France and Spain in 1793, the first battalion was attached to the Army of Rosellon, and fought at the battle of Masdeu and played a prominent part in the capture of Argeles and Thuir. In July 1793 it took part in the attack on the French positions at Perpignan.

In September 1793 the first battalion of the Hibernia formed part of the allied expedition to Toulon and, after capturing the port, played a prominent part in its defence. When the allied force evacuated Toulon in December 1793, the battalion re-joined the Army of Rosellon.

1794   In April the regiment took part in the unsuccessful assault against the Heights of Serat. During the retreat, it took part in the successful counter-attack at Nuestra Senora de Roble. Officer casualties had been so high by this time that Sergeant-Major Don Juan Hogan was appointed as temporary battalion commander.

By August the three battalions of the regiment had been re-united and they fought at the battle of Muga on 13 August.

1795   Following the Treaty of Basle in 1795, France and Spain became allies and the Hibernia fought in several engagements with Portuguese forces before becoming part of the Cadiz garrison.

During the period of alliance between Spain and France, the Irish regiments served on the siege lines at Gibraltar.

1808   There was an uprising in Spain against the French and the Hibernia played an important part in the war that followed. The regiment joined the army of General Joaquin Blake in Galicia. In July the Hibernia suffered serious losses at the battle of Rio Seco. It replaced these losses by recruiting large numbers of Galician volunteers, thus diluting the dwindling Irish component of the regiment further. The Hibernia took part in the campaigns in the Asturias and Santander regions.

1809   A detachment of the Hibernia was captured while covering the British retreat to Corunna in January. In March the remainder of the regiment took part in the battle of Monterey and was also present at the siege of Vigo. In May it fought in the battle of Lugo. The regiment played a major role at the decisive Spanish victory at Tamanes on 18 October 1809 where it beat off successive attacks by French cavalry. A company of 102 grenadiers from the Hibernia Regiment was present at the siege of Gerona in 1809, breaking through the French siege lines on the night of 5 September 1809 as part of a relief force. They manned the defences alongside their countrymen in the Ultonia Regiment. By the time that the garrison surrendered, 61 of those Hibernia grenadiers had died.

1810   In the summer months it took part in the campaign against General Soult's army in Castile and Estramadura and was present at the battles at Bienvenida and Canta el Gallo. In October the Hibernia joined the Anglo-Portuguese army at the lines of Torres Vedras in the operations against General Massena.

1812–14   The Hibernia was present at Badajoz and in a three day battle at Puente de Gevora it sustained heavy casualties. Reduced to a single battalion due to its casualties, the Hibernia garrisoned Ciudad Rodrigo following its capture in 1812 and in 1814 it was moved to garrison Cadiz.

By 1818 the majority of the Hibernia's officers were Irish or of Irish descent but the rank and file was made up almost entirely of Spanish soldiers. This fact led to the regiment's disbandment in the post-war reductions as the king could invoke the clause allowing for the disbandment of the Irish regiments if they no longer had large numbers of Irish soldiers. In 1818 the Hibernia was disbanded at Luja in Granada. The other Irish regiments in the Spanish service were disbanded at the same time.

At various phases during the Napoleonic wars it had campaigned alongside Irish regiments in the British army, such as the 87th (Prince of Wales's Own Irish) Regiment of Foot. It is also interesting to note that Napoleon's Irish Legion was part of the army that opposed the Hibernia at the Lines of Torres Verdras in 1810 and at Badajoz in 1811, although it is unclear if elements of these two Irish units ever fought one another.

In December 1943, under the terms of a re-organization of the Spanish army, it was decided that existing regiments would adopt the historical traditions and lineage of disbanded regiments. Tank Battalion No. 27, 'La Cruzada', was authorized to adopt the traditions of the Regiment of Hibernia. This arrangement was maintained until 1960 when the battalion was disbanded at Mallorca.[3]

IRISH REGIMENTS IN THE BRITISH LEGION IN THE CARLIST WAR, 1835–8

In 1833 Ferdinand VII of Spain died and the contentious question of the succession plunged the country into civil war. Before his death, Ferdinand had revoked the Salic Law, which prevented a female heir from succeeding to the Spanish throne. As a result

---

[3] I am indebted to Dr Alicia Laspra-Rodriquez and General Ramos Oliver for this information.

of his action the three-year old Infanta Isabella was pronounced to be the new ruler of Spain, with her mother, Maria Cristina, acting as regent. The child-queen's uncle, Don Carlos, had previously been the heir apparent and he raised an army and embarked on a campaign to secure the throne. This resulted in the First Carlist War of 1833-40.

Foundation of the British Legion
In England, Lord Melbourne's administration pledged itself to supporting the cause of Queen Isabella and, in June 1835, the formation of the British Legion was announced. It was intended to send an 'all arms' legion to Spain under the command of a Limerick-born officer, Colonel George De Lacy Evans (1787-1870). De Lacy Evans was an officer of vast experience and he was be appointed as a general in the Spanish army for the duration of this command. He was later knighted and ended his career as a general in the British army.

Of the original 7,800 recruits of the British Legion, 2,800 were Irish, 1,800 were Scots and the remaining 3,200 were English. The legion consisted of two regiments of lancers, ten battalions of infantry, a rifle corps, a staff corps and also artillery, engineer, medical and commissariat units. Four of the regiments of the Legion were given Irish titles and the majority of the Irish recruits served in these units:

The 2nd Queen's Own Irish Lancers
The 7th Irish Light Infantry
The 9th Irish Regiment
The 10th Munster Light Infantry

These Irish regiments were formed into an 'Irish Brigade', commanded by Brigadier-General Charles Shaw. It should be noted that many Irish soldiers took both their wives and children with them on this campaign.

Operational history
The Legion arrived in Spain in July 1835. Throughout its service in Spain, pay was always in arrears and as a result the Legion was plagued with disciplinary problems and desertion. During its first winter in Spain it suffered losses due to disease and also the attentions of a pro-Carlist baker in Vittoria who poisoned batches of bread bound for the Legion.

Also, Don Carlos had issued his infamous Durango Decree which promised to execute any members of the Legion who were captured. During the course of the campaign, many captured legionnaires were executed, including some Irishmen. Despite these problems, De Lacy Evans moulded the Legion into an effective fighting force and it took part in the following actions between 1835 and 1837:

Unsuccessful attack on Hernani, 30 August 1835; capture of Arlaban, 16 January 1836; successful assault on Carlist siege lines at San Sebastian, 5 May 1836; capture of Passages, 28 May 1836; unsuccessful attack on Fuenterrabia, 11 July 1836; defence of Passages and Alza, 1 October 1836; storming of the

Heights of Ametzagama, 10 March 1837; capture of Loyola, 11 March 1837; capture of the fort of Oriamendi, near Hernani, 15–16 March 1837 (this was part of an unsuccessful assault on Hernani); storming and capture of Hernani, 14 May 1837; capture of Oyarzun and Irun, 16 May 1837; capture of Fuenterrabia, 18 May 1837

The contract of the Legion expired in June 1837. Around 3,400 men were still serving in the Legion's infantry units by this time, 1,746 of whom re-enlisted in July for a further period of service. Around 340 of these men were from the former Irish regiments of the Legion. The new down-sized force was re-christened as the 'British Auxiliary Brigade' and the Irish troops served in a composite Irish regiment. The last remnants of the Legion and its Irish regiments were disbanded in 1839. There is a memorial to the dead of the Legion at San Sebastian.

IRISH VOLUNTEERS IN THE SPANISH CIVIL WAR, 1936–9

On the outbreak of civil war in Spain in 1936 a large number of volunteers from various European countries travelled to Spain to play their part in this clash of political ideologies. The largest interventions came from Germany, Italy and Soviet Russia.

Other smaller groups of volunteers travelled from different countries and Ireland was no exception. A small number of Irishmen served on both sides in Spain's civil war. Co-incidentally, both the two opposed Irish units carried the numerical designation 'XV' – one serving as the XV Bandera of the Nationalist Tercio while the other served with the XV International Brigade.

XV BANDERA, LEGIÓN EXTRANJERA
(PRO-NATIONALIST IRISH BRIGADE)

Formation
Despite the Irish government's policy of non-intervention in the Spanish Civil War, recruiting for this unit began in August 1936. The recruits were mostly ex-members of the right-wing Army Comrades Association or 'Blueshirts'.

They were led by General Eoin O'Duffy, ex-commissioner of An Garda Síochána and previously leader of the Blueshirts. While O'Duffy travelled to Spain and was appointed as inspector-general of the Bandera with the local rank of 'general de brigada', he was rarely with his men, a fact that would later result in much internal dissent.

Operational history
In the winter of 1936, volunteers made their way to Spain either singly or in groups and travelled with the intention of aiding the Nationalists under General Franco in their campaign against the Spanish Republic.

In December 1936 the last volunteers arrived and they eventually numbered over 650 men. Some other volunteers joined the brigade in early 1937, most notably a 20-

man pipe band that had been raised in St Mary's parish in Dublin. They were based at Cáceres for initial training and acclimatization.

It was originally intended that this Irish bandera would serve with the ultra-Catholic Carlist requetés. Instead of this they were incorporated into the Spanish Foreign Legion, the 'Legión Extranjera', more commonly referred to as 'the Tercio'. Organized in four companies, they were officially designated as the XV Bandera of the Tercio, although they were still commonly referred to in the Irish press as the 'Irish Brigade'.

On 17 February 1937 the XV Bandera left Cáceres and was transported to the Jarama Valley to take part in the Nationalist spring offensive. They experienced their first action on 19 February when they advanced on the town of Ciempozuelos, suffering casualties in a 'friendly fire' incident with another Nationalist unit from the Canary Islands. Two members of the Bandera were killed. They relieved the Moorish garrison at Ciempozuelos and remained in the line there until March.

On 13 March 1937, they took part in an attack on the town of Titulcia. Advancing across a canal and the Jarama river, their attack stalled under heavy fire and they fell back. A new attack was scheduled for the next morning but, after a debate among the Irish officers, representations were made to the local Nationalist headquarters and the attack was called off.

On 23 March the Irish left Ciempozuelos and were re-assigned to a section of the line at La Marañosa, on the northernmost section of the Jarama salient. Here they served alongside Moorish and Carlist troops and helped repulse a Republican attack in early April 1937.

By April 1937, however, the commander of the Tercio, Colonel Juan Yagüe, had expressed his dissatisfaction with the Irish troops under his command. This was largely due to the refusal of the Irish officers to renew the attack at Titulcia. The XV Bandera itself was riven with internal dissent, many being opposed to O'Duffy's style of non-leadership.

On 9 April O'Duffy wrote to Franco requesting that the Irish Bandera be disbanded, a request that Franco accepted with alacrity.

By 10 May the XV Bandera was back in Cáceres and they boarded ship in Lisbon on 17 June, bound for Dublin. They arrived in Dublin on 21 June 1937. In the course of their campaign in Spain the Irish Bandera lost six men killed in action. Some members opted to remain in Spain and served throughout the remainder of the war in different Nationalist units.

16th BRITISH BATTALION, XV INTERNATIONAL BRIGADE (REPUBLICAN ARMY)

Formation
This unit drew its volunteers from the ranks of the Communist Party of Ireland and the Republican Congress. Frank Ryan, an experienced IRA veteran, emerged as the

prime organizer of this movement. He travelled to Spain where he was appointed as a staff officer to the International Brigades.

During the winter of 1936 small groups and individual volunteers made their way to Spain and on their arrival volunteered for service in the newly-formed International Brigades. The majority of the Irish volunteers were incorporated into the 16th British Battalion of the XV International Brigade. This initial Irish contingent was around 100 men. During the course of the war, other volunteers travelled to Spain and the nominal rolls of the International Brigades contain the names of just over 200 Irish volunteers.

Operational history

1936 The XV Brigade was based at Madrigueras, north of Albacete, for its initial training. Despite the fact that the volunteers were not fully trained, occasional calls were made for volunteers to serve in *ad hoc* groups. One such group of volunteers, commanded by Kit Conway, took part in an attack on Nationalist positions on 26 December 1936 at Lopera, near Andújar. Eight men were killed in this unsuccessful attack.

1937 Around 10 January another volunteer company was rushed to the Madrid front where it took part in the Republican counter-attack at Las Rozas. At the same time there was a certain amount of tension developing within the 16th Battalion. Some of the Irish members objected to its 'British' designation and wished to form a separate Irish unit. Their objections increased when it was discovered that some of the British volunteers had served with the Black and Tans in Ireland during the War of Independence. In January 1937 a faction split from the 16th British Battalion and joined the American Lincoln Battalion. Both of these battalions served within the XV International Brigade. The Lincoln faction is often referred to as the 'James Connolly Column' or the 'James Connolly Company'. The majority of the Irish volunteers would appear to have been persuaded by Ryan to remain in the 16th British Battalion. Despite these internal difficulties the Irish volunteers played a full part in the Jarama battle in February 1937. On 12 February the XV Brigade was positioned to oppose the spearhead of the Nationalist advance, Kit Conway's company defending a crucial position alongside the San Martín-Morata road. Conway was mortally wounded in this action. When Republican forces were pushed back, Ryan commanded an important counter-attack on 14 February. The Irish volunteers in the Lincoln Battalion were also involved in this battle, taking part in a number of actions on the Pingarrón Heights. In a final assault on the heights on 27 February, they lost several men. After the Jarama battle, the Irish contingent and the rest of the XV Brigade took up positions in the trenches opposite Morata de Tajuña. They were relieved in June 1937 and a period of leave followed.

During the battle of Brunete, which began on 6 July, the XV Brigade formed part of the Republican centre column. The Irish contingent distinguished itself in the attack on Brunete itself before storming the town of Villanueva de la Cañada, suffering heavy casualties.

Following another period of leave the unit went back into the lines on the Aragon front, near Zaragoza. During the August offensive along the Ebro river, the Irish contingent attacked the village of Quinto, which it captured. They then held a section of the line near Mediana and repulsed Nationalist reinforcements that were advancing to the aid of the Belchite garrison. They joined a Canadian battalion in an unsuccessful attempt to breach the Nationalist defences near Fuentes del Ebro. As the Aragon offensive petered out and the advance on Zaragosa was abandoned, the XV Brigade left the line for a period of recuperation.

In December 1937 they took part in the Teruel campaign and were rushed into the line on 31 December to defend against a Nationalist counterattack. They took part in operations against enemy lines of communications at Atalaya and Pedregosa. By the end of this campaign, which was fought in Arctic conditions, the XV Brigade had been reduced to less than 100 men.

1938 A series of reverses followed for the Republican army and on 31 March over 100 members of various International Brigades were captured near the village of Calaceite. These prisoners included several Irishmen and Frank Ryan was among their number. He died in Germany in June 1944.

Reinforced by drafts of new volunteers, the XV Brigade took part in the Ebro offensive of July 1938 which was mounted in the hope of reducing Nationalist pressure on Valencia. The XV Brigade was given the town of Gandesa as its objective. This town had also been identified as a key point by the Nationalist command and had been reinforced by units of the Tercio and also Moorish troops. Despite their best efforts, the XV Brigade was unable to take the town and the whole offensive later stalled. The Republican units were forced back to their starting points by mid-September.

In the aftermath of the failed Ebro offensive, the Republican government decided to disband the International Brigades. This disbandment parade took place at Barcelona on 29 October 1938. Only fifteen Irishmen were fit for service and able to attend. In the course of the war almost sixty Irish volunteers were killed in action while serving with the International Brigade. Some of the Irish members of the International Brigade remained in Spain and fought until final Republican collapse in March 1939.

CHAPTER 5

Irish regiments in Italian service, 1702–1862

While many people are aware that there was an Irish battalion in Italy during the 1860 war in the Papal States, there has been little historical interest in the Irish troops who served in different Italian armies in the eighteenth century. Italy, as we know it today, did not exist until the final unification of various states, republics and communes in 1870. In the early eighteenth century, it was composed of numerous states and these all maintained armies. For the Irish soldiers who had left Ireland at the end of the seventeenth century, this situation represented an ideal source of employment.

There were Irish soldiers serving on the Italian peninsula from the late 1600s and these men formed part of a wider 'Wild Geese' tradition. In 1691, William Luttrell was granted permission by William III to raise a force of 1,500 Irish Catholics for the service of the Venetian republic.[1] Virtually nothing is known of the subsequent history of this Irish unit. The Duke of Parma established an Irish bodyguard in 1702 while the Regiment of Limerick was transferred from the Spanish to the Neapolitan service in 1735. The available literature on these eighteenth century Irish units is extremely scanty but an attempt has been made to outline their histories in the entries that follow.

It can only be hoped that Irish or Italian scholars will further explore the history of these Irish regiments. Due to the perennial problem of finding research funding in Ireland for such projects, these hopes might be purely aspirational. The available literature indicates that the Italian military connection was extremely important and that it was part of a wider network that connected Irish exiles in France, Spain and Italy. It remains to be seen if this network will be explored further by later generations of scholars.

THE IRISH BODYGUARD OF THE DUKE OF PARMA, 1702–33

Formation
In 1694, Francesco Farnese succeeded as the Duke of Parma and Piacenza. He was a cousin of Mary d'Este Stuart, wife of James II. Throughout his reign he was sympathetic to the Jacobite cause and to the plight of James III (the Old Pretender). At the outbreak of the War of the Spanish Succession in 1701, the Duke of Parma proclaimed himself to be a vassal of Pope Clement XI and stated that he was neutral in the conflict.

---

1 J.G. Simms, 'The Irish on the Continent, 1691–1800' in T.W. Moody and W.E. Vaughan (eds), *A new history of Ireland* (1986), iv, 630–1.

From 1701 both the French and Imperial (Austrian) armies were active in Italy. On the French side, these included the Irish regiments of Berwick, Dillon, Galmoy, Burke and Sheldon. As military activity increased on the Italian peninsula, the Duke of Parma was pressured by both sides in the war to increase his armed forces and thus guarantee the neutrality of his duchy by denying it to outside troops. He began this process by obtaining 1,000 papal troops while also raising militia and independent companies. The names of Irish soldiers appear on the muster lists for various units such as the 'Barattieri Company' in Piacenza and the 'Company-of-Fortune of the Five Gates of Piacenza'. Many of these Irish soldiers later passed into the Irish company of the Duke's personal bodyguard.

In the autumn of 1702, the Duke decided to form new company to serve with his bodyguard, for the 'defence of his own person and to guard the ducal palace'. There already existed a company of archers, a mounted company of young noblemen and a company of around 70 German dragoons.

The Duke decided to use Irish soldiers to form this new company due to their reputation in battle and also in the hope that they would remain loyal in any attack on his person.

On 29 October 1702, Augustine O'Gill was appointed as captain of the Irish Company in bodyguard of the Duke of Parma. It is unclear where the initial Irish officers and men came from but in all probability they were exiled Irish Jacobites or Irish troops who had been discharged or deserted from the French army.

In the terms of organization for this new company ('the capitulations'), it was specified that the officers were to take orders only from the Duke himself and that they were not subject to other officers in the ducal army. They were excused from regular patrols and were under the Duke's orders for his own protection and for any special duties that he might require to have carried out. The company was commanded by a captain and had a total establishment of 100 men. The company's establishment provided for a captain, a lieutenant, an ensign, three sergeants and three corporals. Five lance-corporals were later added to the establishment. The initial contingent of just over 60 men were all Irish. The captain of the Irish company was also paid more than any other officer in ducal service with a salary of 4,608 lire a year.

Operational history

1703   During this year, 54 soldiers of the company obtained their discharge, perhaps leaving to enlist in the Irish regiments in the French service. A further 28 deserted, many not returning from periods of leave. To make up these losses a number of non-Irish soldiers were recruited. These included Germans, Italians and Swiss. A system of appointing 'reformed' or reserve officers was begun in 1703. These officers were used to fill vacancies in the Irish company and also other units.

1706   Captain O'Gill led the contingent from the Duke's bodyguard that was involved in the arrest of Count Felice Landi, whose political activities were thought to be putting the duchy in danger.

1707	In the reforms of the ducal army, the Irish company was the only unit not to be reduced in size. The men of the company carried out regular garrison and escort duties in Parma, Piacenza and at the Duke's summer palace in Colorno. At this time, there were also Irish troops and officers serving in the other companies in ducal service.
1711	In May a boundary dispute broke out with the neighbouring Duke of Modena and around 6,000 Farnese troops were sent to expell Modenese troops from where they had made an incursion on the Enzo river. This force was led by Captain D'Hervey, then commander of the Irish company.
1713	The territory of the duchy was extended under the terms of the Treaty of Utrecht.
1714	Elizabeth Farnese of Parma became the second wife of Philip V of Spain and this would have ramifications for the later succession in the duchy of Parma.
1715	Due to the expansion of Turkish power and the fall of Corinth, the Duke of Parma dispatched his first expedition in aid of the Venetian Republic. He raised five companies and these included some Irish officers.
1716	These companies were initially billeted on the Lido in Venice before taking part in an expedition to liberate Corfu from Turkish rule.
1717	A second expedition of seven companies was sent to Venice, and some Irish served with this force. It was stationed in Dalmatia and also served with the Venetian fleet in the Aegean. In 1717, the Spanish invaded Sardinia and Sicily, creating further tension on the Italian peninsula. This conflict ended with the Treaty of the Quadruple Alliance in 1720.
1718	A third expedition of just one company was sent to Venice. The Treaty of Passarowitz, which was signed on 21 July 1718, ended hostilities between Venice and the Ottoman Empire.
1720–6	During this period 57 new soldiers enlisted in the Irish company to bring it back up to strength.
1727	Duke Francesco Farnese I, the founder of the Irish Company, died in February. He was succeeded by his younger brother Antonio who became the new Duke of Parma. The Irish company's officers at this time were Captain D'Hervey (officer commanding), Lieutenant-Captain John Loghnan and Ensign Thaddeaus FitzPatrick. Some of the old soldiers of the company were transferred to form the garrison at Piacenza.
1728	Around this time Captain D'Hervey was referred to as the 'Chevalier D'Hervey' in official documents. Contemporary manuscripts also mention the solemnization of St Patrick's Day with a special mass. During 1728 James III and Prince Charles Edward Stuart visited the duchy, the prince then being only eight years old.
1731	Duke Antonio died, plunging the duchy into a succession crisis. His wife, the Dowager Duchess Enrichetta proclaimed her wish to be appointed regent, claiming that she was three months pregnant with the Duke's child at the time of his death. This claim of a pregnancy proved to be false and in December

1731 it was decided that the Spanish royal Infante, Charles Bourbon, was the rightful heir as his mother was Elizabeth Farnese of Parma. He would later rule Spain as Charles or Carlos III (1759–88). In his absence, the Duchess Dorotea Bourbon took control as curator of the duchy on behalf of her grandson. The Irish company continued to guard the Dowager Duchess Enrichetta at Colorno until the succession was settled.

1732 The Infante, Charles Bourbon (also referred to as Don Carlo) took possession of the duchy and the Irish company formed part of the new Duke's bodyguard. In November it was used to put down an uprising of newly raised and discontented troops.

1733 The new Bourbon regime decided to raise new units including a Royal Bourbon Farnese Regiment. As a result of this, it was decided to disband all other units. Therefore, the Irish company was disbanded on 27 March 1733.

At the time of its disbandment all of its officers were still Irish. These included Captain Benedict D'Hervey, Lieutenant Thaddeus Fitzpatrick and Ensign Francis D'Hervey. The chaplain was Fr Thomas Glasco. The officers and several Irish soldiers remained in the Bourbon service and were transferred to the newly-raised regiments.

Captain D'Hervey later served as governor of Piacenza and he, and other Irish officers, followed Charles Bourbon to Naples in 1734, remaining in his service.

Commanding officers
1702   Captain Augustine O'Gill
1706   Captain Benedict D'Harvey (until disbandment)

Chaplains
1703   Fr Malachy Stanton
1706   Fr Thomas Dillon, a Dominican originally from Mullingar
1707   Fr Thomas Glasco, a Domincan originally from Naas (served until disbandment)

The main source for the history of this unit was the unpublished thesis of the late Ms Patricia Ann O'Sullivan. This thesis was submitted for examination for the degree of Master of Arts at University College Dublin in 1959. The author gratefully acknowledges the assistance of Ms Mary Byran, who kindly made her late sister's thesis available for consultation.

REGIMENTO INFANTERIA DEL REY
(previously the Regiment of Limerick)

Formation
The details of the history of this regiment are extremely scarce. It was originally a regiment in the Spanish service and as such it was titled as the Regiment of Limerick.

According to some sources this regiment was transferred into the army of the King of Naples in 1718. The Marquess McSwiney carried out extensive research on Irish troops in the Neapolitan service in the early eighteenth century and was convinced that the regiment entered Neapolitan service around 1735. This would make more sense as the Kingdom of the Two Sicilies, which included Naples, was returned to the king of Spain in 1734.[2]

In 1735, the Regiment of Limerick was stationed on Elba and in 1737 the regiment moved to Capua, north of Naples. Surviving archives indicate that the regimental title was changed in the summer of 1737 and from August of that year it was referred to as the Regimento Infantería del Rey (King's Regiment). It was later often referred to as the 'King's Irish Regiment'. In 1794, this regiment was increased in size when a third battalion was added.

Operational history
Due to the few details that are readily available, this regiment's history on campaign remains largely unknown. It would seem almost certain that it took part in the campaigns and battles of the War of the Austrian Succession (1740–8) as there were significant actions on the Italian peninsula and in Sicily. McSwiney stated that it fought in the battles of Velletri, Tortona, Parma and Piacenza.

Its earlier history, as the Regiment of Limerick in the Spanish service, is equally obscure but if it did not transfer into Neapolitan service until 1735, it is possible that it served in the earlier campaigns in Sicily (1718), Gibraltar (1727–8) and Oran (1732). Surviving service records of its officers indicate that this was so.

Officers
On the transfer of this regiment into the Neapolitan service in 1735, all of its officers were Irish or of Irish descent. It was commanded by Colonel Don Raymundo de Burke and he was succeeded by Colonel Don Juan O'Dea in 1739. The numbers of Irish NCOs and enlisted men remains unknown and requires further research.

Many of the officers had previous service in the other Irish regiments in the Spanish service. Some officers had served in the French service before joining the Spanish service and from there had progressed into the Regimento del Rey.[3] McSwiney has identified a large number of Irish officers who served with this regiment throughout the eighteenth century. By the early 1800s, however, the number of Irish had declined. He also identified Irish officers who served with other Neapolitan regiments such as the Regimento Real Estranjero, the Regimento Cavalleria de Sicilia and the Regimento Cavalleria de Rossellon. (The Regimento Cavalleria de Rossellon had previously served in the Spanish service.)

---

2 Following the Treaty of Utrecht in 1713, the kingdom had been ruled by the Austrian Hapsburgs until being returned to Spain in 1734.   3 Don Jeremiah Dean, described as being Irish, had begun his career as a cadet in the Regiment of Berwick in 1712, had transferred to the Ultonia Regiment in 1729 and then the Regimento del Rey in 1738, successively serving in the French, Spanish and Neapolitan armies.

Regimental colours
Details of these are not known. A contemporary document survives that shows a regimental insignia. This incorporates a crowned oval design surrounded by war trophies. The central motif within this oval was a harp.

Note
The main archives for this regiment are held in the Archivio di Stato in Naples. The documents are written mostly in Spanish but there are also some manuscripts in Italian and Latin. Many of these documents have been microfilmed and are held in the National Library of Ireland. The Marquess McSwiney spent several years working on these archives with the intention of writing a book on the regiment. His research notes are held in the library of the Royal Irish Academy in Dublin and he also published an article on his initial research.[4]

THE ST PATRICK'S BATTALION, 1860
AND THE ST PATRICK'S COMPANY, 1860–2

Formation
Following the outbreak of the Second War of Italian Independence in 1859, it became increasingly obvious to Pope Pius IX that Italian revolutionaries and the army of Piedmont would eventually devote their attention to liberating the Papal States. He issued an appeal to the Catholics of Europe and asked for volunteers to come to Italy to serve in the Papal army. Ultimately thousands of Austrians, French, Belgians and Swiss went to Italy and formed new regiments in the Papal army.

In Ireland, A.M. Sullivan of *The Nation* began a campaign in support of Pius IX and members of the Catholic hierarchy also encouraged their parishioners to volunteer. An Austrian army officer, Baron Francis Ferdinand Guttemberg, travelled to Dublin to arrange for the transportation of volunteers to Italy. While such volunteering was technically illegal under the terms of the Foreign Enlistment Act, parties of volunteers travelled from Ireland and the first group arrived in Italy in June 1860. They represented an interesting cross-section of Irish society and included clerks, students, farm labourers, ex-soldiers and militia and even some members of the Irish Constabulary and Dublin Metropolitan Police.

By the beginning of July 1860 they numbered 1,300 men and were initially commanded by an Irish officer in the Austrian service named Fitzgerald. This number would eventually be reduced to around 1,100 men when some malcontents were sent home in July. When Fitzgerald returned to serve in the Austrian army, Major Myles William O'Reilly, a captain in the Louth Rifles Militia, took command. The Irish

---

[4] The Marquies McSwiney, 'Notes on some Irish regiments in the service of Spain and Naples in the eighteenth century', in *Proceedings of the Royal Irish Academy*, Series C, vol. XXXII (Dublin, 1924–7), 158–74.

contingent was officially designated as the 'St Patrick's Battalion', although in the Irish press it was often referred to as the 'Irish Brigade'. The men of the battalion were formally sworn into the Papal service in July 1860.

The battalion was split into two groups with four companies at Ancona to the north of Rome and four companies at Spoleto to the south. They never served together as a full battalion. They also had serious supply problems. In theory they were to be issued with a Zouave-style uniform in green with gold trimmings. Few, if any, members of the battalion ever received this. They were only gradually armed with obsolete smooth bore muskets while most members of the battalion lacked haversacks and belt equipment at the beginning of the campaign in 1860. Despite these shortcomings, the Irish proved themselves to be among the best of the Papal troops during the subsequent campaign and members of the battalion won many Papal medals while also earning the praise of senior officers in both the Papal and Piedmontese armies.

On the invasion of the Papal States on 11 September 1860 the St Patrick's Battalion was disposed as follows:

two companies at Spoleto, commanded by Major M. W. O'Reilly
four companies at Ancona, commanded by Captain Count Russell of Killough
one company attached to the garrison at Perugia, commanded by Captain James Blackney
one company attached to General de la Moricière's field army, commanded by Captain Martin Kirwin.

Operational history
Ultimately, the campaign of 1860 was extremely brief but the Irish contingent distinguished itself at the following actions:

13 September: The defence of Perugia
   Following a morning of confused street fighting, the garrison surrendered the same afternoon. The opposing Piedmontese army numbered over 12,000.

17 September: The defence of Spoleto
   The Irish companies manned the north wall and also defended the crucial gatehouse. This action lasted the whole day and the garrison resisted a number of determined Piedmontese assaults. Without any hope of reinforcement, Major O'Reilly negotiated a surrender on favourable terms that evening.

18 September: The Battle of Castelfidardo
   The Irish company attached to General de la Moricière's field army took part in this battle and were prominent in the defence of the position known as the 'Upper Farm'. Later in the battle, when several gunners had become casualties or had deserted, they helped haul artillery into position under fire. Following the defeat of the Papal forces they fled to Loreto, where they surrendered the next day.

18 to 28 September: The siege of Ancona
The four Irish companies stationed at Ancona served throughout this siege and helped repulse a series of land and sea assaults. The garrison numbered just 6,000 men against 34,000 Piedmontese troops. Due to their performance under fire, the Irish companies were often sent to defend crucial positions in the city's defences. When the seaward defences were finally breached on the 28 September, the garrison surrendered.

The loss of Ancona effectively ended the campaign and the Papal States became part of the unified Italy. The men of the Irish battalion were marched as prisoners to Genoa and were eventually repatriated to Ireland. Many of their wounded remained in Italian hospitals for some months before they could return to Ireland. Due to the confused nature of the fighting and the fact that no official casualty reports were ever submitted, the number of Irish casualties during the 1860 campaign can only be estimated. It has been estimated that around 70 men were killed and wounded in the various actions of the campaign.[5]

In the aftermath of the war the Papal army was much reduced. On 8 November 1860 the St Patrick's Company was formed and several officers, NCOs and men of the previous battalion elected to serve in it. The most senior of these was Count Russell. It never attracted a large number of recruits and its maximum strength was only 46. By 1862, this had dwindled to just 22 men. The St Patrick's Company was therefore disbanded on 30 September 1862, the majority of its members electing to serve with the Papal Zouaves or the Papal Carabineers. Several members of the battalion went on to have distinguished careers during the American Civil War, many of them reaching high rank. These included Lieutenant Myles Walter Keogh who fought at Ancona and later became a brevet colonel in the Union Army during the Civil War. Keogh subsequently served with the 7th Cavalry and died with General Custer at the Little Big Horn in 1876.[6]

---

[5] G.F-H. Berkeley, *The Irish Battalion in the Papal Army of 1860* (Dublin and Cork, 1929), p. 242. [6] David Murphy, 'Little Big (Irish)man' in *History Ireland*, 13:5 (September/October 2005), 66.

CHAPTER 6

Irish regiments in North and South America

Irishmen and women emigrated to the Americas since the foundation of the first British colonies there in the seventeenth century. Throughout succeeding centuries, a steady flow of Irish emigrants headed across the Atlantic. It is not surprising, therefore, that Irishmen began to serve in military formations in America and we can identify Irish individuals who served in colonial militias, and the later the Continental Army, during the French and Indian War (1754–63), the American War of Independence (1775–83) and the War of 1812 (1812–15).

It is also likely that Irishmen formed themselves into local companies and an early example of this can be seen in the Loyal Irish Volunteers formed in Boston in 1775. Such trends were not confined only to north America. In the early decades of the nineteenth century, Irish regiments served in campaigns in Brazil, Bolivia and also Mexico.

The large numbers of Irish who later emigrated to America in the mid-nineteenth century resulted in a number of Irish formations. During the early decades of the nineteenth century, a number of Irish volunteer companies were established and typical of these was the Hibernia Greens, founded in Philadelphia in 1821. This company later split into a different factions and a later companies were founded with titles such as the Montgomery Guards, the Patterson Guards, the Emmet Guards and the Sarsfield Rifle Company.[1] Many similar units still survived in the 1860s and these would form the cadres of Civil War units.

These Irish companies were to be found in both the north and the south and they later would later serve in both the Union and Confederate armies. In the north, the Irish population was centred around large urban centres such as New York, Boston, Chicago and Philadelphia. In the south, the Irish tended to work as dockers and rail workers and as a result their communities were centred around cities such as New Orleans and Mobile.

The American Civil War saw thousands of Irishmen enlist to fight for their adopted state, whether a Union or Confederate one. Due to the larger number of Irish in the north, Irish recruits were formed into regiments and then brigades.

In the south they usually served in company-size units. At several engagements, Irish units faced each other on opposing side, most notably at battles such as 1st Bull Run, Freeman's Farm, Corinth and Fredericksburg.

---

1 *Irish Sword*, 19:77 (Summer 1995), 160. The subject of these antebellum Irish volunteer companies is one that would benefit from further research.

In the decades that followed the American Civil War, large numbers of Irish continued to serve in the US Army. At the battle of the Little Bighorn in 1876, for example, there were 128 Irishmen serving with the 7th Cavalry, representing the largest foreign contingent within that regiment.[2] It was not US Army practice to designate units as being specifically Irish, the notable exception being the 69th New York. So while Irish regiments have largely disappeared in the U.S. Army, Irishmen, or men of Irish descent, have continued to serve in the cause of their adopted country up to the present day.

THE VOLUNTEERS OF IRELAND OR LOYAL VOLUNTEERS OF IRELAND

later, the 105th (King's Irish) Regiment of Foot, 1777–84

Formation

This regiment was raised by the British to serve in the American Revolutionary War. It was formed to serve the Crown and fought in the Loyalist cause and it is arguable that it should be included in the section dealing with British regiments. Due to the fact that it was raised in America, however, it has been included in this section on American regiments. It was perhaps the earliest-known regiment raised in America exclusively from among the Irish population.

There is comparatively little known about the Volunteers of Ireland. It was raised in 1777, although no muster rolls exist from before 1778. It was raised from among the Irish Loyalist community of Philadelphia and recruits were also drafted in from two earlier regiments; the Roman Catholic Volunteers and the New Jersey Volunteers.[3]

An entry in a 1775 orderly book for Boston also mentions the formation of a company referred to as the 'Loyal Irish Volunteers'. This had been raised by 'some Irish merchants residing in the town' and it had its HQ near the Mill Bridge in Boston. It is not known if there was any connection with the later Volunteers of Ireland raised in Philadelphia but it does suggest that more than one Irish unit was raised in the Loyalist cause.

Operational history

1777   The regiment was raised in Philadelphia by Lord Moira and recruited from among that town's Irish community.

1778   The earliest muster roll for the regiment dates from December 1778 when it was based in New York.

1779   In May, the regiment was re-designated as the 2nd American Regiment (Volunteers of Ireland) and was placed on the American establishment. It consisted of ten companies.

---

2 Douglas D. Scott, P. Willey and Melissa A. Connor, *They died with Custer* (Norman, OK, 1998), p. 92.
3 There are muster rolls for this regiment in the National Archives of Canada and the National Archives in Kew, London.

1780   The regiment was sent to South Carolina where it served in the campaign there. On arrival it was based at Charleston and later saw much service during this campaign.

1782   The regiment was placed on the regular British establishment as the 105th (King's Irish) Regiment of Foot.

1783   In April, the officers and NCOs of the regiment were sent to Ireland to recruit a new contingent of soldiers. The remaining men were transferred to the Prince of Wales American Regiment, the New Jersey Volunteers and De Lancey's Brigade.

1784   Due to the conclusion of a peace treaty in 1783, it was decided to disband the regiment and the Volunteers of Ireland were disbanded in England in January.

Colonel, officers and men

Due to its comparatively short history, the regiment only had one commanding officer, Lord Moira, who served as regimental colonel. He would later be promoted to general and was created 1st Marquess of Hastings.

Several Irish officers commanded companies of the regiment. These included Major John Despard, who was later promoted to major-general.[4]

Other companies were commanded by Lt.-Col. Welbore Ellis Doyle, Captain William Barry and Captain John Doyle. The surviving muster rolls reveal the names of numerous Irish soldiers.

IRISH TROOPS IN THE ARMY OF SIMÓN BOLÍVAR, 1817–21

Formation

From 1817 a large number of Irishmen served in the armies of Simón Bolívar during his campaigns to end Spanish Royalist rule in South America.

In the aftermath of the end of the Napoleonic Wars in 1815 the British government sought to reduce the size of its army. At the same time emissaries of the Patriot movement in South America had travelled to London to hold discussions with the government about their plans to recruit volunteers. In August 1819, the Foreign Enlistment Bill was passed which effectively forbade British citizens to serve in foreign armies. Before this bill became law, over 5,500 volunteers had left Britain and Ireland and travelled to Venezuela. The majority were ex-British army officers and soldiers and many came from Ireland.

This first contingent of volunteers were formed into the First British Legion (1817–19). Recruiting still continued in England and Ireland and a further 2,172 men had been raised by 1819. These were formed into the Second British Legion (1819–

---

[4] Major John Despard was the brother of Colonel Edward Marcus Despard, who was convicted of treason and executed in 1803 for heading a conspiracy to seize the Tower of London and the Bank of England and also to assassinate George III.

21). Also, in 1820 General John D'Evereux raised an exclusively Irish force of 1,700 men and these were formed into an Irish Legion and this was later incorporated into the remnants of the British Legion. Apart from combat casualties, these contingents lost a large number of men due to disease and by 1821, the combined British and Irish Legions could only field 800 officers and men. The men of the British and Irish Legions fought at the following engagements:

> the battle of Pantano de Vargas (1819)
> the battle of Boyce (1819)
> the failed assault on Cumana
> the battle of Carabobo (1821)

It should also be noted that a number of Irish officers held high appointments in Simón Bolívar's army. These included Colonel James Rooke, General Daniel O'Leary, Colonel William Ferguson and Colonel Arthur Sandes. Apart from serving as staff officers, these officers were also occasionally made responsible for raising and training new regiments. Throughout his later campaigns to liberate modern-day Venezuela, Colombia and Ecuador, Simón Bolívar was rarely without an Irish officer on his staff.

THE IRISH REGIMENT IN BRAZIL, 1826–8

Formation

In 1826 the newly independent Brazil was involved in a dispute with Argentina over the province of Banda Oriental. At this time Brazil's army was tiny and an Irish officer in the Brazilian service, Colonel Cotter, was sent to Ireland in October 1826 to recruit a regiment of Irish soldiers. These men enlisted for a term of five years and travelled to Brazil with their families. Around 2,400 people, men, women and children, left Ireland for Brazil.

On their arrival in Rio de Janeiro they initially found themselves without quarters but were eventually housed in the Praya Vermelha Barracks.

They were poorly trained and badly equipped, uniformed and fed. Also, their pay was constantly in arrears. Serious disciplinary problems were the result of these deficiencies and these often resulted in clashes with the local population. Disease and desertion further thinned the ranks of this Irish unit.

Disbandment

In June 1828, around 200 members of the Irish regiment joined with German troops in a mutiny over long-term grievances. As a result of this mutiny the regiment was disbanded in late June.

In early July 1828 two contingents of these Irish soldiers were shipped back to Ireland, numbering around 400 people. However, many soldiers remained in Brazil with their families, the largest Irish community being established in the Province of Bahia.

SAN PATRICIO BATTALION, 1846–8

Formation
This Mexican unit, which served in the Mexican-American War, still continues to be the focus of much debate. Many historians have dismissed it as a band of renegade Irishmen who had deserted from the American army. Closer scrutiny reveals a much more complex picture.

The unit was raised in April 1846 and was originally titled as the 'Legión de Estrangeros' (the Legion of Foreigners). It was initially of company strength and served as an artillery unit. It was made up not only of deserters but also of Americans and Europeans who were living in Mexico when the war broke out. By August 1846 there were just over 200 men serving with the unit and it was reorganized as an infantry battalion. There were various nationalities represented in the battalion's ranks and these included Germans, Poles and Scots. The Irish contingent was the largest, however, and the battalion took on an Irish identity as the 'San Patricio Battalion'. Many of the Irish soldiers had deserted from the American army due to the harsh discipline and the anti-Catholic sentiments of the Nativist faction.

Operational history
During the course of the Mexican-American War, the San Patricios were present at the following engagements.

1846	the siege of Fort Texas
	the battle of Resaca de Palma (Guerrero)
	the battle of Monterrey
1847	the battle of Buena Vista
	the battle of Cerro Gordo
	the battle of Churubusco

Churubusco and after
The San Patricios suffered heavy casualties at the battle of Churubusco and also a large number of them were taken prisoner; 67 were found to have previously served in the American army and were court-martialled; of these, 50 were later hanged (these included 21 Irishmen); 11 others were flogged and then branded on the cheek with the letter 'D' for deserter.

Despite these losses the battalion was reformed and while the war ended in February 1848, the San Patricios were not disbanded until August 1848.

Officers
The most famous member of the San Patricios was John Riley (sometimes spelt Reilly or O'Reilly). He was born in Clifden in Co. Galway and had deserted from the American army before the outbreak of war. He initially served as a lieutenant in the

San Patricios and served with the unit throughout the war, being awarded the Mexican Cross of Honour.

It would appear to have been Riley who actively recruited Irishmen into the unit, thus giving it an Irish identity. He was captured at Churubusco but escaped the death penalty on the technicality that he had deserted before the actual declaration of war. He was flogged, however, and branded on both cheeks. Riley was subsequently promoted to lieutenant colonel in the Mexican army and returned to command the reformed San Patricios until their disbandment in 1848.

The San Patricios were initially commanded by a succession of Mexican regular army officers. These officers were:

Major José María Calderón
Lieutenant-Colonel Francisco Rosendo Moreno
Lieutenant-Colonel Francisco Shafino

Regimental colours
There are varying descriptions of the colour carried by the San Patricios. According to one account it was a green silk banner with an image of St Patrick on one side in silver embroidery. On the other side it bore a harp and shamrock.

Another account states that it was a green banner with images of St Patrick, the Mexican eagle and an inscription reading 'Erin Go Bragh'. This main colour of the San Patricos was captured and various historians have made attempts to trace it to various American museums and also the cadet chapel at West Point.

An unusual colour survives at the Museo de Intervenciones in Mexico. It is a green banner with the Mexican coat of arms bordered by what appear to be shamrocks. It has been suggested that this was another battle flag of the San Patricios.

In Mexico, the San Patricios have been commemorated with a memorial at San Angel, near where members of the battalion were executed. Commemorative coins and medals have also been minted and a school and town have been named in their honour. There are annual commemorations in their memory. In 1993 there was a commemoration ceremony in Ireland and a plaque was unveiled at Clifden, Co. Galway, the birthplace of John Riley.

IRISH REGIMENTS IN THE UNION ARMY, 1861–5

At the outbreak of the American Civil War, there was a huge Irish population living in the northern states. During the course of the war, thousands of them joined the Union army and some of these men were formed into specifically Irish regiments while the remainder served in non-Irish regiments within the Union army. Debate still rages as to the exact number of Irishmen who served in the Union army. Some historians suggest a figure of 180,000 while others support a more modest figure of 144,000. A general consensus would suggest that between 144,000 and 160,000

Irishmen served in the Union army. It must also be stressed that these figures are of soldiers who were Irish-born and they do not include soldiers of Irish descent – those who were second or third generation Irishmen.

Given such a huge recruiting base, a number of Irish regiments were formed but here again there is debate as to the actual number. Different historians claim that anywhere between 18 and 38 Irish regiments existed within the Union army. This is a subject, therefore, that still requires much research but an attempt has been made to outline the histories of the more prominent regiments in the section that follows.

What is certain is that a large number of Irish officers held senior appointments with the Union army, both as regimental commanders and general officers.[5] The best-known and perhaps most flamboyant of these was Brigadier-General Thomas Francis Meagher who began recruiting for the regiments of his Irish Brigade in 1861. This brigade consisted of the 63rd, 69th and 88th New York Regiments and was later joined by the 28th Massachusetts and 116th Pennsylvania Regiments. Attached to the Army of the Potomac, this Irish Brigade took part in every major campaign of the war up to the Confederate surrender. While the individual regiments are treated separately in this section, the main actions in which the brigade fought are listed below.

1862	Siege of Yorktown	Malvern Hill
	Seven Pines	(Fair Oaks)Antietam
	Seven Days battles	Fredericksburg
1863	Chancellorsville	Auburn
	Gettysburg	Bristoe's Station
1864	The Wilderness Campaign	Tolapotomy Creek
	Todd's Tavern	Cold Harbour
	Po River	1st and 2nd Petersburg
	1st and 2nd Spottsylvania	Yellow Tavern
	North Anna River	Strawberry Plains
1865	Skinner's Farm	
	Present at the Confederate surrender	
	at Appomatox Courthouse	

While Meagher's Irish Brigade was the largest Irish formation of the war, Colonel Michael Corcoran began recruiting his own brigade, or rather Irish Legion, in 1862 and this formation is noticed separately. During the course of the war, therefore, numerous Irish regiments served with some distinction in the Union army and their service is outlined, regiment by regiment, in the section that follows. The regiments are arranged in order of the date that they were raised.

5 For a list of same see Dean B. Mahin, *The blessed place of freedom: Europeans in Civil War America* (Brassey's, 2002). See also *Irish Sword*, 23:91 (Summer 2002), which was a special issue devoted to the subject of Ireland and the American Civil War.

69th NEW YORK VOLUNTEER INFANTRY REGIMENT, 1849–2006

The 69th Regiment of New York is one of the most famous Irish formations in the world. One of its companies (A Company, 1st Battalion) can trace its history back to the 8th Company of 1st New York Infantry Regiment of the Continental Army that was raised for service with the Continental Army in 1775. In 1849, the official lineage of the 69th Regiment begins. Even to the initiated, its early history can be somewhat confusing as there were actually three units during the American Civil War that bore the designation '69th' and the current 69th Regiment is directly descended from all three. These were:

- the 69th Regiment New York State Militia (later the name was changed to the 69th New York National Guard Infantry Regiment)
- the 69th New York Volunteer Infantry (also known as the 1st Regiment of the Irish Brigade)
- the 69th New York National Guard Artillery Regiment (later to be called the 182d New York National Guard Infantry Regiment

The three regiments are considered part of the modern regiment's lineage.

THE 69th NEW YORK STATE MILITIA

This regiment was formed in 1849 and is the nucleus from which the other 69th Regiments were formed during the American Civil War. Originally formed from independent companies of the First Irish Regiment the and called the 9th New York Regiment in 1850, it later merged with younger regiment which was formed in 1851 from the Second Irish Regiment and called the 69th Regiment.

For many years the founding date of the Regiment was considered 1851 since that is the first time the name '69th Regiment' was used but recently the Army decided the 69th Regiment's lineage could be traced to the earlier date of 1849.

In 1860 the Regiment's commanding officer, Colonel Michael Corcoran, refused to parade the regiment in honour of the Prince of Wales who was then visiting America, much to the approval of New York's Irish community. At the outbreak of the Civil War (1861), Corcoran was awaiting court martial but charges were set aside as he and his regiment volunteered for active service.

Operational history
At the outbreak of the war, the strength of the 69th Regiment of the NY State Militia was only 245 men, all ranks. It was brought up to strength with new recruits and on 23 April 1861 was mustered into Federal service for a term of three months. It was initially used to man the defences of Washington, DC. Despite the fact that the regiment had exceeded its term of enlistment, the men of the 69th volunteered to stay

with the army and fought at the battle of 1st Bull Run (1st Manassas) on 18 July 1861, during which Colonel Corcoran was wounded and captured.

On its return to New York, this regiment was mustered out of Federal service on 3 August 1861. During its short active service in the war, this regiment lost 45 men killed in action while 6 other soldiers died of disease.

This militia or National Guard unit would be called to active duty on several occasions during the war and it was the nucleus around which the other two 69th Regiments were formed.

As a militia unit, it was mustered into service on three occasions during the war. In 1862, it served on garrison duties at Washington, DC. During General Lee's invasion of the north in 1863, it served on garrison duties in Maryland. It then returned to New York to help quell the New York Draft Riots. In 1864, it was mustered into service for a third and final occasion and served on guard duties at Washington and New York before being mustered out of service on 6 October 1864 for the last time.

THE 69th NEW YORK VOLUNTEER INFANTRY

On the return of the 69th New York State Militia from 1st Bull Run, many veterans of the original militia regiment decided to form a new volunteer regiment for active service in the war. This regiment was one of those raised by Colonel (later Brigadier-General) Thomas Francis Meagher in November 1861 and it was designated as the 69th New York Volunteer Infantry but was also known as the '1st Regiment, the Irish Brigade'.

It mustered into Federal service on 18 November 1861 and was brigaded with the 88th and 63rd New York Volunteer Infantry regiments and this brigade was later joined by the 28th Massachusetts and 116th Pennsylvania regiments (see entries for those regiments). This formation was referred to as the 'Irish brigade'. In 1862, the brigade was assigned to the 1st Division of the 2nd Corps, of the Army of the Potomac and in this formation the 69th New York Volunteer Infantry went on to serve in every major campaign in the east up to the Confederate surrender at Appomattox Courthouse. It was General Robert E. Lee who referred to the regiment as 'that fighting Sixty-Ninth' and this apt sobriquet has been associated with the 69th NY Regiment ever since.

Operational history
1862   In March it was attached to the 2nd Brigade, 1st Division, 2nd Corps, Army of the Potomac. It took part in the siege of Yorktown and was engaged at the battles of Seven Pines, Gaine's Mill, Savage Station, Allen's Farm, the Peach Orchard (Fair Oaks), White Oak Swamp, Malvern Hill, Antietam and Fredericksburg.
1863   With the other regiments of Meagher's Irish Brigade, the 69th New York fought at the battles of Chancellorsville, Gettysburg, Auburn and Bristoe's

1864	(Bristow's) Station. By the battle of Gettysburg the regiment had been reduced to just 75 men and was commanded by Captain Richard Moroney. In June it was attached to the Consolidated Brigade, 1st Division, 2nd Corps, the Army of the Potomac. During this year of almost constant campaigning it fought in the battles of the Wilderness Campaign and also the battles of Todd's Tavern, Po River, 1st and 2nd Spottsylvania, Ream's Station, North Anna River, Tolapotomy Creek, Cold Harbour, 1st and 2nd Petersburg, Yellow Tavern and Strawberry Plains. In November it was brigaded with the 2nd Brigade, 1st Division, 2nd Corps, Army of the Potomac.
1865	In this final year of the war, it fought in the battles of Skinner's Farm and Hatcher's Run and was present at Lee's surrender at Appomatox Courthouse. At the end of the war the 69th Volunteers were released from Federal service, being mustered out on 30 June 1865.

During the American Civil War, the 69th NY Volunteer Infantry lost 259 men killed in action while a further 142 died of disease.

69th NEW YORK NATIONAL GUARD ARTILLERY REGIMENT, SERVING AS INFANTRY (182nd NEW YORK INFANTRY REGIMENT, CORCORAN LEGION)

In November 1862, Colonel Corcoran, who had recently been released from captivity by the Confederates, raised the 69th New York National Guard Artillery. Despite being designated as an artillery unit, this regiment served as infantry. The Regiment called themselves the 69th New York Artillery Regiment so they would not be confused with the 69th Infantry Regiment, which was the 1st Regiment of Meagher's Irish Brigade.

The regiment was attached to Corcoran's Irish Legion and was later re-designated as the 182nd New York Infantry Regiment. It became the senior regiment in Corcoran's Irish Legion and served in Virginia and on garrison duty at Washington in 1863. In 1864 it was attached to the Army of the Potomac and served in the campaign in Virginia, serving in several actions including Cold Harbour (3 June 1864), at which it suffered heavy casualties. This regiment served until the Confederate surrender and, in July 1865, it mustered out of service (see separate entry on this regiment under Corcoran's Irish Legion).

1898	The regiment was activated for the Spanish-American (Cuban) War. At the end of the war the regiment was based in Florida awaiting deployment.
1906	The 69th Regiment moved to new headquarters at the Armory on Lexington Avenue, New York, where it continues to be based.
1916	The regiment took part in the Mexican border campaign.

The First World War

1917   On America's entry into WWI, the regimental designation was changed to 165th Infantry although its members continued to refer to themselves as the 'Fighting 69th'. It was attached to the 42nd (Rainbow) Division, which was made up of the best units of the National Guard:

1918   Re-organized into three battalions, the regiment served in the following sectors and campaigns:

Lorraine	St. Mihiel Offensive
Champagne	Argonne Offensive
The defence of Chalons-sur-Marne	The battle for Hill 332, near Sedan
The battle of Ourcq	

1919   At the end of the war, the regiment formed part of the army of occupation in Germany and was stationed at Remagen. It returned to New York in April 1919 where is resumed service in the reserves. During the course of its service in WWI, the regiment lost 644 men killed in action.

The Second World War

1940   The regiment went on active service and was assigned to the 27th (New York) Infantry Division.

1942   After training and duties in the U.S., the regiment it was posted to Hawaii.

1943   Its first action came in November 1943 when it took part in the assault on Makin Atoll in the Gilbert Islands.

1944   The regiment took part in the difficult and costly assault on Saipan in the Marianas Islands.

1945   The regiment's last action of WWII was in the assault and capture of Okinawa. These three Pacific campaigns entailed not only the initial assault on these islands but also a series of follow-up battles as the regiment fought inland. In total, the regiment lost 454 men killed in these Pacific battles. The unit returned to National Guard service.

1951   It celebrated the centenary of its formation. (The lineage of the unit was subsequently changed to reflect a formation date of 1849.)

1963   The 165th Infantry designation was abolished by order of the Secretary of the Army, Cyrus Vance. The regiment re-adopted its historical title as the 69th Infantry and was allowed to use its traditional designation of the 'Fighting Sixty-Ninth'. In the same year, President John F. Kennedy visited Ireland and presented one of the regiment's Civil War battle flags. This colour remains on display at Leinster House in Dublin as a gift from the 69th Infantry.

1993   The 69th was converted into an Air Defence Artillery regiment.

1996   The regiment was reorganized and converted to mechanized infantry.

2001   Following the attacks on the World Trade Centre on 9 September, the 69th NY Regiment was the first military unit to arrive at the scene of the destruction.

Iraq

2004　The 69th Infantry was preparing for active service in Kosovo. In March, it received a warning order to prepare for deployment in Iraq. After months of intensive training, the regiment was deployed in Kuwait in October 2004 and the force being given the title 'Taskforce Wolfhound'. On 28 October, it deployed in Iraq and was assigned to an area of operations 50km northwest of Baghdad at Taji.

2005　The unit was redeployed to Camp Liberty in Baghdad and took over responsibility for a route that ran from the airport to the international zone. This route was named 'Route Irish'.

In September the unit returned to the United States, turning responsibility for its area of operations over to the Iraqi forces.

During the course of its deployment in Iraq, the regiment suffered several fatal casualties while other soldiers were also wounded.

Medal of honour

The Medal of Honour is the highest award for valour in action against an enemy force which can be bestowed upon an individual serving in the Armed Services of the United States. Generally presented to its recipient by the President of the United States of America in the name of Congress, it is often called the *Congressional Medal of Honor*. To date seven members of the regiment have been awarded the Medal of Honour:

Private Peter Rafferty, American Civil War
Private Timothy O'Donoghue, American Civil War
Sergeant-Major Joseph Keele, American Civil War
Sergeant Richard W. O'Neill, World War 1
Sergeant Michael A. Donaldson, World War 1
Lieutenant-Colonel William Joseph Donovan, World War 1
Sergeant Alejandro R. Renteria Ruiz, World War 2

Regimental colours

During the course of its long and distinguished history the 69th Infantry has used a series of regimental colours. Its present colour is a standard U.S. Army Infantry battalion/regimental colour. This incorporates battle streamers and battle rings authorized for the unit. The regiment has recently been awarded the 'Operation Iraqi Freedom' streamer in recognition of its service in Iraq.

The Common Council of New York presented a regimental colour in 1857. It depicted a shield design with representations of the American flag, an Irish harp and an Irish round tower in its sections. An American eagle and stars surmounted this. A pair of Irish wolfhounds supported the shield device with the motto 'Gentle when stroked, fierce when provoked' in a scroll underneath. This design of shield, wolfhounds and motto was repeated on an early cap badge.

One of the original colours (the 'Prince of Wales's Flag') was presented to the 69th Volunteers in November 1861 and it was carried to the first battle of the Civil War, Bull Run. The Irish Brigade carried the first Irish Colour in 1862 but by the end of the year it was already showing battle damage. It was returned to New York just before the battle of Fredricksburg in December 1862. A second Irish Colour was presented to the regiments of the Irish Brigade on December 15, 1862. It is the second colour of the 69th New York State Volunteers that was presented to Leinster House by President J.F. Kennedy in 1963.

It is a green silk banner of around five feet square with all inscriptions in gold lettering. It has a Irish harp in the upper left corner and this is surmounted by a sunburst and has a shamrock design beneath. Beneath this harp, sunburst and scroll of shamrocks was the regimental motto: 'Riamh nar druid osbairn lann' (Who never retreated from the clash of spears).

The dedication reads 'Presented by the Citizens of New York to the 69th NYV (1st Regiment of the Irish Brigade) Brigadier General Thomas Francis Meagher Commanding. In grateful appreciation of their gallant and brilliant conduct on the battlefields of Virginia and Maryland in the war to maintain the National Domain and the American Union. Nov.1862'.

The battle honours on this colour are Fredericksburg, Chancellorsville, Yorktown, Fair Oaks, Gaine's Mill, Allen's Farm, Savage's Station, White Oak Bridge, Glendale, Malvern Hills, Antietam, Gettysburg, Bristoe's [sic] Station. The battle names of Fredricksburg, Chancellorsville Gettysburg, and Bristoe's Station were not on the original colour but were added after the war.

Regimental mascot
The 69th Regiment adopted the Irish wolfhound as their official mascot.

Regimental music
While the band of the regiment played various martial Irish tunes such as *St Patrick's Day* and *The Wearing of the Green*, it is the tune of *Garryowen* that is usually associated with the 69th New York Regiment and it is considered to be the official Regimental March.

Regimental mottos
There are two mottos associated with the 69th Infantry. The official Regimental motto is 'Gentle when stroked, fierce when provoked'. The motto 'Riamh nar druid osbairn lann' (Who never retreated from the clash of spears) appeared on the Civil War colours.

Regimental nicknames
The Fighting 69th   The 69th New York

7th MISSOURI VOLUNTEER INFANTRY REGIMENT, 1861–4
('THE IRISH SEVENTH')

Formation

From the 1850s, there was an Irish volunteer unit based at St Louis and this was known as the 'Washington Blues'. It was one of several Irish volunteer companies set up across the United States at the suggestion of John Mahoney, the commander of 5th NYSM and also head centre of the Fenian Brotherhood. Mahony proposed that the Irish community should establish state militia companies with the idea of creating a corps of experienced soldiers that could be used for a later rebellion in Ireland.

The Washington Blues served in the Border War and the Southwest expedition of 1860 under Sterling Price. On outbreak of American Civil War, there was a split within the Washington Blues. Some joined 5th Missouri Confederate Infantry while the remainder went on to form the 7th Missouri State Volunteers in the Union Army.

In May 1861, a call was made for volunteers from among the Irish community of St Louis in the *Missouri Democrat*. These recruits were to be used to form an 'Irish Brigade' and Colonel John O'Fallon was initially destined to command this unit. The recruiting for this new unit focused on the Irish community in St Louis, which was centred on South Levee and on Poplar, Chesnut and Cherry Streets. Designated as the 7th Missouri Volunteer Infantry, Colonel John D. Stevenson was eventually appointed to command and the regiment was accepted into Federal service on 14 June 1861.

Operational history

1861   During an initial period of training the regiment was based at Booneville, Missouri. It then carried out garrison duties in various tons including Rolla, Syracuse, Sedalia and Otterville. Three companies based at Kansas City operated against William Quantrill and his Missouri raiders.

1862   In February it was assigned to the Army of the West under General Fremont. The regiment took part in the expedition to Blue Springs and, in February, was engaged at the skirmish at Mingo Creek near St Francisville. Companies of the 7th Missouri were also absent on garrison duties at Kansas City. The regiment garrisoned Lexington before being re-assigned to General Grant's Army of Tennessee. It was based at Pittsburg Landing and later Jackson. It was then attached to the 4th Brigade of the 1st Division. In December it was re-assigned to the 4th Brigade of the 3rd Division before being attached to the 3rd Brigade, 3rd Division, 17th Army Corps. It remained with this formation until April 1864. The regiment took part in the battles of Medon Station and Cornith.

1863   The 7th Missouri played an active part in the Vicksburg campaign and was present at the battles of Port Gibson (1 May), Raymond (12 May), Champion's Hill (16 May) and Big Black River Bridge (17 May). It took part in the assaults on Vicksburg on 19 and 22 May 1863. In these attacks, the regiment took part in the assault on Fort Hill at Vicksburg and found itself opposed by remnants of the 5th Missouri Confederate Infantry, in which several former comrades from the Washington Blues were serving. On the surrender of Vicksburg, the regiment took possession of Fort Hill. The 7th Missouri later took part in the expeditions to Monroe, Canton and Bogue Chitto Creek.

1864   The regiment took part in the expedition to Sunnyside Landing in Arkansas before serving in the Meridian Campaign in March. For a brief period it was attached to the 30th Missouri Regiment, which was also Irish, and the two regiments formed a demi-brigade which was often referred to as the 'Missouri Irish Brigade'.

From April, the regiment served in a succession of Federal formations. These included the 16th and 19th Army Corps. Soldiers who had enlisted on three year contracts were mustered out of service in June 1864. The remainder of the regiment carried out various garrison duties in Louisiana, Arkansas and Tennessee before being absorbed into the remnants of the 30th Missouri to form a consolidated battalion. This was officially referred to as the Consolidated Battalion, 7th and 30th Missouri Volunteers. It was more generally known as the 'Missouri Irish Battalion'. This amalgamation was ended in 1864 when the 7th Missouri was sent to Franklin, Tennessee. The regiment mustered out of service on 17 December 1864 at Nashville, Tennessee.

During the course of the war, the regiment had lost four officers and 52 men killed. A further two officers and 128 men had died of disease.

Regimental colours
The colour of the Washington Blues consisted of a green field with a gold harp device. In a scroll there was he motto 'What Washington did for America we will do for Ireland'. It is not clear what became of this colour.

The colour of the 7th Missouri Volunteer Infantry consisted of a green field with a sunburst device at the centre. Superimposed on this sunburst device was a harp and also images of Irish round towers and wolfhounds. There was a scroll of shamrocks beneath the central device. On the reverse of this colour, there was a scroll with the motto 'Faugh a Ballagh' (Clear the Way). These colours have been preserved and are held at the Missouri State capital building in Jefferson City.

9th MASSACHUSETTS VOLUNTEER INFANTRY REGIMENT, 1861–4

Formation
This regiment was raised from among Boston's Irish community in June 1861 and it was sent to Washington DC where it was attached to General William T. Sherman's brigade in the Army of the Potomac. In March 1862 it was attached to the 2nd

Brigade, 1st Division, 3rd Corps of the Army of the Potomac and it would continue to serve with this army until its disbandment in 1864.

Operational history

1861　After mustering into Federal service, the 9th Massachusetts formed part of the garrison of Washington, DC.

1862　While serving with the Army of the Potomac, the regiment took part in numerous engagements including the skirmish at Howard's Bridge, Virginia, and the siege of Yorktown. It also took part in the battles of Hanover, the Seven Days battles, Mechanicsville, Gaine's Mill, Malvern Hill, Groveton, 2nd Bull Run (2nd Manassas), Antietam and Fredericksburg.

1863　The 9th Massachusetts was engaged at the battles of Chancellorsville and Gettysburg.

1864　The regiment took part in the battles of the Wilderness Campaign and also 1st and 2nd Spottsylvania, North Anna River and Cold Harbour. On 10 June 1864 the regiment was ordered out of the line and mustered out of service on 21 June.

During the course of its numerous engagements, the 9th Massachusetts lost 209 men killed in action and another 69 died of disease.

Regimental colours

A surviving colour of the 9th Massachusetts consists of a green field with an elaborate central device that incorporates arms of the United States, an eagle and also a shamrock scroll. A scroll bears the inscription 'As aliens and strangers thou didst us befriend. As sons and patriots we do thee defend'. It is known that this colour was carried at the battle of Gaine's Mill in June 1862.

23rd ILLINOIS VOLUNTEER INFANTRY REGIMENT, 1861–5 ('MULLIGAN'S IRISH BRIGADE')

Formation

This regiment was raised from among the Irish community in Chicago and it was officially mustered into Federal service on 15 June 1861. Numbered as the 23rd Illinois Infantry Regiment, it was originally commanded by Colonel James A. Mulligan and was referred to as 'Mulligan's Irish Brigade', the 'Chicago Irish Brigade' or simply as the 'Irish Brigade'.

It was initially hoped that this regiment would form the nucleus of another Irish brigade but enough recruits were not forthcoming and it served as a single regiment during the war. It was originally based at Kane's Brewery on West Polk Street Chicago and was then moved to Quincy, Illinois before being sent to Missouri. G Company of the 23rd Illinois was named as the 'Mahony Guard'.

Operational history

1861   The 23rd Illinois took part in the siege of Lexington, Missouri, in September. Following Confederate counterattacks, the regiment was captured by the army of General Price and was subsequently paroled. On 8 October 1861, the 23rd Illinois was mustered out of service and it seemed that its short history was over. By order of General McClellan, the regiment was restored in December and it remained in existence for the rest of the war. For its part in the defence of Lexington, the regiment was formally thanked by Congress.

1862   The 23rd Illinois re-assembled in Chicago and was used to guard POWs at Camp Douglas. It then undertook garrison duties at Harper's Ferry and in the defences along the Upper Potomac. In November three companies of the regiment attacked the Confederate army of General Imboden and captured 40 prisoners and a quantity of supplies.

1863   The regiment was attached to the 5th Brigade, 1st Division, 8th Corps in the Army of West Virginia and in December was re-assigned to the 2nd Brigade of the 2nd Division. The 23rd Illinois fought in the engagements at Greenland Gap, Phillippi and Hedgeville.

1864   In April 300 men of the regiment re-enlisted on the expiration of their original contracts, this time negotiating signing contracts as veterans. Thereafter the regiment was officially referred to as the 23rd Regiment Illinois Veteran Volunteer Infantry.

The 23rd Illinois served with the Army of West Virginia and also the Army of the James. It was present at the sieges of Petersburg and Richmond and took part in the battles of Leetown, Maryland Heights, Snicker's Gap and Kernstown. At this last action, Colonel Mulligan was killed in action.

During General Sheridan's Shenandoah campaign, the 23rd Illinois fought in the battles of Cedar Creek, Winchester, Charlestown, Halltown, Berryville, Opequan Creek, Fisher's Hill and Harrisonburg.

1865   The regiment fought in the battle of Hatcher's Run and was present at the Confederate surrender at Appomatox Courthouse. It was mustered out of service on 30 July 1865.

During the war the 23rd Illinois lost 54 men killed in action while 95 men died of disease.

A cavalry unit raised by Captain Patrick Naughton in Missouri in 1861 and named as the 'Irish Dragoons' was originally attached to this regiment. This cavalry unit later served with other formations. (See separate entry for that regiment.)

63rd NEW YORK VOLUNTEER INFANTRY REGIMENT, 1861–5

Formation

This regiment also consisted of volunteers from the Irish community in New York. It enlisted its initial recruits between August and November 1861 and was originally referred to as the 'Independent Irish Regiment'. On completing its recruiting it was attached to Meagher's Irish Brigade in November 1861. It was also referred to as the '3rd Regiment, Irish Brigade' while operating within this larger formation. Its wartime history mirrored that of other regiments within this brigade and it took part in the same actions.[6]

Operational history

1861   Attached to Meagher's Irish Brigade, General Sumner's Division, Army of the Potomac.

1862   In March, the regiment was attached to the 2nd Brigade, 1st Division, 2nd Corps, Army of the Potomac. During this year it took part in numerous actions including the siege of Yorktown and the battles of Seven Pines (Fair Oaks), Seven Days, Malvern Hill, Antietam and Fredercksburg.

1863   With the other regiments of Meagher's Irish Brigade, the 63rd New York was engaged in the battles of Chancellorsville, Gettysburg, Auburn and Bristoe's (Bristow's) Station. At Gettysburg it numbered 75 men and was commanded by Lt.-Col. Richard C. Beutley.

1864   In January, with the rest of the Irish Brigade, the regiment formed part of the Consolidated Brigade, 1st Division, 2nd Corps, Army of the Potomac. This brigade was re-designated as the 2nd Brigade in November. During this year the regiment was almost in constant action and it fought in numerous battles including those of the Wilderness Campaign and also the battles of Todd's Tavern, Po River, 1st and 2nd Spottsylvania, North Anna River, Tolapotomy Creek, Cold Harbour, 1st and 2nd Petersburg, Yellow Tavern and Strawberry Plains.

1865   In the final year of the war the regiment fought at the battle of Skinner's Farm and was present at the Confederate surrender at Appomatox Courthouse. On 30 June the regiment was mustered out of service.

During the course of the war, the 63rd New York Infantry lost 156 men killed in action while a further 93 died of disease.

88th NEW YORK VOLUNTEER INFANTRY REGIMENT, 1861–65

Formation
This regiment was raised at Fort Schuyler, New York, in December 1861 and was one of the original regiments of Meagher's Irish Brigade. This brigade was initially attached to General Sumner's Division in the Army of the Potomac and the regiment was also referred to as the '5th Regiment of the Irish Brigade' or 'Meagher's Own'.

---

6 For a more complete list of these engagements, see the entry for the 69th NY Regiment.

Operational history

1862 With the rest of the Meagher's Irish Brigade, the 88th New York was attached to the 2nd Brigade, 1st Division, 2nd Corps of the Army of the Potomac. During 1862, it took part in several engagements including Gaine's Mill, Savage Station, the Peach orchard, Malvern Hill, Antietam and Fredericksburg.

1863 The 88th New York fought with Meagher's Irish Brigade in the battles of Chancellorsville, Gettysburg, Auburn and Bristoe's (Bristow's) Station. Due to casualties on campaign, the regiment numbered just 90 men at the battle of Gettysburg and was commanded by Captain Denis F. Burke.

1864 During this year, the Irish Brigade was in almost constant action and the 88th New York was engaged at numerous battles including those of the Wilderness Campaign and also Todd's Tavern, 1st and 2nd Spottsylvania, 1st and 2nd Petersburg and Cold Harbour. In June the brigade was re-designated as the Consolidated Brigade of the 1st Division, 2nd Corps of the Army of the Potomac but it was re-named as the 2nd Brigade of the same formation in November.

1865 The regiment was present at the battle of Skinner's farm and the Confederate surrender at Appomatox courthouse. The 88th New York was mustered out of service on 30 June 1865.

Between 1862 and 1865, the regiment lost 151 men killed in action while a further 72 died of disease.

THE IRISH DRAGOONS, 1861–5

Formation
This cavalry unit was raised by Captain Patrick Naughton in St Louis, Missouri, in August 1861, being officially mustered into service on 1 September. Named as the 'Irish Dragoons', it was originally attached to the Colonel Mulligan's Irish Brigade which was later re-named as the 23rd Illinois Volunteer Infantry Regiment (see separate entry for that regiment). During the course of the war, however, the Irish Dragoons were attached to other formations.

Operational history

1861 In September the unit was attached to Colonel White's Prairie Scouts, Missouri Volunteers and took part in the attack on Springfield, Missouri, on 25 October. In December the Irish Dragoons became Company L of the Curtis Horse, later re-designated as the 5th Regiment of Cavalry, Iowa Volunteers.

1862 From March until June 1862, the company served in Kentucky guarding telegraph lines. In August and September it took part in the capture of

Confederate stores and facilities in Tennessee at Cumberland and Clarksville. On 6 November the Irish Dragoons took part in an engagement at Garretsburg, Kentucky in which one of its officers was killed.

1863   The unit took part in engagements in Tennessee at Guy's Gap, (25 June), Wartrace (5 October) and Sugar Creek (9 October).

1864   In January, many of the troopers terms of enlistment expired but the majority re-enlisted. The regiment was re-designated as the 5th Regiment of Veteran Cavalry, Iowa Volunteers. The Irish Dragoons still formed Company L. In July it was attached to the division of Major-General L.H. Rousseau and took part in a number of raids into Alabama and Georgia. The Irish Dragoons took part in engagements at Ten Islands, Alabama (14 July) and Chewa Station, Georgia (18 July). The unit transferred under the command of Brigadier-General Edward M. McCrook and took part in further engagements in Georgia at Campbell town (28 July), Lovejoy's Station (29 and 30 July) and Newnan (30 July). At this last action the regiment was surrounded and almost captured.

On 8 August 1864, the remnants of this cavalry regiment, including the Irish Dragoons, were amalgamated with the 5th Regiment of Infantry, Iowa Volunteers. This new unit was re-designated as the 5th Regiment of Veteran Cavalry Consolidated, Iowa Volunteers. It was attached to the 3rd Cavalry Division of the Military Division of the Middle. It took part in further actions in Georgia at Fairburn (18 August), Bear Creek Station (26 August) and Jonesboro (31 August to 1 September). It then moved into Tennessee and was present at actions at Columbia (24 to 28 November), Franklin (30 November), Nashville (15–16 December) and Pulaski (25 December).

1865   The regiment took part in a raid into Alabama and Georgia. In Alabama it was present at engagements at Five Mile Creek (28 March), Montevallo (31 March) and Ebenezer Church (1 April). The Irish Dragoons fought their last action at Columbus, Georgia, on 16 April 1865. On 11 August 1865, the entire regiment, including the Irish Dragoons, was mustered out of service at Nashville, Tennessee.

9th CONNECTICUT INFANTRY, 1861–5

Formation

This volunteer regiment was raised at Camp English, New Haven, Connecticut, in September and October 1861. The regiment's original commanding officer was Colonel Thomas W. Cahill. The 9th Connecticut was moved to Boston and then sent by steam ship to Mississippi where it was stationed at Ship Island from December 1861 to April 1862. It formed part of the New Orleans Expeditionary Corps and then was attached to the army of the Department of the Gulf.

In 1862 it served as part of the garrison of New Orleans and during the rest of the war mostly served with the army of the Department of the Gulf but would later serve with several army corps including those of the Department of the East, the Department of Virginia and North Carolina and also with the Army of the Shenandoah.

Operational history

1862 The regiment took part in the expedition to Biloxi, taking part in the actions at Pass Christian and Biloxi. It then served in the siege of Vicksburg and was also present at the battles of New Orleans and Baton Rouge. In a general order written after the battle, it was stated that 'Connecticut, represented by the sons of the ever-green shamrock, fought as their brothers did at Boyne Waters'.[7]

1864 The 9th Connecticut fought in the battles of La Fourche Crossing, Chattahoola Station, Pass Manchac, Bayou des Allemands, Deep Bottom, Winchester, Fisher's Hill and Cedar Creek. After these battles, the regiment was reduced to a battalion of four companies due to wartime casualties and also the loss of soldiers whose enlistment contracts had expired.

1865 After service in Virginia, the regiment was sent to Georgia where it was based in Savannah and Hilton Head and operated against local guerrilla fighters. The 9th Connecticut mustered out of federal service at Savannah, Georgia, on 3 August 1865 and returned to New Haven.

The 9th Connecticut served in some of the most unhealthy theatres of the war and as a result lost 243 men to disease. Conversely, the regiment lost only 10 men killed in action.

Regimental colours
A surviving colour of the 9th Connecticut incorporates the coat of arms of the United States and a harp device, the whole surmounted by an eagle. The field of this colour is green and bears the motto 'Erin Go Bragh' in a scroll. It is known that this colour was carried at the battle of Baton Rouge in 1862.

28th MASSACHUSETTS INFANTRY, 1861–5

Formation
This regiment, which also formed part of Meagher's Irish Brigade, was raised in Boston, Massachusetts, in December 1861, its original recruits being raised from among that city's Irish community. In January 1862 it was sent to New York and the regiment was attached to the Department of the South in April. In December 1862, it was attached to Meagher's Irish Brigade and it operational history after this date would mirror that of the other regiments of that brigade.

7 General Order No. 57, Department of the Gulf.

Operational history

1862   In April the regiment was attached to the 1st Brigade, 2nd Division, Department of the South, transferring in July to the 1st Brigade, 1st Division, Army of the Potomac. In December it was re-attached to Meagher's Irish Brigade, which was officially designated as the 2nd Brigade, 1st Division, 2nd Corps, Army of the Potomac. During 1862 it fought in the battles of Secessionville, 2nd Bull Run (2nd Manassas), Chantilly, Antietam and Fredericksburg.

1863   With the other regiments of Meagher's Irish Brigade, the 28th Massachusetts took part in the battles of Chancellorsville, Gettysburg, Auburn and Bristoe's (Bristow's) Station. At Gettysburg it numbered 224 men and, commanded by Colonel R. Byrnes, was the largest unit in the Irish Brigade.

1864   In June the regiment was re-assigned to the 1st Brigade, 1st Division, 2nd Corps, Army of the Potomac, being re-assigned to the division's 2nd Brigade in November. During this year of constant campaigning it took part in the battles of the Wilderness Campaign, 1st and 2nd Spottsylvania, Cold Harbour and Petersburg, among others.

1865   The regiment was present at the Confederate surrender at Appomatox Courthouse on 9 April. The 28th Massachusetts was mustered out of service on 29 June 1865.

During the course of the war, the 28th Massachusetts lost 250 men killed in action while a further 137 died of disease.

37th NEW YORK VOLUNTEER INFANTRY REGIMENT, 1861–3

'The Irish Rifles'

Formation

This volunteer regiment was raised from among New York's Irish community and was mustered into service in June 1861. It had its roots in the old 75th New York State Militia, which had been raised in 1856 by Colonel John McCunn and Lt.-Col. James Heggerty. This regiment had been disbanded but was raised again in 1861 and was given a new designation as the 37th New York Volunteer Infantry.

Alongside its numerical title, it also adopted the title of 'The Irish Rifles' and was mustered into Federal service in New York on 7 June 1861.

It was sent to Washington DC where it initially served General Hunter's Brigade in the Army of the Potomac. It would later serve with General Richardson's Brigade in the Army of the Potomac and also in the Third Army Corps.

Operational history

1862   In March, the 37th New York ('The Irish Rifles') were attached to the 3rd Brigade, 3rd Division, 3rd Corps of the Army of the Potomac. In July they

1863 were re-assigned to the 1st Division of the same formation. During 1862 they were present at several engagements including the siege of Yorktown and the battles of Williamsburg, Seven Pines (Fair Oaks), Oak Grove, Malvern Hill, Groveton, 2nd Bull Run (2nd Manassas), Chantilly and Fredericksburg.

1863 The regiment was heavily engaged at the battle of Chancellorsville. On 22 June the 37th New York was mustered out of service as the majority of its recruits had enlisted for two years in 1861. Those men who had signed on for three years were transferred to the 40th New York Infantry Regiment.

In its relatively short history the 37th New York lost 119 men either killed in action or due to disease. Three soldiers of the regiment, James R. O'Beirne, Timothy Fallon and Martin Conboy, were awarded the Medal of Honour for acts of gallantry during the war.

Commanding officers
1861   Colonel John H. McCunn (to August)
1861   Colonel Samuel B. Hayman (to June 1863)

Other Regimental officers
Lt.-Col. John Burke   Major Patrick H. Jones
Lt.-Col. Gilbert Riordan   Major William De Lacy
Major Denis C. Minton

Regimental colours
A colour of the 37th New York survives and this consists of a green field with a central harp device and also shamrock motifs, in gold. Two scrolls above and below the harp bear the inscription 'The 37th Regiment Irish Rifles New York Volunteers'.

A further scroll below reads 'The First Regiment of Irish Volunteers in the Field'. It bears the battle honours Williamsburgh (*sic*) and Fair Oaks and was presented to the regiment in time to be carried at the battle of Chancellorsville in 1863.

69th PENNSYLVANIA VOLUNTEER INFANTRY REGIMENT, 1861–5

Formation
The 69th Pennsylvania Infantry was raised in Philadelphia in August 1861 by Colonel Joshua T. Owen who had previously commanded the 24th Pennsylvania Volunteers. The 69th Pennsylvania was recruited from among Philadelphia's Irish community and the regiment was mustered into Federal service on 19 August.

Colonel Owen took command with Lt.-Col. Dennis O'Kane serving as the regiment's second-in-command. The 69th Pennsylvania initially formed part of the garrison at Washington DC, before being attached to the General Baker's brigade in the Army of the Potomac.

Operational history

1862   In March the regiment was attached to the 2nd Brigade, 2nd Division, 2nd Corps, the Army of the Potomac. It was present at several major engagements that year including the siege of Yorktown and the battles of Fair Oaks (Seven Pines), the Peach Orchard, Savage Station, Glendale, Malvern Hill, Chantilly, Antietam and Fredericksburg.

1863   The regiment fought in skirmishes at Thoroughfare Gap and Haymarket in in June. The 69th Pennsylvania was heavily engaged at the battle of Gettysburg where on 2 July it was positioned in a crucial position on Cemetery Ridge, where it resisted a Confederate attack. On 3 July it occupied a section of the line that was the target of the Confederate attack more commonly known as 'Pickett's Charge'. It held its section of the line and the regiment succeeded in repelling the attack. The commanding officer of the 69th Pennsylvania, Colonel O'Kane, was mortally wounded. The regiment had begun the battle with just 284 men. A total of 143 of these were either killed or wounded during the battle.

1864   In June the regiment was attached to the 3rd Brigade, 2nd Division, 2nd Corps, Army of the Potomac. During this year of hard campaigning it took part in the battles of the Wilderness Campaign and also fought in numerous other actions including Po River, 1st and 2nd Spottsylvania, 1st and 2nd Petersburg, North Anna River, Cold Harbour, Ream's Station and 1st Hatcher's Run.

1865   The 69th Pennsylvania took part in the final campaign of the war and fought at the battles of 2nd Hatcher's Run (Dabney's Mills), Watkins House and the fall of Petersburg. The regiment was present at the Confederate surrender at Appomatox Courthouse on 9 April. The 69th Pennsylvania was mustered out of service on 1 July 1865.

The regiment lost 178 men killed in action and 110 men to disease.

116th PENNSYLVANIA VOLUNTEER INFANTRY REGIMENT, 1862–5

Formation
This regiment was raised from among the Irish community of Philadelphia between June and September 1862. It initially served on garrison duties in Washington DC and at Harper's Ferry before being attached to Meagher's Irish Brigade in October 1862. Thereafter, it took part in all the major engagements in which the Irish brigade was engaged.

Operational history

1862   In October, attached to Meagher's Irish Brigade; the 2nd Brigade, 1st Division, 2nd Corps, Army of the Potomac. With that brigade it was engaged at the battle of Fredericksburg.

1863   The 116th Pennsylvania fought in the battles of Chancellorsville and Gettysburg. At the time of the battle of Gettysburg, the regiment had been reduced to just 66 men and was commanded by Lt.-Col. St Clair A. Mulholland.

1864   During this year of constant campaigning, the regiment was present at numerous battles including those of the Wilderness campaign and the battles of 1st and 2nd Spottsylvania and Cold Harbour. In June the regiment was re-assigned to the 4th Brigade, 1st Division, 2nd Corps, Army of the Potomac.

1865   The regiment continued to serve up to the Confederate surrender at Appomatox Courthouse. It was mustered out of service on 30 June 1865.

During the war, the 116th Pennsylvania lost 145 men killed in action while a further 89 died of disease.

30th MISSOURI VOLUNTEER INFANTRY REGIMENT, 1862–5

'The Shamrock Regiment'

Formation

This regiment was formed at St Louis, Missouri, in October 1862 and initially carried out garrison duties at Pilot Knob and Davidson before being moved to Helena, Arkansas, where it joined the forces under General William T. Sherman. During the war, it would see extensive service in the western theatre of operations.[8]

Operational history

1863   The 30th Missouri fought in the battle of Chickasaw Bluff and the battle and siege of Arkansas Post. In May the regiment took part in the siege of Vicksburg, taking part in a series of assaults on the Confederate stronghold, including the actions at Haines and Drumgoulds Bluff. The 30th Missouri was then sent to Louisiana where it repulsed two Confederate assaults in the vicinity of Natches.

1864   The regiment returned to Vicksburg in April and later joined the 7th Missouri to form the 'Missouri Irish Brigade'. It was present at the action at Clinton, Louisiana. As the contracts began to expire for the regiment's original contingent, it was amalgamated with the 7th Missouri to form the Consolidated Battalion 7th and 30th Missouri Volunteers. This formation

---

[8] There would also appear to have been an Irish company in the 14th Missouri.

was usually just referred to as the 'Missouri Irish Battalion'. In December, this arrangement was ended and the 30th Missouri was ordered to join the army besieging Mobile, Alabama.

1865   On 9 April, the 30th Missouri took part in the assault and capture of Fort Blakeley. This was its last action of the war and it was mustered out of service in August 1865.

17th WISCONSIN INFANTRY REGIMENT, 1862–5
'Wisconsin Irish Brigade'

Formation
This regiment was raised at Camp Randall, Madison, Wisconsin, in March 1862 and initially served at St Louis, Missouri, before being moved to Pittsburg Landing (Shiloh) in Tennessee, where it formed part of the garrison. It was commanded by Colonel John L. Doran.

Alongside its official title, it was also referred to as the 'Wisconsin Irish Brigade', perhaps suggesting that a larger formation was originally envisaged. In July 1862 it was attached to the 1st Brigade, 6th Division of the army of the District of Corinth. It would later serve with both the 16th and 17th Army Corps.

Operational history

1862   The 17th Wisconsin took part in the advance upon Corinth and served in the siege and battle of that town. It then took part in General U.S. Grant's campaign on the central Mississippi.

1863   The regiment fought in the battles of Port Gibson, Champion's Hill and also in the siege and assaults on Vicksburg.

1864   The 17th Wisconsin took part in the assault on Kenesaw Mountain and also the siege and battle of Atlanta. It later fought in the battle of Jonesboro and the siege of Savannah.

1865   In this final year of the war, the regiment fought in the battle of Bentonville and was present at the surrender of General Johnson and his army in April. The 17th Wisconsin mustered out of service at Louisville, Kentucky, on 14 June 1865.

During the war the regiment lost 41 men killed in action while a further 228 men succumbed to various diseases.

Regimental colours
A surviving colour of the 17th Wisconsin Infantry Regiment consists of a green field with a central device incorporating a Hibernia and harp motif and the coat of arms of the United States. This device is surmounted by an eagle while a scroll bears the motto 'Faugh a Ballagh' (Clear the Way).

A further scroll bears the inscription 'Wisconsin Irish Brigade'. This colour was carried at the battle of Cornith, after which the regiment's commanding officer, Colonel John Doran, remarked that 'the regiment was greeted with as hearty a cheer as was ever raised for the Sons of Erin'.

CORCORAN'S IRISH LEGION, 1862–5

Formation
This Irish Legion was the brainchild of Colonel Michael Corcoran, a Sligo-born officer in the service of the Union. Corcoran had previously served in the 69th New York Regiment and had achieved a level of fame when he refused to parade his regiment during the visit of the Prince of Wales (later Edward VII) to New York in 1860. While this act of defiance endeared him to the wider Irish-American community, he still faced the possibility of court-martial proceedings when war broke out in 1861. The matter was dropped when his regiment volunteered for service but Corcoran was wounded and captured at the 1st Battle of Bull Run (1st Manassas) on 21 July 1861.

He was not repatriated until August 1862, but on his release, he was promoted to brigadier-general and authorized to raise a new brigade of volunteers in New York. This brigade was initially composed of eight regiments and was referred to as the 'Irish Legion'. In contemporary sources it was also referred to as 'Corcoran's Irish Legion' or simply as the 'Corcoran Legion'.[9] The original regiments of the Irish Legion were as follows:

1st Regiment
  The first regiment of the Irish Legion was recruited from the 69th Regiment National Guard of the State of New York, which was mustered out of Federal service in September 1862. All of its companies were raised in Manhattan and all its officers had previously served in the 69th NGSNY.

2nd Regiment
  This regiment was raised in the 4th Senatorial District of New York. The majority of this regiments recruits also came from Manhattan and two companies were raised in Brooklyn.

3rd Regiment
  The third regiment of the legion was the 155th Regiment, also known as the Buffalo Irish Regiment, which had been raised in early August 1862 in New York City.

4th Regiment
  This regiment was composed of a company from the 25th Regiment NGSNY which had mustered out of Federal service in early September 1862. Further recruits were raised in Albany, West Troy and Cohoes.

9 In August 2006, a memorial to Corcoran was unveiled in his home town of Ballymote.

5th Regiment
This unit had originally been raised to serve in Senator Francis B. Spinola's 'Empire Brigade' but was transferred to serve in the Irish Legion. Company A of this regiment was known as the 'Corcoran Zouvres' at some stage in its early history.

6th Regiment
This regiment raised its recruits in Manhattan, Brooklyn and also the counties of Kings, Queens, Suffolk and Richmond.

7th Regiment
This regiment had originally been the Phoenix Regiment of the Empire Brigade and it traced its origins back to a Fenian organization of 1858. All of its companies were raised in Manhattan.

8th Regiment
This regiment was referred to as the Cosmopolitan Guard and was recruited citizens from any foreign country. Apart from Irish, it recruited English, Dutch, Hungarian, French, German, Italian, Polish, Scottish and Spanish soldiers.

Some of the above regiments were more successful in raising recruits than others and it was decided to re-organize the legion and amalgamate the above regiments into the following five regiments. These were known as the 1st to 5th Regiments of the Corcoran Brigade but were officially designated as:

> 69th New York National Guard (Colonel Matthew Murphy)
> 155th New York Volunteer Infantry (Colonel William McEvily)
> 164th New York Volunteer Infantry (Colonel James E. McMahon)
> 170th New York Volunteer Infantry (Colonel Peter McDermott)
> 175th New York Volunteer Infantry (Colonel Michael K. Bryan)

The 175th New York Volunteer Infantry ultimately did not serve with the Corcoran Legion, although it was raised to serve with it. This regiment was assigned to other formations and never served with the other regiments of the Legion. The Corcoran Legion, therefore operated as a four regiment brigade (69th, 155th, 164th, 170th NY Volunteer Infantry Regiments).

Operational history
The 69th New York National Guard was officially the 182nd New York Regiment but due to its connections with the original 69th NGSNY it in fact retained the 69th numerical title. It was raised in New York City in November 1862 and left for Newport, Virginia, later in the same month. In December it was attached to the Corcoran Brigade in the Division of Suffolk, Virginia.

The 155th New York Volunteers was raised in New York City and was mustered into service in November 1862. It was sent to Newport and was initially attached to the department of Virginia before being re-assigned to the Corcoran Brigade in December 1862.

The 164th New York Volunteers were also known as the 'Corcoran Guard' and the regiment was raised in New York City between September and October 1862. It was officially mustered into service on 19 November 1862 and was sent to Newport in the Department of Virginia. In December it was attached to the Corcoran Brigade in the Division of Suffolk.

The 170th New York Volunteers, was also referred to as the '4th Corcoran Legion' and it was organized in New York. Mustered into service at Staten Island on 7 October 1862, it initially formed part of the garrison of Washington DC. In December it was assigned to the Corcoran Brigade in the Division of Suffolk, Virginia.

The 175th New York Volunteers was raised in New York in September 1862 and during its first month absorbed men recruited for other regiments that had not come up to full strength. These included men originally destined for the 171st New York Volunteers. The regiment recruited in New York City in the districts of Albany, Castleton, Troy, Glen Falls and Knox, among others. It mustered into the Federal service in September and October 1862, its recruits signing three-year contracts. Although it was intended to attach this regiment to the Corcoran Legion, it actually served with other formations including the army of the Department of the Gulf and later the 19th Corps.

The Corcoran Brigade, usually referred to as Corcoran's Irish Legion, was initially designated as the 3rd Brigade, 1st Division, 7th Corps, Department of Virginia. In 1863 it was re-assigned to 22nd Corps, Department of Washington. It would remain with the 22nd Corps until May 1864 when it was attached to the 2nd Corps, Army of the Potomac. In June 1864 it was serving as 2nd Brigade, 2nd Division, 2nd Corps, Army of the Potomac.

1863   The Corcoran Legion's first engagement was against Confederate forces commanded by General Roger Pryor at 'Deserted House' on the Blackwater River, Virginia on 29 January 1861. Thereafter it served in the siege of Suffolk and the engagement at Edgerton Road in April. Garrison duties followed at Suffolk, Portsmouth and Fairfax Courthouse. Corcoran died after being thrown from his horse on 22 December and Colonel Matthew Murphy succeeded to command of the Legion.

1864   The Legion was employed on guard duties on the Orange and Alexandria Railroad. It then took part in the battles of the Rapidian Campaign and the battles of 1st and 2nd Spottsylvania, Cold Harbour, 1st and 2nd Petersburg, Ream's Station and Hatcher's Run.

1865   During this last year of the war, the Legion took part in the battles of 2nd Hatcher's Run and Skinner's Farm. It was present at the Confederate surrender at Appomatox Courthouse.

From May 1864, the Irish Legion was brigaded with Meagher's Irish Brigade and fought alongside them at several engagements including Spotsylvania, Cold Harbour and Skinner's Farm. At the end of the war, the regiments of the legion were mustered out of service on 15 July 1865. The casualties of the Legion's regiments were:

> 69th NGSNY (or 182nd NY Infantry): 73 killed in action, 53 died of disease.
> 155th NY Volunteer Infantry: 114 killed in action, 73 died of disease.
> 164th NY Volunteer Infantry: 126 killed in action, 129 died of disease.
> 170th NY VolunteerInfantry: 129 killed in action, 98 died of disease.

The 175th NY Volunteer Infantry, which served with other formations, incurred 14 fatal combat casualties while a further 121 men died of disease.

IRISH UNITS IN THE ARMY OF THE CONFEDERATE STATES OF AMERICA, 1861–5

By 1860 there was quite a large Irish population in the southern states of America and there were significant Irish communities in towns such as Charleston, Memphis and Richmond.[10] The Irish population in what became the Confederate states stood at 83,874. Around a third of these lived in Louisiana, mostly centred around New Orleans. A further 16,512 Irish lived in the state of Virginia while 12,498 lived in Tennessee.[11]

Despite this large Irish population, the Confederacy never formed Irish regiments or brigades on the same scale as the Union Army. There were, however, a large number of Irish units and these were usually organized as company-sized units. Several of these had been raised as pre-war volunteer militia companies and they were incorporated into larger state regiments in 1861. The Confederate command also realized that there was a large transient Irish population working on railroad projects. As a result of this, Irish railroad workers were recruited in large numbers at the major railheads such as Mobile and Manassas Junction, while the Irish dock workers of New Orleans also became the focus of a recruitment drive. Estimates vary as to the numbers of Irish that served in the Confederate army. In 1863, John Mitchell claimed that 40,000 Irish soldiers were serving in the Confederate army but this is now generally held to be a vastly inflated figure. Modern estimates as to the number of Irish soldiers in the Confederacy range from 11,000 to 20,000. Numerous Irishmen held senior rank in the Confederate army, the most prominent being Cork-born Major-General Patrick Ronayne Cleburne, who was one of only two foreign-born major-generals in the Confederate army.[12]

---

10 1860 census figures: Charleston 3,263 Irish (40,578 Total Population); Memphis 4,159 Irish (22,623); Mobile 3,307 Irish (29,258); New Orleans 24,398 Irish (168,675); Richmond 2,294 Irish (37,910); Savannah 3,145 Irish (22,292): Ella Lonn, *Foreigners in the Confederacy*, p. 481. 11 Dean B. Mahin, *The blessed place of freedom*, pp 77–83. 12 For a list of same see Mahin, op. cit., 243–4. See *Irish Sword*, 23:91 (Summer

The Irish companies that were raised often adopted Irish-sounding titles and there were a number of units named the 'Emmet Guard' or 'Emmet Guards'.[13] In a similar vein, various state regiments had companies which called themselves the 'Emerald Guard' or the 'Irish Volunteers'. It is now generally accepted that these Irish troops performed well on the whole, despite the fact that they may have been prone to occasional lapses of discipline. Many Irish companies were appointed as the colour guards of their parent regiments. At several engagements, such as Antietam and Fredericksburg, Irish Confederate units faced other Irishmen who were fighting on the Union side.

As the war progressed and their parent regiments suffered heavy casualties, the Irish companies were absorbed within their parent regiments and brigades. While the Irish units in the Union army have been the focus of much research, there has been considerably less scholarly interest in the Irish units in the Confederate Army. The regiments listed below were the main Irish units or contained large Irish contingents. The 6th Louisiana and the 10th Tennessee are dealt with separately as they have been the subject of modern regimental histories. Thereafter, all Confederate units are listed, state by state.

6th LOUISIANA VOLUNTEERS

Formation
In the 1860 census, the Irish population of New Orleans, Louisiana, was 24,398 out of a total population of 168,675. It is therefore not surprising that the state of Louisiana raised more Irish units than any other Confederate state. The Confederate regiment with the largest Irish contingent was the 6th Louisiana Volunteers, which was raised in 1861 in New Orleans. It had originally been intended to raise an 'Irish Brigade' and two Irish-born officers, Captains Joseph Hanlon and William Monaghan, both raised companies of Irish recruits. These were initially designated as Companies A and B of the 'Irish Brigade' but they were later incorporated as Companies I and F of the 6th Louisiana Volunteers. The regiment assembled at Camp Moore in early June 1861 and was composed of 10 companies. Of the men who made up the original contingent, 468 were Irish-born and they represented the largest single ethnic group. Only 163 men of the regiment gave Louisiana as their place of birth.

Apart from the two original Irish companies, the Calhoun Guards (Company B, 6th Louisiana Volunteers) was also largely Irish with further Irish soldiers scattered through the regiment's other companies. The 6th Louisiana Volunteers was attached to Brigadier-General Hay's Brigade in the Army of Northern Virginia. It fought in all of the army's major battles and three of its colonels, including Monaghan, were killed in action.[14]

2002). 13 Often spelt 'Emmett' rather than 'Emmet'. 14 Col. Isaac Gurdon Seymour, killed at Gaine's Mill; Col. Henry B. Strong, Irish-born, appointed 16 August 1862, killed at Sharpsburg, 17 Sept. 1862; Col. William Monaghan, Irish-born, appointed 7 November 1862, killed near Shepardstown, VA, 25 August 1864.

List of major engagements of the 6th Louisiana Volunteers

1861 1st Manassas (Bull Run)

1862 Front Royal   Cedar Mountain
      Middletown   Bristoe Station
      1st Winchester   2nd Manassas
      Cross Keys   Chantilly
      Port Republic   Harper's Ferry
      Gaine's Mill   Sharpsburg
      Malvern Hill   Fredericksburg

1863 2nd Winchester   Rappahannock Station
      Gettysburg   Mine Run
      Raccoon Ford

1864 Battle of the Wilderness   Kernstown
      1st and 2nd Spotsylvania   3rd Winchester
      Cold Harbour   Cedar Creek
      Monocacy

1865 Hatcher's Run
      Fort Steadman
      Surrendered at Appomatox
      Court House, April 1865

10th TENNESSEE INFANTRY REGIMENT (IRISH) CONFEDERATE STATES VOLUNTEERS

This regiment was raised in April 1861 at Nashville and was just one of sixteen volunteer units that were raised in that town. It was officially designated as D Company, Tennessee Home Guards and the prime-mover behind its organization was a local politician named Randal William McGavock. McGavock had also been involved in the formation of a St Patrick's Club in 1858, and he was later appointed as an officer in the Confederate States Army.

By end of summer 1861 the company actually had enough recruits to form a regiment and, on 1 September 1861, 720 officers and men mustered into Confederate service in 10 companies at Fort Henry. The new regiment was designated as the Tenth Tennessee Infantry Regiment of Volunteers (Irish). The regimental colonel was Colonel Adolphus Heiman and Randal W. McGavock was appointed as regimental lieutenant-colonel, effectively acting as the regiment's commanding officer.

Following the surrender of Fort Donelson in February 1862, the entire regiment of 720 men was taken prisoner. When these men were paroled, or escaped, the regiment was reformed although it never again numbered more than 254 men. During the course of the war, the 10th Tennessee's service was concentrated in the Western theatre of operations and it campaigned with the Army of the West, the Army of the Mississippi and the Army of Tennessee.

List of major engagements of the 10th Tennessee:

1862　Fort Henry　　　　　　　　　Chickasaw Bluffs
　　　Erin Hollow　　　　　　　　　1st assault on Vicksburg
　　　Fort Donelson

1863　Snyder's Bluff　　　　　　　　Chickamauga
　　　2nd assault on Vicksburg　　　Missionary Ridge
　　　Raymond

1864　The battles of the Atlanta Campaign:
　　　Rocky Face Ridge　　　　　　Decatur
　　　Resaca　　　　　　　　　　　Utoy Creek
　　　New Hope Church　　　　　　Jonesborough

1864　Cassville　　　　　　　　　　Franklin
　　　Peach Tree Creek　　　　　　　Murfreesborough
　　　Pine Mountain　　　　　　　　Nashville
　　　Kennesaw Mountain

1865　Bentonville

Following the Confederate defeat at Bentonville, General Joseph E. Johnston surrendered to General William T. Sherman outside Durham, North Carolina, on 9 April 1865, bringing the war in the Western theatre to an end.

By late 1864, the 10th Tennessee had been reduced to just 36 men. During the war 66 men had died while on service; 30 of these had been killed in action while a further 10 had died of disease; the remaining 26 fatalities occurred in Union POW camps. A further 91 men were seriously wounded in action. These were heavy casualties when one considers that for much of the war the regiment numbered less than 260 men.

Commanding officers
Colonel Randal W. McGavock commanded until being killed in action at the battle of Raymond on 12 May 1863. Thereafter the 10th Tennessee was commanded by both Colonel William Grace and Lt.-Col. John G. O'Neill who alternated in command until Grace was mortally wounded at Jonesborough in 1864. Thereafter O'Neill commanded the regiment until the Confederate surrender.

Regimental colours
The original colour was presented to the 'Sons of Erin' Irish volunteer company that Colonel McGavock raised in Nashville and which was later re-designated as Company H, Tenth Tennessee Infantry Regiment (Irish). On one side this colour was in green

colour with a central harp motif and the inscription 'Sons of Erin' and 'Go Where Glory Waits You!' On the other side was the Confederate 'Stars and Bars' flag.

This colour was captured by the Union army at Fort Donelson in 1862 and was later presented as a trophy to the 69th New York Regiment. It has since been returned to its native Tennessee where it is held in the State Museum in Nashville. During the 1960s it was restored as part of the Civil War Centennial commemorations.

Nicknames
Due to the inscription on the regimental colour, the Tenth Tennessee was usually referred to as the 'Sons of Erin'. Also, due to its high casualty rate, it was sometimes referred to as the 'Bloody Tenth'.

A LIST OF IRISH UNITS IN THE ARMY OF THE CONFEDERATE STATES OF AMERICA
(ALPHABETICAL ORDER, BY STATE)

ALABAMA

The Alabama Light Dragoons/the Mobile Dragoons. These two units are believed to be the same one but with different designations. It was a volunteer company raised in 1860 by captains Theodore O'Hara and J.H. Marshall. It became part of the 56th Alabama Cavalry, Army of the Mississippi.

The Emerald Guards, Company I, 8th Alabama Regiment, General Wilcox's Brigade, Army of Northern Virginia. This unit was raised from among the fire brigade companies of Mobile and was present at Seven Pines, Fredericksburg, Gettysburg, battle of the Wilderness, Spotsylvania, Yorktown, Frazier's Farm, Chancellorsville. It surrendered at Appomatox Couthouse. This company wore dark green uniforms and carried a flag with a harp and shamrock motif with 'Erin go bragh' and 'Faugh a ballagh' inscribed upon it. The company was the colour guard of its regiment.

The Emmet Guards, Company B, 24th Alabama, raised in Mobile. Attached to the Army of Tennessee.

The Irish Volunteers, raised in Montgomery.

ARKANSAS

The Irish Company, 12th Arkansas Battalion of Sharpshooters. This unit is believed to be the company that delayed the advance of the Union army at Port Gibson.

GEORGIA

The Irish Jasper Greens of Savannah. This volunteer unit was raised in 1842. It formed companies A and B of the 1st Georgia Volunteers and served with the

Western Army. Its traditions are maintained by Battery A, 230th Field Artillery Battalion of the U.S. National Guard.

An Irish artillery unit, 'Frazier's Battery', raised in Savannah.

The Emmet Rifles, Company B, 1st Georgia (Regulars), General Anderson's Brigade, Army of Northern Virginia. A pre-War militia company it was heavily engaged at Sharpsburg.

The Irish Volunteers, Company C, 1st Georgia Infantry, Army of Tennessee. Raised in Augusta.

The Jackson Guards, Company B, 19th Georgia Regiment, General Archer's Brigade, Army of Northern Virginia. Raised in Atlanta, this company carried a green flag with a harp and shamrock motif. It was engaged at Bentonville, 2nd Manassas, Fredericksburg (Prospect Hill) and the Seven Days battles. It surrendered with General Joseph Jackson in April 1865.

The Montgomery Guards, Company K, 20th Georgia Regiment, General Toombs's Brigade, Army of Northern Virginia.

The McMillan Guards, Company K, 24th Georgia Regiment, General Cobb's Brigade, Army of Northern Virginia. Raised in Hubersham County, Georgia, it defended the Sunken Road at Fredericksburg against the attacks of Brigadier-General Meagher's Irish Brigade in the Union army.

The Lochrane Guards, Company F, Phillip's Georgia Legion, General Cobb's Brigade, Army of Northern Virginia. Raised in Macon, Georgia, July 1861. Named after Osborn A. Lochrane, an Irish immigrant and later supreme justice of the Georgia Supreme Court. This company fought at Antietam, defended the Sunken Road at Fredericksburg and also fought at Gettysburg. It was later re-named as the Lochrane Light Infantry.

In 1864 Irish Union prisoners in Georgia formed 2nd Foreign Battalion or 'Brookes Battalion' – later the 8th Confederate Battalion. They were disbanded after the defence of Savannah.

LOUISIANA

The Emmet Guards, Company D, 1st Louisiana Regiment, General Hay's Brigade, Army of Northern Virginia. Raised in Orleans parish.

The Montgomery Guards, Company E, 1st Louisiana Regiment, General Hay's Brigade, Army of Northern Virginia. Raised Orleans Parish, this company was heavily engaged at 2nd Manassas. When the its men ran out of ammunition, they threw rocks at advancing Union troops.

The Orleans Light Guards, Company F, 1st Louisiana Regiment, General Hay's Brigade, Army of Northern Virginia. Raised in New Orleans.

The Moore Guards, Company B, 2nd Louisiana Regiment, General Hay's Brigade, Army of Northern Virginia. Raised in Rapides parish.

The 6th Louisiana Volunteers. This was the largest Irish unit in the CSA. Raised in 1861, three of its companies were Irish:
    The Calhoun Guards, Company B, 6th Louisiana
    'Irish Brigade', (Company A) Company I, 6th Louisiana
    'Irish Brigade', (Company B) Company F, 6th Louisiana
There was also a significant Irish contingent in the other companies of the regiment. (See separate entry for 6th Louisiana Volunteers above).

The Sarsfield Rangers, Company C, 7th Louisiana Regiment, General Hay's Brigade, Army of Northern Virginia. Raised in Orleans Parish.

The Virginia Guards, Company D, 7th Louisiana Regiment, General Hay's Brigade, Army of Northern Virginia. Raised in Orleans parish.

The Irish Volunteers, Company F, 7th Louisiana Regiment, General Hay's Brigade, Army of Northern Virginia. Raised in Assumption parish.

The Virginia Blues, Company I, 7th Louisiana Regiment, Hay's Brigade, Army of Northern Virginia. Raised in Orleans parish.

The Cheneyville Rifles, Company H, 8th Louisiana Regiment, General Hay's Brigade, Army of Northern Virginia. Lost its colours at Cemetery Hill, Gettysburg.

The Emerald Guards, Company E, 9th Louisiana Regiment, General Hay's Brigade, the Army of Northern Virginia. Also known as the Milliken Bend Guards, raised in Madison parish.

The Shepherd Guards, Company A, 10th Louisiana Regiment, General Starke's Brigade, Army of Northern Virginia. Raised in Orelans parish.

The Derbigny Guards, Company B, 10th Louisiana Regiment, General Starke's Brigade, Army of Northern Virginia.

The Hewitt's Guards, Company C, 10th Louisiana Regiment, General Starke's Brigade, Army of Northern Virginia. Present at Spotsylvania and Petersburg.

The Hawkins' Guards, Company D, 10th Louisiana Regiment, General Starke's Brigade, Army of Northern Virginia.

The Orleans Blues, Company H, 10th Louisiana Regiment, General Starke's Brigade, Army of Northern Virginia. Raised in Orleans parish.

The Dillon Guards, 11th Louisiana Regiment.

The Avengo Zouaves or 'Governor's Guards', the 13th Louisiana Regiment. This regiment had a large Irish contingent and later incorporated two other Irish companies – the Southern Celts and St Mary's Volunteers.

The 14th Louisiana Regiment, General Starke's Brigade, Army of Northern Virginia. This regiment had a large Irish contingent, the remainder of the troops being Germans, Poles and French.

The 15th Louisiana Regiment. 7 of 10 companies raised in New Orleans. Over 100 Irish but no distinct Irish company

The 20th Louisiana Regiment. This regiment had four Irish companies.

The 2nd Louisiana Battalion of Infantry or 1st Louisiana Special Battalion is more commonly known as 'Wheat's Tigers' or the 'Louisiana Tigers'. This Zouvre regiment had a large Irish contingent recruited from among the dock workers at New Orleans in 1861 by Major Roberdeau Chatham Wheat. Attached to General Taylor's brigade, it fought at 1st Manassas and was present at Front Royal, Port Republic and Gaine's Mill. It was amalgamated into other Louisiana regiments in 1862 after Wheat's death.

Donaldsonville independent companies – these two companies had a large Irish contingent.

A number of pre-war militia units: The Shamrock Guards, the O'Brien Light Infantry and the Loughlin Light Guards were amalgamated to form the Louisiana Irish Regiment, commanded by Colonel P.B. O'Brien.

The Irish Brigade, Company F, 1st Louisiana Cavalry. Present at the battle of Big Hill, Richmond, Kentucky. Also known as 'the Copperheads'.

MISSISSIPPI

The Jasper Greys, Company F, 16th Misssippi Regiment, General Featherstone's Brigade, Army of Northern Virginia. Raised in the Irish catholic enclave at Paulding, Mississippi in April 1861.

The Adams Light Guard, Company D, 16th Mississippi Regiment.

The O'Connor Rifles, Company B, 2nd Mississippi Regiment.

MISSOURI

Irish battery, General Price's army.

The Shamrock Guards, General Price's army.

Two Irish companies served under General Bevier, one of these in the 5th Missouri Regiment.

NORTH CAROLINA

Company H, 40th North Carolina (3rd North Carolina Artillery), formed at Wilmington.

SOUTH CAROLINA

Three different companies called themselves the 'Irish Volunteers':

1. The 'Old Irish Volunteers'. This was a militia company formed in 1860 for state service.
2. The Irish Volunteers, Company K, 1st Regiment of South Carolina Volunteers, General Gregg's Brigade, Army of Northern Virginia. This was the first Charleston unit to volunteer for war service. Its blue silk flag was made by the Ursuline nuns of Charleston. The company acted as the regimental colour guard and was present at Cold Harbour.
3. The Irish Volunteers, Company C, Charleston City Militia (or Charleston Infantry Battalion). This battalion was amalgamated with the 1st Carolina Sharpshooters in 1863 to form the 27th South Carolina Infantry. It was attached to General Hagood's Brigade, Army of Northern Virginia. It formed part of the garrison at Battery Wagnar and Fort Sumter and fought at Cold Harbour and Petersburg.

The 'Irish Artillery' – two batteries at Fort Sumter in 1861 with large Irish contingents.

The Meagher Guards, Charleston. Named in honour of Thomas F. Meagher, it was later re-named as the Emerald Light Infantry when Meagher aligned himself with the Union cause. It was disbanded 1862.

TENNESSEE

The following Tennessee units had large Irish contingents:

2nd Tennessee Infantry.

10th Tennessee Infantry Regiment (Irish). (See earlier entry for this regiment)

19th Tennessee Infantry

Company I, 21st Tennessee, later re-designated as Company B 5th Confederate Infantry or 5th Confederate Tennessee.

TEXAS

Captain Redwood's Company, 'Irish Company', Rio Grande Regiment.

Company F, 1st Texas Heavy Artillery, the Davis Guards. This unit was composed of a number of Irishmen and was commanded by Major Richard ('Dick') Dowling who had been born in Tuam, Co. Galway. This company formed the garrison at Fort Griffin, overlooking the Sabine Pass. On 8 September 1863, Dowling and his men repulsed a large Union invasion force that was attempting to force the Sabine Pass, capturing one ship and over 300 Union troops. Two other ships in the Union fleet were badly damaged. It was one of the most one-sided engagements in the war and

Dowling and his men were later awarded a special medal: the 'Davis Guards' medal, the only gallantry medal ever instituted by the Confederate states.[15]

Company I, 'San Patricio Company', Terry's Texas Rangers (8th Cavalry). This company was raised in San Patricio parish, Texas, and had a number of Irish troopers.

10th Texas Infantry. This regiment had a large Irish contingent and served in Cork-born General Patrick R. Cleburne's division at Missionary Ridge.

VIRGINIA

The Montgomery Guard, Company C, 1st Virginia Regiment General Kemper's Brigade, Army of Northern Virginia. This unit was raised as a volunteer company in 1850 by Patrick T. Moore who later commanded the 1st Virginia. It had a distinctive green uniform and a flag that incorporated a harp device. Some of its members were veterans of the Crimean War. Present at the battle of Fredericksburg.

1st Virginia Battalion, Provost Guard. With the exception of Company A, this was almost an entirely Irish battalion. The men for this battalion were raised in Norfolk, Alexandria, Covington, Richmond and Lynchburg. 200 Irishmen were recruited in Covington alone. It served as the provost guard for General Thomas J. Jackson's corps.

The Jeff Davis Guards, Company H, 11th Virginia Regiment, General Kemper's Brigade, Army of Northern Virginia. Raised in Lynchburg from among the railroad workers, this unit contained many Irish and also Germans, Italians and Swiss.

The Emmet Guard, Company F, 15th Virginia Regiment, General Corse's Brigade, Army of Northern Virginia. This company was raised in Richmond and was present at Williamsburg and Grove Landing. It was disbanded in 1862 after a series of disciplinary problems.

The Emmet Guards, Company G, 17th Virginia Regiment, General Corse's Brigade, Army of Northern Virginia. A light infantry company raised in Alexandria, they wore green uniforms.

The O'Connell Guards, Company I, 17th Virginia Regiment, General Corse's Brigade, Army of Northern Virginia. A light infantry company raised among railroad workers in Alexandria.

The Montgomery Guards, Company F, 19th Virginia Regiment, General Garnett's Brigade, Army of Northern Virginia. Raised in Charlottesville, this unit was present at Williamsburg, Gettysburg and Slaughter's Gap.

The Virginia Hibernians, Company B, 27th Virginia Regiment, General Paxton's Brigade, Army of Northern Virginia. A light infantry company raised in Alleghany County, it was the colour guard of the regiment and fought at Fredericksburg.

---

15 Having survived the war, Dowling died of yellow fever in 1867. There is a statue of Dowling in Houston, Texas, where there is also a street and a school named after him. There is a memorial in Sabine City and a further statue of Dowling at the Sabine Pass battleground park. In 1998 a plaque was unveiled in Tuam.

The Emerald Guard, Company E, 33rd Virginia Regiment, General Paxton's Brigade, Army of Northern Virginia. Raised in the New Market of Shenandoah County, it was composed of Irish railroad workers from Manassas Junction. It was present at the battles of Gettysburg, Fredericksburg and Spotsylvania.

19th Battalion of Heavy Artillery, an Irish unit raised at Alexandria.

THE FENIANS IN AMERICA

The Fenian Brotherhood, the American sister-organization to the Irish Republican Brotherhood, was founded in New York in 1859. During the years that followed, many of its members served in volunteer companies in America and later in Union Army during the American Civil War. Their leaders saw this as a means of gaining experience for an eventual rebellion in Ireland. After the end of the American Civil War, the focus of their plans switched to Canada, where it was felt the movement could strike a blow directly against British power. This activity led to failed incursions into Canada in 1866, 1870 and 1871. The Fenians had acquired around 10,000 rifles but never had enough recruits. It is estimated that there were 7,000 men in different groups along the Canadian border but they had no cavalry and artillery. The movement's secretary of war was Brigadier-General Thomas Sweeny, a one-armed veteran of American Civil War.

The first Fenian raid set out from the Niagara River, outside Buffalo on 1 June 1866. It was led by Colonel John O'Neill who had previously served in the Union Army. Some accounts state that the force consisted of just 600 men while others state that 1,200 Fenians set out for Canada. Most wore their everyday work clothes but many also wore green shirts. The force's officer core contained some veterans of the Army of the Potomac, who wore their Union Army uniforms. This force occupied the village of Fort Eyrie inside the Canadian border.

The Fenians had been planning action against Canada for some time and British forces in Canada had been at high alert since the spring of 1866. The arrival of a gunboat on the river prevented more supplies getting through and the Fenians had to forage for food. Two British columns moved against them; Lt.-Col. George Peacocke had 'several hundred' men while Lt.-Col. Alfred Booker advanced with 900 men.

Ultimately Booker was the first to make contact and he engaged the Fenians at Ridgeway on 2 June 1866 in what came to be known as the 'Battle of Ridgeway'. Around twelve men were killed on the British side while a further 40 were wounded. The Fenians lost eight men killed and twenty wounded while a further 60 were taken prisoner. When they re-crossed the river into America, O'Neill and around 700 Fenians were arrested. On 7 June another Fenian column crossed the border with around 1,000 men and occupied some small villages before being pushed back the next day.

On his release, O'Neill continued to plan raids into Canada. He led a two further small raids in may 1870 and October 1871, being arrested on both occasions.

1 (*above*) A private and officer of the Regiment of Dillon, *c*.1724. After the end of the Jacobite wars in Ireland, thousands of Irish soldiers travelled to the Continent, where they served in Irish regiments in the French, Spanish and Austrian armies. (Courtesy of the Service Historique de la Défense.)

2 (*above, right*) A trooper of the cavalry Regiment of Fitzjames, *c*.1740. Originally formed as the Regiment of Sheldon, this regiment was disbanded in 1762 after suffering heavy casualties at the battle of Wilhemstal. (Courtesy of the artist, Seán Ó'Brógáin.)

3 A private in the Irish company of Quebec, 1756. This company was formed from Irish prisoners of war who offered their services to General Montcalm. The company was sent to France in 1757 where it would appear that its personnel were split up among the Irish regiments. (Anne S.K. Brown Military Collection, Brown University, Providence, USA. Photo: René Chartrand.)

4 (*left*) Contemporary illustration of an officer and private of Napoleon's Irish Legion. Formed in 1803 the officer corps of this unit was formed by exiled United Irishmen while its rank and file were of other nationalities. After campaigning in Spain and in eastern Europe, the legion was finally disbanded in 1815. (Author's collection.)

5 (*below*) A voluntary hospital during the Franco-Prussian War. During the course of this war, many foreign volunteers travelled to France. An Irish infantry company and an Irish volunteer ambulance company served in the war in the French army. (Author's collection.)

6 Uniforms and colours of the Spanish regiments of Irlanda and Hibernia, *c*.1740. In the early eighteenth century Irish regiments transferred from the French to the Spanish service. They retained their traditional red coats as shown here and their colours displayed Irish devices. (Anne S.K. Brown Military Collection, Brown University, Providence, USA. Photo: René Chartrand.)

7 Uniforms of the Spanish regiments of Ultonia, Irlanda and Hibernia after 1802. In 1802, the Irish regiments in the Spanish service were issued new uniforms. They wore a new tunic in light blue and the regiments were distinguished by different colour facings. (Courtesy Dr Alicia Laspra Rodriquez.)

8 (*above*) An 1802 illustration of the regiment of Hibernia. This contemporary illustration shows soldiers of the Hibernia in their new light blue uniform. The style of bicorn hat is particularly Spanish. These Irish regiments were disbanded in 1818. (Author's collection.)

9 (*below*) The British Legion in action during the First Carlist War of 1833–40. During this war in Spain, the British sent a volunteer legion to assist the cause of the Infanta, Queen Isabella. Commanded by Sir George De Lacy Evans from Co. Limerick, the Legion contained over 2,000 Irish volunteers who were formed into Irish regiments such as the 2nd Queen's Own Irish Lancers and the 7th Irish Light Infantry. (Author's collection.)

10 (*above, right*) Count Maximilian Ulysses Browne (d.1757), an Irish officer in the Austrian service. While Irish regiments in the Austrian service were somewhat short-lived, many Irish officers reached high rank within the Austrian military. Browne, who successfully defended Prague against the Prussians was just one of several high ranking Irish officers of this period. (Author's collection.)

11 (*above, left*) A grenadier of the 18th Royal Irish Regiment at Namur, 1695. This regiment was one of the earliest Irish regiments formed in the British service. The grenadier-style cap worn here did not impede the wearer while throwing grenades, the original battlefield task of a grenadier. (Courtesy of the artist, Seán Ó' Brógáin.)

12 (*above*) Sergeant Masterson of the 87th Foot capturing the French eagle at Barrosa, 1811. On seizing the French standard he is reputed to have called out 'Bejabers boys! I have the cuckoo'. During the Peninsular War some newly raised Irish regiments served with distinction. The 87th Foot later became the 1st Bn of the Royal Irish Fusiliers. (Author's collection.)

13 (*left*) An officer of the Inniskilling Dragoons, *c*.1825. This regiment traced its lineage back to the Jacobite wars in Ireland and was formed out of troops of cavalry raised in the cause of William of Orange. This officer wears mounted review order of the early nineteenth century. (Author's collection.)

14 Troopers of the 8th King's Royal Irish Hussars in the Crimea, 1854. In the 1850s photography was still in its infancy. The Crimea was the first war to produce images of troops on active service. This group is interesting as one of the men's wives is included in the group. (Author's collection.)

15 Uniforms of the 86th (Royal County Down) Regiment of Foot during the Indian Mutiny, 1857. The uniforms of the army in India were often not suited to the climate and on campaign and soldiers took on a much more dishevelled appearance. The 86th Foot was later a battalion of the Royal Irish Rifles. (Author's collection.)

16 The colours of the 89th Foot (later the 2nd Bn of the Royal Irish Fusiliers) in 1866. These serve as an example of British regimental colours of the period. The Queen's Colour was essentially a Union flag with a royal cipher while the Regimental Colour had the Union flag in the upper quarter near the flagstaff and also incorporated regimental battle honours. (Author's collection.)

17 A Simkin illustration of 1897 showing uniforms of the Irish regiments. From left to right: a drummer of the Royal Dublin Fusiliers, a bandsman of the Leinster Regiment and a private of the Royal Inniskilling Fusiliers. In the background, a mounted trumpeter of the 4th Royal Irish Dragoon Guards. (Author's collection.)

18 The landings from the *River Clyde* at Gallipoli in 1915. The 1st Bn Royal Munster Fusiliers and the 1st Bn Royal Dublin Fusiliers took part in these ill-fated landings at V-Beach on 25 April 1915, both battalions being decimated by Turkish fire. (Author's collection.)

19 V-Beach at Gallipoli, as seen from the *River Clyde*. Dead and wounded fill the barge in front of the River Clyde while further dead litter the shore line. Troops from the Irish battalions can also be seen taking cover on the landing beach. The 10th (Irish) Division would also later serve in this campaign. (IWM Q50473.)

20 The Tyneside Irish going over the top at the Somme 1916. This was a 'pals' brigade formed from among the Irish community on the Tyne. In this somewhat eerie photograph they can be seen advancing on the first day of the Somme battle. Many of them appear to be walking towards the German lines with their rifles shouldered. (IWM Q53.)

21 Men of the 1st Bn Royal Irish Regiment in Palestine in 1917. This battalion had been based in India in 1914 and during the war served with the 27th Division before joining the 10th (Irish) Divison. They have been issued with slouch hats to combat the heat of the Middle East. (IWM Q32128.)

22 The Liverpool Irish entering Lille at the end of WWI. The Liverpool Irish were a Territorial (Reserve) unit of the British army activated for active service. The extreme youth of some of these soldiers is apparent. (IWM Q9572.)

23 Disbandment parade of the Irish regiments at Windsor in June 1922. Following the formation of the Irish Free State, several Irish regiments that recruited in southern Ireland were disbanded. At a disbandment parade their colours were handed over to King George V for safekeeping. The colours were lodged in Windsor Castle, where they remain. (IWM Q31523B.)

24 Lord Gort and General Georges inspect the 2nd Bn Royal Inniskilling Fusiliers in France in 1940. This battalion formed part of the BEF (British Expeditionary Force) in France and Belgium. It is being inspected here just weeks before the German Blitzkrieg of 1940. (IWM F3959.)

25 Stuart tanks of the 8th King's Royal Irish Hussars in Egypt, 1941. These M3 Stuart light tanks had been supplied by the Americans and are seeing here being put through their paces in the Western Desert. (IWM E5066.)

26 Riflemen of 2nd Bn Royal Ulster Rifles, Normandy, June 1944. Taken just after the D-Day landings, some of these riflemen still wear inflatable lifejackets under their web equipment. (IWM B5039.)

27 The pipe bands of the 38th (Irish) Brigade, Rome, June 1944. Following the liberation of Rome, this Irish brigade held a special parade on 12 June 1944. Having served in North Africa, the brigade served throughout the difficult campaigns in Sicily and Italy. (IWM NA16179.)

28 Uniforms of the 69th New York National Guard, 1853. While this unit would wear the blue uniform of the Union during the American Civil War, their earliest uniforms included green tunics. (Anne S.K. Brown Military Collection, Brown University, Providence, USA. Photo: René Chartrand.)

29 Recruiting for the 'Irish Zouaves', 1862. The 5th New York Volunteers or 'Duryee's Zouaves' were not officially an Irish regiment but surviving muster rolls include a large number of Irish names, a fact apparently alluded to by the original reporter in this case. (Author's collection.)

30 The colour of the 69th New York Volunteers. During the American Civil War, Irish units on both sides carried distinctive colours. These usually incorporated a green field, superimposed on which were Irish devices such as harps, shamrocks, round towers and even wolfhounds. This colour was presented to the Oireachtas by President John F. Kennedy and is on display in Leinster House. (Courtesy of the Houses of the Oireachtas.)

31 Captain (later Brigadier-General) Thomas Francis Meagher, 1861. This contemporary illustration of Meagher shows him as an officer of the Zouave company (Company K) of the 69th New York Militia. He would later go on to recruit and command an Irish volunteer brigade for the Union. (Anne S.K. Brown Military Collection, Brown University, Providence, USA. Photo: René Chartrand.)

32 A modern illustration of a private of the 69th New York National Guard, 1861. This unit was also designated as the 182nd NY Infantry Regiment and formed part of Corcoran's Irish Legion. It served in numerous engagements including the 2nd battle of Cold Harbour in 1864. (Anne S.K. Brown Military Collection, Brown University, Providence, USA. Photo: René Chartrand.)

33 The battle of Fredericksburg, 1862. This contemporary illustration shows the defence of Marye's Heights by Confederate forces. In the distance Meagher's Irish Brigade can be seen advancing. At Fredericksburg the Confederate troops commanded by General Cobb also contained some Irish companies. (Author's collection.)

34 Major-General Patrick R. Cleburne, Confederate States Army. Cleburne, who had been born in Cork, was the most senior Irish soldier in the army of the Confederacy. He was killed at the battle of Franklin in 1864. It is estimated that between 15,000 and 20,000 Irish soldiers served in the Confederate army. (Author's collection.)

35 Confederate guerrilla fighters firing on paddle steamers on the Union-controlled Mississippi River. While the Unions army formed Irish regiments and brigades, the Irish units in the Confederate army tended to be company-sized units. Over forty such units served in the war. (Author's collection.)

36 A soldier of the Fenian 1870 raiding force into Canada. Between 1866 and 1871, there were three Fenian raids into Canada. This modern illustration by Ron Volstad shows a Fenian of the 1870 raid wearing a green tunic. (Courtesy of the History & Heritage Directorate, Canadian Department of National Defence.)

37 Officers and men of the Hibernian Rifles, 1913. In the early years of the twentieth century, the Ancient Order of Hibernians formed a number of volunteer rifle companies. This photograph was taken at Newport, Rhode Island in 1913. The unit's colour appears to include an Hibernia and harp device. (Courtesy of William H. Gibson.)

38 Boer forces firing on British troops during the 2nd Anglo-Boer War, 1899–1902. During this war, the Boer army raised two units, or commandos, of Irish volunteers. Raised from among the Irish community at Johannesburg, they excelled at guerrilla warfare. (Author's collection.)

39 Officers of the South African Irish Regiment, North Africa, 1941. This unit was first raised at the outbreak of the First World War and served again during the Second World War, seeing much service in North Africa. It still exists as part of the South African reserve, or Citizen Force, and is based at Johannesburg. (IWM SAF348.)

40 Pipers of the Irish Regiment of Canada entering Ravenna, 1944. Irish regiments in Canada were raised around the outbreak of the First World War. During the Second World War the Irish Regiment of Canada served in Italy and the Low Countries. It survives as part of the Canadian army reserve and is based at Sudbury, Ontario. (IWM NA21941.)

CHAPTER 7

Irish regiments in the British army, 1685–2006

While large numbers of Irish soldiers served in the French, Spanish and other armies from the seventeenth century onwards, it was in the British army that the largest number of Irishmen served during the period covered by this gazetteer and it is within that army that we find the largest number of Irish regiments.

The history of the Irish soldier within the British Army developed in various phases from 1685. Following the 'Glorious Revolution' of 1685, some existing Irish regiments declared for William III while further new regiments were raised in Ireland during the Jacobite War. These regiments included the 4th Royal Irish Dragoon Guards, the 6th Inniskilling Dragoons and the 18th Royal Irish Regiment.

Following the outbreak of war between Britain and France in 1793, further Irish regiments were raised and these included the 83rd and 86th Regiment of Foot, which both later became battalions of the Royal Irish Rifles. New Irish regiments were therefore raised in various phases on the outbreak of various wars in the years following 1685.

From the mid-1600s onwards the Honourable East India Company raised numerous regiments to protect its ever-expanding territory on the sub-continent. Thousands of Irishmen served in these regiments in the centuries that followed and some regiments, such as the Royal Madras Fusiliers, were largely composed of Irish soldiers.

Some of the better-known Irish regiments in the British Army date from the Cardwell army reforms of 1881. This vast reform of the army linked existing battalions to form new regiments and these included Irish regiments such as the Royal Dublin Fusiliers, the Royal Munster Fusiliers and the Leinster Regiment. The reformed army structure included former battalions of the East India Company army and these battalions were included in the amalgamations that formed Irish regiments. The new structure linked the regiments with specific recruiting districts in Ireland while the new regiments absorbed the battalions of the Irish Militia as their reserve battalions. Irish cavalry regiments, and later the Irish Guards, recruited on a 32-county basis.[1]

Alongside the regular army regiments, there was also a long history of further reserve or volunteer units being raised in Ireland as Fencible, Volunteer, Militia or Yeomanry units. This tradition continued in the mid-nineteenth century with the

---

1 The Royal Artillery and Royal Engineers also recruited on a 32-county basis.

growth of the Volunteer Rifle movement and some later Irish Territorial Army battalions, such as the London Irish Rifles, could trace their lineage back to these units. Later Irish units, such as the Irish Imperial Yeomanry companies of the 2nd Anglo-Boer War, were raised in direct response to government appeals for volunteers, usually after some kind of military defeat.

This section includes entries on the most significant Irish regiments within the British Army. There were also further regiments that had very brief histories and about which very little is known. These regiments included those listed below:

20th Inniskilling Light Dragoons (1759–63)
23rd Light Dragoons or Colonel William Fullerton's Regiment (1794–1802)
24th Light Dragoons or 'Colonel William Loftus's Regiment (1794–1802)
33rd (Ulster) Light Dragoons (1794–6)
76th Regiment of Foot (1756–63)
83rd Foot (later a battalion of the Royal Irish Rifles)
90th Irish Light Infantry (1759–63)
96th (Queen's Royal Irish) Regiment (1793–6)
97th (Earl of Ulster's) Regiment of Foot (later the 2nd Battalion, Royal West Kent Regiment)
99th Prince of Wales's Tipperary Regiment of Foot (1805–18)
100th Prince Regent's County of Dublin Regiment of Foot (later a battalion of the Leinster Regiment)
101st (Irish) Regiment of Foot (1794–5)
101st The Duke of York's Irish Regiment (1806–17)[2]
102nd (Irish) Regiment of Foot (1793–5)[3]
103rd (King's Irish Infantry) Regiment of Foot (1781–3)
105th Regiment of Foot (1777–1783, raised in Philadelphia)
124th Regiment of Foot (The Waterford Regiment) (1794–5)
134th (Loyal Limerick) Regiment of Foot (1794–5)
135th Limerick Regiment (1795–6)

LARGER IRISH FORMATIONS IN THE BRITISH ARMY, 1899–2006

Despite the fact that so many Irish regiments served within the British army, they were rarely brigaded together in larger formations. It was not until the end of the nineteenth century that it became more common practice to group Irish units together within the army as brigades or divisions. The most significant Irish formations are listed below.

---

[2] The 101st Foot designation was later associated with the Royal Munster Fusiliers.   [3] The 102nd Foot designation was later associated with the Royal Dublin Fusiliers.

THE 2nd ANGLO-BOER WAR, 1899–1902

The 5th, or Irish Brigade
Commanded by Major-General Fitzroy Hart, this brigade was formed at Durban in 1899 and was composed of:
- 1st Battalion, Royal Inniskilling Fusiliers
- 1st Battalion, Royal Dublin Fusiliers
- 1st Battalion, Connaught Rangers
- 1st Battalion, the Border Regiment

This brigade took part in several actions, including the disastrous battle of Colenso in December 1899, where it suffered heavy casualties.

THE FIRST WORLD WAR, 1914–18

The 10th (Irish) Division
Raised and initially commanded by Lieutenant-General Sir Bryan T. Mahon. The division was composed of:

29th Brigade
- 5th Battalion, Royal Irish Regiment
- 6th Battalion, Royal Irish Rifles
- 5th Battalion, Connaught Rangers
- 6th Battalion, the Leinster Regiment

30th Brigade
- 6th Battalion, Royal Munster Fusiliers
- 7th Battalion, Royal Munster Fusiliers
- 6th Battalion, Royal Dublin Fusiliers
- 7th Battalion, Royal Dublin Fusiliers

31st Brigade
- 5th Battalion, Royal Inniskilling Fusiliers
- 6th Battalion, Royal Inniskilling Fusiliers
- 5th Battalion, Royal Irish Fusiliers
- 6th Battalion, Royal Irish Fusiliers

This Irish division took part in the campaigns in Gallipoli and Salonika before being transferred to fight on the Palestinian front.

The 16th (Irish) Division
Initially commanded by Lieutenant-General Sir Lawrence Worthington Parsons who was succeeded by Major-General William Bernard Hickie in 1915. The division was composed of:

47th Brigade
- 6th Battalion, Royal Irish Regiment
- 6th Battalion, the Connaught Rangers
- 7th Battalion, the Leinster Regiment
- 8th Battalion, Royal Munster Fusiliers

48th Brigade
- 7th Battalion, Royal Irish Rifles
- 9th Battalion, Royal Munster Fusiliers
- 8th Battalion, Royal Dublin Fusiliers
- 9th Battalion, Royal Dublin Fusiliers

49th Brigade
7th Battalion, Royal Inniskilling Fusiliers   7th Battalion, Royal Irish Fusiliers
8th Battalion, Royal Inniskilling Fusiliers   8th Battalion, Royal Irish Fusiliers

This division served throughout the war on the Western Front and fought in numerous actions including the battles of the Somme, 3rd Ypres, Cambrai, Messines and the 'Kaiserslacht', the German offensive of March 1918.

The 36th (Ulster) Division
This division was initially commanded by Major-General C.H. Powell who was succeeded by Major-General Sir Oliver S.W. Nugent in 1915. It was composed of the following battalions:[4]

107th Brigade[5]
    8th Battalion, Royal Irish Rifles (East Belfast Volunteers)
    9th Battalion, Royal Irish Rifles (West Belfast Volunteers)
    10th Battalion, Royal Irish Rifles (South Belfast Volunteers)
    15th Battalion, Royal Irish Rifles (North Belfast Volunteers)

108th Brigade
    11th Battalion, Royal Irish Rifles (South Antrim Volunteers)
    12th Battalion, Royal Irish Rifles (Central Antrim Volunteers)
    13th Battalion, Royal Irish Rifles (1st Co. Down Volunteers)
    9th Battalion, Royal Irish Fusiliers (Armagh, Monaghan and Cavan Volunteers)

109th Brigade
    9th Battalion, Royal Inniskilling Fusiliers (Tyrone Volunteers)
    10th Battalion, Royal Inniskilling Fusiliers (Derry Volunteers)
    11th Battalion, Royal Inniskilling Fusiliers (Donegal and Fermanagh Volunteers)
    14th Battalion, Royal Irish Rifles (Young Citizens Volunteers of Belfast)

The 36th Ulster Division took part in numerous actions during the war, being one of the few divisions to reach its first-day objective at the beginning of the battle of the Somme. It later served in the battles of 3rd Ypres, Cambrai and Messines, among others, and fiercely resisted the German offensive of March 1918, the 'Kaiserslacht'.

THE SECOND WORLD WAR, 1939–45

38th (Irish) Brigade, 78th Infantry Division
This was the largest Irish formation within the British Army during the war. It was composed of:

---

[4] The 36th Ulster battalion titles here include pre-war Ulster Volunteer Force designations as this force provided the majority of the division's recruits.   [5] The British army in Northern Ireland has retained this historical title of 107th Brigade within its current organization.

6th Battalion, Royal Inniskilling Fusiliers
1st Royal Irish Fusiliers
2nd London Irish Rifles

This brigade was initially attached to the 6th Armoured Division before joining the 78th Division. It took part in numerous actions in North Africa, Sicily and Italy, its most famous being the attack on the hilltop town of Centuripe, Sicily, in 1943.

The Irish Guards Battle Group
This was composed of the 2nd and 3rd Battalions of the Irish Guards. The 2nd Battalion served as a tank regiment while the 3rd Battalion fought as lorried infantry. This battle group served in Europe following the Normandy landings in 1944 and later took part in the campaign in the Rhineland.

Due to the gradual disappearance of many of the Irish regiments through post-WWII amalgamation, Irish brigades or divisions have not operated within the British Army since 1945. However, during operations in Iraq in 2003 and 2005, the Royal Irish Regiment formed a battle group which served in the British zone.

THE 18th ROYAL IRISH REGIMENT, 1684–1922

Formation
This regiment was raised in Ireland on 1 April 1684 as part of Charles II's reforms of the Irish military establishment. It was formed out of a number of independent units of infantry and cavalry that already existed and were being used to garrison important towns around Ireland. It was raised by the Earl of Granard and, following the practice of the time was known by the name of its colonel as the 'Earl of Granard's Regiment of Foot'.

It was taken on the English establishment in 1689 and was named as the Royal Regiment of Ireland in 1695. It more usual to refer to the regiment by the name of its colonel and in official correspondence it was often referred to by name of successive colonels. In 1747 when it was ranked as the 18th Foot and, in 1751, was re-designated as the 18th (or Royal Irish) Regiment of Foot. This was changed again in 1782 when the regiment was re-designated as the 18th (The Royal Irish) Regiment of Foot. Due to its foundation in 1684, it was ranked as the oldest Irish infantry regiment in the regular British army.

Operational history
Jacobite War/Nine Year War
At the 'Glorious Revolution' of 1688, the regiment was based at Hertfordshire and the officers and men declared their support of William III. During the years that followed, the regiment served in the war in Ireland and was then sent to the Continent where it saw continued service until the end of this war.

1690   While it was present at the battle of the Boyne, according to regimental records, it was not directly engaged. The regiment took part in the first siege of Limerick.

1691   It was present at the siege of Athlone and the battle of Aughrim.

1692   The regiment was sent to England and from there to the Low Countries where it remained for the rest of the war. During this period its men were used as marines on Royal Navy warships.

1695   The regiment played a distinguish role in the siege of Namur being awarded special colours and the battle honour 'Namur', the first such battle honour authorized for regiments of the British army.

1697   At the end of the war, the regiment was returned to Ireland and was based at various locations including Cork and Waterford.

The War of the Spanish Succession, 1701–14

1701   The regiment returned to the Low Countries and during this war saw service there and in Germany.

1704   Campaigning with the army of the Duke of Malborough, it fought in decisive actions including the capture of Schellenburg and the victory at Blenheim.

1706   The regiment took part in the battle of Ramillies and the siege of Menin.

1708   It fought in the battle of Oudenarde and the siege of Lille.

1709   The regiment was present at the siege of Tournai and the battle of Malplaquet. In the final stages of the war, it served in the sieges of Aire (1710) and Bouchain (1711). It remained in the Low Countries as part of the garrison of Ghent until 1715.

1715   The regiment returned to England and was initially based in Gloucester.

1718   It was posted to Minorca.

1727   A detachment of the regiment was sent to Gibraltar where it formed part of the garrison during the siege of that year.

1742   The regiment returned from Minorca and was based at various locations in England.

1745   The regiment was sent to the Low Countries during a brief period of service in the **War of the Austrian Succession** (1740–8). It arrived too late to take part in the battle of Fontenoy and on the outbreak of the Jacobite Rebellion in Scotland, was rushed back to England. It then served as part of the garrison of Scotland being based at Fort Augustus, Edinburgh, Stirling and other locations.

1749   It was returned to Ireland and initially based in Enniskillen. It later served in various locations around the country including Waterford and Dublin. Apart from the years 1755–6 when it was based in England and Scotland, the regiment remained in Ireland until 1767.

1767   The regiment was sent to America, being initially based at Philadelphia.

War of American Independence, 1775–83

The regiment was on active service during the first year of this war and took part in the retreat from Concord and Lexington and the battle of Bunker Hill (1775).

1776 The regiment returned to England and was based at Dover, playing no further part in the American War of Independence.
1782 Based in the Channel Islands.
1783 In October the regiment was sent to Gibraltar where it remained as part of the garrison until 1793.

French Revolutionary and Napoleonic Wars, 1793–1815

1793 The regiment took part in the expedition to Toulon. It would later serve during the campaign in Corsica (1794).
1798 It was based at Gibraltar where it formed part of the garrison.
1800 The regiment took part in the Egyptian campaign and was later posted to Elba.
1802 The regiment returned to Ireland and was initially based at Armagh.
1803 A second battalion was formed and the two battalions of the regiment served on garrison duties in various locations. The 1st Battalion was sent to Jamaica while the 2nd served in the Channel Island. Between 1807 and 1810, the 2nd Battalion also served in the West Indies before being disbanded in 1814.
1817 The remaining 1st Battalion returned to England and served on garrison duties in England and, from 1818, in Ireland.
1821 The regiment was sent to Malta. It then served in the Ionian Islands (1824–32).
1832 It was returned to England and served on garrison duties in England and Ireland (1834).
1836 Detachments of the regiment were sent to Ceylon (Sri Lanka) the remainder of the regiment following.
During this assignment to the East, the regiment took part in the **1st China or Opium War** (1839–42), serving throughout this campaign. At the end of the war, the regiment was based at Chusan and Kulangsu in China.
1845 The regiment was based at Hong Kong.
1847 The regiment was moved to India and was based initially at Calcutta. It would later serve in various locations including Meerut and Dum Dum. Between 1852 and 1853, it served in the **2nd British-Burmese War**, returning to India at the end of the campaign.
1853 In December, the regiment boarded ships for England. On arrival, it was based at Chatham.

The Crimean War, 1854–6

1854 The regiment remained in England until December and was not part of the initial expeditionary force. It landed at Balaclava on 30 December.
1855 It remained in the Crimea until peace was declared in 1856 and served throughout the siege of Sevastopol. It lost a large number of casualties in this siege and also to disease.

The Indian Mutiny, 1857–9

1856 The regiment returned to Ireland at the end of the war.

1857 A detachment left Cork for Bombay and this was later followed by the rest of the regiment. On its arrival it was based at Poona. During the rest of the rebellion, it was split into several detachments and these took part in numerous campaigns against the rebels.

1858 A second battalion of the regiment was raised at Enniskillen.

1st Battalion
The regiment's first battalion remained in India until 1866 when it was returned to England. In 1868 it was moved to Ireland where it remained until 1872 when it was sent to Malta. In 1874 it was sent to India where it remained until 1884, taking part in the **2nd Afghan War** (1878–80).

2nd Battalion
The newly raised 2nd Battalion was moved to England in 1859 before being posted to the Channel Islands in 1862. In 1863 it was posted to New Zealand where it saw prolonged service in the **2nd Maori War** (1860–79). This battalion returned to England, via Australia in 1870. It remained on garrison duty in England until 1876, when it returned to Ireland. In 1879 it was moved to England where it served as the garrison unit at various locations.

1881 Under the terms of the Cardwell army reforms of this year, the regiment was re-designated as the Royal Irish Regiment, being reorganized as the county regiment of Kilkenny, Tipperary, Waterford and Wexford. The following battalions of the Irish Militia also became reserve battalions of the regiment under the terms of the 1881 reforms.

3rd Battalion (Wexford Regiment of Militia, 1881–1908)
4th Battalion (2nd, North Tipperary Light Infantry, 1881–1908)
5th Battalion (Kilkenny Fusiliers Regiment of Militia, 1881–1908)[6]

The movements of the post-1881 regular battalions were as follows:

1st Battalion
This battalion remained in India until 1885 when it was sent to Egypt and took part in the Gordon Relief Expedition. It returned to England in 1886 and was sent to Ireland in 1891 where it remained until the outbreak of the 2nd Anglo-Boer War in 1899. In 1896 a detachment was sent to South Africa and served as mounted infantry in the Mashonaland Expedition.

2nd Battalion
The regiment's second regular battalion was sent to Egypt in 1882 where it took part in Lord Wolseley's campaign against the rebel forces of Arabi Pasha.
    During this campaign it fought in the battles at Kassassin and Tel-el-Kebir. In 1883 it was sent to Malta before returning to England. The battalion was sent to Malta again in 1884 and proceeded to India in 1885.

---

6 These Militia battalions were further re-organized in 1908.

2nd Anglo-Boer War, 1899–1902

The regiment's 1st Battalion was sent to South Africa in December 1899 where it was initially attached to the 12th Brigade. It saw extensive service in this war as a regular battalion while detachments of the regiment later served as mounted infantry. The men of the 1st Battalion took part in numerous engagements including the Relief of Mafeking (1900) and the battles at Slabbert's Nek (1900) and Monument Hill (1901).

The First World War, 1914–18

During the course of the war, the regiment's reserve battalions were activated and also new service and garrison battalions were formed. In total, ten battalions of the regiment saw service in the war and fought in numerous actions including early actions in 1914 such as Le Cateau and the Marne. Apart from extensive service on the Western Front, battalions of the Royal Irish Regiment also served in Gallipoli, Macedonia, Egypt and Palestine. In 1914, the regimental depot was in Clonmel.

1st Battalion

This regular battalion was in India at the outbreak of war and was based at Nasirabad. It was attached to the 82nd Brigade of the 27th Division and was posted to the Western Front in December 1914. In 1915, it was sent to Salonika and was later attached to the 10th (Irish) Division. In September 1917 it was sent to Egypt and took part in the Palestine campaign of 1917–18. The battalion was based at Nablus in October 1918 at the time of the armistice with Turkey.

2nd Battalion

The regiment's second regular battalion was based in Devonport at the outbreak of the war and was attached to the 8th Brigade of the 3rd Division, BEF. It landed in France in August 1914 and fought in the first actions of the war. It remained on the Western Front for the rest of the war, serving with several divisions including the 4th, 7th, 16th (Irish) and 63rd Divisions.

3rd (Reserve) Battalion

This battalion was activated at Clonmel on the outbreak of war and served at various locations in Ireland during the war. In April 1918, it was sent to Larkhill in England where it joined the Irish Reserve Brigade.

4th (Extra Reserve) Battalion

Activated at Kilkenny on the outbreak of war, this battalion served in both Ireland and England between 1914 and 1918. In April 1918, it was sent to Larkhill where it joined the Irish Reserve Brigade.

5th (Service) Battalion (Pioneers)

This K1 battalion was formed in Clonmel in August 1914. It was attached to the 29th Brigade of the 10th (Irish) Division and after training in Ireland and England was sent to Gallipoli where it took part in the Suvla landings. It later served in Salonika and was returned to France in April 1918 where it was attached to the 50th Division.

6th (Service) Battalion

This K2 battalion was formed at Clonmel in September 1914. It was attached to the 47th Brigade of the 16th Irish Division and was augmented by a company from the Guernsey Militia. It served throughout the war on the Western Front and was disbanded in France in February 1918, its remaining personnel being sent to the 2nd and 7th Battalions.

7th (South Irish Horse) Battalion

This battalion was formed in France on 1 September 1917 and it incorporated the personnel from the 1st and 2nd South Irish Horse as these cavalrymen had been dismounted to serve as infantry. The battalion was attached to the 49th Brigade of the 16th (Irish) Division and was reduced to cadre strength in April 1918. The battalion was later re-formed using personnel from the Royal Dublin Fusiliers, the Royal Munster Fusiliers and the Royal Irish Regiment. (See separate entry on the South Irish Horse).

8th (Service) Battalion

This battalion was formed in France in May 1918 by the re-naming of the regiment's 2nd Garrison Battalion. It was attached to the 121st Brigade of the 40th Division.

1st Garrison Battalion

This battalion was formed in Dublin in August 1915 and was stationed in Holyhead and Devonport before being sent to the island of Mudros in September 1915. From October 1915, detachments of this battalion were sent to serve on the Gallipoli peninsula. In February 1916, the battalion was sent to Egypt where it remained for the rest of the war.

2nd (Home Service) Garrison Battalion

This battalion was formed in Dublin in March 1916 and remained in Ireland until April 1918 when it was re-named as the 2nd Garrison Battalion and was sent to France, joining the 178th Brigade of the 59th Division. In May 1918, it was re-named as the 8th Battalion (see above) and later served with the 40th Division.

Following the armistice in 1918, the wartime battalions of the Royal Irish Regiment were disbanded over a period of some months. The 1st Battalion remained in Germany as part of the army of occupation while the 2nd Battlion was sent to India. Following the foundation of the Irish Free State in 1922, the regiment was disbanded, its colours being laid up in Windsor Castle during the Irish regiments' disbandment parade in 1922.

Colonels-in-chief

1898   Field-Marshal Lord Wolseley, 1st Viscount Wolseley
1913   Field-Marshal Sir John Denton Pinkstone French

Colonels

1684	Lieutenant-General Arthur Forbes, 1st Earl of Granard
1686	Colonel Arthur, Lord Forbes
1688	Colonel Sir John Edgeworth
1689	Colonel Edward Brabazon, 4th Earl of Meath
1692	Major-General Frederick Hamilton
1705	Lieutenant-General Richard Ingoldsby
1712	Brigadier-General Robert Sterne
1717	Brigadier-General William Cosby
1732	Colonel Sir Charles Hotham
1735	Major-General John Armstrong
1742	General Sir John Mordaunt
1747	Lieutenant-General John Folliott
1762	General Sir John Sebright
1794	General Sir James Murray
1811	General John Hely-Hutchinson, 2nd Earl of Donoughmore
1832	General Matthew Aylmer, Lord Aylmer
1850	Field-Marshal Sir John Foster Fitzgerald
1877	Lieutenant-General Clement Alexander Edwards
1882	General Sir Alexander Macdonnell
1886	General Sir Richard Denis Kelly
1889	General George Frederick Stevenson Call
1895	General Robert Walter McLeod Fraser
1895	Lieutenant-General Sir Henry M. Havelock-Allen, VC
1897	Major-General Charles Frederick Gregorie
1918	Major-General John Burton Foster (to disbandment)

Battle honours

Namur 1695, Blenheim, Ramilles, Oudenarde, Malplaquet, Egypt, China, Pegu, Sevastopol, New Zealand, Afghanistan 1879–80, Tel-el-Kebir, Egypt 1882, Nile 1884–5, South Africa 1900–2, Mons, Le Cateau, Retreat from Mons, Marne 1914, Aisne 1914, La Bassée 1914, Ypres 1915, Ypres 1917, Ypres 1918, Bazentin, Delville Wood, Guillemont, Ginchy, Messines 1917, Pilckem, Langamarck 1917, St Quentin, Rosières, Arras 1918, Drocourt-Quéant, Hindenburg Line, Canal du Nord, St Quentin Canal, Struma, Macedonia 1915–17, Suvla, Landing at Suvla, Gallipoli 1915, Gaza, Jerusalem, Tell 'Asur, Nablus, Palestine 1917–18

Motto

Virtutis Namurcensis Praemium (The Reward for Virtue at Namur)

Regimental music

Tunes associated with the regiment included 'St Patrick's Day' (1st Bn) and 'The War March of Brian Boru' (2nd Bn). The tune 'Garryowen' was the quick march used by both battalions.

Nicknames
'The Namurs' and 'Paddy's Blackguards'

4th ROYAL IRISH DRAGOON GUARDS, 1685–1922

Formation

This regiment was raised in the north of England in January 1685 by the Earl of Arran, heir to the dukedom of Hamilton. It initially consisted of just a troop of heavy cavalry or cuirassiers and this was amalgamated with a number of other units from London, Lichfield, Durham, Granthan and Morpeth. The regiment was ranked as the 6th Horse and was titled as the Earl of Arran's Cuirassiers. It would later also be known under the name of nine different regimental colonels. This was a regiment raised in the service of James II and after the Glorious Revolution of 1688, it was selected to guard the king, queen and the Prince of Wales. It was one of the regiments, however, that defected to the Williamite cause and after a series of disbandment and amalgamations of regiments, was re-designated as the 5th Horse in 1690. It would later be re-titled several times before being designated as the 4th (Royal Irish) Dragoon Guards in 1788.

Operational history

Nine Years War, 1688–97

1691–7 The regiment was sent to Flanders in 1691 where it served with the Williamite army present at the battles of Steenkirk and Landen and took part in the siege of Namur.

1697 The regiment returned to England at the end of the Nine Years War

1698 It was stationed in Ireland where it would remain for almost a century.

1746 The regiment was transferred to the Irish establishment and renamed as the **1st Horse**. Due to the blue facings of the regiment's uniform, it was also known as the 'Blue Horse'.

1788 In February of this year the regiment's title was changed to **4th Dragoon Guards** but this was changed in April to **4th (Royal Irish) Dragoon Guards**.

French Revolutionary and Napoleonic Wars, 1793–1815

1793 The regiment was stationed in England.

1795 Early in the year the regiment returned to Ireland, before taking part in an expedition to Brittany. At the end of this expedition the regiment returned to Ireland, where it was active during the suppression of the 1798 Rebellion.

1799 The regiment was stationed in England.

1802 It was based in Ireland.

1804 The regiment returned to garrison duty in England. During these years of garrison duty, the regiment was used to suppress miners' protests in Durham and Northumberland.

1805	The regiment established a 'St Patrick's Fund' to provide ex-members with financial assistance.
1811	In June the regiment was based in Bristol and was ordered to supply six troops for service in the Peninsula. These troops boarded ship for Lisbon where they arrived on 4 August. This contingent formed part of a heavy cavalry brigade which was commanded by Major-General John Le Marchant. During the closing months of the year, the regiment was decimated by sickness.
1812	The regiment took part in the sieges of Badajoz and Ciudad Rodrigo in January before joining the brigade of Major-General John Slade. It took part in the pursuit of the French army after the capture of Badajoz in April but, because Slade lost his way, missed the battle at Villagarcia, near Llerena. In June the regiment was ordered to re-join Le Marchant's brigade but the men and horses seem to have been in poor condition as only a squadron was with the brigade by the time of the battle of Salamanca (22 July 1812). It was based in Madrid before taking part in the retreat to Portugal following the abandonment of the siege of Burgos. On its arrival in Portugal in November, the regiment could parade 311 men but only 89 horses.
1813	On St Patrick's Day the regiment was ordered to hand over its remaining horses to other cavalry regiments and to march to Lisbon to baord ship. It had lost 2 officers, 239 men and 445 horses during the campaign; all through sickness. It sailed from Lisbon in April and was stationed in England on its return.
1814	The regiment was stationed in Ireland.
1818	It was based in England. It then continued on garrison duties in England and Ireland until 1854 (Ireland, 1822; England, 1826; Ireland, 1832; England, 1835; Ireland, 1841; England, 1845; Ireland, 1851).
1837	The regiment attended the coronation of Queen Victoria and was granted the Harp and Crown badge and the motto 'Quis Separabit'.
1839	It was called out to disperse Chartist protesters in Birmingham.

Crimean War, 1854–6

1854	At the outbreak of the Crimean War, the regiment was stationed in Dublin, under the command of Lieutenant-Colonel E.C. Hodge. It was sent to the Crimea as part of the Heavy Cavalry Brigade under the command of Brigadier-General John Scarlett and it took part in the Charge of the Heavy Brigade on 25th October 1854 during the battle of Balaclava.
1855	The regiment remained in the Crimea and, much reduced due to casualties and illness, served throughout the siege of Sevastopol (Sebastopol).
1856	At the end of the war, the regiment returned to England and performed garrison duties there and in Ireland until 1882 (Ireland, 1861; England, 1867; Ireland, 1872; England, 1878).

Egypt, 1882: Arabi Pasha Rebellion

1882   The regiment formed part of the Major-General Drury Lowe's Cavalry Divison during the expedition to Egypt to quell the rebellion of Arabi Pasha. It took part in the battle of Tel-el-Kebir and the capture of Cairo. On its return, the whole regiment was treated to a dinner at the Royal Pavilion in Brighton.

Egypt and the Sudan, 1884–5: Gordon Relief Expedition

1884   The regiment provided a detachment for the Heavy Division of the Camel Corps and served in Egypt and the Sudan during the failed Gordon Relief Expedition.

1886   The regiment returned to England and was based at Manchester. It remained on garrison duties in England and Ireland until 1894 (Ireland, 1888; England, 1891).

1891   The regiment was ordered to carry out its first tour of India and was initially stationed at Rawalpindi, before moving to Muttra in 1902. It was used for frontier patrols in India and, while some members of the regiment volunteered to serve in South Africa, the regiment did not serve in the 2nd Boer War.

1904   It was posted on garrison duty to South Africa and was based at Middelburg, Cape Colony.

1908   The regiment returned to home station. Squadrons of the regiment were based at Brighton and Shrapnel Barracks, Woolwich.

1910   It was based at Tidworth where it remained at the outbreak of the First World War in 1914.

First World War, 1914–18

1914   The regiment was attached to the 2nd Cavalry Brigade of the Cavalry Division of the British Expeditionary Force (BEF). It landed at Boulogne on 16 August 1914. In September the divisional designation was changed and it became the 1st Cavalry Division. The regiment remained in the 2nd Cavlary Brigade, 1st Cavalry Division until the end of the war.

On the morning of 22 August 1914, C Squadron of the regiment made contact with a patrol of the German 4th Cuirassier Regiment between Maisières and Casteau on the Soignies Road, taking prisoners after an exchange of fire. This encounter was the first clash between British and German troops during the war.

The regiment took part in several actions in 1914 including Mons, Le Cateau, the retreat from Mons and the battles of the Marne, La Basée, Messines and Armentières and 1st Ypres. During these battles it fought in both a mounted and dismounted capacity.

1915–18 During the rest of the war, the regiment was often in reserve awaiting the promised breakthrough. Nevertheless, it also provided dismounted contingents which served in the trenches. In 1918 it took part in the pursuit of the retreating German army to Mons. Following the Armistice, it was the first British regiment to cross the Hohenzollern Bridge at Cologne in December 1918, becoming the first regiment of the army of occupation.

Post-war service and amalgamation

1919   The regiment was stationed in Ireland before returning to Tidworth in July.

1921   On 1st January the regimental title was changed to **4th Royal Irish Dragoon Guards**. Later in the same year it was posted to India.

1922   On 22 October, the regiment was amalgamated with the 7th Dragoon Guards (Princess Royals) to form the 4th/7th Dragoon Guards. While many of the regiment's personal continued to serve with this new amalgamated regiment, it had effectively ceased to be an Irish regiment. The 4th/7th Dragoon Guards had a distinguished career in the Second World War, serving in France, the D-Day campaign and the campaign in Germany. In 1992 it was amalgamated with the 5th Royal Inniskilling Dragoon Guards to form the Royal Dragoon Guards.

Colonels

Year	Name
1685	Lieutenant-General James Hamilton, 4th Duke of Hamilton and Earl of Arran
1688	Colonel Charles Hamilton, 2nd Earl of Selkirk
1688	Colonel Charles Godfrey (following 'Glorious Revolution')
1693	Lieutenant-General Francis Langston
1713	Lieutenant-General George Jocelyn
1715	Major-General Sherington Davenport
1719	Lieutenant-General Owen Wynne
1732	Lieutenant-General Thomas Pearce
1739	Field-Marshal James O'Hara, Lord Kilmaine
1743	Lieutenant-General John Brown
1762	General James Johnston (senior)
1775	General James Johnston (junior)
1778	General George Warde
1803	Lieutenant-General Miles Staveley
1814	General Sir Henry Fane
1827	General Sir George Anson
1849	General Richard Pigot
1868	General Sir James Charles Chatterton
1874	General Sir Edward Cooper Hodge
1894	Lieutenant-General William Godfrey Dunham Massy
1896	Lieutenant-General Sir Henry Clement Wilkinson
1908	Lieutenant-General Sir Edward Cecil Bethune

Commanding officers

Year	Name
1823	Lieutenant-Colonel Robert Ross
1831	Lieutenant-Colonel James Charles Chatterton
1848	Lieutenant-Colonel Edward Copper Hodge

1859   Lieutenant-Colonel William Charles Forrest (transferrs to 11th Hussars, in 1859)
1859   Lieutenant-Colonel Arthur Cavendish Bentick
1871   Lieutenant-Colonel Frank Chaplin
1877   Lieutenant-Colonel James Gunter
1882   Lieutenant-Colonel Thomas Bradley Shaw-Hillier
1886   Lieutenant-Colonel Philip Edward Pope
1888   Lieutenant-Colonel Hugh McCalmont
1892   Lieutenant-Colonel Philip Kavanagh Doyne
1896   Lieutenant-Colonel George Digby Filmer Sulivan

Regimental colours
The guidon of the regiment was of crimson silk, edged with gold. In the centre there was a harp and crown device above the star of St. Patrick and the inscription IV DG. The central device was enclosed by a circle containing the regimental title in gold letters. Beneath a wreath device there was the regimental motto and battle honours.

Battle Honours
At the time of the regiment's amalgamation, its battle honours were:

Peninsula, Balaklava, Sevastopol, Tel-el-Kebir, Egypt 1882, Mons, Le Cateau, Retreat from Mons, Marne 1914, Aisne 1914, La Bassée, Messines 1914, Armentières 1914, Ypres 1914, Ypres 1915, St Julien, Frezenberg, Bellewaarde, Somme 1916, Somme 1918, Flers-Courcelette, Arras 1917, Scarpe 1917, Cambrai, 1917, Cambrai 1918, St Quentin, Rosières, Amiens, Albert 1918, Hindenburg Line, Pursuit to Mons, France and Flanders 1914–18.

Motto
'Quis Separabit' (Who shall separate us?)

Regimental music
The regimental quick march was ' St Patrick's Day'. The slow march was the '4th Dragoon Guards', which was also known as 'The Blue Horse'.

Nicknames
The Buttermilks, The Mounted Micks.

6th INNISKILLING DRAGOONS
Later the 5th Royal Inniskilling Dragoon Guards, 1689–1992

Formation
This regiment was another raised to serve the Williamite cause during the Jacobite Wars in Ireland. In August 1689, Colonel Sir Albert Conyngham was authorized to raise a dragoon regiment of twelve troops but would seem to have anticipated this

order and had begun forming a regiment sometime earlier. He raised this regiment using volunteers from the various independent troops of horse that had been formed in Enniskillen, Co. Fermanagh, and also enlisted volunteers from Co. Donegal. The regiment was originally known as 'Conyngham's Regiment of Dragoons' or just as 'Conyngham's Dragoons'. In contemporary accounts the regiment was also referred to as the 'Inniskilling Horse' or the 'Inniskilling Dragoons'.

In 1690 it was ranked in the numerical sequence as the 7th Dragoons but this was changed to the 6th Dragoons in 1691. In terms of the regiment's official title the practice until 1751 was to adopt the name of the regimental colonel. For example, when Colonel Robert Echlin took command of the regiment in 1691, it became known as 'Echlin's Regiment of Dragoons' and sometimes as 'Echlin's Inniskillings'.

Operational history

The Jacobite War in Ireland, 1689–91

1690   The regiment fought in numerous actions during this war and played a prominent part in the battle of the Boyne on 1 July.

1691   It fought at the battle of Aughrim on 12 July. The regiment remained in Ireland at the end of the war.

1708   The regiment was moved to England.

1709   Squadrons of the Inniskillings were based at Perth, Fife, Drmfermline, Falkland and Forfar. The regiment remained stationed in northern England of Scotland for the next number of years.

The Jacobite Rebellion, 1715–16

1715   By now the regiment was referred to as the 'Black Dragoons', presumably because they were mounted on black horses. During the suppression of the Jacobite rebellion, the regiment fought in the engagement at Dunblane (Sheriffmuir) in November 1715.

1716   After the end of the rebellion the regiment was kept on the English-Scottish border for a long period and was quartered at various places including Stranraer and Glasgow.

1725   The regiment was used to put down disturbances near Glasgow.

1728   The Inniskillings were moved south to England and initially stationed at Reading. They were later quartered at various locations including Windsor, Maidenhead and Staines. They remained on home service, being stationed in English and Scottish towns until 1742.

The War of the Austrian Succession, 1742–8

1742   In August the regiment boarded ship at Woolwich and was landed in Ostend. It would remain in Flanders and Germany for the rest of the war.

1743   The Inniskillings fought in the battle of Dettingen

1744   Although war was officially declared between France and England during this year, the regiment remained inactive in Flanders, finishing the year in quarters in Ghent.

1745   The regiment was present at the British defeat at Fontenoy.

1746	It fought in the battle of Rocoux.
1747	The regiment fought in the battle of Laffeldt.
1749	At the end of the war, the regiment returned to home service, being quartered initially at Shrewsbury and Stafford.
1750	Stationed at Norwich and Yarmouth.
1751	Re-designated as the **6th (Inniskilling) Dragoons**. Based at Canterbury and Rochester.
1752	The Inniskillings were stationed initially at Maidstone and Town Malling and later had troops at various locations including Hastings, Lewes and Cuckfield.
1754	Based in Dorset on anti-smuggling duty.
1755	A 'light troop' (a troop of light cavalry) was added to the regimental establishment.

The Seven Years War, 1757–63

1758	The regiment took part in an expedition to St Malo, before being sent to Germany where it arrived at Emden in July. It would remain on the Continent for the rest of the war.
1759	The Inniskilling Dragoons took part in the battle of Minden and, on the night of 26–27 August, raided the camp of General Wetter, taking over 400 prisoners.
1760	The regiment was present at the battles of Warburg and Zierenberg and took part in the expedition to Wesel, which began in October.
1761–3	The Inniskilling Dragoons took part in the protracted operations in Germany and fought in the battles of Kirk Denkern (1761), Wilhelmstahl (1763) and Groebenstein (1763).
1763	At the end of the war, the regiment boarded ship for England in January. On its arrival, it was stationed in Northamptonshire. The regiment's light troop was disbanded in April. For the next 30 years the regiment remained on home service and was stationed at various towns around England.

French Revolutionary and Napoleonic Wars, 1793–1815

1792	While war did not break out between England and France until the following year, the regiment was brought up to wartime establishment.
1793	The regiment joined the expedition of the Duke of York in Flanders, and arrived on the Continent in June. It took part in the battles of Marquion, Hondschoote, Courtrai and Cysoing.
1794	In May the Inniskilling Dragoons fought in the battle of Willems.
1795	During the year's campaigning the Duke of York suffered a series of reverses and, harried by French armies, the regiment took part in a number of actions during the retreat into Germany. In late 1795 it boarded ship for England and in its arrival was quartered at Norwich.
1809	After a period of home service in England, the regiment returned to Ireland and was initially quartered in Dundalk. This marked the regiment's return to Ireland after an absence of 101 years!

1810	Stationed in Dublin.
1811	The regiment was stationed in Ballinasloe. It later was quartered in Belturbet and Tullamore.
1814	The Inniskilling Dragoons moved to Dublin and took ship to England where they were quartered in Liverpool and York. During the winter of 1814–15, squadrons of the regiment were based at Nottingham, Derby and Mansfield.
1815	During the Waterloo campaign, the Inniskilling Dragoons were attached to the 2nd Brigade of Heavy Cavalry under General Sir William Ponsonby. This brigade included the 1st Royal Dragoons and the 2nd North British Dragoons (Scots Greys) and was commonly known as the Union Brigade. With this brigade, the regiment was heavily engaged at the battle of Waterloo and suffered heavy casualties. The regiment remained in France at the end of the campaign as part of the army of occupation.
1816	The Inniskilling Dragoons returned to England in January and were stationed at Salisbury. This marked the beginning of a long period of home service and the regiment rotated through a succession of stations. This period included several tours in Ireland (1819–23, 1829–33, 1838–41 and 1846–51).

The Crimean War, 1854–6

1854	At the outbreak of the war, the regiment was based at York, Newcastle and Leeds. A service squadron was formed and attached to the Heavy Cavalry Brigade, which was under the command of Brigadier-General Scarlett. After a period spent in Bulgaria, the British expeditionary force arrived in the Crimea in September and, on 25 October, the regiment took part in the successful, but often forgotten, Charge of the Heavy Brigade.
1855	The regiment remained in the Crimea for the rest of the war and was later awarded the battle honour 'Sevastopol' for the part it played in the siege.
1856	The Inniskilling Dragoons returned to England in January and began a period of home service.
1858	The regiment was ordered to India, arriving at Bombay in October. It remained in India until 1867, being stationed at various posts including Kirkee, Mhow and Meerut.
1867	The Inniskilling Dragoons returned to England and were stationed at Colchester before being moved to York.
1871	The regiment was moved to Ireland where it remained until 1877. During this time it was stationed at the Curragh, Newbridge, Dublin and Dundalk.
1873	The regiment was based in the Curragh at the same time that the 27th Inniskilling Regiment was based there. This was the first time that the two regiments had been in the same location since Waterloo.
1875	The 6th Inniskilling Dragoons returned to its home town of Enniskillen. At this time the 27th Inniskilling Regiment was also based there. This was the first time since the seventeenth century that these two regiments were in Enniskillen at the same time.

1877 The regiment was moved to Scotland being based in Edinburgh and then Glasgow.
1880 Based at Leeds and Norwich.

1st Anglo-Boer War, 1880–1

1881 In light of the outbreak of war in South Africa, the regiment took ship in January. While it was in transit from Durban to Newcastle, Natal, the British forces suffered a disastrous defeat at Majuba Hill. By the time it arrived in Natal in March, an armistice had been signed. The Inniskilling Dragoons remained on garrison duty in South Africa until 1890 and served on operations in Buchuanaland and Zululand.
1890 The regiment returned to England and was stationed at Brighton. It was subsequently stationed at Aldershot, Manchester and Edinburgh.
1897 The Inniskilling Dragoons were moved to Ireland being stationed at Dundalk and then the Curragh.

2nd Anglo-Boer War, 1899–1902

1899 At the outbreak of the war, the regiment was based at the Curragh. Ordered to South Africa, the regiment arrived at Cape Town in November and December. The Inniskilling Dragoons were attached to the 1st Cavalry Brigade which formed part of General French's force. The regiment would later serve with the 2nd Cavalry Brigade.
1900 The regiment took part in actions at Colesberg, Poplar Grove and Vredes Verdrag. It also took part in the advance from Krondstad and the captures of Johannesburg, Pretoria and Middlelburg.
1901 As the war descended into a phase of bitter guerrilla fighting, the regiment took part in extended operations in the South-Eastern Transvaal and the Orange River Colony.
1902 As the war reached its final phase, the Inniskillings took part in a series of 'drives', designed to push the surviving Boer 'bitter-enders' onto British positions. These drives resulted in the capture of the remaining men from several Boer commandos. At the end of the war, the regiment returned to the Curragh.
1904 The regiment was based in Dublin.
1906 It was sent to Egypt.
1908 The Inniskilling Dragoons returned to India for another period of overseas service. Attached to the Mhow Cavalry Brigade, it was stationed in Mhow and then Muttra.

The First World War, 1914–18

1914 The regiment was based in India at the outbreak of the war and sailed from Bombay in December.
1915 On its arrival in France it was attached to the Mhow Cavalry Brigade of the 2nd Indian Cavalry Division. In common with the majority of the cavalry regiments in the allied armies during the war, the Inniskilling Dragoons were

often held in reserve in expectation of a decisive breakthrough. Dismounted squadrons were sometimes detached for 'tactical duties' and these could range from serving as front line parties or as reconnaissance units.

1916   In November, the 2nd Indian Cavalry Division was re-designated as the 4th Cavalry Division.

1917   In the wake of the German counter-offensive at Cambrai in late November, the regiment had a rare chance for mounted action. The Inniskilling Dragoons took part in a costly charge on German positions at Guislain Ridge on 1 December, losing 169 men killed and wounded, while 271 horses were killed.[7]

1918   In March the regiment was assigned to the 7th Cavalry Brigade of the 3rd Cavalry Division.

A service squadron of the 6th (Inniskilling) Dragoons was raised in Enniskillen in November 1914 and was attached to the 36th Ulster Division as divisional cavalry. This squadron arrived in France in October 1915 and was attached to the cavalry regiment of X Corps in June 1916. In 1917 it was dismounted and its personnel were posted to the 9th Battalion, the Royal Irish Fusiliers, 108th Brigade, 36th Ulster Division.

The Inter-War Years

1921   The regiment was re-titled as the **Inniskillings (6th Dragoons)** and was based at York in England.

1922   It was amalgamated with the 5th Dragoon Guards (Princess Charlotte of Wales's) to form **5th/6th Dragoons**. Based in Cairo.

1923   Stationed at Risalpur, India.

1927   Under the terms of a further re-organization, the regiment was re-titled as the **5th Inniskilling Dragoon Guards**.

1928   Based at York.

1930   Colchester.

1935   Re-designated as the **5th Royal Inniskilling Dragoon Guards**.

1938   The regiment gave up its horses and was mechanized, being equipped with light tanks.

The Second World War, 1939–45

1939   On the outbreak of the war, the regiment was equipped with MK VI B light and went to France as part of the BEF where it initially acted as the divisional reconnaissance regiment to the 3rd and then the 4th Divisions.

1940   The Inniskilling Dragoon Guards were re-assigned to 2nd Light Armoured Reconnaissance Brigade and the regiment was tasked with guarding crossings over the Louvain Canal. During the retreat to Dunkirk it took part in several rearguard actions at Assche, Morbeque, Neuve Chapelle, Bergues and on the Ringsloot Canal.

---

7 Gavin Hughes, 'A Cambrai charge: the 6th (Inniskilling) Dragoons at Guislain Ridge, 1 December 1917', in *Irish Sword*, 22:87 (Summer 2000).

1940–3 During a prolonged period of training and re-equipping in England, the regiment served with the 3rd Motor MG Brigade and then the 28th Armoured Brigade.

1944–5 The regiment was assigned to the 22nd Amoured Brigade of the 7th Armoured Division and, following the D-Day landings, took part in the in the bocage country. The Inniskilling Dragoon Guards later served in 'Operation-Market Garden' and in the campaign in Germany. The regiment remained in Germany after the war as part of the army of occupation.

Korean War, 1950–3

1951 The regiment was posted to Korea and was attached to the 1st Commonwealth Division.

1952 The Inniskilling Dragoon Guards took part in the defence of 'the Hook' feature in the allied lines during determined Chinese attacks on 18–19 November.

1953 At the end of the war, the regiment was posted to Egypt.

Since 1953, the Royal Inniskilling Dragoon Guards have served on numerous tours in England and abroad. These included extended periods with the British Army of the Rhine (BAOR) and are outlined below.

1954	England	1969	Germany (BAOR)
1957	Germany (BAOR)	1974	England
1962	England	1976	Germany (BAOR)
1964	Aden, with squadrons in Bahrein and Hong Kong	1981	Northern Ireland
		1981	Germany
1965	Libya	1984	England
1966	Cyprus	1986	Germany
1968	England		

1992 As part of the 'Options for Change', the 5th Royal Inniskilling Dragoon Guards were amalgamated with the 4th/7th Royal Dragoon Guards to form a new regiment with the title of the **Royal Dragoon Guards**. While this new regiment maintains the Inniskillings' traditions to some degree, this last amalgamation effectively ended the separate history of a regiment that could trace its lineage back to 1689.

Colonels-in-Chief

1897 Field-Marshal, HRH the Duke of Connaught
1922 Field-Marshal, HM Albert I, King of the Belgians
1937 HM Leopold III, King of the Belgians
1985 HRH Prince Charles, the Prince of Wales

Colonels

1689 Colonel Sir Albert Conyngham
1691 Colonel Robert Echlin

1715	General John Dalrymple, 2nd Earl of Stair
1734	Colonel Charles, Lord Cadogan
1743	Field-Marshal John Dalrymple, 2nd Earl of Stair
1745	Major-General John Leslie, 8th Earl of Rothes
1750	Major-General the Hon. James Cholmondeley
1775	Lieutenant-General Edward Harvey
1778	Lieutenant-General James Johnston
1797	Major-General George Augustus, 11th Earl of Pembroke
1827	Lieutenant-General Sir William Lumley
1840	Lieutenant-General Sir Joseph Straton[8]
1840	Lieutenant-General Sir George Pownall Adams
1856	Major-General Sir James Jackson
1860	Major-General Thomas Marten
1868	Major-General Lewis Duncan Williams
1874	Major-General Henry Darlrymple White
1886	General Charles Cameron Shute
1904	Lieutenant-General Edward Arthur Gore
1912	Major-General Sir Michael Frederick Rimington
1922	Lieutenant-General Sir George T.M. Bridges
1937	Major-General Roger Evans
1947	General Sir Charles Frederic Keightley
1957	Colonel Sir Michael Picton Ansell
1962	General Sir John D'Arcy Anderson
1967	Brigadier-General Arthur Carr
1972	General Sir Cecil Blacker
1981	Brigadier-General William F.A. Findlay
1986	Major-General Richard Charles Keightley
1991	Major-General Patrick Guy Brooking

Battle honours
Dettingen, Warburg, Willems, Waterloo, Balaklava, Sevastopol, South Africa, 1899–1902; Somme 1916, Somme 1918, Morval; Cambrai 1917; Cambrai 1918, St Quentin, Avre, Lys, Hazebrouck, Amiens, Hindenburg Line, St Quentin Canal, Beaurevoir, Pursuit to Mons, France and Flanders 1914–18, Withdrawal to Escaut, St Omer-La Bassée, Dunkirk 1940, Mont Pincon, St Pierre La Vielle, Lisieux, Risle Crossing, Lower Maas, Roer, Ibbenburren, North-West Europe 1940, North-West Europe 1944–45, The Hook 1952, Korea 1951–52.[9]

Motto
5th Inniskilling Dragoon Guards: Vestigia Nulla Retrorsum (We do not retreat).

---

8 General Straton died in October 1840. 9 Any battle of the period 1689 to 1922 refers to the 6th (Inniskilling) Dragoons before its first amalgamation in 1922.

Regimental music
The quick marches associated with the regiment are 'Fare ye well Inniskilling', 'Sprig of Shillelagh' and 'St Patrick's Day'. The slow march is 'the Soldier's Chorus'.

Nicknames
The Old Inniskillings, the Skins.

27th (INNISKILLING) REGIMENT OF FOOT
Later the Royal Inniskilling Fusiliers, 1689–1968

Formation
The Inniskilling Fusiliers was another regiment that was founded against the turbulent backdrop of the Jacobite War in Ireland. As early as 1688, infantry companies were formed from among the Protestant community of Enniskillen, Co. Fermanagh, and they proclaimed their allegiance to William III. By early 1689, this force consisted of ten companies and numbered over 700 men. There was also a troop of horse and this cavalry unit would later form the nucleus of the 6th Royal Inniskilling Dragoons (see separate entry for that regiment).

From June 1689, the Enniskillen infantry regiment or 'Inniskilling Regiment' was commanded by Colonel Zechariah Tiffin and was officially known as Tiffin's Regiment. In January 1690, it was placed on the regular army establishment and until 1751 it was known by the name of its colonel. In 1751 this was changed to 27th (Inniskilling) Regiment of Foot. Despite these various official designations, throughout its early history the regiment was often referred to as the 'Inniskilling Regiment'. This must represent the longest use of a territorial title by any regiment of the British army. While the town name is actually spelt 'Enniskillen', the spelling 'Inniskilling' became standard in the regimental title around 1840. Following the Cardwell reforms of 1881, it was amalgamated with the 108th Regiment of Foot (Madras Infantry), the original regiment forming the 1st Battalion of the re-named Royal Inniskilling Fusiliers.

Operational history
The Jacobite War, 1689–91 (Ireland)
The Nine Years War or the War of the League of Ausburg, 1689–97 (Europe)
During the Jacobite War in Ireland, the original Enniskillen companies and later Tiffin's Regiment took part in numerous battles including Lismella, Belleek, Belturbet, Cornagrade, Lisnaskea, Newtownbutler, the Boyne, Aughrim and the siege of Limerick.

When the war in Ireland was over, the regiment remained in service to fight in William's European campaigns.

1692 The regiment was based in Portsmouth but was then moved to Flanders where it took part in the battle of Steenkirk.

1693   Duties at the Tower of London were followed by re-embarkation for Flanders.
1695   The regiment was present at the siege of Namur.
1697   Following the Treaty of Ryswick, the Inniskillingers were returned to serve on garrison duty in England and Ireland. It would later form part of the garrison at Minorca.
1739–40   The regiment took part in the expedition to the West Indies, losing a large number of men due to illness.

Jacobite Rebellion, 1745–6

1745   Following the outbreak of rebellion in Scotland, the regiment was sent to join Lieutenant-General Hawley's forces and took part in the battle of Falkirk.
1746   The regiment took part in the battle of Culloden. At the end of the rebellion, the regiment was returned to Ireland.
1747   The regiment was ranked as the 27th Foot.
1751   The regiment was re-designated as the 27th (Inniskilling) Regiment of Foot.

The Seven Years War, 1756–63

1756   On the outbreak of war with France and in preparation for a campaign in North America, the Inniskilling Regiment was shipped to New York.
1758   The regiment took part in the siege operations at Ticonderoga.
1759   Attached to the army of General Amherst, the regiment fought in the actions at Crown Point and in the taking of Montreal.
1761   The Inniskilling Regiment took part in operations in Nova Scotia before being sent to Barbados.
1762   The regiment took part in the captures of Martinique and Grenada. War was declared against Spain in May and the Inniskilling Regiment took part in the capture of Cuba in June. It was then posted to New York in October where it formed part of the garrison.
1765   The regiment was posted to Canada (then British North America) and formed part of the garrisons of Quebec, Trois Rivières and Montreal.
1767   In August, the regiment was embarked for the home station and it was based in Ireland until 1775, forming the garrisons at Dublin and Limerick.

The American War of Independence, 1775–83

1775   On the outbreak of war in America, the regiment was shipped to Boston where it arrived in October.
1776   It was then posted to Halifax, Nova Scotia, before taking part in the landings at Long Island, Staten Island and Rhode Island. It also fought in the actions at White Plains, Fort Washington and King's Bridge.
1777   During this year, the Inniskilling Regiment formed part of the garrison of Rhode Island.
1778   The regiment took part in the battles at Quintin's Bridge and Hancocks' Bridge before being posted to the West Indies, where it took part in the capture of St Lucia.

1779   The regiment took part in the abortive mission to relieve Grenada.
1780   The Inniskilling Regiment formed part of the garrison of St Lucia.
1781   The regiment was moved to Barbados and remained in the West Indies until 1785 when it was returned to home station, serving as the garrison in various locations in Scotland and Ireland.
1789   The regiment was returned to Ireland and served in Dublin, Galway and Cork until the outbreak of the wars with France.

French Revolutionary and Napoleonic Wars, 1793–1815

While much of Europe had been at war since 1792, Britain did not declare war on France until 1793. In 1812, Britain also found itself at war with America in the War of 1812, a war that did not end until 1815.[10]

At the outbreak of hostilities, the 27th (Inniskilling) Regiment of Foot was a single battalion regiment. During these wars, two further battalions were raised and the three battalions of the Inniskillings saw distinguished service in the West Indies, Egypt, the Peninsula, America and the Low Countries. While the regiment already had a enviable record in 1793, it was during the numerous campaigns of these wars that it established itself as one of the finest regiments in the British Army.

1st Battalion

Between 1794 and 1795, the 1st Battalion of the 27th Inniskilling Regiment took part in the expeditions to the Low Countries before being sent to the West Indies. In 1796 it played an important part in the capture of St Lucia and was later allowed to fly its own flag above the captured fortress for an hour before the Union flag was hoisted. The battalion returned to England in 1798 before campaigning in the Low Countries and in Egypt, where it fought at the battle of Alexandria in 1801.

After a period of garrison duty in Malta, the 1st Battalion was sent to Naples in 1805 and took part in the campaign in Sicily. In 1806 the battalion fought in the capture of Maida and remained in the Italian theatre until 1811 when it was sent to the Peninsula, where it remained until 1814. In 1814, it joined the regiment's other two battalions in Bordeaux before being sent to Canada and then Plattsburg on the Mississippi, where it served in the 'War of 1812' against the Americans.

The battalion was returned to Europe for the Waterloo campaign. Attached to brigade of Major-General Sir John Lambert, the battalion fought in the battle of Waterloo, suffering heavy casualties while defending its position on the Charleroi road. Out of 698 men at Waterloo, 478 were either killed or wounded. This battalion remained in France until 1817, before being returned to Ireland.

---

10 The Anglo-American War or the War of 1812 was officially terminated with the Treaty of Ghent in December 1814, but news of this did not reach America until February 1815. In the meantime the American and British armies had fought a significant battle at New Orleans on 8 January 1815, a major American victory.

2nd Battalion

This battalion was first raised in 1800 from volunteers from Donegal and Fermanagh militia units. It took part in the Egyptian campaign and, with the 1st/27th, fought at the battle of Alexandria in 1801. Following the Peace of Amiens (1802), several battalions were disbanded and the 2nd/27th was one of these. A resumption of hostilities with France led to it being but re-formed in 1804 and it joined Lord Cathcart's army in Hanover in 1805. It later served in Sicily (1806) and Malta (1807) before taking part in the expedition to Naples in 1809.

In 1811 it was sent to the Peninsula where it took part in numerous actions including Alsafara, Biar, Castalla, the siege of Tarragona and the battle of Ordell. In 1814, having met with the regiment's other battalions in Bordeaux, it was sent to Ireland and provided drafts of replacements for the 1st Battalion in America before being disbanded in Dublin in April 1817.

3rd Battalion

The recruits for this battalion were raised in Belfast, Omagh and Enniskillen. Many of these were young men and this resulted in the battalion being known as the 'Young Inniskilleners'. The battalion was embodied at Glasgow in September 1805 and was returned to Ireland in 1806 and was based at Enniskillen in 1807. During this time it recruited new drafts for the 1st and 2nd Battalions, which were both serving in the Mediterranean.

In 1808 it was sent to the Peninsula where it remained until 1814. The 3rd/27th saw distinguished service with Wellington's army and fought in numerous actions including the capture of Badajoz and the battles of Busaco, Cuiudad Rodrigo, Salamanca, Vittoria, Orthez and Toulouse, among others. In 1814, it met the regiment's 1st and 2nd Battalions in Bordeaux before being sent to Canada and then to Mississippi where it served alongside the 1st/27th . It returned to the Low Countries in 1815 and formed part of the garrison of Paris. Having supplied drafts to the 1st/27th, this battalion returned to Canterbury, where it was disbanded in February 1816.

1817	After an absence of over 20 years on foreign service, the regiment, now just of one battalion again was returned to Dublin. It later served in Waterford and Cork.
1819–23	The 27th Foot was stationed in Gibraltar.
1824–30	The regiment was based in the West Indies and formed the garrison at various locations including Barbados, St Vincent and Grenada.
1831	The regiment was returned to Ireland and served on garrison duty in towns such as Fermoy, Limerick and Buttevant and its home town of Enniskillen.
1835–48	During these years the 27th Foot was stationed in South Africa and took part in several campaigns including the 6th Kaffir War of 1835. In 1842 a detachment of two companies under Major T.C. Smith was sent to Port Natal in a costly expedition to back up Britain's seizure of the port from

	the Boers. Following a long and difficult siege, Smith's force was relieved and Natal was claimed for the British Crown. This forced the Boer population to trek further inland in an attempt to escape this unwelcome British interference.
1848	The regiment returned to home station, being based at Edinburgh and Glasgow. It would remain in Scotland for two years.
1850	The 27th Foot returned to Ireland and was stationed in Belfast.
1852	The regiment was based in Dublin.
1853	The 27th Foot was based at Enniskillen. During this phase of home service, it would later be stationed in Dublin and Cork.
1854	In June the regiment was ordered to India. During this voyage, one of the regiment's transport ships, the *Charlotte*, was wrecked in a storm at Algoa Bay in Port Elizabeth, South Africa, on the night of 20 September. Over 100 men of the regiment, and some of their wives, were killed. The first detachment arrived in India in September and was stationed at Dum Dum.
1857	During the Indian Mutiny, detachments of the regiment took part in several actions against the Sepoy rebels. The 27th Foot remained in India until 1864, being based at various barracks including those at Umballa, Gwalior and Gondah.
1864	The regiment returned to England and was based at Portsmouth. It remained in England until 1873, being based at different locations that included Chatham, Colchester, Aldershot and Gosport.
1873	The 27th Innskillings returned to Ireland and were based at the Curragh where the 6th Innsiskilling Dragoons were also stationed. The two regiments had not been in the same location since the battle of Waterloo in 1815. Detachments of the 27th were later based in Londonderry.
1875	In September, the regiment was moved to its home town of Enniskillen. At the same time, a detachment of the 6th Inniskilling Dragoons was also sharing the same station. This was the first time since the seventeenth century that the two regiments had been in their home town at the same time.
1876	The regiment remained at Enniskillen with detachments in Londonderry, Sligo and Boyle.
1881	Under the terms of the Cardwell army reforms of 1881, the 27th (Inniskilling) Regiment of Foot was amalgamated with the 108th Regiment of Foot (Madras Infantry) to form the Royal Innskilling Fusiliers. Under this new arrangement, the old 27th (Inniskilling) Regiment of Foot became the 1st Battalion of the Royal Innskilling Fusiliers while the 108th Regiment of Foot (Madras Infantry) became the new regiment's 2nd Battalion.
	After this army reforms, the regiment was also assigned recruiting district No. 27, which included counties Donegal, Derry, Tyrone and Fermanagh. The 108th Regiment of Foot (Madras Infantry) had been raised in India in 1853 and had initially been designated as the 3rd Madras European Regiment in the East India Company service. A large number of

its original recruits were from Ireland and subsequent drafts of replacements joined the regiment in succeeding years. It served in the Indian Mutiny and, in 1861, was re-designated as the 108th Regiment of Foot (Madras Infantry).

In 1881 and 1882, regiments of the Militia of Ireland were re-designated as militia battalions of the regiment. These battalions were:

3rd Battalion (Fermanagh Light Infantry, 1881–1908)
4th Battalion (Londonderry Light Infantry, 1881–1882)
4th Battalion (Royal Tyrone Fusiliers, 1882–1908)
5th Battalion (Prince of Wales's Own Donegal Militia, 1882–1908)

On the establishment of the Territorial Force in 1908, the designations of these reserve battalions changed once again.

3rd Battalion (Royal Tyrone Fusiliers, 1908–53)
4th Battalion (Fermanagh Light Infantry, 1908–53)

Pathan War, 1897–8

1897 The 2nd Battalion, Royal Inniskilling Fusiliers too part in this campaign against the Pathans on the North-West Frontier of India.

The 2nd Anglo-Boer War, 1899–1902

1899 The 1st Battalion of the regiment was sent to South Africa and was attached to General Fitzroy Hart's Irish Brigade. As part of this formation it took part in the disastrous battle of Colenso (December).

1900 The 1st Battalion took part in the relief of Ladysmith and the campaign in the Transvaal. The regiment's 2nd Battalion was also sent to South Africa and the two battalions took part in the last phase of the war. At the end of the war, the 1st Battalion returned to Enniskillen while the 2nd Battalion was sent to Egypt.

In the years preceding First World War, the 1st Battalion served in Crete, China and was in India at the outbreak of the war.
The 2nd Battalion served on home station in Dublin, Aldershot and Dover.

The First World War, 1914–18

Alongside the regiment's two regular battalions, eleven further battalions were raised for service in the war. The various battalions of the Royal Inniskilling Fusiliers saw service not only on the Western Front but also in Gallipoli, Egypt, Macedonia and Palestine.

1st Battalion

This regular battalion was based at Trimulgherry in India at the outbreak of the war. It arrived in England in January 1915 and was attached to the 87th Brigade of the 29th Division. In April 1915 it arrived at Mudros and subsequently took part in the landings at Gallipoli on 25 April. The battalion was evacuated from

Gallipoli in January 1916 and was sent to France where it remained for the rest of the war. In February 1918 it was transferred to the 109th Brigade of the 36th (Ulster) Division.

2nd Battalion

This regular battalion was based in England at the outbreak of the war and was sent to France in December, initially serving as GHQ troops. In January 1915 it was attached to the 5th Brigade of the 2nd Division and it would later serve with the 5th, 32nd and finally the 36th (Ulster) Division.

3rd (Reserve) Battalion

This wartime battalion was raised at Omagh in August 1914 and was later based at Lough Swilly and Derry. In April 1918 it was amalgamated with the 4th and 12th Battalions of the Royal Inniskilling Fusiliers and remained at Oswestry in West Lancashire for the remainder of the war.

4th (Extra Reserve) Battalion

This battalion was raised at Enniskillen on 4 August 1914 and was later stationed at Lough Swilly, Buncrana and Clonmany. It was amalgamated with the 3rd Battalion in April 1918.

5th (Service) Battalion

This service battalion was raised at Omagh in August 1914 and was a K1 battalion. It was attached to the 31st Brigade of the 10th (Irish) Division and took part in the Gallipoli, Salonika and Palestine campaigns. In May 1918 it left the 10th (Irish) Division and was sent to France, subsequently serving with the 66th Division.

6th (Service) Battalion

This K1 battalion was formed at Omagh in August 1914. After initial training in Dublin and at the Curragh, it was attached to the 31st Brigade of the 10th (Irish) Division and served in Gallipoli, Salonika, Egypt and Palestine. In May 1918 it was sent to France and subsequently servedwith the 14th, 34th and 50th Divisions.

7th (Service) Battalion

This K2 battalion was formed at Omagh in October 1914 and was attached to the 49th Brigade of the 16th (Irish) Division. After training in Tipperary and Finner Camp, it was sent to England and from there to France in February 1916. Due to its losses on the Western Front, it was amalgamated with the 8th Battalion, Royal Inniskilling Fusiliers, in August 1917 to form the 7th/8th Battalion. Its remaining personnel were transferred to the 2nd Battalion Royal Irish Regiment in early 1918 and it was reduced to cadre. In June 1918 the 7th/8th Battalion was reformed using troops from the 8th Rifle Brigade and this battalion later served with the 30th Division in Belgium.

8th (Service) Battalion
This K2 battalion was formed at Omagh in October 1914 and was attached to the 49th Brigade of the 16th (Irish) Division. From August 1917 it was amalgamated with the 7th Battalion (see above).

9th (Service) Battalion (Co. Tyrone)
This battalion was raised in Omagh in September 1914 and was formed by men of the Tyrone Volunteers, UVF. It was attached to the 36th (Ulster) Division and following training in Ireland and England was posted to France in October 1915. It remained with the 36th (Ulster) Division until the end of the war, taking part in numerous battles including the Somme and Messines.

10th (Service) Battalion (Derry)
Raised in Omagh in September, this battalion was formed by men from the Derry Volunteers, UVF. It was attached to the 36th (Ulster) Division and went to France in 1915. Following numerous engagements with this division, the battalion was disbanded in France in January 1918, its remaining men (7 officers and 150 men) being transferred to the 2nd Battalion, Royal Inniskilling Fusiliers.

11th (Service) Battalion (Donegal and Fermanagh)
This battalion was also raised at Omagh in September 1914 and was formed by men from the Donegal and Fermanagh units of the UVF. It was attached to the 36th (Ulster) Division and from 1915 served on the Western Front. In February 1918 it was disbanded, its remaining men being absorbed by the 9th Battalion, Royal Inniskilling Fusiliers.

12th (Reserve) Battalion
This battalion was formed in Enniskillen in April 1915 using men from the depots of the 9th, 10th and 11th Battalions. It remained in Ireland until April 1918 when it was amalgamated with the 3rd Battalion.

13th (Service) Battalion
In June 1918, the 11th Garrison Guard Battalion in France was re-designated as the 13th (Garrison) Battalion, Royal Inniskilling Fusiliers. From July 1918, the 'Garrison' designation was dropped and the battalion remained attached to the 40th Division until the end of the war.

At the end of the First World War, the regiment's wartime battalions were disbanded. During the course of the war, the various battalions of the regiment had fought in numerous actions in various theatres of the war, amassing over 50 new battle honours while eight men of the regiment were awarded the Victoria Cross.

The Interwar Years
1st Battalion, 1919 to 1939
The regiment's 1st Battalion was stationed successively in Ireland, Iraq, Shanghai and Singapore and was moved to India following the outbreak of the Second World War.

1922   When it was announced that the Royal Irish Fusiliers were to be disbanded along with other Irish regiments, the Royal Inniskilling Fusilier's decided to disband its second battalion and this incredible act of generosity allowed the Royal Irish Fusiliers to survive on the army establishment.

1937   The regiment's 2nd Battalion was re-established as war seemed increasingly likely.

The Second World War, 1939–45

Alongside the two regular battalions of the Royal Inniskilling Fusiliers, four wartime battalions were also raised, the 5th, 6th, 30th and 70th Battalions. The 1st, 2nd and 6th Battalions served in various campaigns while the remaining wartime battalions acted as home defence, recruiting or training units for the Inniskilling battalions overseas. During the course of the war, battalions of the regiment served in Africa, Europe and Burma.

1st Battalion, 1939–45

This battalion was based in Singapore on the outbreak of war and was moved to India following Japan's entry into the war in 1941. During the campaigns in Burma in 1942, it took part in actions at Yenangyaung on the River Irrawaddy.

In 1943 it took part in the campaign on the Arakan peninsula where it was cut off by Japanese forces. The men of the battalion split into small groups in order to evade capture, but the battalion that re-formed at the end of the campaign was much depleted.

2nd Battalion, 1939–45

This battalion formed part of the BEF in 1939 and was attached to 13th Brigade of the 5th Division. Following the German Blitzkrieg of 1940 it was involved in many desperate rearguard actions and the remains of the battalion was evacuated from Dunkirk.

It was later to the Middle East and served in Madagascar, India, Syria and Egypt. In 1943 it took part in the invasion of Sicily and served for the rest of the campaign in Italy. At the end of the war, this battalion formed part of the garrison in Austria and was then disbanded.

6th Battalion, 1939–45

This battalion was attached to the 38th (Irish) Infantry Brigade in 1942, which initially formed part of the 1st Division.

The brigade was then attached to the 78th Infantry Division and, within this formation, the 6th Battalion served in the campaigns in North Africa, Sicily and Italy, taking part in numerous actions including the assault on Centuripe and the battle of Monte Cassino ('Cassino II'). The battalion was disbanded in July 1944.

During the Second World War, the various battalions of the Royal Inniskilling Fusiliers suffered 1,152 fatal casualties, the largest number lost by any Irish regiment during the war.

1945	At the end of the war, all of the other wartime battalions of the regiment were disbanded and the surviving 1st Battalion, Royal Inniskilling Fusiliers returned to India and was later stationed in Hong Kong and Malaya, where it was engaged in anti-terrorist duties.
1949	The 1st Battalion was stationed in the West Indies.
1951	The battalion was returned to home station.
1952	The 1st Battalion was granted the freedom of Enniskillen before being sent to the Suez Canal Zone. It then served in Kenya as part of the campaign against the Mau Mau. Following its service in Kenya, the regiment was granted the freedom of Nairobi, being the first British regiment to be so honoured by a colonial city. To date, no other regiment has been awarded a similar honour. The regiment's 2nd Battlion was also re-established in 1952 and served in Suez and Cyprus before being disbanded for the final time (1956).
1955	The 1st Battalion was returned to England and afterwards served in Germany.
1960	The battalion had detachments based in Kenya and Bahrain.
1961	The Royal Inniskilling Fusiliers were stationed in Kuwait following as the area was threatened by Iraq.
1962	The battalion was stationed at Gravesend in England.
1964	The Royal Inniskilling Fusiliers joined the UN force in Cyprus.
1965	Stationed in Berlin.
1967	The battalion returned to England and was stationed at Worcester.
1968	Detachments of the regiment were ordered to Bermuda but had returned to Worcester by June. On 30 June 1968, the regiment was effectively disbanded when it was amalgamated with other surviving Irish battalions to form the Royal Irish Rangers.[11] The Royal Irish Rangers were subsequently amalgamated with the Ulster Defence Regiment to form the Royal Irish Regiment in July 1992.

Colonels

1689	Brigadier-General Zechariah Tiffin
1702	General Thomas Whetham
1725	Field-Marshal Richard Molesworth, 3rd Viscount Molesworth
1732	Lieutenant-General Archibald Hamilton
1737	Lieutenant-General William L. Blakeney, 1st Baron Blakeney
1761	General Hugh Warburton
1771	Lieutenant-General Sir Eyre Coote
1773	General Eyre Massey, 1st Baron Clarina
1804	General Sir Francis Rawdon Hastings, 1st Marquess of Hastings
1826	General Sir Galbraith Lowry Cole

11 This new regiment formed by the amalgamation of the Royal Inniskilling Fusiliers, the Royal Ulster Rifles and the Royal Irish Fusiliers.

1842 Lieutenant-General Sir John Maclean
1848 General Sir William Francis Patrick Napier
1853 Lieutenant-General Edward Fleming
1860 Lieutenant-General John Geddes
1864 General James Robertson Craufurd
1870 General Randal Rumley
1881 General Randal Rumley (1st Battalion)
General Sir Edward Harris Greathead (2nd Battalion)
General Sir Arthur Edward Hardinge (2nd Battalion, from November)
1886 Lieutenant-General Sir James Talbot Airey (2nd Battalion)
1891 Lieutenant-General John Neptune Sargent (1st Battalion)
1898 Lieutenant-General William Roberts
1902 General Nathaniel Stevenson
1911 General Sir Archibald James Murray
1923 Lieutenant-General Sir Travers Edward Clarke
1941 Field-Marshal Sir Claude John Eyre Auchlinleck
1947 Brigadier-General Eric E.J. Moore
1960 Major-General Denis Grattan Moore
1966 Major-General Ewing H.W. Grimshaw

Battle honours
Martinique 1762, Havannah, St Lucia 1778, South Africa 1835, South Africa 1846–47, Relief of Ladysmith, South Africa 1899–1902, Le Cateau, Retreat from Mons, Marne 1914, Aisne 1914, Messines 1914, Messines 1917, Armentières 1914, Aubers, Festubert 1915, Somme 1916, Somme 1918, Bazentin, Guillemont, Ginchy, Ancre 1916, Arras 1917, Scarpe 1917, Ypres 1917, Ypres 1918, Pilckem, Langemarck 1917, Polygon Wood, Broodseinde, Poelcappelle, Cambrai 1917, Cambrai 1918, St Quentin, Rosières, Hindenburg Line, Beaurevoir, Courtrai, Selle, Sambre, France and Flanders 1914–18, Kosturino, Struma, Macedonia 1915–17, Helles, Landing at Helles, Krithia, Suvla, Landing at Suvla, Scimitar Hill, Gallipoli 1915–16, Egypt 1916, Gaza, Jerusalem, Tell 'Asur, Palestine 1917–18, Defence of Arras, Ypres-Comines Canal, North-West Europe 1940, Two Tree Hill, Bou Arada, Oued Zarga, Djebel Bel Mahdi, Djebel Tanngoucha, North Africa 1942–43, Landing at Sicily, Solarino, Simeto Bridgehead, Adrano, Centuripe, Simeto Crossing, Pursuit to Messina, Sicily 1943, Termoli, Trigno, San Salvo, Sangro, Garigliano Crossing, Minturno, Anzio, Cassino II, Massa Tambourini, Liri Valley, Rome, Advance to Tiber, Trasimene Line, Monte Spaduro, Argenta Gap, Italy 1943–45, Middle East 1942, Yenangyaung 1942, Donbaik, Burma 1942–43

Motto
Nec Aspera Terrent (Nor do difficulties deter or By difficulties undaunted)

Nicknames
The Skins (27th Foot), The Lumps (108th Foot)

5th ROYAL IRISH LANCERS, 1689–1922

Formation

This regiment was just one of six regiments that were raised under the terms of a royal warrant of 1 January 1689. All of these regiments, five cavalry and one infantry regiment, were raised at Enniskillen. The regiment's first colonel was James Wynne who raised and initially commanded the regiment.

Initially simply referred to as Wynne's Inniskillen Dragoons it was officially designated as the 5th Dragoons in 1690 and, in 1704, was re-designated as the Royal Dragoons of Ireland. In 1751 the regiment was re-titled as the 5th Regiment of Dragoons, this being changed to 5th (or Royal Irish) Regiment of Dragoons in 1756. As was common practice at the time, during the early period of its history, the regiment was often referred to using the name of its colonel.

Operational history

The Jacobite War in Ireland

1689   The regiment fought at the battle of Newtownbutler on 31 July.
1690   It took part in the battle of the Boyne, 1 July 1690.
1691   Detachments of the regiment were based at Ballyshannon and Belturbet. The regiment was also present at the capture of Athlone in June 1691. It fought at the battle of Aughrim on 12 July and later served in mopping-up operations in Sligo.
1692   The regiment formed part of the garrison at Fermoy.

Nine Years War, 1688–97

1694   In April the regiment boarded ship for Flanders where it remained until 1697, taking part in several engagements. Following the Treaty of Ryswick, it returned to Ireland .

War of the Spanish Succession, 1701–14

1702   The regiment sailed to reinforce Malborough's army in Holland where the regiment was known among the army as 'Ross's Dragoons', after its commanding officer.
1704   The regiment was officially re-named as the Royal Dragoons of Ireland and two more troops were sent to Holland.

During the course of this campaign, the regiment was present at all the major battles, including Brenham (1704), Ramillies (1706), Oudenarde (1708) and Malplaquet (1709). At Ramillies it charged alongside the Scots Greys and captured two regiments of French grenadiers; the Regiment du Roi and the Regiment de Picardie. The regiment was allowed to wear grenadier distinctions, including mitre head-dress, as a result of this action.

1713   The regiment was placed on the Establishment of Ireland and suffered as a result. It was broken up into squadron and troop detachments and posted at different barracks all over the country, only coming together once or twice a

	year for reviews. It also suffered due to financial strictures and morale plummeted.
1796	The regiment was stationed in Ireland for the rest of the 18th century and in 1796 it assembled at Bantry Bay to oppose the expected French invasion, which never materialized.
1798	At the time of the rebellion, the regiment was split up among various barracks around the country. Morale was low and its proficiency was in doubt. It was deemed that it had not responded effectively to the rebellion and rumours that it had been infiltrated by large number of United Irishmen led to an investigation. While it was found that only a handful of men were sympathetic to the rebel cause, it was decided to disband the regiment. The disbandment parade took place at Chatham in April 1799.
1858	In accordance with a decision to augment the British cavalry by adding two new regiments, on 9 January 1858 the regiment was re-raised as the 5th (Royal Irish) Light Dragoons (Lancers). Due to its previous disbandment, however, it lost its seniority in the list of regimental precedence.
1860	The re-formed regiment left depots at Newbridge and the Curragh and transferred to Aldershot.
1863–74	The regiment was stationed at Cawnpore in India.
1874	The regiment returned to England where it performed garrison duties in various stations.
1884	The 5th Royal Irish Lancers provided a detachment for the Heavy Division of the Camel Corps, assigned to the Gordon Relief Expedition. This detachment took part in the battle of Abu Klea, where its commanding officer, Major L. Carmichael, and six troopers were killed.
1885	Two squadrons of the regiment took part in the Gordon Relief Expedition and took part in several actions including Hasheen, Tamai and Suakin. At the end of the campaign it was awarded the battle honour 'Suakin 1885', the regiment's first battle honour since Malplaquet, over 170 years previously.
1888–98	The regiment was stationed in India, being based at various stations including Meerut and Muttra. In January 1898 it was ordered to South Africa as war seemed increasingly likely. On its arrival in South Africa in February, the regiment was initially stationed at Ladysmith and Pietermaritzburg.

2nd Anglo-Boer War, 1899–1902

During the course of this war, the 5th Royal Irish Lancers took part in several major campaigns and battles including the siege of Ladysmith and the battle of Belfast. Perhaps its most important action was at Elandslaagte in October 1899 where it took part in a charge against Boer forces.

1902	At the end of the Anglo-Boer War the regiment returned to England, where it was based at Colchester, York and Aldershot.

1910   The regiment was posted to Dublin. Due to the poor performance of the regimental officers in a number of reviews, the inspector-general designated the regiment as being 'unfit for service'.

1914   The regiment was stationed at the Curragh Camp as part of the 3rd Cavalry Brigade. The regiment's officers were implicated in the Curragh Mutiny, 18 out of 20 threatening to resign if ordered to implement government policy in Ireland.

The First World War, 1914–18

1914   The regiment was based in Dublin at the outbreak of the war. It was assigned to 3rd Cavalry Brigade of the Cavalry Division in August and went to France as part of the BEF. In September 1914, it was transferred to Major-General Sir Hubert Gough's command, which was later designated as the 2nd Cavalry Division, of which it formed the 3rd Brigade.

        The regiment took part in the retreat from Mons, being the last cavalry regiment to leave the town. During 1914 it also took part in the battles of Mons, Le Cateau, the Marne, the Aisne, Messines and the first battle of Ypres.

1915–18   While the regiment formed part of the cavalry reserve and waited for the decisive breakthrough promised by the generals, it also took turns serving as infantry in the trenches. In this capacity it distinguished itself in several actions, most notably Guillemont Farm (June 1917) and Bourlon Wood.

        It took part in the pursuit of the retreating German army to Mons and was allowed the honour of being the first regiment to re-enter the town when it was retaken. This event was later the subject of a painting by Caton-Woodville. In November 1918 the regiment was attached to the Canadian Corps.

Post-war and amalgamation

The regiment was stationed with the army of occupation in Germany until November 1919 when it was sent to India, having taken part in the victory parade in London. On its arrival in India it was based at Risalpur and later Peshawar.

By 1921 rumours began to circulate that the regiment was to be disbanded. The officers were offered the choice of either becoming a battalion of the Royal Tank Corps or being disbanded. They chose the latter option and the regiment was disbanded in July 1921.

    Due to a change in policy it was decided to re-form the regiment in April 1922 and to amalgamate it with the 16th Lancers. This reversal in policy was carried out but by then the majority of the units officers and enlisted men had transferred into other units. The 5th Royal Irish Lancers provided the officers and men for D Squadron of the new amalgamated regiment which was titled as the 16th/5th Queen's Royal Lancers, the 16th Lancers taking precedence in the title due to the 5th Royal Irish Lancers previous disbandment in 1799.

This amalgamation effectively ended the regiment's history as a distinct Irish regiment, although efforts were made to maintain the Irish contingent in D squadron. This regiment had a distinguished record in the Second World War, serving with the 6th Armoured Division in North Africa and Italy. During the Cold War it served in Germany with the British Army of/on the Rhine (BAOR).

The 16th/5th Lancers were further amalgamated with the 17th/21st Lancers in 1993 to form the Queen's Royal Lancers. D Squadron maintains the traditions of the 5th Lancers.

Colonels

1689	Brigadier-General James Wynne
1695	General the Hon. Charles Ross
1715	Colonel the Hon. Thomas Sydney
1729	General the Hon. Charles Ross
1732	Lieutenant-General Owen Wynne
1737	Richard, Viscount Molesworth
1758	General John Mostyn
1760	General Sir Joseph Yorke, Lord Dover
1787	General Robert Cuninghame, Lord Rossmore
1799	Regiment disbanded, re-instated in 1858
1858	General Sir James Charles Chatterton
1868	General Edward Pole
1872	General Henry Darby Griffith
1887	Lieutenant-General the Hon. Somerset John Gough-Calthorpe
1892	Lieutenant-General the Hon. Charles Wemyss Thesiger
1896	Lieutenant-General William Godfrey Dunham Massy
1906	Major-General Thomas Arthur Cooke
1908	Major-General Sir Henry Jenner Scobell
1912	Field-Marshall Sir Edmund Henry Hynman Allenby, 1st Viscount Allenby

Lieutenant-colonels (commanding officers)

To 1695	Lieutenant-Colonel Charles Ross (commanded the regiment before 1695)
1695	Lieutenant-Colonel Owen Wynne
1705	Lieutenant-Colonel Robert Hunter
1707	Brevet-Colonel Hugh Caldwell
1709	Brevet-Colonel Jonathan Hill
1711	Lieutenant-Colonel Richard Gore
1715	Lieutenant-Colonel Thomas Sydney (also Sidney)
1719	Lieutenant-Colonel Wriothy Betton
1729	Lieutenant-Colonel Alex Rose
1740	Lieutenant-Colonel William Cope
1749	Lieutenant-Colonel Christopher Clarges
1760	Lieutenant-Colonel William Hill

1768   Lieutenant-Colonel Hugh Cane
1778   Lieutenant-Colonel James Stewart
1797   Lieutenant-Colonel Charles William Stewart
1798   Lieutenant-Colonel Alex J. Goldie
1799   Regiment disbanded, re-instated in 1858
1858   Lieutenant-Colonel George Augustus Filmer Sulivan
1861   Lieutenant-Colonel Robert Portal
1871   Colonel William Godrey Dunham Massy
1879   Colonel William Lloyd Browne
1885   Colonel William Ward Bennett
1889   Colonel Alfred Bissel Harvey
1893   Lieutenant-Colonel Cecil F. Johnstone-Douglas
1894   Colonel James Scott-Chisholme
1899   Lieutenant-Colonel James F. Malcolm Fawcett
1901   Colonel Henry Jenner Scobell
1902   Colonel Edmund Henry Hynman Allen by (later Viscount Allenby)
1905   Lieutenant-Colonel Herman W. Gore Graham
1909   Lieutenant-Colonel George Francis Milner
1913   Colonel Arthur Parker
1917   Lieutenant-Colonel James Bruce Jardine
1919   Lieutenant-Colonel Herbert Anderson Cape

Regimental colours
Cavalry regiment do not carry large regimental standards as these are not practical. Sometimes a small cloth flag, or guidon, was attached to a lance and carried as a form of standard. An illustration of 1800 depicts a guidon of the 5th Royal Irish Dragoons with a blue flag, on which there was a gold harp and crown device.

Battle honours
At the time of the regiment's amalgamation in 1922, its battle honours were:

Blenheim, Ramillies, Oudenarde, Malplaquet, Suakin 1885; Defence of Ladysmith, South Africa 1899–1902; Mons, Le Cateau, Retreat from Mons, Marne 1914; Aisne 1914, Messines 1914, Ypres 1914, Ypres 1915, Gheluvelt; St Julien, Bellewaarde, Arras 1917, Scarpe 1917, Cambrai 1917; Somme 1918, St. Quentin, Amiens, Hindenburg Line, Canal du Nord, Pursuit to Mons, France and Flanders 1914–18.

Motto
'Quis Separabit' (Who shall separate us?)

Regimental music
Marches associated with the regiment include 'Let Erin Remember', 'The harp that once through Tara's Halls', the Wearing of the Green' and the 'Garryowen'.

Nicknames

Due to the red plastron fronts of the regiment lancer tunics, they were known as 'the Redbreasts'. Another nickname was 'the Daily Advertisers'.

8th KING'S ROYAL IRISH HUSSARS, 1693–2006

(From 1958, the Queen's Royal Irish Hussars and, from 1993, the Queen's Royal Hussars (the Queen's Own and Royal Irish))

Formation

Raised in February 1693 and recruited from Irish protestants. The regiment was raised by Sir Albert Conyngham who had previously raised a regiment of dragoons in Enniskillen in 1689. This earlier regiment evolved into the 6th Inniskilling Dragoons.

He gave command of the new regiment to his son, Lieutenant-Colonel Henry Conyngham, and it was known as 'Conyngham's Regiment of Irish Dragoons'. Many of the officers and men of Conygnham's Dragoons had seen service during the Jacobite Wars in Ireland and were experienced cavalry soldiers who had fought at Derry, Limerick, the Boyne and Aughrim.

Operational history

1693–7 Troops of the regiment stationed at Blessington, Baltinglass, Newry, Dundalk, Four Mile House and Castle Roche. At the Termination of the Nine Years' War in 1697, the regiment was reduced to peace time establishment.

1698 In June 1698 there were detachments of the regiment stationed at Cavan, Killeshandra, Belturbet, Enniskillen, Strabane, Letterkenny, Rathmullen, Limavady, Muff, Coleraine, Navan and Kells.

1700 Four troops of the regiment were disbanded and the remainder dismounted in the post-war reduction of the army.

1701 Two new troops were raised. In August 1701, funds were allocated to buy new horses.

1702 Detachments of the regiment were quartered at Limerick where they took part in a campaign to end the activities of bands of rapparees.

1703 The regiment was stationed at Nenagh.

War of the Spanish Succession, 1704–14

1704 Troops of the regiment stationed at Athlone, Nenagh, Charleville, Cappoquin and Mallow with smaller detachments in numerous other locations. The regiment re-assembled at Cork and embarked for Portugal 31 October 1704 where they arrived in November. Due to a shortage of horses, they remained in garrison at Lisbon and St. Ubes.

1705 The regiment formed part of Lord Peterborough's expedition to Catalonia and was present at the successful siege of Barcelona. In December they were stationed in Lerida.

1706 Present at the raising of the siege of St Mateo, the battle of San Estevan de Litera, the captures of Nules and Valencia (January–February 1706)

From April 1706, the regiment took part in the defence of Barcelona and the raising of the siege there. In July it took part in the capture of Origuela. Around 150 men of the regiment captured after the French captured Elche in October.

1707 A squadron of the regiment was present at the battle of Almanza, 15th April, where the allies were badly defeated by superior French forces. 31 men were killed including the regiment's commanding officer, Brigadier-General Killigrew. Lieutenant-Colonel John Pepper was appointed as the new colonel of the 8th Hussars.

1708 A dismounted detachment was based at Barcelona and the remainder of the regiment was quartered at Montblanco and Constantino. The regiment took part in the capture of Tortosa and a dismounted detachment formed part of General Stanhope's successful expedition to Minorca in September.

1709 The 8th Hussars spent the beginning of the year in Catalonia, encamped on the Segre river. In August it captured Balaguer and Ager and subsequently formed the garrions of these fortresses.

1710 In June and July the 8th Hussars took part in skirmishes against the French and Spanish at Balaguer and Portella. On 27 July they took part in the rout of French and Spanish cavalry at Almenara. In the aftermath of the battle the men of the regiment equipped themselves with the cross belts of the fallen enemy cavalry. One of the regimental nicknames – 'the Cross-belts'– dates from this event. On 20 August they took part in the battle of Saragossa. In early December 1710 the regiment was quartered at Brihuega and was besieged by a superior enemy force. The town surrendered on 9 December and the whole regiment was taken prisoner, along with the rest of the British force.

1711–12 The officers, NCOs and men of the regiment were returned in a series of prisoner exchanges, the last members of the 8th Hussars were not exchanged until December 1712.

1714 The remainder of the regiment returned to Ireland in April. Extra troops that had been raised for war service were disbanded. After the end of the War of Spanish Succession, the whole regiment was disbanded in the post-war reductions of the army under a warrant issued on 9 March 1714.

1715 After the ascension of George I and the Jacobite rebellion of 1715, a warrant ordering that the 8th Hussars be re-formed was issued in July 1715. By the end of August, six troops had been raised and were stationed in the south of England. On 6 October, they took part in a raid on Oxford during which several Jacobite sympathizers were arrested. They then went into winter quarters at Warwick and Banbury.

1717 The regiment was transferred to the Irish establishment.

1719 The 8th Hussars arrived in Ireland and troops were stationed at Roscommon, Castlebar, Headford, Portumna and Loughrea.

1735	Troops of the 8th Hussars stationed at Granard, Mullingar, Navan and Philipstown.
1736	The entire regiment was quartered in Dublin.

War of the Austrian Succession, 1740–8

1743	A detachment of the regiment sent to Flanders.
1744	A further draft from the 8th Hussars sent to Flanders while further troops were sent to Coventry, Warwick and Stratford.
1745	In December the 8th Hussars were sent to Doncaster to join the force that was assembling to march against the Jacobite army of Prince Charles Edward Stuart, the 'Young Pretender'. On 13 December they entered Preston, just missing the Jacobite army which had left a few hours earlier. Later in the day they fought a skirmish with the Jacobite rearguard at the village of Clifton. They took part in the successful siege of Carlisle.
1746	On 3 April they were present at the relief of Blair Castle. The regiment was then stationed at Earn and took no part in the battle of Culloden. After the battle they were stationed in a succession of Scottish towns and hunted down Jacobite fugitives. In August the 8th Hussars were stationed at Dunfries.
1748	Troops of the regiment stationed at St. Andrews, Dundee, Montrose and Aberdeen.
1748	Following the Peace of Aix-le-Chapelle, the regiment was reduced in size in a series of post-war reductions and returned to Ireland.
1749	Troops at Colooney, Longford, Granard and Sligo.
1750	Troops of the 8th Hussars at Charleville, Mallow, Cappoquin and Tullough.
1751	Troops at Loughrea, Headford and Portumna. Under the terms of a royal warrant of July 1751, the regiment was re-designated as the **8th Dragoons**.
1752	Troops as Tallow, Nenagh, Charleville and Doneraile.
1755	The entire regiment was stationed in Sligo town.
1763	The 8th Dragoons took no part in the Seven Years War but at the end of this war, it was reduced in size.
1768	The 8th Dragoons was stationed in Dublin and reviewed in the Phoenix Park on 28 May.
1769	Troops of the regiment stationed at Mallow, Tallaght and Cappoquin.
1771	Stationed at Loughrea.
1772	Stationed at Birr.
1773	The regiment was reviewed at Cavan and Belturbet and then went into barracks at Navan.
1775	Stationed at Athlone. The regiment was re-designated as the **8th Light Dragoons**.
1777	The regiment was re-designated as the **8th King's Royal Irish Light Dragoons**. The regiment was stationed at Clonmel and Clougheen.
1778	Stationed at Cork and Bandon. In October reviewed at Kinsale.
1779	Remained in Cork with detachments at Mallow.

1780	Stationed at Longford and Charleville.
1781	Troops stationed at Charleville, Bruff, Middleton, Castle Martyr, Tallaght and Cloyne. Some members of the regiment were engaged in recruiting men for the war in America.
1784	Stationed at Kilkenny
1785	Reviewed at Nenagh
1786	Stationed at Cashel
1787	At Mallow
1788	Reviewed at the Curragh
1790	Stationed at Ballinrobe

The French Revolutionary and Napoleonic Wars, 1793–1815

1792   While many of the countries of Europe were at war with France, Britain did not declare war until 1793. In 1792, the regiment was stationed at Longford.

1793   The regiment was increased to an establishment of 351 men, all ranks.

1794   In May the regiment was embarked aboard 12 ships in Dublin harbour and was landed in Liverpool, before marching to London. In April they boarded ships again and arrived at Ostend on 26 April 1794. As part of the Duke of York's expeditionary force in Flanders, they were attached to the Hanoverian division of Major-General Hamerstein. On 18 May they took part in an unsuccessful attempt to clear the French from the village of Bousbecque, losing 186 men killed, wounded or captured. On 8 June the regiment captured a bridge at Langemark. On 14 June it took part in the unsuccessful attack on Ghits. It subsequently formed part of the garrison at Nieuport, which it later left hurriedly on the advance of the French. Some of the regiment remained in the town and while the majority were later evacuated, 22 men were taken prisoner when the town fell. On 6 July, picquets of the regiment were driven out of Alost. Later in July it took part in a series of actions around Duffel. By this time it had been reduced to a single squadron of around 100 effectives. On 14 September, the regiment was based in Boxtel when it was attacked by the French and over-run. They then covered the withdrawal of Abercrombie's army until it had retreated across the Waal River. In November, it was based at Rheinswonde and took part in several skirmishes along the Waal River.

1795   During the early months of this year, the regiment and the whole army retreated from Holland and endured the terrible winter. In February, it crossed the Ems River and in May was quartered in Bremen where it acquired new horses and recruits. In November the regiment was ordered to return to England, arriving at Newcastle on 24 December.

1796   In January, it was based at Manchester. Having being moved to Coventry, it was ordered to join the British expedition to the Cape of Good Hope and embarked for South Africa on 11 August. The regiment disembarked at Cape Town on 11 November, where it was attached to the army of General Craig.

1797   The regiment spent the year encamped around Cape Town. There were delays in paying the men and morale and discipline suffered accordingly.

1798   When the Dutch colonists in the Cape refused to agree to an oath of loyalty to George III, a military expedition formed at Stellenbosch. This force included the 8th Light Dragoons and left Stellenbosch in September to begin operations in the interior. To prevent disturbances among the Dutch population, detachments were stationed in various hamlets such as Graaf Reinet and Bergvliet. During the night of 22 November, a fire swept through the dragoons' stables in Cape Town and also destroyed a large quantity of government stores.

1799 In February, members of the regiment were involved in quelling fresh disturbances at Graaf Reinet. The regiment remained in South Africa until 1802.

1801 In February the regiment received orders to send a troop to Egypt and it left Cape Town on 24 February. In September this detachment was encamped with the army at Rosetta.

1802 The detachment of the 8th Light Dragoons left Egypt for India in June. The 309 men of the regiment remaining in South Africa embarked at Cape Town on 11 October, destined for India.

First Mahratta War, 1803–5

1803 One troop was based at Vellore while the majority of the regiment was based in Bengal. The Vellore troop later rejoined the main body of the regiment, which had been increased to the full Indian establishment of 690 men. On 1 November, the 8th Light Dragoons took part in the battle of Leswari, during which its commanding officer, Col. Vandeleur was killed. After the battle the regiment returned to Cawnpore where they formed part of the town's garrison.

1804 In October it moved to Agra and on 17 November the regiment was present at the storming of the camp of the mahratta chief, Holkar, at Farakhabad and routing his army. In December the 8th Light Dragoons were present at the siege and capture of the fortress of Dig.

1805 On 2 March the regiment took part in a successful charge on the army of Amir Khan at Afzulgerh and then pursued him to Bhartpur, covering over 700 miles in 44 days. During the night of 29/30 March, it took part in another attack on the Holkar's camp, this time near Futtypore. In April the Raja of Bhartpur signed a treaty and the 8th Light Dragoons returned to Agra and went into quarters at Secundra, outside the city. In October, the regiment re-joined the army of General Lake in his campaign against Holkar and pursued him as far as the Bias River, near Armritsar.

1806 On 7 January, Holkar signed a peace treaty and the regiment returned to Secundra. At the end of the campaign, the regiment was awarded its first battle honour 'Leswarree'

1807 In January, the 8th Light Dragoons moved into quarters at Cawnpore.

1808 The regiment was marched to Khoundoghaut in a show of strength against the Sikhs and later returned to Cawnpore.

1809 Early in the year the regiment again marched into Sikh territory as far as the Sutlej River. It went into quarters at Ludhiana.

1812	A detachment of the regiment took part in the campaign in Bundelkhand and was present at the captures of the brigand forts at Kalinjar and Ajaygerh. In September the 8th Light Dragoons were sent to Benares in a show of strength against the Pindaris.
1813	The regiment returned to Cawnpore in April.

Anglo-Nepal War, 1814–16

1814	The 8th Light Dragoons took part in an expedition against the Gurkhas of Nepal and a squadron was sent to Saharanpur to join the force of General Gillespie. They occupied the town of Dehra and took part in the attack on the hill fort at Kalunga. During this attack on 31 October 1814, the 8th Light Dragoons fought dismounted but the assault failed and siege operations began. Kalunga fell on 27 November. The regiment then assembled at Meerut and were later based at Delhi in an effort to stop further unrest among mahratta chiefs in that area.
1815	Attached to the army of Major-General Dyson Marshall.

Second Mahratta and Pindari (or Pindaree) War, 1816–18

1817	In February, the regiment took part in the siege of Hatras and when the fortress fell, returned to Meerut. In October the regiment was assigned to General Donkin's army and took part in the campaign against the Pindaris.
1818	At the conclusion of these campaigns, the regiment returned to quarters at Meerut.
1820	The regiment moved to Cawnpore.
1822	It was ordered that the regiment be equipped and clothed as hussars and be re-designated as the **8th (The King's Royal Irish) Hussars**. In August they were ordered to return for home service and 280 men of the regiment were transferred to the 16th Lancers.
1823	The regiment boarded ship on 11 January and reached England on 5 May. On arrival it was quartered at Norwich and Ipswich. The regiment later moved to Romford.
1824	The regiment received its first issue of hussar uniforms. Quartered at Dorchester and Christchurch.
1825	At Hounslow and Hampton Court.
1826	At Brighton and Canterbury.
1827	The regiment returned to Ireland and was quartered at Dundalk
1828	At Newbridge
1829	Dublin
1830	Longford
1831	Manchester
1832	Newcastle
1833	Gloucester
1834	Coventry
1835	Hounslow
1836	Dublin
1837	Newbridge
1838	Dublin
1839	Dundalk and then to Leeds
1840	Norwich
1841	Manchester
1842	Hounslow and Hampton Court
1843	York (detachments at Newcastle and Leeds)

1844   Dundalk. In September, the regiment was moved to Dublin.

1845   Moved from Dublin in September and had headquarters at Longford with detachments at Athlone, Mohill, Clone and Dunmore.

1846   Moved to Cahir with detachments at Limerick, Dungarvan and Clonmel.

1847   In September, moved to Ballincollig, with detachments in Cork, Bandon and Fermoy.

1848   In July, the regiment moved to Newbridge with detachments in Dublin and Kilkenny. During the Young Ireland rebellion, a detachment of the regiment joined Major-General McDonald's flying column and operated around Ballingarry.

1849   The 8th Royal Irish Hussars moved to the Royal Barracks in Dublin and carried out various duties during Queen Victoria's visit that year. The regimental headquarters later moved to Newbridge and a further detachment was based at Carlow.

1850   In May the regiment moved to England and was based at Brighton with detachments at Dorchester and Towbridge.

1851   At Hampton Court and Hounslow.

1852   Troops of the regiment at Nottingham, Sheffield, Mansfield and Loughborough. A squadron of the regiment and the regimental band formed part of the Duke of Wellington's funeral procession in October.

1853   The regiment attended the large-scale exercises on Chobham Common.

The Crimean War, 1854–6

1854   In April the 8th Royal Irish Hussars were assigned to the Light Cavalry Brigade under the command of Lord Cardigan. The regiment moved to Exeter while a depot company was sent to Newbridge. It sailed from Plymouth in late April and arrived at Constantinople (Istanbul) on 20 May. From there it progressed to Varna to take part in operations against the Russians on the Danube. On 25th June, a squadron of the 8th Hussars took part in Lord Cardigan's expedition to the Danube, later dubbed 'the soreback reconnaissance'. On 31 August and 1 September, the regiment re-embarked on ships bound for the Crimea, where it landed on 16 September. It was present at the skirmish on the Bulganak River and after the battle of the Alma, pursued the fleeing Russian army. On 25 October, it took part in the Charge of the Light Brigade during the battle of Balaclava, losing 66 men killed and missing in action. The regiment was present at the battle of Inkerman on 5 November but was not engaged.

1855   On the arrival on reinforcements for the Light Brigade in April, the 8th Hussars joined the 10th and 11th Hussars and the 17th Lancers to form a Hussar Brigade. The regiment served throughout the siege of Sevastopol. In May a detachment of the 8th Hussars took part in General Sir George Brown's expedition to Kertch. In November the regiment boarded ship and was transported to Ismail where it went into winter quarters.

1856 In April the 8th Hussars boarded ship and returned to England where they were reviewed by Queen Victoria at Osborne House on 12 May. Five troops of the regiment were later based at Dundalk with one at Belfast. The regiment was awarded the Crimean War medal with the clasps 'Alma, Balaclava, Inkerman, Sevastopol'. It was awarded the same citations as battle honours.

The Indian Mutiny, 1857–9

1857 While detachments of the 8th Hussars had previously volunteered to go to India on the outbreak of the mutiny, the whole regiment received orders to embark for India in September. It sailed from Queenstown (Cobh) on 8 October and reached Bombay on 16 December.

1858 The regiment was then moved from Bombay to Bhooj, the capital of Cutch, which it reached in February. The 8th Hussars were present with General Roberts' brigade at the siege of Kotah, which fell on 30 March. It was heavily engaged with rebel sepoys at the captures of Morar and Gwalior in June. During the course of these actions, a member of the regiment killed the rebel leader, the Rani of Jhansi. A detachment of the regiment fought dismounted at the siege of Powrie, which fell on the 23 August. Another squadron engaged a force of mutineers at Beejapore on 5 September and inflicted heavy casualties. On 14 August, the 8th Hussars were present at the battle of Kotarrhea and again caused heavy casualties when the sepoy force broke and fled. Detachments of the regiment were present at the battles of Sindwaha (19 October) and Koorwye (25 October). On 14 November, detachments took part in the attack on a mutineer camp at Koondrye. A further detachment of the 8th Hussars were present at the battle of Chota Oodeypoor in December, an action that saw resulted in a decisive defeat for the rebel leader, Tantia Topee.

1859 The early part of the year was spent in the pursuit of several large bands of rebel sepoys. On 5 April the regiment took part in the battle of Boordah. In May the 8th Hussars went into quarters, some of its detachments having covered over 4,000 miles in the course of the campaign. The regiment was awarded the Indian Mutiny medal with the clasp 'Central India, 1857–58'. It was also awarded the battle honours 'Hindoostan' and 'Central India, 1857–8'.

1861 The 8th Hussars transferred to the Bengal presidency and was quartered at Meerut.

1863 The regiment was ordered to England in November.

1864 The first detachment of the regiment boarded ship at Calcutta on 9 January and reached England on 2 May and was later quartered at York.

1865 Based at Aldershot

1866 Detachments at Birmingham, Coventry, Weedon and Northampton.

1867 Headquaters at Manchester with detachments at Burnley, Bury and Ashton-under-Lyne.

1868 In Scotland at Hamilton and Perth.
1869 The regiment returned to Ireland and was based at Dundalk with squadrons in Belfast and Belturbet.
1870 At the Curragh Camp. Later in the year moved to Dublin to Islandbridge and Portobello barracks.
1871 In August the 8th Hussars were present at a grand review in the Phoenix Park in honour of the Prince of Wales (later Edward VII). At the end of the year it had detachments at the Curragh, Newbridge and Dublin.
1872 In May the regiment moved to the Curragh for annual manoeuvres. The headquarters were later based at Longford with detachments at Athlone, Gort, Dunmore and Castlebar. The regiment remained with its headquarters at Longford until 1875 and lived in poor conditions while there was an outbreak of glanders among the horses. Morale plummeted and many officers and NCOs either left the service or transferred to other regiments.
1875 The regiment was ordered to England and arrived at Aldershot in April.
1876 Regimental headquarters remained at Aldershot and the regiment attended large-scale exercises at Pointington Down and Salisbury.
1877 The regiment attended a royal review at Windsor Castle and then exercises at Ascot Heath. In September it moved to Hounslow Heath with a squadron at Hilsea. A small detachment served at orderlies at the Horse Guards in London.

Second Afghan War, 1878–1880

1878 The first detachment of the regiment left Portsmouth on 15 December.
1879 The forward part of the 8th Hussars reached Bombay on 15 January and proceeded to Muttra where it established regimental headquarters. In December the regiment was ordered to move to Hassan Abdul.
1880 Having passed through Meen Meer, Umballa, Jhelum and Rawlpindi, the 8th Hussars reached Hassan Abdul on 7 January and were ordered to Peshawar where it joined the cavalry brigade of the reserve division. It joined the Khyber Line Force under General Bright in March and undertook line of communication duties. Detachments of the 8th Hussars operated against the forces of the 'Moollah Fakir' around Maijena in May, pursuing them to the Safed Koh Mountains. At the end of May the regiment was ordered to return to India and in August they were stationed at Rawlpindi and detachments were later sent to Murree.
1881 The 8th Hussars were awarded the battle honour 'Afghanistan, 1879–80'.
1882 Reviewed at Rawlpindi.
1883 Stationed at Meerut.
1889 The 8th Hussars remained based at Meerut until July 1889 when it was ordered to prepare to leave for England. The first contingent of the regiment arrived at Portsmouth on 20 November and it was later stationed at Shorncliffe.

1890 The regiment moved to Aldershot while another detachment was based at Norwich.
1891 Stationed at Norwich. The 8th Hussars remained here until 1893 and built up a good relationship with the local inhabitants and also helping to extinguish a fire in the town on one occasion. On leaving they were presented with commemorative vases, a mess room clock for the NCOs mess and also illuminated addresses. A benefit concert was held for the regimental band on 14 July 1893.
1893 The 8th Hussars moved to Aldershot and after annual manoeuvres were moved to Hounslow.
1894 Stationed at Hounslow with a detachment at Hampton Court.
1895 The regiment took part in large-scale manoeuvres at Aldershot, reservists having been mobilized for this series of exercises. Headquarters remained at Hounslow. In September the regiment moved to Leeds with a detachment at York.
1896 Regimental headquarters remained at Leeds.
1897 The 8th Hussars returned to Ireland with headquarters at Cahir.
1898 The men of the regiment helped extinguish a fire at the Cahir flour mills and the town's inhabitants later presented the 8th Hussars with an address and a commemorative cup.
1899 Headquarters remained at Cahir while squadrons of the regiment took part in annual manoeuvres at the Curragh. It later took part in large-scale manoeuvres in the south of Ireland. On 26 December, the regiment received orders to mobilize for war.

2nd Anglo-Boer War (or the South African War), 1899–1902

1900 On 13 February the headquarters squadron and A and C squadrons embarked at Queenstown (Cobh) while B squadron embarked at Albert Docks, London, on 17 February. The regiment landed at Cape Town in March and was initially attached to the 4th Cavalry Brigade under General Dickson. During the course of the war, it took part in the following actions:

Occupation of Bloemfontein, 13 March
Skirmish at Karree, near Bloemfontein, 29 March
Relief of Wepener, the attack on Kromspruit Farm and Lewkop (or Leeuw Kop), 22 April
Thabanchu Mountain, 24 April
Occupation of Thabanchu, 28 April
Hout Nek, 1 May
Advance to Pretoria, May 1900
Sand River, 10 May
Klip River, 27 May
Action at Johannesburg, 28 May
Action at Dornkop, 29 May

Kalkheuvel, 3 June
Capture of Pretoria, June 1900
Diamond Hill, 11 June
Olifantsfontein, 11–17 July
Capture of Pan Station, 27 July
Capture of Wonderfontein Station, 1 August
Battle and capture of Belfast, SA, 26–27 August
Olifants Nek, 23 December

1901 Regiment based at Johannesburg, January 1901
Battle of Kaalfontein Station, 12 January
Battle of Nondweni, Zululand, 28 August
1902 Defence of Cork Farm, 13 January

At the signing of the Peace of Vereenniging, the regiment was based at Vlakfontein. It moved to Pretoria where it stayed until October 1903 when it embarked for England, where it was based at Aldershot. For its service in the 2 Anglo-Boer War the regiment was awarded the single battle honour 'South Africa'.

1903 Aldershot
1904 Aldershot and Southampton
1905 Memorial to South African War dead erected in St Patrick's Cathedral, Dublin. The regiment was remained at Aldershot.
1906 At Aldershot. Took part in army corps manoeuvres.
1907 Moved from Aldershot to Colchester.
1908 The regiment remained at Colchester.
1909 In October the regiment embarked for India, the leading elements arriving at Lucknow in November.
1910 Remained at Lucknow with a detachment at Calcutta. In late 1910, the 8 Hussars made a tour of Bengal in a demonstration against potential dissidents.
1911 The regimental HQ remained at Lucknow while detachments carried out special duties in Calcutta.
1912 Remained at Lucknow but marched to Calcutta for special duties.
1913 Lucknow.
1914 Until the outbreak of the First World War, the regiment served with the Lucknow Cavalry Brigade, based at Ambala.

The First World War, 1914–1918

The regiment began mobilizing for war at Ambala on 31 August. It embarked at Bombay and sailed for Marseilles were its leading elements arrived on 10 November and were based at La Valentine, outside Marseilles.

The 8th Hussars were initially attached to the Ambala Cavalry Brigade of the 1st Indian Cavalry Division. In 1916 it transferred to the 2nd Indian Cavalry Division and in November 1916, this division was re-designated as the 5th Cavalry Division.

In October 1918 the regiment joined the 1st Brigade of the 1st Cavalry Division. It remained horsed and in France and Flanders for the entire war.

The regiment was awarded the following battle honours in the First World War:

Givenchy, 1914	St Quentin	Hindenburg Line
Somme, 1916–18	Bapaume, 1918	St Quentin Canal
Bazentin	Rosières	Beaurevoir
Flers-Courcelette	Amiens	Pursuit to Mons
Cambrai, 1917–18	Albert, 1918	France and Flanders, 1914–18

1919 At the end of the war the regiment formed part of the army of occupation in Germany, being based at Grottenhorton from January to March in 1919. On 28 March the 8th Hussars boarded ship at Antwerp sailed for England. On their arrival they were based at Shorncliffe. On 18 November the regiment boarded ship for India, reaching Lucknow on 12 December.

1920 Due to an outbreak of disturbances in Mesopotamia (modern-day Iraq), the regiment boarded ship on 12 October at Bombay and sailed for Basra. On its arrival in Mesopotamia it proceeded to Kut-el-Armara and from there to Bagdhad. In November it was moved to Mandali on the Persian (Iranian) border. In December the regiment was moved to Nineveh, near Mosul.

1921 The 8th Hussars took part in operations around Tel-el-Far and Pesk Kabur. In September the regiment moved back to Bagdhad. It left Basra on 26 November, bound for Bombay. Shortly after reaching India, it re-embarked for Egypt, where it arrived in December. The regiment was billeted at Helmieh, a suburb of Cairo, and patrolled the city in order to put down political disturbances. Two squadrons were later billeted on Gezireh, an island in the Nile.

1922 In April the regiment moved to barracks at Abbassia to the north-east of Cairo and due to continued disturbances a detachment was later sent to Gezireh again. In September, the regiment was under orders to move to Constantinople (Istanbul) as it was feared that Turkish forces would try to re-take the city. As tensions eased, this move did not take place.

1923 In August the regiment received orders to return to England. Departing from Alexandria, it arrived at Southampton on 12 September. The 8th Hussars were stationed at York and would remain there until 1926.

1924 At York. In June members of the regiment who had served in Iraq were issued with the General Service Medal and the clasp 'Iraq'.

1925 At York. Took part in the military tattoo at Wembley.

1926 At York. During the general strike, the regiment was called out in May to aid the civil power. In June, the 8th Hussars took part in a military tattoo in York and, in July, a detachment was present at a ceremony to mark the anniversary of the battle of the Boyne. This ceremony took place at Leeds. A draft of the regiment was dispatched to Egypt in September to reinforce the 3rd Hussars. In December the regiment moved to Wiesbaden as part of the army of occupation in Germany.

1934　The regiment was moved to Egypt where it remained until the outbreak of WWII.

The Second World War, 1939–45

At the outbreak of war the regiment was equipped with MK III and MK VI light tanks but the regiment later received both Grant and Stuart tanks. It was assigned to the 7th Armoured Brigade and saw extensive service during the North African campaign of 1940–2, serving in numerous battles including Sidi Barrani, Buq Buq, Sidi Rezegh, Gazala, Mersa Metruh and El Alamein.

In 1943 the 8th Royal Irish Hussars was assigned to the 7th Armoured Division and served in Italy before returning to England to prepare preparation for the Normandy landings.

From 1944 it served in Europe and during the Normandy campaign, it saw heavy fighting the bocage country. The 8th Royal Irish Hussars remained in the European theatre for the rest of the war and fought in numerous other battles including Mont Pincon, the Dives Crossing and the campaign on the Rhineland in 1945. During the course of its WWII service, the regiment suffered 196 fatal casualties.

1947　The regiment returned to England after service with the army of occupation in Germany.

The Korean War, 1950–3

1950　The 8th King's Royal Irish Hussars was sent to Korea where it was attached to the 29th Infantry Brigade Group and later the 1st Commonwealth Division. It took part in several actions in this war including the battle at Hill 327 and the during the Imjin campaign.

1952　The regiment was returned to Germany where it served with BAOR.[12]

1958　The regiment was amalgamated with the 4th Queen's Own Hussars to form the **Queen's Royal Irish Hussars**. Following this amalgamation, the new regiment served in England and also in Germany with the BAOR. Overseas service also included tours of Aden (1961) and Malaya (1962).

1st Gulf War, 1990–1

1990　The regiment was posted to the Persian Gulf where it formed part of the 7th Armoured Brigade. It took part in the operations in Iraq in 1991 and was awarded the battle honours 'Wadi al Batin' and 'Gulf 1991'.

1993　The Queen's Royal Irish Hussars were amalgamated with the Queen's Own Hussars to form the **Queen's Royal Hussars (Queen's Own and Royal Irish)**. Since 1993, this new amalgamated regiment has served in Germany (BAOR), England and Northern Ireland while also completing tours in Bosnia (1996) and Kosovo (2001).

---

12 BAOR = British Army of the Rhine.

Iraq, 2003

2003   The regiment was deployed in Iraq in 2003 as part of 20th Armoured Brigade.
2004   The regiment carried out a further tour of Iraq as part of 1st Mechanised Brigade.
2006   In May 2006, the Queen's Royal Hussars were deployed in Iraq for another tour.

The regiment maintains its HQ and depot in the Regent's Park Barracks in London and includes Northern Ireland in its recruiting area. The traditions of the 8th King's Royal Irish Hussars are maintained by the regiment (Queen's Royal Hussars).

Colonels-in-chief

1953   Field-Marshal, HRH, Prince Philip, the Duke of Edinburgh (remained as colonel and joint colonel after 1958 and 1993 amalgamations)
1993   HM Queen Elizabeth, the Queen Mother (Colonel of the Queen's Own Hussars; remained as joint colonel after 1993 amalgamation)

Colonels

1693   Major-General Henry Conygham
1706   Major-General Robert Killigrew
1707   Major-General John Pepper
1719   Major-General Phineas Bowles
1722   Brigadier-General Richard Munden
1725   Field-Marshal Sir Robert Rich
1731   Major-General Charles, 8th Baron Cathcart
1733   Brigadier-General Sir Adolphus Oughton
1737   Lieutenant-General Clement Neville
1740   Lieutenant-General Richard St George
1755   General John, 3rd Earl of Waldegrave
1758   General Joseph (Yorke), 1st Baron Dover
1760   General John Severne
1787   General Charles, 1st Earl Grey
1789   General Francis Lascelles
1797   General Charles, 1st Earl Grey (reappointed)
1799   General Sir Robert Laurie
1804   General Sir John Floyd
1818   General Sir Banastre Tarleton
1833   General Sir William Keir Grant
1839   Lieutenant-General Sir Joseph Straton
1840   Lieutenant-General Philip Philpot
1843   General Sir John Brown
1855   Field-Marshal Charles (Bingham), 3rd Earl of Lucan

1865 General Lawrenson
1868 General John Charles Hope Gibsone
1875 Lieutenant-General Rodolph De Salis
1880 General William Charles Forrest
1886 Lieutenant-General Sir Charles Craufurd Fraser, VC
1895 Major-General William Mussenden
1910 General Sir Bryan Thomas Mahon
1930 Brigadier-General John Van Der Byl
1948 Colonel (Air Marshal) Sir John E.A. Baldwin (continued as joint colonel with Sir Winston Churchill after 1958 amalgamation)
1958 Sir Winston Churchill (colonel of 4th Queen's Own Hussars; continued as joint colonel until his death in 1965)
1965 Lt.-Col. George Jardine Kidston-Montgomerie of Southannan
1969 General Sir John Winthrop Hackett
1975 Major-General John M. Strawson
1985 General Sir Brian L.G. Kenny
1993 Major-General Richard E. Barron
1999 Major-General David J.M. Jenkins
2004 Major-General Arthur George Denaro

Lieutenant-colonels, 8th King's Royal Irish Hussars, 1750–1924
1750 Lt.-Col. John Severne
1760 Lt.-Col. William Lushington
1768 Lt.-Col. Francis Lascelles
1780 Lt.-Col. Andrew Lyon
1781 Lt.-Col. the Hon. Robert Henry Southwell
1788 Lt.-Col. Richard St George
1789 Lt.-Col. Richard Rich Wilford
1794 Lt.-Col. Thomas Pakenham Vandeleur
1803 Lt.-Col. John Sullivan Wood
1807 Lt.-Col. Robert Rollo Gillespie
1813 Lt.-Col. the Hon. Henry Westenra
1824 Lt.-Col. Lord George William Russell
1828 The Hon. George Berkeley Molyneux
1841 Lt.-Col. James McCall
1847 Lt.-Col. Frederick George Shewell
1856 Lt.-Col. Rodolph De Salis
1865 Lt.-Col. Francis Edmund Macnaghtan
1871 Lt.-Col. John Puget
1874 Lt.-Col. William Mussenden
1879 Lt.-Col. John Worthy Chaplain, VC
1883 Lt.-Col. Hugh Langtry
1887 Lt.-Col. Thomas Astell St Quentin

1892 Lt.-Col. James Davidson
1897 Lt.-Col. Peter Legh Clowes
1901 Lt.-Col. Charles Edward Duff
1905 Lt.-Col. Henry Newman Morgan Thoyts
1909 Lt.-Col. Henry Foulkes Deare
1913 Lt.-Col. Francis William Mussenden
1917 Lt.-Col. Guy Macaulay Mort
1920 Lt.-Col. John Van Der Byl
1924 Lt.-Col. Andrew Curell

Battle honours, 8th King's Royal Irish Hussars and Queen's Royal Irish Hussars
Leswaree, Hindoostan, Alma, Balaclava, Inkerman, Sevastopol, Central India, Afghanistan 1879–80, South Africa 1900–2, Givenchy 1914, Somme 1916, Somme 1918, Bazentin, Flers-Courcelette, Cambrai 1917, Cambrai 1918, St Quentin, Bapaume 1918, Rosières, Amiens, Albert 1918, Hindenburg Line, St Quentin Canal, Beaurevoir, Pursuit to Mons, France and Flanders 1914–18, Villers Bocage, Mont Pincon, Dives Crossing, Nederrijn, Best, Lower Maas, Roer, Rhine, North-West Europe 1944–5, Egyptian Frontier 1940, Sidi Barrani, Buq Buq, Sidi Rezegh 1941, Relief of Tobruk, Gazala, Bir el Igela, Mersa Matruth, Alam el Halfa, El Alamein, North Africa 1940–2, Seoul, Hill 327, Imjin, Kowang-San, Korea 1950–1, Wadi al Batin, Gulf 1991.

Regimental music
Tunes associated with the regiment include 'St Patrick's Day', 'A galloping 8th Hussar' and the 'March of the Scottish Archers'.

Motto
Pristinae Virtutis Memores (Mindful of former valour or The memory of former valour)

Nicknames
'The Cross Belts'. This nickname was adopted after the regiments actions at the battle of Alemara in 1710. 'The Twenty-Fives.'[13]

THE ROYAL IRISH ARTILLERY, 1755–1801

Formation
While a 'train of artillery' was established in Ireland by royal warrant on 22 March 1687, there was no permanent artillery regiment until the mid-eighteenth century. In

---

[13] Through the 1958 and 1993 amalgamations further mottos, music and nicknames have been added to the regimental list. Only those referring to the original regiment are included here.

1755 an officer and a party of 24 NCOs and men were sent from Woolwich to form the nucleus of a new artillery in Ireland.

One of this original contingent was Captain John Straton (or Stratton), who remained associated with the regiment until its amalgamation with the Royal Regiment of Artillery in 1801. For the rest of 1755, the artillery train in Ireland was re-organized and received new equipment and a series of reviews and drills took place in the Phoenix Park.

Operational history

1756   The official warrant for the formation of this warrant was issued on 1 April 1756, the unit being designated as the 'Artillery Company in Ireland'. Another draft of 60 NCOs and men was sent from Woolwich under the command of a major. The company was based in Dublin and Kilkenny during the year, carrying out a series of exercises in the Phoenix Park.

1757   The company remained in Dublin with its HQ in Dublin Castle. Artillery pieces were assigned to every infantry battalion in Ireland.

1758   The unit remained in Dublin but attended a military camp in Wicklow. Target practices took place in the Phoenix Park and in Ringsend.

1759   During the refurbishment of the Royal Barracks (now Collins Barracks) in Dublin, the company was billeted in a camp in the Phoenix Park.

1760   In February a warrant was passed increasing the establishment of the unit to four companies and re-designating it as the 'Regiment of Royal Irish Artillery'. Later in the same month, a detachment of the regiment was sent to Carrickfergus to oppose the French landing there but arrived after the French had left. In May a detachment attended the 'camp of exercise' in Cahir. In a warrant of September the regiment was allocated the 'King's House in Chapelizod' to use as its HQ and barracks.

1761   The regiment's new HQ at Chapelizod was renovated while stores and equipment were moved from Dublin Castle. From July to October the regiment was encamped in the Phoenix Park and a series of target practices were carried out. In late 1761, the regiment was in cantonments in Maynooth and Chapelizod.

1762   The firing range in the Phoenix Park was extended while further houses were leased in Chapelizod for accommodation. At the end of the year, the regiment numbered 432, all ranks.

1768   One of the members of the regiment, David Blakeney, made a series of complaints about the administration of the unit. After a court-martial, he was sentenced to 200 lashes. The regiment remained based at Chapelizod and carried out a series of exercises and reviews in the Phoenix Park. At the end of the year, the regiment numbered 228, all ranks.

1770   Detachments of the regiment were sent to Limerick, Cork and Dungannon Fort.

1771   Two members of the regiment were tried and found guilty of highway robbery and were transported for life.

1774 In July the regiment took part in a series of manoeuvres in the Phoenix Park with other regiments.

American War of Independence, 1775–83

1775 In August 47 men of the regiment volunteered for service in America.

1776 A detachment of the regiment was sent to Cork.

1777 In March, another draft of 70 men of the regiment was sent to America. A further 175 men were recruited into the regiment. On 19th September, the detachment in America fought in the First Battle of Saratoga at the action at Freeman's Farm. On 7 October they took part in the Second Battle of Saratoga and were in the action at Bemis Heights.

1778 In January 150 officers and men volunteered for the campaign in America. Further detachments were sent to Charlesfort and Dungannon Fort. Under the terms of a warrant of April 1778, the regiment was increased from four to six companies. Detachments were later sent to Clonmel, Kinsale, Belfast, Charlesfort and Clogheen. Members of the regiment also manned floating batteries in Dublin harbour. At the end of 1778, the regiment's strength was 534, all ranks.

1779 Detachments of the regiment were sent to Carrickfergus and Limerick while other detachments were garrisoned the Magazine Fort and also manned floating batteries in Dublin harbour. The regiment numbered 612 men, all ranks, at the end of the year.

1780 Detachments continued to man the floating batteries in Dublin harbour.

1781 Detachments were sent to Cork and Castlebar.

1782 While the floating batteries in Dublin continued to be manned, detachments were sent to Cork.

1783 Detachments of the regiment were stationed in Cork and Carlow. In September 1783, under the terms of a royal warrant, the regiment was reduced from 701 to 386 men. The discharged men were encouraged to join the army of the East India Company.

1784 The regiment remained in Dublin for next number of years, carrying out exercises in the Phoenix Park and also providing troops to garrison the Magazine Fort.

French Revolutionary and Napoleonic Wars, 1793–1815

1793 The establishment of the regiment was raised from six to ten companies. In August, two companies were sent to join the Duke of York's expedition to the Low Countries. They later took part in the siege of Dunkirk. In November another company was sent to the West Indies.

1794 Three further companies were sent to Flanders where they joined the Duke of York's army. Further drafts were later sent as reinforcements. The company in the West Indies took part in the captures of Martinique, Guadaloupe and St Lucia. It lost many men due to illness. In August 1794 the regimental strength was 910 men, all ranks. Further recruits were enlisted later in the

	year and several drafts were sent to England. By October 1794, the regiment had been enlarged to 20 companies and numbered over 2,000 men.
1795	During this year, there were companies of the regiment on foreign service on the continent and in the West Indies. In September, 17 companies of the regiment were at different stations in Ireland and numbered 1,528 men, all ranks.
1796	Detachments of the regiment were based at various barracks in the country. In December, they joined forces in Bantry Bay on receiving news of the arrival of the French Fleet off the Irish coast.
1797	In June, a detachment of 176 men, all ranks, was sent to the West Indies to reinforce the company of the regiment stationed there.
1798	A detachment of 159 men was sent to Chatham. In July, there were 15 companies based in Ireland and 5 in the West Indies. During the 1798 Rebellion, detachments of the regiment served in the field with other Crown forces and were present at a number of engagements with the United Irishmen. On 29 May, two of the regiment's howitzers were captured after an action near Wexford. Three more guns were captured at Gorey on 4 June but these were recovered at Vinegar Hill on 21 June. Companies of the regiment were present at the battle of Castlebar on 27 August and six of their guns were captured by the French. These were recovered at Ballinamuck on 8 September. Some members of the regiment were captured by the United Irishmen and made serve guns at New Ross and Vinegar Hill. One captured gunner was later court-martialled and executed for aiding the United Irishmen during the rebellion. In September the regiment was re-organized into two brigades (a light and heavy brigade).
1799	In early 1799 there were 15 companies of the regiment in Ireland and 5 in the West Indies, numbering 2,032 men, all ranks. In November, a further detachment of 108 officers and men was sent to Martinique and Barbados.
1800	A party of 96 officers and men left Ireland in January for the West Indies. In Ireland, detachments of the regiment were stationed at Islandbridge, Naas, Arklow, Wexford, Charlemount, Belfast, Derry, Coleraine, Dundalk, Enniskillen, Cork, Clonmel, Bandon, Limerick, Tarbet, Waterford, Kilkenny, Athlone, Galway, Carrick-on-Shannon, Castlebar, Lough Swilly and Carrickfergus,
1801	Following the Act of Union, the regiment was reduced to ten companies and was incorporated into the Royal Regiment of Artillery as it seventh battalion. The regiment's band and invalid company was also absorbed into the Royal Regiment of Artillery. Many officers, NCOs and men of the regiment continued to serve with the Royal Artillery for the remainder of the Napoleonic Wars and took part in the campaigns in the West Indies, the Low Countries, the Peninsula and France.

Regimental officers

Colonels in chief
1760	James, Marquis of Kildare	1797	Henry, Earl of Carhampton
1766	Richard, Earl of Shannon	1800	The Hon. Thomas Pakenham
1770	Charles, Marquis of Drogheda		

Colonels 'en seconde'
1760	Bernard Hale	1797	The Hon. Thomas Pakenham
1789	Henry, Earl of Carhampton	1800	Marcus Beresford

Colonels Commandant
1783	John Straton	1795	Richard Bettesworth

Second Colonels
1795	William Brady	1800	John Pratt
1795	Lucius Barber		

Lieutenant-Colonels Commandant
1760	John Rutter	1795	John D. Arabin
1762	Daniel Chenevix	1795	William Buchanan
1776	John Straton	1797	John Bourchier
1783	Richard Bettesworth	1800	Joseph Walker
1795	William Wright		

Lieutenant-Colonels
1793	William Brady	1795	William Buchanan
1793	Lucius Barber	1795	Richard Legge
1795	John Pratt	1795	John Bourchier
1795	William Wright	1795	John Walker
1795	John D. Arabin	1800	Joseph Sneyd
1795	Charles Moore	1800	Hugh Swayne

18th KING'S IRISH HUSSARS, 1759–1821

Formation

By 1858 three regiments had borne the title of 18th Light Dragoons/Hussars. Only one of these was officially designated as an Irish regiment. In 1759 a regiment of light dragoons had been raised in England and designated as the 18th Light Dragoons. In 1763 it was re-numbered as the 17th Light Dragoons and would later be re-designated as the 17th (Duke of Cambridge's Own) Lancers.

In 1759 another regiment of light dragoons was raised in Ireland by the Marquis of Drogheda. This regiment, commonly known as the Drogheda Light Horse, was originally designated as the 19th Light Dragoons but was re-numbered in 1763 as the 18th Light Dragoons. During the Peninsular War, it was often referred to as 'Drogheda's Cossacks'. After much campaigning in the Napoleonic wars, it was disbanded in 1821. This second regiment was distinctly Irish in its composition but this association did not continue after the disbandment of 1821.

The third incarnation of the 18th Light Dragoons came in 1858 when the regiment was re-raised at Leeds and designated as the 18th Hussars. While it was allowed to retain the peninsular battle honours of the disbanded 18th King's Irish Hussars, it was no longer an Irish regiment. Therefore, for the purposes of this gazetteer, it is only the Irish 18th Light Dragoons/Hussars of 1759 to 1821 that will be dealt with. It is of interest to note that the Duke of Wellington commanded a troop of this regiment early in his career (1792–3).

Operational history

1759   The regiment was raised in Ireland by Charles Moore, 1st Marquess of Drogheda. It was initially designated as the 19th Light Dragoons and was known locally as the 'Drogheda Light Horse'.

1763   The regiment was renumbered as the 18th Light Dragoons.

French Revolutionary and Napoleonic Wars, 1793–1815

1795   The regiment served in Ireland until 1795 when it was sent to the West Indies and took part in the Maroon War. Decimated by ill-heath, it returned to Ireland in 1798 under the command of the regimental surgeon.

1799   It was attached to the command of the Duke of York and served in the campaign in Holland.

1807   The regiment was re-designated as an hussar regiment and was re-equipped and uniformed accordingly. It took the new title of **18th King's Irish Hussars**.

1808   It was sent to the Peninsula as part of General Sir John Moore's army. From October 1808 the regiment was active with the army in Spain, capturing a large party of French at Rueda. It then took part in actions at Valladolid, Sahagun and Benevente. During the retreat to Corunna, the remnants of the regiment took part in numerous rearguard actions, only to be ordered to shoot their horses on the beach before taking ship for England. A greatly reduced regiment re-assembled at Deal in Kent in 1809 and began the long process of recruiting and re-organization.

1813   On New Year's Day the regiment was ordered to march to Portsmouth for embarkation. It sailed on 19 January and arrived at Belem on 3 February. It was initially stationed at Luz and Benfica but due to the inactivity during the winter months, and the availability of cheap drink, it suffered from severe disciplinary problems. On 31 May 1813 it provided the advanced guard for a crossing of the River Elsa and surprised and captured fifty French dragoons. In a short and violent action at Morales on 2 June, it took part in a skirmish with the French rearguard.

At the battle of Vittoria (21 June 1813), the regiment played a prominent role, attacking and breaking a French infantry square and then harrying the retreating French army through the town of Vittoria and beyond.

It also captured the baggage train of the King Joseph of Spain and the French generals. A Lieutenant Dolbell, was placed in charge of the captured baggage but allowed his men to loot it. This event, combined with the fact that the Duke of Wellington discovered some troopers of the 18th drunk and looting in Vittoria, led to a severe reprimand. Wellington estimated that the men of the 18th had helped themselves to around a million pounds sterling in loot, which included Marshal Jourdan's baton. Wellington threatened to dismount them and send them home if they continued to misbehave. The regiment was then paraded and the men were made surrender their loot.

In the aftermath of the Vittoria battle, the regiment took part in the siege of Pamplona before crossing the River Bidassoa and marching to the French frontier. By December 1813 it had crossed onto French soil and was patrolling the River Nive. It later provided a cavalry screen as the army crossed the river and acted as cavalry support for the Spanish army that attacked Mendionde. On 22 December 1813, the regiment marched into winter quarters at Hasparren and would remain here until February 1814.

1814   When the new years campaign season began, the 18th was employed in the cavalry force that harried the French army. On 26 February it clashed with the French rearguard near Puyoo. Following the battle of Orthez (27 February) it remained in contact with the French army after its defeat and retreat. It took part in the siege of Bordeaux but was inactive during the battle of Tarbes.

During the operations around Toulouse, it clashed with enemy picquets on the 28 March and, on 8 April, captured the bridge at Croix d'Orade. The regiment took part in the battle of Toulouse on 10 April 1815, capturing a bridge on the River Ers and driving off a large body of French cavalry in the process.

For their part in this campaign, they were awarded just the single battle honour of 'Peninsula'. At the end of the campaign they were sent home to refit and recruit new troops.

1815   During the Waterloo campaign, the regiment formed part of Brigadier-General Vivian's light cavalry brigade which also included the 10th Hussars and the 1st Hussars of the King's German Legion. These regiments were present at the battles of Quatre Bras and Waterloo, the 18th Hussars suffering severe casualties. At Waterloo, troopers of the regiment captured a large number of French horses and these were later sold, some of the proceeds being spent on a pair of silver ceremonial trumpets. Following the Waterloo Campaign, the regiment stayed in Europe as part of the army of occupation.

1821   The regiment returned on home service and in 1821 was posted to Newbridge in Co. Kildare. It was earmarked as one of the regiments that was to be disbanded as part of post-war reductions in the size of the army. On 10 September 1821 the regiment was disbanded. At the time it shared Newbridge Barracks with the 19th Lancers, which was also disbanded.

1858 and afterwards

In 1858 the 18th Regiment of Hussars was re-formed and a series of re-organizations and amalgamations occurred over the next 130 years. In 1992 a final amalgamation with 15th/19th the King's Royal Hussars, formed the Regiment of Light Dragoons. These later regiments were not Irish in composition and form no further part in this study.

THE ROYAL IRISH RIFLES, LATER THE ROYAL ULSTER RIFLES

Formerly the 83rd (County of Dublin) Regiment of Foot and the 86th (Royal County Down) Regiment of Foot, 1793–1968

Formation

The Royal Irish Rifles were formed in 1881 under the terms of the Cardwell army reforms. The regiment was created through the amalgamation of two earlier regiments; the 83rd (County of Dublin) Regiment of Foot and the 86th (Royal County Down) Regiment of Foot, both of which had been raised in 1793 following the outbreak of war between Britain and Revolutionary France.

The 83rd Foot and the 86th Foot became the 1st and 2nd Battalions of the Royal Irish Rifles in 1881.

The 83rd (County of Dublin) Regiment of Foot (later, 1st Battalion, Royal Irish Rifles)

1793   This regiment was raised in September by Lt.-Col. William Fitch. It was raised due to the outbreak of war with France, it initially took the name of its colonel and was known as Fitch's Regiment of Foot. It was later numbered as the 83rd Regiment of Foot and was the third regiment to have borne this designation.[14]

1794   A second battalion was added to the regimental establishment but was later re-designated as the 134th Regiment of Foot.

1795   The 83rd Foot was sent to the West Indies where it served in the suppression of the 'Maroon Rebellion'. Colonel Fitch was killed in action in September. It later served in San Domingo, Jamaica.

1802   The 83rd Foot returned to England and later served as part of the garrison of Jersey.

1804   A second battalion was raised and served on garrison duties in England, the Channel Islands and Ireland.

1806   The 1st/83rd Foot was sent to the Cape, where it remained until 1817.

1809   It had originally been intended to also send the 2nd/83rd Foot to the Cape but in March it was embarked aboard ships at Cobh and sent to Portugal.

---

14 The first 83rd Foot had also been raised in Ireland in 1758 and after services in Portugal had been disbanded in 1763.

	The 2nd Battalion remained in Spain and Portugal until 1814 and took part in numerous actions during the Peninsular campaign, including Talavera, Busaco, Ciudad Rodrigo, Badajos, Salamanca, Vittoria, Nivelle and Toulouse.
1814	Following the end of the war in Europe, the 2nd Battalion was returned to Ireland and served in various stations including Cork, Kilkenny, Dublin and Armagh.
1817	In April, the regiment's 2nd Battalion was disbanded at Armagh and its surplus personnel were sent to the 1st Battalion in the Cape. The 83rd Foot, now just a single battalion regiment, was sent to Ceylon (Sri Lanka) where it took part in the campaign against the insurrection in the islands Kandyan provinces.
1829	The 83rd Foot returned to England and was sent to Sctoland where it was based in Glasgow.
1830	The regiment returned to Ireland and was initially based at Enniskillen. Detachments of the regiment later served in Omagh, Lifford and Sligo. The 83rd Foot remained in Ireland until 1834 and was based in various locations including Dublin, Westport and Ballinew.
1834	The 83rd Foot was sent to Canada where it served as part of the garrison of Halifax and later Montreal. It remained in Canada until 1843.
1843	The regiment returned to England and initially based at Gosport.
1845	The 83rd Foot returned to Ireland.
1849	The regiment was ordered to India and was initially based at Poona. It later served in stations at Bombay and Kurrachee.

Indian Mutiny 1857–9

The 83rd Foot took part in numerous actions during the Mutiny, many of its detachments being used to disarm rebel sepoys. The regiment took part in the siege and attack on the fortified town of Awah and the capture of Kotah, among other actions.

1859	The regiment remained in India at the end of the Mutiny. In October it was given the new title of 83rd (County of Dublin) Regiment of Foot, the new territorial designation being reference to the regiment's Irish origins.
1862	The 83rd Foot returned to England and remained on home station for five years, serving in the garrisons of various stations including Aldershot, York, the Curragh, Armagh and Sligo.
1867	The regiment was sent to Gibraltar.
1870	The 83rd Foot returned to India, being initially stationed at Poona.
1881	The regiment was sent to South Africa but arrived too late to play any effective part in the 1st Anglo-Boer War. In July, under the terms of the army reforms, it was re-designated as the 1st Battalion, Royal Irish Rifles. It returned to England in November 1881. Following this re-organization of the army, the regiment was assigned recruiting district No. 83, which included counties Antrim, Down and Louth.[15]

15 Co. Louth was later included in the recruiting area of the Leinster Regiment. By WW1, the Royal Irish Rifles recruiting district also took in Belfast and Tyrone.

1882   The 1st Battalion, Royal Irish Rifles was stationed at Dover. It would later serve on duties in the Channel Islands, England and Ireland.

1896   A detachment of the regiment was sent to serve as mounted infantry in Matabeleland in Rhodesia (Zimbabwe).

1897   The 1st Battalion was sent to South Africa being stationed at Durban and Ladysmith.

1899   The battalion returned to India and was based at Dum Dum and Calcutta. Detachments volunteered for service in South Africa during the 2nd Anglo-Boer War of 1899–1902, but the battalion itself remained in India.

1904   The battalion furnished a machine detachment for the British expedition to Tibet. This detachment was commanded of Lt Bowen-Colthurst.

1914   This battalion was based in Aden on the outbreak of the First World War.

The 86th (Royal County Down) Regiment of Foot (later, 2nd Battalion, Royal Irish Rifles)

1793   This regiment was also raised following the outbreak of war with France.

            It was originally raised by Colonel (later General Sir) Cornelius Cuyler as a corps of volunteers. It was raised in Shrewsbury and included men from Shropshire, Yorkshire, Lancashire and Cheshire. It was initially known as 'Cuyler's Shropshire Volunteers'.

1794   The regiment was moved to Kilkenny and was numbered as the 86th Foot on the regular establishment and was more usually just referred to as the 'Shropshire Volunteers'.[16] The regiment's initial services were as marines and detachments served on board various Royal Navy ships in the Channel and the Mediterranean between 1794 and 1796.

1796   The 86th Foot took part in the expedition to the Cape and remained in South Africa until 1799.

1799   The regiment was posted to India where detachments served in Madras and Bombay, a further detachment being sent to Ceylon (Sri Lanka).

1800   In a series of detachments the regiment was sent to Egypt where it took part in the campaign against the French. It remained in Egypt until 1802 and was present at the captures of Alexandria and Cairo.

1802   The regiment returned to India in July and was initially based at Bombay. It later took part in the campaign in Gujerat and the 2nd Mahratta War of 1803–5. It was present with Lord Lake's army in the assault on Bhurtpore in 1805.

1806   The regiment was re-designated as the 86th (Leinster) Regiment of Foot. In April it was sent to the Portuguese possession of Goa where it remained until 1809.

1809   The 86th Foot returned to Madras to help put down a mutiny among native troops of the Madras presidency.

---

16 Two other regiments had previously been ranked as the 86th Foot, the first of which had been raised in Ireland in 1759 but was disbanded in 1763.

Irish regiments in the British army, 1685–2006

1810   The regiment played a prominent part in the capture of the French-held island of Bourbon off the east African coast. It remained on station on Bourbon and Mauritius until 1812.

1812   The 86th Foot returned to the Madras presidency. It was re-named as the 86th (Royal County Down) Regiment of Foot.

1814   A second battalion was formed and initially earmarked for service in Holland. Following the end of hostilities, this battalion was disbanded. The 86th Foot remained in India until 1819 when it returned to England. It later served on garrison duty in England and in various locations in Ireland including Waterford, Kilkenny, Wexford, Athlone and Drogheda.

1826   The 86th Foot was sent to the West Indies where it was based in Trinidad, Tobago, Antigua and Barbados.

1837   The regiment returned to England and served at various locations, before being sent to Ireland in 1840.

1842   The 86th Foot returned to India and took part in the 1st Sikh War of 1845–6.

Crimean War, 1854–6

1855   While the main body of the regiment remained in India, a large detachment was sent to Aden due to fears of a Russian invasion there. This detachment was recalled to India on the outbreak of the Indian Mutiny.

Indian Mutiny 1857–9

The regiment played an active part in the suppression of the sepoy revolt and was attached to the Central India Field Force. It took part in the storming of both Chandaree and Jhansi. In 1858 it took part in the capture of Gwalior and then served with various flying columns until February 1859. At the end of the Mutiny the regiment returned to England.

1859   The regiment returned to home station and initially served on garrison duty in England before being sent to Ireland.

1864   The 86th Foot was posted to Gibraltar.

1867   The regiment was initially ordered to Mauritius but as a fever epidemic had broken out there, it was remained at the Cape for some time before being moved to Mauritius in late 1867.

1871   The 86th Foot was sent to the Cape where it remained until 1875.

1875   The regiment returned to England where it served on garrison duties in England and Ireland.

1880   The 86th Foot was sent to Bermuda.

1881   In July, under the terms of the Cardwell army reforms, the regiment was re-designated as the 2nd Battalion, Royal Irish Rifles. At the same time, several regiments of the Militia of Ireland were re-designated as militia or reserve battalions of the Royal Irish Rifles. These were:

3rd Battalion (Royal North Down Rifles, 1881–1908)
4th Battalion (Antrim Militia (Queen's Own Royal Rifles), 1881–1908)

5th Battalion (Royal South Down Light Infantry, 1881–1953)
6th Battalion (Louth Rifles, 1881–1908)

1883   The 2nd Battalion, Royal Irish Rifles was sent to Halifax, Nova Scotia.
1886   The battalion was sent on garrison duty to Gibraltar.
1888   The 2nd Battalion took part in the expedition to Egypt.
1891   The battalion was stationed in Malta and returned to India where it remained until 1899.

2nd Anglo-Boer War, 1899–1902

1899   The 2nd Battalion, Royal Irish Rifles arrived in South Africa in November and were sent to Queenstown in the division of General Sir W.F. Gatacre.
1900   The battalion took part in the disastrous actions at Stormberg and Reddersburg and at the latter engagement a large number of men were taken prisoner. Much reduced in numbers, the battalion served on garrison work in the Orange River Colony for most of the rest of the war. It also formed two companies of mounted infantry.
1903   The 2nd Battalion returned to Ireland and stationed in Dublin. From 1903, the battalion served on duty in Ireland and England. It was based at Tidworth on the outbreak of war in 1914.

First World War, 1914–18

During the course of the war, battalions of the regiment were present at just about every major battle, from the opening engagements of 1914 to the final battles of 1918. Alongside the two regular battalions, a series of service, reserve and garrison battalions were also raised. In total, 21 battalions of the Royal Irish Rifles served in the war with several different divisions in all the major theatres of the war. On the outbreak of war, the regimental depot was in Belfast.

1st Battalion
This regular battalion was in Aden on the outbreak of the war. It was returned to England where it was attached to the 8th Division. It served on the Western Front from November 1914 and was attached to the 36th (Ulster) Division in February 1918.

2nd Battalion
The second regular battalion was in England at Tidworth on the outbreak of war. It was attached to the 3rd Division of the BEF and landed in France on 14 August 1914. It served throughout the first difficult campaign of the war and was present at the Mons and Le Cateau battles. It remained on the Western Front for the rest of the war and was later attached to the 25th and 36th (Ulster) Divisions.

3rd (Reserve) Battalion
This battalion was activated at Belfast on 4 August 1914. It served in Ireland

until 1918 when it was moved to Larkhill in England. It later absorbed the personnel from the disbanded 17th, 18th, 19th and 20th Battalions.

4th (Extra Reserve) Battalion
Activated at Newtownards on 4 August 1914, this battalion remained in Ireland for much of the war, being employed on coastal defence duty at Carrickfergus. In April 1918 it was moved to Larkhill in England where it joined the Irish Reserve Brigade.

5th (Extra Reserve) Battalion
This battalion was activated at Downpatrick on 4 August 1914 and served on garrison duties in Ireland until April 1918 when it was sent to Larkhill in England, where it was attached to the Irish Reserve Brigade.

6th (Service) Battalion
This K1 battalion was formed in Dublin. After training in Ireland and England it was attached to the 10th (Irish) Division and arrived Mudros in July 1915. With the 29th Brigade of the 10th (Irish) Division, it landed at ANZAC Cove on Gallipoli as part of renewed operations in September 1915. It later served in Salonika, Egypt and Palestine and was disbanded in April 1918.

7th (Service) Battalion
This battalion was formed in Belfast in September 1914. After training in Ireland and England it absorbed a draft of 230 officers and men from the Royal Jersey Militia. Attached to the 16th (Irish) Division it landed in France in December 1915 and it later served with the 36th (Ulster) Division. It served entirely on the Western Front and fought in battles including the Somme, Messines and Cambrai. In November 1917, its remaining personnel were absorbed by the 2nd Battalion.

8th (Service) Battalion (East Belfast Volunteers)
Raised in Belfast in September from the men of the Belfast Volunteers, UVF. It was attached to the 107th Brigade of the 36th (Ulster) Division and served on the Western Front in battles such as the Somme, Messines and 3rd Ypres, among others. In August 1917 it was amalgamated with the 9th Battalion to form the 8th/9th Battalion. This amalgamated battalion was disbanded in February 1918.

9th (Service) Battalion (West Belfast Volunteers)
This battalion was raised in September 1914 in Belfast and also recruited men from the UVF. It was attached to the 107th Brigade of the 36th (Ulster) Division and served on the Western Front, being amalgamated with the 8th Battalion in August 1917.

10th (Service) Battalion (South Belfast Volunteers)
Raised in Belfast in September from men of the UVF, this battalion was attached to the 107th Brigade of the 36th (Ulster) Division. Its war service was entirely on the Western Front and it was later attached to the 4th Division. It was disbanded in France in February 1918.

11th (Service) Battalion (South Antrim Volunteers)
This battalion was raised in Co. Antrim in September 1914 and included men from Antrim units of the UVF. It was attached to the 108th Brigade of the 36th (Ulster) Division and served throughout the war on the Western Front. In November 1917 it was amalgamated with the 13th Battalion to form the 11th/13th Battalion. It was disbanded in France in February 1918.

12th (Service) Battalion (Central Antrim)
This battalion was also raised in September 1914 and recruited from Co. Antrim units of the UVF. It was attached to the 108th Brigade of the 36th (Ulster) Division and landed in France in October 1918. It remained on the Western Front for the rest of the war and fought in numerous actions including the Somme, Messines and the defence against the German March 1918 offensive, the 'Kaiserslacht'. It was stationed in Belgium at the armistice in 1918.

13th (Service) Battalion (1st Co. Down)
This battalion was raised in September 1914 and recruited men from the Co. Down units of the UVF. It was attached to the 108th Brigade of the 36th (Ulster) Division and served on the Western Front. In November 1917 it was amalgamated with the 11th Battalion, the amalgamated battalion being disbanded in February 1918 in France.

14th (Service) Battalion (Young Citizen Volunteers)
This battalion was raised in Belfast in September 1914 and recruited among the Young Citizen Volunteers of the UVF. It joined the 109th Brigade of the 36th (Ulster) Division and landed in France in October 1915. It remained on the Western Front for the rest of the war and fought in numerous actions before being disbanded in February 1918.

15th (Service) Battalion (North Belfast)
This battalion was also raised from recruits from UVF units. It was formed in September 1914 and was attached to the 107th Brigade of the 36th (Ulster) Division. At the armistice in 1918 it was at Mouscron in Belgium, having served throughout the war on the Western Front.

16th (Service) Battalion (2nd County Down) (Pioneers)
This battalion was raised in Lurgan in September 1914 and recruited men from the Co. Down units of the UVF. It was attached to the 36th (Ulster) Division as its pioneer battalion and served up to the armistice on the Western Front.

17th (Reserve) Battalion
This battalion was raised in Newcastle, Co. Down, in March 1915. It absorbed the depot companies of the 8th, 9th and 10th Battalions and was attached to the 15th (Ulster) Reserve Brigade. It was moved to Larkhill in England in April 1918 and was absorbed into the 3rd Battalion.

18th (Reserve) Battalion
This reserve battalion was raised in Holywood, Co. Down in April 1915 and absorbed men from the depot companies of the 11th and 12th Battalions. It was attached to the 15th (Ulster) Reserve Brigade and later moved to Larkhill in England where it was absorbed into the 3rd Battalion.

19th (Reserve) Battalion
This battalion was formed in Newcastle, Co. Down, in October 1915. It absorbed men from the depot companies of the 14th and 15th Battalions. It was attached to the 15th (Ulster) Reserve Brigade, before being moved to Larkhill, England, in April 1918 where it was absorbed by the 3rd Battalion.

20th (Reserve) Battalion
Formed in Holywood, Co. Down, this battalion absorbed men from the depots of the 13th and 16th Battalions. It served with the 15th (Ulster) Reserve Brigade but was absorbed into the 3rd Battalion at Larkhill in May 1918.

1st Garrison Battalion
This battalion formed in Dublin in November 1915 and was sent to India in February 1916.

Inter-War Period

At the end of the war the remaining wartime battalions of the regiment were gradually disbanded, the last of them being disbanded in 1920.

The two regular battalions remained after the war and the 1st Battalion served as part of the army of occupation in Germany, while the 2nd Battalion served in Mesopotamia (Iraq).

As some form of self-government appeared to be increasingly likely for the southern part of Ireland, it was decided to change the regiment's title. In January 1921, it was changed to Royal Ulster Rifles. On the establishment of the Irish Free State in 1922, County Louth was lost from the regiment's traditional recruiting district.

During the inter-war years the regiment's regular battalions served on numerous stations at home and abroad. These included Germany, Palestine, Egypt and Hong Kong (1st Battalion) and Egypt, Constantinople (Istanbul), India and Palestine (2nd Battalion). In 1937 the London Irish Rifles were added to the regiment's organization as a Territorial Army battalion (see separate entry on that regiment).

The Second World War, 1939–45

1st Battalion
The 1st Battalion, Royal Ulster Rifles was based in India on the outbreak of war and was sent to England in 1940. In 1941 the battalion was re-trained as gliderborne airborne infantry and was assigned to the 6th Airborne Division in 1943. It took part in the D-Day operations in 1944 and, as part of 'Operation Mallard', the battalion was near Ranville and took part in actions at Longueval and St Honorine. The 1st Battalion's next airborne action was during 'Operation Varsity' on 24 March 1945 when it landed near Hamminkeln on the River Ussel. During

this action it captured a vital bridge and many German POWs. The 1st Battalion served for the rest of the war in Germany.

2nd Battalion
On the outbreak of war, this battalion was in Palestine but was rushed back to England where it joined 9th Brigade, 3rd Division of the BEF. Following the fall of France in 1940, the 2nd Battalion was evacuated from Dunkirk. The battalion was re-trained as amphibious infantry at the Combined Operations Training Centre at Inverary. On D-Day 1944, the 2nd Battalion was assigned to the 3rd (British) Infantry Division and landed at Queen Red Beach, a sub-section of Sword Beach. It then took part in actions at Cambes, Colombelles and Caen. During 'Operation Market-Garden', the 2nd Ulster Rifles were engaged in action on the Escaut Canal. It continued to serve for the remainder of the war in the Low Countries and Germany.

The Royal Ulster Rifles also formed three reserve battalions and these served as home defence battalions during the war while other wartime battalions served as training units.

Following the end of the war, the wartime battalions were disbanded while the two regular battalions were sent to Palestine.

1948   The regiment was reduced to just a single battalion, its 2nd Battalion being disbanded. It adopted the new title of 1st Battalion, The Royal Ulster Rifles (83rd and 86th).

Korea, 1950–1
The Ulster Rifles were attached to the 29th Independent infantry Brigade Group and sent to Korea under United Nations command. The regiment served in the Korean War from November 1950 to October 1951. It fought in numerous actions including the battle in 'Happy Valley', north of Seoul in 1951. In April 1951 it fought in the battle on the Imjin.

In the years following the Korean War, the Royal Ulster Rifles served on various assignments in Cyprus, Borneo, with the BAOR in Germany and on home station. In July 1968, the Royal Ulster Rifles were amalgamated with the Royal Inniskilling Fusiliers and the Royal Irish Fusiliers to form the Royal Irish Rangers (see separate entry on the Royal Irish Rangers).

Colonels of the Royal Irish Rifles/Royal Ulster Rifles from 1881
1881   General Gustavus Brown (1st Battalion)
1881   Field-Marshal Sir John Michel (2nd Battalion)
1886   General Wilmot Henry Bradford
1914   General Sir Charles John Burnett
1915   Field-Marshal Sir Henry Hughes Wilson
1922   General Sir Alexander Godley
1937   Lieutenant-General Sir Denis J.C.K. Bernard
1947   General Sir James Stuart Steele

1957   Brigadier-General Ian Henry Hart
1962   Major-General Ian Cecil Harris (until amalgamation in 1968)

Battle honours
This list includes the honours of the 83rd and 86th Foot, the Royal Irish Rifles and the later Royal Ulster Rifles.

Cape of Good Hope 1806, Talavera, Bourbon, Busaco, Fuentes d'Onor, Ciudad Rodrigo, Badajoz, Salamanca, Vittoria, Nivelle, Orthes, Toulouse, Peninsula, Central India, South Africa 1899–1902, Mons, Le Cateau, Retreat from Mons, Marne 1914, Aisne 1914, La Bassée 1914, Messines 1914, Messines 1917, Messines 1918, Armentières 1914, Ypres 1914, Ypres 1915, Ypres 1917, Ypres 1918, Nonne Bosschen, Neuve Chapelle, Frenzenburg, Aubers, Somme 1916, Somme 1918, Albert 1916, Bazentin, Pozières, Guillemont, Ginchy, Ancre Heights, Pilckem, Langemarck 1917, Cambrai 1917, St Quentin, Rosières, Lys, Bailleul, Kemmel, Courtrai, France and Flanders 1914–18, Struma, Macedonia 1915–17, Suvla, Sari Bair, Gallipoli 1915, Gaza, Jerusalem, Tell 'Asur, Palestine 1917–18, Dyle, Dunkirk 1940, Normandy Landing, Cambes, Caen, Troarn, Venlo Pocket, Rhine, Bremen, North-West Europe 1940, North-West Europe 1944–45, Seoul, Imjin, Korea 1950–51.

Motto
Quis Separabit? (Who shall separate us?)

Regimental music
There are several tunes associated with the Royal Irish Rifles or the previous 83rd and 86th Regiments. For the 83rd Regiment, the regimental tunes were 'Garryowen' and 'Off! said the stranger'. Tunes associated with the 86th Regiment were 'the Kinegar Slashers' and 'St Patrick's Day'. Following amalgamation in 1881, the tune 'St Patrick's Day' was adopted as the regimental march of the Royal Irish Rifles. Other tunes associated with the regiment include 'God Bless the Prince of Wales' and, somewhat oddly, the pre–1917 Russian National Anthem.

Nicknames
The 83rd Foot was known as 'Fitch's Grenadiers'. The 86th Foot came to be known as the 'Irish Giants' during their time in India.

THE ROYAL IRISH FUSILIERS (PRINCESS VICTORIA'S)

Formerly the 87th (or Royal Irish Fusiliers) Regiment of Foot and the 89th (Princess Victoria's) Regiment of Foot, 1793–1968

Formation
This regiment was created under the terms of the Cardwell reforms in 1881. It was formed through the amalgamation of the 87th (or Royal Irish Fusiliers) Regiment of

Foot and the 89th (Princess Victoria's) Regiment of Foot and these regiments formed the 1st and 2nd Battalions of the new regiment respectivley. Both of the regiment's founding battalions could trace their histories back to 1793 and had served with distinction in the Napoleonic Wars and the various campaigns of the nineteenth century.

THE 87th (OR ROYAL IRISH FUSILIERS) REGIMENT OF FOOT, LATER THE 1st BATTALION, PRINCESS VICTORIA'S (ROYAL IRISH FUSILIERS)

Two regiments had previously been designated as the 87th Foot and had been raised and disbanded between 1759 and 1783. On the outbreak of war between England and France in 1793, the size of the army was increased and in September 1793 another 87th Regiment of Foot was raised in Ireland by Colonel (later General) Sir John Doyle. Colonel Doyle obtained permission from the Prince of Wales (the future Geroge IV) to name the regiment in his honour.

Ranked as the 87th Foot, its original title was 87th (The Prince of Wales's Irish) Regiment of Foot.

Operational history
French Revolutionary and Napoleonic Wars, 1793–1815

1st Battalion

1794   The regiment was sent to the Low Countries as part of Lord Moira's expedition. It saw its first action against the French at Alost.

1795   It formed part of the garrison at Bergen-op-Zoom and the entire battalion was captured when the town surrendered to the French. The regiment was re-formed in England and was posted to the West Indies. It remained in the West Indies until the Peace of Amiens in 1802.

1807   The 1st Battalion took part in Sir Samuel Auchmuty's expedition to South America and fought in the battles of Montevideo and Buenos Aires.

1810   The battalion was sent to the Cape in South Africa and form there to Mauritius, where it remained until 1815.

1811   The regiment was re-designated as the 87th (Prince of Wales's Own Irish) Regiment of Foot.

1815   The 1st Battalion was ordered to India where it served in the Gurkha or **Nepal War** of 1815–16. In 1817 it took part in the campaign against the Pindarees and was present at the capture of Fort Hattrass.

2nd Battalion

1804   Under the terms of the Additional Forces Act, a second battalion was raised for this regiment in Ireland. It was raised and commanded by Colonel Sir Charles Doyle, the son of the regiment's original colonel.

1808   After garrison duty in Ireland, England and Guernsey, the regiment was ordered to Portugal in December.

1809   On its arrival in Portugal, the 2nd Battalion joined the army of Lord Wellesley. It went on to see distinguished service during the Peninsular campaign and took part in the battles of Talavera, Tarifa, Barrosa, Vittoria, Nivelle, Orthes and Toulouse. The battalion achieved huge status by capturing a French Eagle standard at the battle of Barrosa in 1811. The prized standard was captured from the French 8e de Ligne by Sergeant Patrick Masterson who, on seizing the Eagle, is reported to have shouted 'Bejabers Boys! I have the cuckoo!' This was the first French Eagle captured during the Peninsular campaign.

1817   On 1 February, the regiment's 2nd Battalion was disbanded at Colchester following the end of the war in 1815 and the reduction of the size of the army.

1825   The remaining 1st Battalion remained in India and served in the **1st Anglo-Burma War** of 1825–6.

1827   The 1st Battalion returned to home station and in July was re-designated as the 87th Regiment of Foot (or Prince of Wales's Own Irish Fusiliers). In November, this designation was changed again to 87th (or Royal Irish Fusiliers) Regiment of Foot.

1831   The regiment was sent to Mauritius where it remained until 1842.

1842   The 87th Foot returned to home station were initially based in Scotland.

1849   The regiment was sent to India where it remained until 1860. During the Indian Mutiny it was on garrison duty on the North-West Frontier and saw no service in that campaign.

1860   The 87th Foot was sent to China and was based in Hong Kong.

1861   The regiment returned to home station.

1865   The 87th was sent on garrison duty in Gibraltar before being posted to Malta and the Nova Scotia in Canada.

1876   The regiment returned to England where it carried out garrison duties at various locations.

1881   The 87th Foot was based at Aldershot when, under the terms of the Cardwell army reforms, it was re-designated as the 1st Battalion of the Royal Irish Fusiliers. The regiment was assigned recruiting district No. 87, which took in counties Armagh, Cavan and Monaghan.

THE 89th (PRINCESS VICTORIA'S) REGIMENT OF FOOT, LATER THE 2nd BATTALION, PRINCESS VICTORIA'S (ROYAL IRISH FUSILIERS)

The 2nd Battalion of the Royal Irish Fusiliers was also raised in 1793 as a response to the outbreak of war with France. Previously, two other regiments had borne the designation of 89th Foot but both had been disbanded by 1783.

The new 89th Foot was raised in Ireland by Colonel (later Lt-Gen.) William Crosbie and in December 1793 was ranked as the 89th Regiment of Foot.

Operational history

1794   The regiment was attached to Lord Moira's expedition to Flanders where it took part in actions at Alost, Boxtel, Niemegen and Tuyl. Following the failure of this expedition to the Low Countries the regiment returned to England and was initially based at Sunderland in 1795.

1795   The 89th Foot was returned to Ireland where it was garrisoned at various locations including Arklow and Wexford.

1796   The regiment took part in the operations against the abortive French landings in Bantry Bay. It was later based at Fermoy and Clonmel.

1798   The 89th Foot played an active part in the suppression of the United Irishmen rebellion, being present at the battle of Vinegar Hill.

1799   The regiment was sent to Messina, Sicily.

1800   The 89th Foot was based in Malta.

1801   The regiment was attached to General Sir Ralph Abercrombie's expedition to Egypt and fought in the actions at Alexandria and the Nile. On the conclusion of this campaign, it was sent to Gibraltar.

1802   The 89th Foot returned to Ireland and was based at various locations including Youghal and Enniskillen.

1803   A 2nd Battalion of the regiment was formed. The 1st Battalion was then quartered in Athlone and Loughrea.

1805   The 1st Battalion joined an expedition to Holland and then served in England, the Cape (1807) and Ceylon (Sri Lanka, 1808).

1809   Following a mutiny by the Madras army, the 1st Battalion was sent to India.

1810   The 1st/89th Foot took part in the expedition to the Isle de France and then the expedition to Java (1811), where it fought in several actions.

1812   The 1st Battalion was sent to Sumatra and then returned to India, where it was still posted at the end of war with France in 1815.

2nd Battalion

1803   The regiment raised a 2nd Battalion in Ireland and this remained on home service before joining the garrison in Gibraltar.

1812   On the outbreak of war with America, the so-called **War of 1812**, the battalion was sent to Halifax, Nova Scotia.

1813   The 2nd/89th was based at Quebec and later played an active part in the war, fighting in the actions at Christler's Farm (1813) and Blackrock (1813), the battle of Niagara (1814) and the siege of Fort Erie (1814).

1816   At the conclusion of the war with America, the 2nd Battalion was returned to England where it was disbanded in November, its remaining personnel being transferred to the surviving 1st Battalion.

1817   The remaining 1st Battalion was still based in India at the end of the Napoleonic wars. It served in the **Mahratta and Pindaree War** of 1816–18 and took part in the storming of several fortresses.

1824 | The regiment took part in the **1st Anglo-Burmese War** of 1824–6 and fought in several engagements.
1831 | The 89th Foot was ordered back to England and was initially based at Canterbury.
1833 | The regiment returned to Ireland and was based at Cork.
1835 | The 89th Foot was posted to the West Indies, being based at Barbados.
1841 | The regiment was moved to Canada and was based at Amhertsburg. It was later based at various locations including Halifax and Quebec.
1847 | The regiment was returned to England and was based in various stations including Liverpool and Manchester. During this period the regiment was deployed in aid of the civil power and helped suppress the chartist riots. It was moved to Ireland in 1848.
1854 | The 89th Foot was moved to Gibraltar and from there it joined the 3rd Division in the Crimea in 1855. It served during the remainder of the **Crimean War** where it served in the siege of Sevastopol.
1856 | At the end of the Crimean War, the regiment returned to Gibraltar and from there was sent to the Cape in South Africa.
1857 | On the outbreak of the **Indian Mutiny** the 89th Foot was rushed to India where it took part in expeditions against the sepoys in 1858 and 1859. It remained in India at the end of the mutiny and was ordered to England in 1865, where it was initially based at Shorncliffe.
1866 | The regiment was re-designated as the 89th (The Princess Victoria's) Regiment of Foot.
1867 | On the outbreak of the Fenian Rebellion in Ireland, the regiment was ordered to the Curragh Camp.
1870 | The regiment returned to India and was based at Cannanore. It remained in India until 1876, when it was sent to join the garrison in Burma.
1880 | The 89th Foot returned to India and was based at Belgaum.
1881 | Under the terms of the Cardwell army reforms, the regiment was re-designated as the 2nd Battalion of Princess Victoria's (Royal Irish Fusiliers). At the same time, battalions of the Irish Militia were re-designated as reserve or militia battalions of the new regiment. These battalions were:

3rd Battalion (Armagh Light Infantry)
4th Battalion (Cavan Light Infantry)
5th Battalion (Monaghan Regiment of Militia)

PRINCESS VICTORIA'S (ROYAL IRISH FUSILIERS)

In the years preceding the First World War, both regular battalions of the Royal Irish Fusiliers saw extensive service.

1st Battalion

1882   The 1st Battalion was sent to Egypt as part of Lord Wolseley's expedition and took part in the battle of Tel-el-Kebir. The battalion returned to home station in the same year.

1883   The battalion was sent to India.

1898   The 1st Battalion returned to Egypt as part of Lord Kitchener's army where its Maxim gun detachment was present at the battle of Omdurman.

1899   The battalion left Egypt in September 1899 and sailed for South Africa where it served during the **2nd Anglo-Boer War** of 1899–1902. During this war it fought in the battles of Talana Hill and Nicholson's Nek and the relief of Ladysmith. After the end of the Anglo-Boer, the 1st Battalion was sent on garrison duties and at the outbreak of the First World War it was based in Shorncliffe in England.

2nd Battalion

1884   The battalion remained in India until being sent to Egypt. During the campaign against the Mahdists in 1884 it fought in the battles of El Tab and Tamai. It then returned to garrison duty in England and Ireland.

1899   On the outbreak of the **2nd Anglo-Boer War** of 1899–1902, the 2nd Battalion was ordered to the Cape in October. On arrival it joined the 6th, or Fusilier, Brigade under Major-General Barton. It took part in attempts to relieve Ladysmith and also in the battle of Pieter's Hill. It later took part in the defence of Machadodorp in 1900. A detachment of the battalion, serving as mounted infantry, was ambushed on the Blood River in September 1901, suffering 20 casualties. At the end of the war, the 2nd Battalion returned to regular garrison duty and was based in Quetta on the outbreak of the First World War.

The First World War, 1914–18

During the course of the war, 12 new battalions of the Royal Irish Fusiliers were raised. Alongside the two existing regular battalions, these new battalions served as service, reserve and garrison units.

Battalions of the regiment served with various divisions including the 4th, 27th, 10th (Irish) and 36th (Ulster) Divisions. They served in all theatres of the war and took part in numerous actions, a fact evidenced by the large number of battle honours awarded to the Royal Irish Fusiliers after the war. On the outbreak of war, the regimental depot was in Armagh.

1st Battalion

This regular battalion was based at Shorncliffe and the outbreak of the war. It was attached to the 10th Brigade of the 4th Division, BEF, and landed in France on 23 August 1914. It took part in the opening engagements of the war and was later attached to the 36th (Ulster) Division. All of its service was on the Western Front.

2nd Battalion

The regiment's second regular battalion was based at Quetta in modern-day Pakistan on the outbreak of the war. It was returned to England and then sent to France in December 1914 as part of the 27th Division. In November 1915 it was sent to Salonika where it joined the 10th (Irish) Division. It later served in Egypt and Palestine.

3rd (Reserve) Battalion

This battalion was activated at Armagh on 4 August 1914. It remained in Ireland until 1918 when it was sent to England where it was attached to the West Riding Reserve Brigade.

4th (Extra Reserve) Battalion

This reserve battalion was activated in Cavan on 4 August 1914. It served in various locations around Ireland until 1918 when it was sent to England and its personnel were absorbed into the 3rd Battalion.

5th (Service) Battalion

This K1 battalion was formed at Armagh in August 1914. It was attached to the 31st Brigade of the 10th (Irish) Division and took part in Suvla Bay landings in 1915. It served in Salonika, Egypt and Palestine and, in May 1918, was sent to France where it joined the 66th Division. At the end of the it was serving with the 16th (Irish) Division in Belgium.

6th (Service) Battalion

This K1 battalion was formed at Armagh in September 1914. It was attached to the 10th (Irish) Division and served in Gallipoli and Salonika before being absorbed into the 5th Battalion in 1916.

7th (Service) Battalion

This battalion formed slightly later in September 1914 and was therefore classed as a K2 battalion. It joined the 16th (Irish) Division and served on the Western Front. Due to casualties incurred during the Somme battles, it was amalgamated with the 8th Battalion in October 1916 to form the 7th/8th Battalion. It was disbanded in France in early 1918, having been decimated in the battles of 1917.

8th (Service) Battalion

This K2 battalion also formed at Armagh in September 1914. It was attached to the 16th (Irish) Division and served in the Somme battles of 1916. In October 1916 it was amalgamated with the 7th Battalion and this combined battalion was disbanded in February 1918.

9th (Service) Battalion

This battalion was raised in September 1914 and included men from the Armagh, Monaghan and Cavan units of the Ulster Volunteer Force. It was attached to the 36th (Ulster) Division and all of its service was on the Western Front, including the battles of the Somme, Messines and Cambrai. In September 1917 it absorbed

B and C Squadrons of the 2nd North Irish Horse and was re-designated as the 9th (North Irish Horse) Battalion, Princess Victoria's (Royal Irish Fusiliers). It was based near Tourcoing in Belgium at the end of the war.

10th (Reserve) Battalion

This battalion was formed at Lurgan in September 1915 as a local reserve battalion, incorporating dept staff of the 9th Battalion. It formed part of the (Ulster) Reserve Brigade and it was moved to England in 1918 where its personnel were absorbed by the 3rd Battalion.

11th (Service) Battalion

This battalion was formed in England in June 1918 using men from the regiment's garrison battalion and also 7th Battalion, Royal Dublin Fusiliers. It was attached to the 48th Brigade of the 16th (Irish) Division and sent to France, where it was absorbed by the regiment's 5th Battalion in August.

1st Garrison Battalion

Formed in Dublin in September 1915, this battalion served on garrison duties in India and then Burma.

2nd Garrison Battalion

This battalion was raised in Dublin in April 1916. In August 1916 it was posted to Salonika where it was later attached to the 28th Division. It remained in Macedonia until the end of the war, serving on line of communication duties.

3rd (Reserve) Garrison Battalion

This battalion was raised in Dublin in December 1916. It served on garrison duties in Ireland and England during the war. Some of its personnel may have been used to form the 11th Battalion in 1918 as both battalions were then stationed near West Hartlepool.

At the end of the war, the wartime service battalions were disbanded. The regiment's regular battalions remained and during the inter-war period served on Garrison duties in England, Egypt and India.

1921	On 1 January, the regimental title was changed and the new designation was as the Royal Irish Fusiliers (Princess Victoria's).
1922	On the establishment of the Irish Free State, the regiment lost Cavan and Monaghan from its recruiting district. It was initially scheduled for disbandment but in an incredible act of generosity, the Royal Inniskilling Fusiliers disbanded its 2nd Battalion. This allowed the Royal Irish Fusiliers to survive as a single battalion regiment.
1938	As war seemed increasingly likely, the regiment formed a 2nd Battalion.

The Second World War, 1939–45

The regiment raised a second battalion in 1938, before the outbreak of the war, and between 1939 and 1945, a further three battalions were raised to serve as home defence and training units.

1st Battalion

This regular battalion of the Royal Irish Fusiliers was attached to the BEF in France on the outbreak of the war, serving with 25th Brigade of the 50th (Northumbrian) Division. During the battle for France in 1940 it took part in several rearguard actions and was heavily engaged in the fighting on the La Basée Canal. Following evacuation from Dunkirk, the battalion was re-organized in England and later served in the campaigns in North Africa, Sicily and Italy, serving within the 38th (Irish) Brigade and fighting in numerous engagements including Centuripe, Cassino II and the Liri Valley actions. It formed part of the army of occupation in Austria after the end of the war.

2nd Battalion

This battalion was based in Malta in 1939 and remained there until 1943, playing a role in defending this strategic island during the prolonged siege. In 1943 it was sent to Egypt, Syria and Palestine, before joining the ill-fated expedition to Leros in the Dodecanese, where it suffered numerous casualties. In the aftermath of this operation, the regiment's 6th Battalion was re-designated as the 2nd Battalion, Royal Irish Fusiliers in June 1944.

Post-War Period, 1945–68

The 2nd Battalion of the Royal Irish Fusiliers served in Egypt and Palestine and was disbanded in 1948. The 1st Battalion served in Palestine, the Suez Zone in Egypt, Jordan and with the British Army in Germany. During the Korean War, detachments of the regiment joined the Royal Ulster Rifles in Korea.

In 1954, the battalion was posted on garrison duty in Korea before being sent to Kenya in 1956 during the Mau Mau disturbances. After Kenya, the 1st Battalion later served with the British Army of the Rhine (BAOR) and also in Libya, Swaziland and Aden. On 1 July 1968, it was amalgamated with the Royal Ulster Rifles and the Royal Inniskilling Fusiliers to form the Royal Irish Rangers (see separate entry for that regiment).

Colonels-in-chief
1910   Field-Marshal HM King George V

Colonels
1881   General Sir Charles Hastings Doyle (1st Bn)
1881   General John Arthur Lambert (2nd Bn)
1887   General Augustus H. Ferryman
1897   Lieutenant-General Sir Alexander H. Cobbe
1899   Major-General Thomas R. Stevenson
1923   Lieutenant-General Sir Thomas Edwin Scott
1937   Brigadier-General Adrian B. Incledon-Webber
1946   Field-Marshal Sir Gerald W.R. Templer
1960   Major-General Thomas P.D. Scott

Battle honours

In 1881 the Royal Irish Fusiliers adopted the battle honours of its founding battalions and thereafter added a considerable number of honours to this list in its own right.

Egypt, Montevideo, Talavera, Barossa, Tarifa, Java, Vittoria, Nivelle, Niagara, Orthes, Toulouse, Peninsula, Ava, Sevastopol, Tel-el-Kebir, Egypt 1882, Egypt 1884, Relief of Ladysmith, South Africa 1899–1902, Le Cateau, Retreat from Mons, Marne 1914, Aisne 1914, Armentières 1914, Hill 60, Ypres 1914, Ypres 1917, Ypres 1918, Gravenstafel, St Julien, Frezenberg, Bellwaarde, Somme 1916, Somme 1918, Albert 1916, Guillemont, Ginchy, Le Transloy, Arras 1917, Scarpe 1917, Messines 1917, Messines 1918, Langemarck 1917, Cambrai 1917, St Quentin, Rosières, Lys, Bailleul, Kemmel, Courtrai, France and Flanders 1914–18, Kosturino, Struma, Macedonia 1915–17, Suvla, Landing at Suvla, Scimitar Hill, Gallipoli 1915, Gaza, Jerusalem, Tell 'Asur, Megiddo, Nablus, Palestine 1917–18, Withdrawl to Escaut, St Omer-La Bassée, Bou Arada, Stuka Farm, Oued Zarga, Djebel bel Mahdi, Djebel Ang, Djebel Tanngoucha, Adrano, Centuripe, Salso Crossing, Simeto Crossing, Malleto, Termoli, Trigno, Sangro, Fossacesia, Cassino II, Liri Valley, Trasimene Line, Monte Spurdo, Monte Grande, Argenta Gap, San Nicolo Canal, Leros, Malta 1940.

Motto
Faugh-a-Ballagh (Clear the Way)

Regimental music
Tunes associated with the regiment are 'Barrosa', 'Garry Owen' and 'St Patrick's Day'.

Nicknames
Various nicknames have been associated with the founding battalions of the Royal Irish Fusiliers. These include 'the Old Fogs', 'the Faugh-a-Ballagh Boys', 'the Eagle Takers', 'the Rollickers' and 'Blayney's Bloodhounds'. Some of these nicknames refer to the regiment's motto; 'Faugh-a-ballagh'. The nickname 'the Eagle Takers' refers to the capture of the French Eagle at Barrosa. 'Blayney's Bloodhounds' refers to the 89th Foot's actions during the 1798 rebellion.

THE CONNAUGHT RANGERS

Formerly the 88th (Connaught Rangers) Regiment of Foot and the 94th Regiment of Foot, 1793–1922

The Connaught Rangers was perhaps one of the best-known of the Irish regiments in the British army. It was initially raised as the 88th (The Connaught Rangers) Regiment of Foot in 1793. Under the terms of the Cardwell army reforms of 1881, this regiment was amalgamated with the 94th Regiment of Foot, and the 88th and

94th Regiments subsequently formed the 1st and 2nd Battalions of the Connaught Rangers.

88th (THE CONNAUGHT RANGERS) REGIMENT OF FOOT

Subsequently the 1st Battalion, the Connaught Rangers

Formation

Two earlier regiments had previously been numbered as the 88th Foot but had been disbanded. These were the 88th Royal Highland Volunteers (1760–63) and the 88th Foot (1779–83).

The 88th (Connaught Rangers) Regiment of Foot was the third regiment to be assigned that regimental number. It was one of several regiments raised in 1793 on the outbreak of war with revolutionary France. It was raised by Colonel the Hon. John Thomas De Burgh (later the 13th Earl of Clanricarde), under the terms of a commission dated 25 September 1793.

Its original officers were awarded their commissions according to the number of recruits that they brought with them to the regiment and the regiment's first recruits were from the counties of the province of Connaught . Even before being given the numerical designation of '88th Foot', the regiment was already known as the Connaught Rangers due to the composition of the regiment. Also the title of 'Rangers' was a popular one for provincial levies of the period.

Operational history

The Revolutionary and Napoleonic Wars, 1793–1815

1794   The regiment's first experience of action was in the Low Countries and it took part in the campaign under the Duke of York. It returned to England with 543 men sick out of its total strength of 773. Lieutenant-Colonel William Carr Beresford (later Viscount Beresford) was given command of the regiment.

1795   The regiment was sent to the West Indies but the transport fleet was dispersed in a storm and only two companies reached Grenada and St Lucia. The remainder of the regiment returned to Gibralttar and was afterwards posted to Jersey.

1799   The Connaught Rangers were sent to India and afterwards served in Ceylon before being posted to Egypt.

1802   The regiment returned to England and was employed in coastal defence.

1804   A second battalion raised in Ireland under the Additional Forces Act. This new battalion was initially commanded by Lieutenant-Colonel John Alexander Wallace.

1806   The 1st Battalion, Connaught Rangers was sent to the Cape and from there to South America as part of General Whitelock's unsuccessful attempt to take Buenos Aires.

1808 The 1st Battalion was sent to Cadiz in December but as British troops were refused entry into the city, they returned to Lisbon.

1809 The 1st Battalion sent to the Peninsula and attached to the 3rd Division, taking part in the battle of Talavera. A draft of replacements from the 2nd battalion arrived in September under Lt.-Col. Wallace who then took command of the regiment. The 2nd Battalion was sent to Lisbon and then Gibraltar.

1810 The 1st Battalion of regiment played a prominent role in the battle of Busaco, its conduct being commended by the Duke of Wellington. In the aftermath of the battle, one of the battalion's officers encountered French soldiers of Napoleon's Régiment Irlandais among the prisoners.

1811 The 1st Battalion took part in the battle of Fuentes de Oñoro and the sieges of Badajoz and Ciudad Rodriego. The 2nd Battalion of the Connaught Rangers, which had been in garrison in Lisbon and saw action at Sabugal, joined the 1st Battalion after Fuentes de Oñoro and its men were absorbed into the 1st Battalion. Its officers and NCOs were returned to Ireland to recruit and train drafts of replacements. In September the Connaught Rangers fought in the action at El Bodon.

1812 During the storming of Ciudad Rodrigo in January, the Connaught Rangers provided the initial storming party or 'forlorn hope' when the walls had been breached. The regiment also took part in the storming of Badajoz, where the French 88^e de Ligne formed part of the garrison. At the battle of Salamanca it captured the Schellen-baum or 'Jingling Johnnie' of the French 101st de Ligne.[17] Following a period in the garrison at Madrid, the regiment then took part in the difficult and humiliating retreat from Burgos, back into Portugal.

1813 The Connaught Rangers fought in the battle of Vittoria and in November and December in the actions along the Nivelle and Nive rivers.

1814 The regiment fought in the final battles of this campaign at Orthez and Toulouse. As Britain was still at war with America, the regiment was ordered to Quebec where it took part in operations against Plattsburg on Lake Erie.

1815 The Connaught Rangers were ordered back to Europe following Napoleon's escape from Elba but arrived too late to take part in the Waterloo campaign. The regiment formed part of the army of occupation at Valenciennes until 1817.

1816 The 2nd Battalion, Connaught Rangers was disbanded.

1819 The regiment was based at Edinburgh

1825 Posted to the Ionian Islands, thereafter carrying out further garrison duties in the Meditteranean, the West Indies and Canada.

The Crimean War, 1854–6

1854 The regiment joined the expeditionary force being sent to the east and was attached to the 2nd Brigade of the Light Division. It took part in the battles of the Alma and Inkerman.

---

17 This unusual musical instrument was carried by the regiment's band until its disbandment.

1855 For the rest of the war, the Connaught Rangers served in the prolonged siege of Sevastopol.

Indian Mutiny, 1857–8

1857 The regiment was posted to India where it took part in the campaign against the sepoys in Central India. It remained in India until 1870.

1877 The Connaught Rangers were sent to South Africa and served in the 9th Kaffir War (1877–9) and the Zulu War of 1879. In January 1879, the time of the battles of Isandhlwana and Rorke's Drift, the regiment was based at Kingwilliamstown with companies at Pietermaritzburg and on the island of St Helena. The Connuaght Rangers subsequently took part in the second invasion of Zululand in 1879.

1880 The regiment was posted to India where it remained until 1891.

1881 Under the terms of the Cardwell Reforms, the 88th (Connaught Rangers) Regiment of Foot was re-designated as the 1st Battalion, Connaught Rangers. Following this re-organization of the army, the regiment was assigned recruiting district No. 88, which took in counties Sligo, Mayo, Roscommon, Leitrim and Galway.

1891 The 1st Battalion, Connaught Rangers returned to service in the British Isles.

94th REGIMENT OF FOOT

Subsequently the 2nd Battalion, the Connaught Rangers

By 1823, several regiments had borne the numerical designation of the 94th Foot. All of these regiments were only in existence for a relatively short period.

These regiments were:

1. The 94th (Royal Welsh Volunteers) Regiment of Foot (1760–63).
2. The 94th Foot (1779–83). This regiment was raised in Colchester.
3. The 94th Regiment (1793–5). Raised in Ireland by Colonel the Hon. John Hely-Hutchinson (later Earl of Donoughmore).
4. The 94th (or Scotch Brigade) Regiment of Foot (1803–18). This regiment had evolved from the un-numbered corps known as the Scotch Brigade that was raised in 1793.
5. In 1823 a new regiment was raised and designated as the 94th Regiment of Foot.

This last 94th Regiment of Foot that was formed in 1823 was not an Irish regiment. During the course of the 19th century it saw service in the Mediterranean, India, Aden and South Africa. In 1881 it was re-designated as the 2nd Battalion of the Connaught Rangers. On the reorganization of the regiment, the battle honours of the previous 94th regiments were incorporated with those of the Connaught Rangers. Between 1881 and the outbreak of the First World War, the 2nd Battalion,

Connaught Rangers served on garrison duties in England, Malta, Cyprus and Egypt. In 1896 it took part in the Dongola Expedition and later served in India and as part of the home garrison.

The Cardwell reforms of 1881 also allowed for the re-designation of regiments of the Irish Militia. Four Militia battalions subsequently became reserve battalions of the Connaught Rangers. These were:

> South Mayo Rifles Regiment of Militia, became the 3rd Battalion, Connaught Rangers (1881–1908).
> Galway Regiment of Militia, became the 4th Battalion, Connaught Rangers (1881–1908).
> Roscommon Regiment of Militia, became the 5th Battalion, Connaught Rangers (1881–1908)
> North Mayo Fusiliers Regiment of Militia, became the 6th Battalion, Connaught Rangers (1881–89).

Following the formation of the Territorial Force in 1908, only two Militia battalions remained. These were:

> 3rd Battalion, Connaught Rangers (Galway Regiment of Militia)
> 4th Battalion, Connaught Rangers (Roscommon Regiment of Militia)

The 2nd Anglo-Boer War, 1899–1902

1899   The 1st Battalion of the Connaught Rangers was sent to South Africa where it arrived at Cape Town on 28 November, before being sent to Durban. With the 1st Battalion, Royal Inniskilling Fusiliers, 1st Battalion, Royal Dublin Fusiliers and the 1st Battalion, Border Regiment it formed the 5th or Irish Brigade under Major-General Fitzroy Hart. On 15 December, it took part in the disastrous battle of Colenso where it lost 24 men killed, 105 men wounded and a further 25 men missing.

1900   The battalion took part in the battles at Venter's Spruit, Hart's Hill and the relief of Ladysmith before being returned to the Cape Colony.

1901   On 14 July, the battalion repulsed a Boer attack on its positions at Zuurvlakte.

The First World War, 1914–18

Both of this regiment's regular battalions served in the war and four new battalions were also formed to serve as service or reserve battalions. Battalions of this regiment saw service in many theatres including Gallipoli, Egypt, Palestine, Salonika and Mesopotamia (Iraq).

The regiment's battalions also saw extensive service on the Western Front and fought in practically every major battle from 1914, a fact reflected in the numerous battle honours awarded to the Connaught Rangers for their wartime service. On the outbreak of war, the regimental depot was in Renmore Barracks in Galway.

1st Battalion

This regular battalion was based at Ferozepore, India, on the outbreak of the war, and was attached to Ferozepore Brigade of the 3rd (Lahore) Division.

It arrived in Egypt in September but was then moved to France. In December 1914, it was amalgamated with the 2nd Battalion at Le Touret in France. In December 1915, it was attached to the 9th Indian Brigade, 3rd Indian Division, and sent to Mesopotamia (Iraq) and was based at Basra. In February 1916 it was attached to the 7th Indian Brigade. The battalion was sent to Egypt in April 1918 and at the end of the war was based at Nazareth in Palestine.

2nd Battalion

At the outbreak of the war, this regular battalion was based at Barrosa Barracks in Aldershot. It was attached to the 5th Brigade of the 2nd Division and landed at Boulougne on 14 August 1914. It was transferred to the Lahore Division in November 1914 and amalgamated with the 1st Battalion in the following month.

3rd (Reserve) Battalion

This battalion was formed at Galway on 4 August and was later based at Crosshaven and Kinsale in Co. Cork. In November 1917 it was moved to England and was based at Newcastle. In 1918 the battalion was amalgamated with the 4th Battalion and thereafter formed part of the garrison at Dover.

4th (Extra Reserve) Battalion

This battalion was raised at Boyle on 4 August 1914 and was later stationed at Queenstown (Cobh), Bere Island, Fermoy and Crosshaven, all in Co. Cork.

In November 1917 it was moved to Scotland and was based at Nigg in Perthshire and also Fort George. In May 1918 it was amalgamated with the 3rd Battalion and remained at Drover for the rest of the war as part of the garrison.

5th (Service) Battalion

This K1 battalion was formed in Dublin in August 1914 and was attached to the 29th Brigade of the 10th (Irish) Division. After training at Kilworth and the Curragh, it was moved to England in May 1915, where it was based in Basingstoke for further training. It took part in the Gallipoli campaign, being attached to the Australian and New Zealand Corps (ANZAC) for the supplementary landings of August 1915. Following its evacuation from Gallipoli, it served in the Salonika campaign and in Egypt, before being sent to France in June 1918. It served for the rest of the war in the 66th Division.

6th (Service) Division

This battalion was formed at Kilworth in September 1914 and was a K2 unit. It was attached to the 47th Brigade of the 16th (Irish) Division. After training in Fermoy and at Blackdown in England, it was sent to France in December 1915. Its entire war service was on the Western Front and it took part in numerous battles including the Somme, 3rd Ypres and Cambrai. In April 1918 it was reduced to cadre and the majority of its surviving personnel were transferred to the 2nd Battalion of the Leinster Regiment. The cadre staff later served in a training capacity with the 34th and 39th Divisions before being disbanded in August 1918.

At the end of the war, the wartime service battalions were disbanded. The regiment's 2nd Battalion was sent to Silesia as part of the army of occupation. The 1st Battalion, Connaught Rangers, was sent to India. In June 1920 a mutiny broke out among the 1st Battalion at Solan in India. The courts martial that followed sentenced fourteen men to death although only one, Private James Joseph Daly, was actually executed. In 1922, both battalions were returned to England and the regiment was disbanded.

Battle honours
Seringapatam, Egypt, Talavera, Busaco, Fuentes d'Onor, Ciudad Rodrigo, Badajoz, Salamanca, Vittoria, Nivelle, Orthes, Toulouse, Pyrenees,[18] Peninsula, Alma, Inkerman, Sevastopol, Central India, South Africa 1877–9, Relief of Ladysmith, South Africa 1899–1902, Mons, Retreat from Mons, Marne 1914, Aisne 1914, Messines 1914, Messines 1917, Armentières 1914, Ypres 1914, Ypres 1915, Ypres 1917, Langemarck 1914, Langemarck 1917, Gheluvelt, Nonne Bosschen, Festubert 1914, Givenchy 1914, Neuve Chapelle, St Julien, Aubers, Somme 1916, Somme 1918, Guillemont, Ginchy, St Quentin, Bapaume 1918, Rosières, Hindenburg Line, Cambrai 1918, Selle, France and Flanders 1914–18, Kosturino, Struma, Macedonia 1915–17, Suvla, Sari Bair, Scimitar Hill, Gallipoli 1915, Gaza, Jerusalem, Tell Asur, Megiddo, Sharon, Palestine 1917–18, Tigris 1916, Kut al Amara 1917, Baghdad, Mesopotamia 1916–18.[19]

Colonels
1793–1881, 88th (The Connaught Rangers) Regiment of Foot
1881–1922, The Connaught Rangers
1793   General John Thomas De Burgh, 13th Earl of Clanricarde
1794   General John Reid
1807   General Sir William Carr Beresford, 1st Viscount Beresford
1819   General Sir John Gordon Drummond
1824   General Sir Henry Frederick Campbell
1831   General Sir Alexander Wallace
1857   Lieutenant-General Robert Barclay Macpherson
1858   Lieutenant-General Horatio George Broke
1860   General Sir George Buller
1860   Major-General John Cox
1863   General Arthur Alexander Dalzell, 13th Earl of Carnwath
1864   General Montague Cholmeley Johnstone
1874   General Sir Horatio Shirley

18 The battle honour 'Pyrenees' was not awarded until 1910 and was for the service of the 88th Foot.
19 The pre-1881 battle honours were awarded for the service of the 88th and 94th Regiments of Foot.

1879   General William Irwin
1881   General William Irwin (1st Battalion)
        General Sir John Thornton Grant (2nd Battalion)
1889   General Joseph Edwin Thackwell
1900   Lieutenant-General Sir Edward Hotpon
1912   Major-General William Liston Dalrymple (up to disbandment in 1922)

Motto
'Quis Separabit?' (Who shall separate us?)

Regimental music
Quick march 'St Patrick's Day'. Marches associated with 94th Foot 'Blue Bonnets' and 'Argyle is my name'. Other associated marches: 'The Connaught Ranger'.

Nicknames
The Devil's Own, The Fagon Bealachs (88th Foot), The Garvies (94th Foot)

THE ROYAL DUBLIN FUSILIERS, 1881–1922

*Formerly the 102nd Regiment of Foot (Royal Madras Fusiliers)
and the 103rd Regiment of Foot (Royal Bombay Fusiliers), 1644–1881*

Formation
The Royal Dublin Fusiliers was formed as a two battalion regiment in 1881 under the terms of the Cardwell army reforms. It was formed through the amalgamation of two regiments from the former East India Company Army; the Royal Madras Fusiliers and the Royal Bombay Fusiliers. Both of these ancient and historic regiments could trace their respective histories back to the seventeenth century and had served in numerous campaigns in India.

The actual Royal Dublin Fusiliers only existed as a regiment between 1881 and 1922 but both of its battalions had accumulated a long list of battle honours during their previous incarnations which covered over 200 years of campaigning in India. The Royal Dublin Fusiliers would later add to this list of battle honours during the 2nd Boer War and the First World War, before being disbanded in 1922.

THE MADRAS EUROPEANS, LATER THE 102nd REGIMENT OF FOOT (ROYAL MADRAS FUSILIERS) AND FROM 1881 THE 1st BATTALION, ROYAL DUBLIN FUSILIERS

This battalion traces its history back to a series of independent companies that were raised by the East India Company in the late 1630s. The earliest of these was raised about 1639 and would have consisted of a mix of musketeers and pikemen.

During this period they were deployed to protect East India Company trading stations and served in places such as Bantam, Bencoolen and on the island of Formosa. In 1644 the Honourable East India Company formed a permanent company to serve as the garrison of Fort St George in Madras and this is unit formed the nucleus of the later Royal Madras Fusiliers.

1742   These independent companies were formed into a 500-strong battalion and was titled as the Madras Europeans. The young Robert Clive was commissioned into this regiment as an ensign at the beginning of his career.

Seven Years War, 1756–63

During the war against the French and Suraj-ud-Dowlah, the Nawab of Bengal, the regiment was present at the battle of Plassey (1757) and also took part in the battles of Condore and Wandewash (1760). It served in the sieges of Masulipatam and Pondicherry and in the relief and defence of Patna. The regiment was enlarged to three battalions in 1760 and later served in the Mysore War (1767–9) and in the Tanjore War (1774), when it was increased to four battalions. In 1766 it was re-designated as the 1st Madras Europeans.

1774   A fourth battalion was added to the regiment and it was re-designated as the 1st Madras European Regiment.

1778–80   It took part in the campaign against the French, and was present at the sieges of Pondicherry and Negapatam. During the extended campaign against Hyder Ali, the regiment took part in a series of battles which included Arcot, Peranbaucum, Wandewash, Porto Novo, Sholingur, Vellore and Cuddalore. Under Lord Cornwallis, the Madras Europeans played a major role in the campaign against the Tipoo Sultan during the Third Mysore War (1789–92) and succeeded in storming and capturing Nundy Droog. In 1791, the Royal Tiger badge and 'Spectamur Agendo' motto was authorized for the regiment. In 1793 the regiment was present the siege of Pondicherry and, in 1796, they took part in the capture of Ceylon (Sri Lanka), before capturing a series of Dutch-controlled islands which included Amboyna and Banda.

1799   The regiment took part in the Fourth Mysore War of 1799 but was not present at the final storming of Seringapatam. Nevertheless, by this stage in its history, the Madras European Regiment had taken part in forty-six general actions and seventy-four sieges during its service in India. It was reduced to a single battalion.

1803   The regiment was based at Cuttack.

1809–10   It took part in the recapture of Amboyna, Terante and Banda and its sapper company served in Java.

1815–16   The regiment was stationed at Tumboodra and Hyderabad.

3rd Mahratta War, 1817–19

The regiment took part in the battles of Manipuri (Mahidput) and Nagpore and also the siege and capture of Asseerghur.

1st Burma War, 1823–6
The regiment served throughout this war in Burma.

1830   Re-titled as Madras (European) Regiment
1839   The regiment was re-designated as the 1st Madras (European) Regiment.
1843   The regiment was re-designated as a fusilier regiment and took the title of 1st Madras (European) Fusiliers.

2nd Burma War, 1852–3
The Madras Fusiliers took part in the 2nd Burma War and would remain in Burma until 1857.

Persia and the Indian Mutiny, 1857–9
In 1857 it boarded ship for Persia and was travelling to the campaign there when the Persian War actually ended. Returning to Calcutta, it arrived in that city ten days after the outbreak of the Indian Mutiny. The regiment distinguished itself greatly during the Mutiny. Under the command of Brigadier John Neill, it served in Benares and Allahabad before taking part in the recapture of Cawnpore. It then took part in the relief, siege and capture of Lucknow before serving in the final campaign in Oude. In 1858 it was re-titled as the 1st Madras Fusiliers.

1861   On the re-organization of the East India Company army in 1861, the regiment passed to the control of the Crown and initially was re-designated as the 1st Royal Madras Fusiliers. In 1862 it was re-titled as the 102nd Regiment of Foot (Royal Madras Fusiliers).[20]
1868   The Royal Madras Fusiliers was sent to England and served on home station for the first time in its long history. It later served at both Gibraltar and Ceylon.
1881   The Royal Madras Fusiliers was amalgamated with the 103rd Regiment of Foot (Royal Bombay Fusiliers) to become the 1st Battalion, Royal Dublin Fusiliers. Under the terms of these reforms the regiment was assigned to recruiting district No. 102, which took in the city and county of Dublin and also counties Kildare, Carlow and Wicklow. The 1st Battalion later served in Egypt (1885), England (1886), and Ireland (1887).

THE BOMBAY EUROPEANS, LATER THE 103rd REGIMENT OF FOOT (ROYAL BOMBAY FUSILIERS) AND FROM 1881 THE 2nd BATTALION, ROYAL DUBLIN FUSILIERS IN 1881

This battalion can trace its origins back to 1661 when a company of Europeans was formed to garrison Bombay, which had been ceded to the British crown as part of the

---

20 Five previous regiments had been designated as the 102nd Foot and these included an earlier Irish regiment and also a regiment from New South Wales.

dowry of Queen Catherine of Braganza, wife of Charles II. Details of its early history are scarce but it would seem that in 1688 it was designated as the Bombay European Regiment and transferred to the control of the Honourable East India Company.

In the early eighteenth century it operated in Bengal and between 1748 and 1754 it campaigned against the French in the Carnatic. It is known that the battalion served under Lord Clive and was present at the battle of Plassey in 1757. It served throughout the campaigns of 1758–64 and was present at the final defeat of Meer Kossim at Buxar on the 23 October 1764. In 1767 the Bombay Europeans took part in the campaign in Persia.

1780   Under General Goddard the battalion took part in the campaign in Guzerat and was present at the storming of Ahmedabad. It took part in the **1st Mahratta War** of 1779–82 and served under Lord Cornwallis during his campaign of 1790–1 during the **3rd Mysore War**, being posted in Goa and at Malabar. The Bombay Europeans played a prominent part in the storming of Seringapatam in 1792 and one of its NCOs, Sergeant Grant, planted the British flag on the walls of Tippoo's fortress having stormed the breach.

1803   The battalion was employed in campaigns in Guzerat and Malwa during the **2nd Mahratta War**.

1817   It took part in the defeat of Bajee Rao, the last peshwar of Poona, while also serving in the **3rd Mahratta War** of 1817–18.

1819   The battalion was present at the capture of Cutch and throughout the 1820s the Bombay Europeans played a prominent part in the campaign against Gulf pirates and slavers, storming the pirate stronghold at Mussooling Bay in March 1821.

1st Burma War, 1823–6

Detachment's of the battalion were employed as marines on board East India Company ships and took part in expeditions to the Rangoon and Irawaddy rivers.

1839   The battalion was sent to take possession of Aden and was involved in a protracted campaign against the Arab tribesmen who tried to re-capture the port. It was re-designated the 1st Bombay (European) Regiment.

1844   The regiment was re-titled the 1st Bombay (European) Fusiliers.

2nd Sikh War, 1848–9

The Bombay Europeans saw extensive service during the 2nd Sikh War and took part in the siege of Mooltan and the final defeat of the Sikhs at Gujerat. Following the defeat of the Sikhs the battalion pursued their Afghan allies as far as the Kyber Pass.

Indian Mutiny 1857–9

During the Mutiny, the Bombay Europeans were stationed in the Bengal Presidency but saw no major action. The regiment transferred to the control of the Crown in 1858 and was re-designated as the 1st Bombay Fusiliers (1859).

1861   As part of further reforms the regiment was re-designated as the 103rd Regiment of Foot (Royal Bombay Fusiliers).[21]

1870   The Royal Bombay Fusiliers were sent to England, serving on home station for the first time in the regiment's history.

1881   Under the terms of the Cardwell reforms, the regiment was amalgamated with the Royal Madras Fusiliers to become the 2nd Battalion, Royal Dublin Fusiliers. It subsequently served in Gibraltar (1884), Egypt (1885) and India (1886)

Under the terms of the Cardwell reforms of 1881, three regiments of the Irish Militia were re-designated as reserve battalions of the Royal Dublin Fusiliers. These were:

3rd Battalion (Kildare Rifles Militia, 1881–1922)
4th Battalion (Queen's Own Royal Dublin City Militia, 1881–1922)
5th Battalion (Dublin County Light Infantry Militia, 1881–1922)

2nd Anglo-Boer War, 1899–1902

1st Battalion

The battalion arrived in Cape Town on 28 November 1899 and was assigned to the 5th or Irish Brigade under Major-General Fitzroy Hart. The 1st Battalion took part in actions at Colenso, Elandslaagte, the Relief of Ladysmith, Alleman's Nek and Amersfort. A detachment of the battalion served as Mounted Infantry at the defence of Fort Itala.

2nd Battalion

The 2nd Battalion was posted to South Africa in 1899 before the outbreak of the war. It took part in actions at Talana Hill, Laing's Nek, Lombards' Kop and three sections of the battalion were present at the ambush of the armoured train outside Frere. The battalion later formed part of Hart's Irish Brigade and took part in the battles of Colenso, Venter's Spruit, Pieter's Hill and the Relief of Ladysmith. They later fought at Zuickerbosch Spruit. In January 1902, they were posted to Aden.

In the years that preceded the First World War, the regular battalions of the RDF served on garrison duty in Malta, the Ionian Islands and India.

The First World War, 1914–18

The two regular battalions of the Royal Dublin Fusiliers served throughout the war while a nine further service, extra reserve and reserve battalions were also raised by 1918. These battalions served most notably with the 10th and 16th (Irish) Divisions. In 1914, the regimental depot was in Naas.

While the majority of men who served with the regiment during the war saw service on the Western Front, battalions of the regiment also served in the campaigns

---

21 Four previous regiments had borne the designation of 103rd Foot, including the 103rd (King's Irish Infantry) Regiment of Foot, which existed between 1781 and 1783.

in Gallipoli, Salonika, Egypt and Palestine. Their wartime services are outlined below.

1st Battalion
This regular battalion was in Madras at the outbreak of the war. It arrived Plymouth on 21 December 1914 and joined 86th Brigade of the 29th Division. During the Galliploi campaign, it landed at Cape Helles, 25 April 1915, form the transport ship *River Clyde* and suffered heavy casualties. It was later amalgamated with the 1st Royal Munster Fusiliers in a composite battalion known as the 'Dubsters'. It transferred to the 16th (Irish) Division and arrived in France in March 1916 and would later serve with the 29th Division.

2nd Battalion
This regular battalion was based at Gravesend on the outbreak of war. It was attached to the 10th Brigade of the 4th Division and landed at Boulogne on 22 August 1914. In late 1916 it was transferred to 48th Brigade of the 16th (Irish) Division and later absorbed the remaining men from the disbanded 8th and 9th Battalions. It was reduced to cadre strength but was reconstituted in June 1918 and later served with the 31st and 50th Divisions.

3rd (Reserve) Battalion
This reserve battalion was activated at Naas, Co. Kildare on 4 August 1914. During the war it served at various home barracks including Queenstown (Cobh), Gateshead, Grimsby, Weelsby and Waltham. Some of its personnel absorbed into the 4th, 5th and 11th Battalions.

4th (Extra Reserve) Battalion
This reserve battalion was activated in Dublin on 4 August 1914. It later served in Cork, Sittingborne, Templemore, Mullingar and Brocklesby near Grimsby. In May 1918 its personnel were absorbed into the 3rd Battalion.

5th (Extra Reserve) Battalion
This reserve battalion was activated 4 August 1914 in Dublin. It served in Queenstown (Cobh), Sittingborne, the Curragh Camp, Longford and Glencorse, near Edinburgh. In May 1918 personnel absorbed into the 3rd Battalion.

6th (Service) Battalion
This K1 battalion was formed at Naas in August 1914 and was attached to the 30th Brigade of the 10th (Irish) Division. With this division it served in the Gallipoli, Salonika, Egyptian and Palestine campaigns. In May 1918 it left the 10th Division and was sent to France where it served with the 66th Division form the rest of the war.

7th (Service) Battalion
This K1 battalion was formed at Naas in August 1914. It was assigned to 30th Brigade, 10th (Irish) Division and served in Gallipoli, Salonika, Egypt and Palestine. In April 1918 it was sent to France where it was reduced to cadre, its surplus personnel being sent to the 2nd Battalion. On 10 June 1918 the cadre

staff joined the 16th (Irish) Division at Samer before returning to England. On 18 June 1918 the cadre staff were absorbed by the newly formed 11th Battalion of the Royal Irish Fusiliers at Greatham, Durham.

8th (Service) Battalion
This service battalion was formed in September 1914 and joined 48th Brigade of the 16th (Irish) Division. It served with this division throughout the Somme campaign and early 1917 before being amalgamated with 9th Battalion to form 8th/9th Battalion in the 48th Brigade. On 10 February 1918 the battalion was disbanded in France, the remaining personnel going to the 1st and 2nd battalions.

9th Service Battalion
This battalion was formed in September 1914 and was attached to the 48th Brigade, 16th (Irish) Division. In September 1915 moved to England and was based at Blackdown before landing at Havre in December 1915. On 24 October 1917 the remaining personnel were amalgamated with 8th Battalion to form 8th/9th Battalion. This battalion disbanded in France in February 1918, the remaining personnel joining 1st and 2nd Battalions.

10th (Service) Battalion
This service battalion was raised in Dublin in late 1915. In August 1916 it was moved to Pirbright, England, before sailing for France in August 1916. It joined 190th Brigade, 63rd Division. In June 1916 transferred to 48th Brigade, 16th (Irish) Division. On 24 October 1917 it absorbed surplus personnel from the amalgamation of the 8th and 9th Battalions. This battalion was disbanded in France on 15 February 1918.

11th (Reserve) Battalion
This battalion was formed in Dublin in July 1916. In January 1918 it was based at Aldershot and in May was absorbed into the 3rd Battalion at Plymouth.

Following the Armistice, the wartime battalions of the regiment were disbanded over the period of some months. The two regular battalions remained and served as part of the armies of occupation, the 1st Battalion being stationed in Germany while the 2nd Battalion was sent to Constantinople in Turkey. Following the foundation of the Irish Free State, the regiment was disbanded in 1922, its colours being laid up in Windsor Castle.

Battle honours
The battle honours of the Royal Dublin Fusiliers include those of the former Royal Madras Fusiliers and the Royal Bombay Fusiliers. This lengthy list reflects not only long service in India but also the extensive service of RDF battalions in various theatres during the First World War.

Arcot, Plassey, Condore, Wandiwash, Pondicherry, Nundy Droog, Amboyna, Ternate, Banda, Maheidpoor, Ava, Pegu, Lucknow, Buxar, Guzerat, Carnatic, Mysore,

Serringpatam, Kirkee, Beni Boo Ali, Aden, Mooltan, Goojerat, Punjaub, Sholinghur, Relief of Ladysmith, South Africa 1899–1902, Le Cateau, Retreat from Mons, Marne 1914, Aisne 1914, Armentières 1914, Ypres 1915, Ypres 1917, Ypres 1918, St Julien, Frezenberg, Bellewaarde, Somme 1916, Somme 1918, Albert 1916, Guillemont, Ginchy, Le Transloy, Ancre 1916, Arras 1917, Scarpe 1917, Arleaux, Messines 1917, Langemarck 1917, Polygon Wood, Cambrai 1917, Cambrai 1918, St Quentin, Bapaume 1918, Rosières, Avre, Hindenburg Line, St Quentin Canal, Beaurevoir, Courtrai, Selle, Sambre, France and Flanders 1914–18, Kosturino, Struma, Macedonia 1915–17, Helles, Landing at Helles, Krithia, Suvla, Sair Bair, Landing at Suvla, Scimitar Hill, Gallipoli 1915–16, Egypt 1916, Gaza, Jerusalem, Tell' Asur, Palestine 1917–18.

Colonels-in-chief (RDF)
1908   Field-Marshal HRH, the Duke of Connaught

Colonels (RDF)
1881   General Sir Robert J.H. Vivian (1st Battalion)
        General Sir William Wyllie (2nd Battalion)
1891   General Sir Robert Walter Macleod Fraser
1895   Lieutenant-General Sir John Blick Spurgin
1903   Major-General William Francis Vetch
1910   Major-General Charles Duncan Cooper (until disbandment)

Motto
'Spectamur Agendo' (Let us be judged by our deeds or By our deeds we are known).

Regimental music
Tunes associated with the regiment include 'The British Grenadiers', 'St Patrick's Day' and 'The Dublin Fusiliers'. Colonel H.C. Wylly's history of the regiment's first battalion, *Neill's Blue Caps*, also included the words and music of a regimental song.

Regimental mascot
During the course of a long history the battalions that later formed the Royal Dublin Fusiliers had many official and unofficial mascots. The most impressive official mascot was a Royal Bengal Tiger, named 'Plassey', who was the mascot of the 102nd Royal Madras Fusiliers during the 1860s and early 1870s, even accompanying the battalion back to England.

At the end of the First World War, the regiment also acquired a German dog which became the regiment's mascot. He had been founded wounded outside a German dugout at Festubert in 1917 and was given the name 'Jack'.

Nicknames
The 102nd Royal Madras Fusiliers, later the 1st Battalion RDF, were known as 'The Sweet Lambs' until the time of the Indian Mutiny. Thereafter they were usually

known as 'Neill's Blue Caps' due to the blue cloth that their commanding officer bought them to cover their shakos. The 103rd Royal Bombay Fusiliers, later the 2nd Battalion RDF, were known as the 'Old Toughs'.

THE ROYAL MUNSTER FUSILIERS, 1881–1922

Formerly the 101st Regiment of Foot (Royal Bengal Fusiliers) and the 104th Regiment of Foot (Bengal Fusiliers), 1756–1881

Formation

The Royal Munster Fusiliers was another regiment that officially dated from the Cardwell reforms of 1881. Both of the two battalions that founded the new regiment, however, had long traditions of service with the East India Company and this was reflected in the numerous battle honours that were awarded for service in wars in India.

101st REGIMENT OF FOOT (ROYAL BENGAL FUSILIERS), LATER THE 1st BATTALION, ROYAL MUNSTER FUSILIERS

This regiment, later a battalion within the Royal Munster Fusiliers, was raised in December 1756 by Lord Clive and was originally designated as the Bengal European Regiment. It was formed by amalgamating a number of independent companies which were then serving in Bengal as part of the army of the East India Company.

The original independent Bengal company had been raised in 1652 and this 'guard of honour' had initially been just thirty men, commanded by an ensign. During the 130 years that followed, the Bengal Europeans saw service in numerous wars as the East India Company extended its power in India and, in so doing, came into conflict with native rulers and also the French and the Dutch. On various occasions it was also expanded to include two or more battalions and one of these additional battalions became the 2nd Bengal European Regiment and later the 104th Bengal Fusiliers. The battles and sieges in which the 101st Royal Bengal Fusiliers served in are listed below.

Operational history

1756   The assault on the fortress of Baj Baj.
1757   The capture of Fort William (Calcutta), the capture of Hugli, the battle of Chitpore and the captures of Chandernagore and Kutwah.
        The battle of Plassey.
1758   The battle of Condore and the captures of Rajamundri and Narsurpore.
1759   The battles of Musulipatam, Patna, Chandernagore and Bederra.
1760   The regiment took part in the defence of Patna and the battles of Seerpore and Beerpore.
1761   The battle of Suan.

1763	The battles of Manjee, Kutwah, Geriah and the captures of Suti and Monghyr.
1764	Battle of Buxar and the assault on Chunar.
1765	The regiment was re-designated as the 1st Bengal Regiment.
1765	The captures of Allahabad and Chunar and the battles of Karrah and Kalpi.
1774	The battle of Kutra.
1781	The battles of Patuta, Porto Novo, Pollilore, Sholinghur, Veracundalore and several other actions.
1782	The battle of Arnee.
1783	The siege of Cuddalore.
1794	The Rohilcund campaign.
1803	The regiment was re-designated as the Bengal European Regiment.
1804	Capture of the fortress at Gwalior. The battle and storming of Deig.
1805	The assaults on Bhurtpore.
1808	Expedition to Macao.
1810	Expedition to Java.
1814	The regiment served in the Nepal War.
1817	The regiment fought in the Pindaree War.
1822	Re-designated as the 1st Bengal European Regiment.
1826	The storming of Bhurtpore.
1830	Re-designated as the Bengal European Regiment.

1st Afghan War, 1839–42

1838	The regiment served in the 1st Afghan War and took part in the storming of Ghuznee (1839) and the capture of Pushoot (1840).
1840	Re-designated as the 1st Bengal (European) Light Infantry.

1st Sikh War, 1845–6

1845	The battle of Ferozshuhur.
1846	Capture of Sobraon. The regiment was re-designated as the 1st Bengal (European) Fusiliers.

2nd Sikh War, 1848–9

1848	The battle of Chillianwallah.
1849	The battle of Gujerat (Guzerat).

2nd Burma War, 1852–3

1852	The capture of Pegu.

The Indian Mutiny, 1857–9

1857	The regiment took part in the storming of Delhi and the battles of Budli-ka-Serai, Subzi Munid, Narnoul and Nujjufghur, among others.
1858	Siege and capture of Lucknow and the battles of Baree and Sahadit.
1861	Re-designated as the 1st Royal Bengal Fusiliers.
1862	The regiment transferred from the East India Company service to the control of the Crown. On doing so it was re-titled again, this time as the 101st

41 The Cork company of the Irish Volunteers, 1914. Some of these volunteers wear the full volunteer uniform while others wear a mixture of civilian and military items. (Military Archives.)

42 Mayo flying column during the War of Independence, 1919–21. Perhaps one of the most evocative photographs from this era. These volunteers have dispensed with volunteer uniform and wear more practical dress for the guerrilla campaign. Lightly equipped, such Flying Columns were able to move across country quickly to attack British columns. (Military Archives.)

43 Colour Party of the National Army at Griffith Barracks, 1922. During the Civil War, the army of the Irish Free State expanded at a rapid rate and included over 60 infantry battalions by 1923. (Military Archives.)

44 Troopers of the Mounted Escort or 'Blue Hussars'. This unit, officially 'An Marc Sluagh' or Mounted Escort, provided escorts for ceremonial occasions between 1931 and 1949. It was not a permanently constituted unit and raised its personnel from the Artillery Corps. Such ceremonial duties are now carried out by a motorcycle escort. (Military Archives.)

45 Pre-war photograph of men of the 2nd Infantry Battalion. This photograph, taken in the 1930s, shows Irish soldiers in the Vickers-type helmet. This, along with the style of tunic of the period, gave Irish troops a distinctly Germanic appearance. (Military Archives.)

46 Parade of troops through Cork during the Emergency. The years of the Second World War or Emergency saw a rapid expansion of both the permanent and reserve forces. This parade included mechanized infantry and also armoured cars. (Military Archives, Hanley Collection.)

47 Light anti-aircraft battery at Cobh during the Emergency. Ireland's air defences were also greatly expanded between 1939 and 1945. Heavy and light AA batteries were established around the country and opened fire on unidentified aircraft on numerous occasions. (Military Archives.)

48 Irish troops boarding a plane at Baldonnel aerodrome bound for the Congo. This was the first UN mission for Ireland and during it Irish troops were involved in heavy fighting in actions at Elizabethville and Jadotville, among other locations. (Military Archives.)

49 Irish troops of the UNICYP force in Cyprus being inspected. This mission was necessary due to tensions between the island's Greek and Turkish communities. The Irish troops here have been issued with a practical lightweight uniform, better suited for the climate. (Military Archives.)

50 Recruiting for the Pearse Battalion of the FCA at Trinity College in the 1960s. The Irish reserve forces have evolved in various stages since the 1920s. On occasion, units were based in Irish universities which were seen as prime recruiting grounds. (Military Archives.)

51 Members of 73rd Battalion UNIFIL in 1993. Lieutenant (now Commandant) Gareth Prendergast and his men take a breather after a patrol in the Irish battalion area in Lebanon. During this mission, which claimed the lives of several Irish soldiers, every day began with a patrol and a sweep for mines. (Courtesy Comdt. Gareth Prendergast.)

52 An Irish mobile patrol in Somalia, part of the UNOSOM II mission. This mission in support of humanitarian operations in war-torn Somalia lasted from 1993 to 1995. (Military Archives.)

53 Members of the Irish army on patrol in East Timor. Between 1999 and 2004 Irish troops served with the various missions in East Timor. They often had to operate in difficult jungle terrain in their efforts to prevent internecine strife between local communities. (Military Archives.)

54 Irish troops prevent civil disorder while serving with KFOR in Kosovo. Due to tensions between the different communities, Irish troops were often called upon to assist the civil power in preventing riots. (*An Cosantóir*.)

55 Irish UNMIL troops on long range patrol in Liberia. The most recent large-scale Irish mission was to this African state. Due to the large areas under Irish control, long range patrols of several days were commonplace. (*An Cosantóir*.)

56 Women members of the Reserve Defence Forces on an artillery potential officers course. Since 1980, women have served in the Defence Forces, initially only as officers. They now serve in all ranks and across all branches of the service. (*An Cosantóir*.)

57 Members of the Army Ranger Wing on exercise. Since the 1960s, Irish soldiers had gone on special forces training abroad. In 1980, the Army Ranger Wing was formed and now carries out special forces and anti-terrorism duties. (*An Cosantóir*.)

58 President Mary McAleese reviews a Reserve Defence Forces guard of honour during the Easter commemorations, 2007. (*An Cosantóir*.)

Regiment of Foot (Royal Bengal Fusiliers). It was the fifth regiment to bear the 101st designation.

1868   The regiment was returned to England for the first time in its history. It later served on garrison duties in Malta, Nova Scotia and Bermuda.

1881   Under the terms of the Cardwell army reforms, it was re-designated the 1st Battalion of the Royal Munster Fusiliers. Under the terms of the same army reforms, the regiment was allocated recruiting district No. 101, which included counties Clare, Kerry, Limerick and both Cork county and city.

104th REGIMENT OF FOOT (BENGAL FUSILIERS), LATER THE 2nd BATTALION, ROYAL MUNSTER FUSILIERS

Three previous regiments had borne the numeral 104th before the designation of this regiment in 1839. Its early history can be traced back to 1765 when the Bengal European Regiment (see above), then over 1,600 strong was further sub-divided. The 2nd Bengal European Regiment was raised as a result of this reform and this regiment was absorbed by the East India Company's Marine Battalion in 1803.

It was re-formed again in 1822 but was absorbed by the 1st Bengal European Regiment in 1830. Using volunteers from te 1st Bengal Europeans, the regiment was re-formed once more in 1839 as the 2nd Bengal (European) Light Infantry and remained in existence until becoming the 2nd Battalion of the Royal Munster Fusiliers in 1881. While the early history of both the 1st and 2nd Bengal Europeans is somewhat confusing, it can be shown that they shared a common history, the establishment of the second regiment being due to the expansion of the original Bengal European Regiment. This made the 1881 linking of these two regiments ultimately very logical.

Operational history

2nd Sikh War, 1848–49

1848   The battle of Chillianwallah.
1849   The battle of Gujerat (Guzerat).
1850   It was re-designated as the 2nd Bengal (European) Fusiliers. The regiment was sent to Burma and served in the **2nd Burma War** of 1852–3.

The Indian Mutiny, 1857–9

1857   The regiment served throughout the mutiny, taking part in the storming of Delhi and the battle of Budli-ka-Serai.
1858   The regiment transferred to the control of the Crown.
1859   It was re-designated as the 2nd Bengal Fusiliers.
1862   The regiment was re-designated as the 104th Regiment of Foot (Bengal Fusiliers). The 104th Bengal Fusiliers remained in India until 1871 when it was sent to England. It later served in Malta, before returning to India.

1881   The regiment was re-designated as the 2nd Battalion, Royal Munster Fusiliers. At the same time, regiments of the Irish Militia were re-designated as militia or reserve battalions of the Royal Munster Fusiliers. These battalions were:

3rd Battalion (South Cork Light Infantry Militia)
4th Battalion (Kerry Militia)
5th Battalion (Royal Limerick County Militia (Fusiliers))

2nd Anglo-Boer War, 1899–1902

1st Battalion

The 1st Battalion of the regiment was sent to the Cape in 1899, before war actually broke out. It was initially attached to the 20th Brigade under the command of Major-General Arthur Paget. The battalion took part in the capture of Bethlehem (1900) and fought in the actions at Warm Baths, near Pretoria (1900) and Rhenoster Kop (1900). In 1901, the battalion served in both the Cape Colony and the Transvaal and detachments later served as mounted infantry, taking part in the action on the Betel-Standerton Road. In January 1902, a detachment of the battalion fought in the successful action near Griquatown. At the end of the war, the battalion was sent to India.

2nd Battalion

The regiment's second battalion was brought from India in December 1901 and served on blockhouse duty for the remaider of the war in the Orange River Colony. At the end of the war, the battalion returned to Ireland.

5th Battalion

The regiment's 5th (Limerick Militia) Battalion was activated during the war and sent to the Mediterranean where it carried out garrison duties. For this service, it was awarded an honour for its battalion colours 'Mediterranean 1901'.

In the years preceding the First World War, the regiment's regular battalions served on garrison duties in India, Ireland and England.

The First World War, 1914–18

Including the regiment's regular battalions, a total of eleven battalions of the Royal Munster Fusiliers served in the Great War. Battalions of the regiment served with various divisions including the 29th, 10th (Irish) and 16th (Irish) Divisions. In 1914, the regimental depot was in Tralee.

These battalions fought in all of the major actions on the Western Front from 1914 onwards while the regiment was also represented in the campaigns in Gallipoli, Salonika, Egypt and Palestine. A detachment of the Royal Munster Fusiliers also served on the Italian Front from 1917 as part of the allied effort to shore up the crumbling Italian army.

1st Battalion

This regular battalion was based at Rangoon on the outbreak of the war and was sent to England where it joined the 86th Brigade of the 29th Division. It took part in the disastrous landings at Cape Helles in April 1915 where it suffered serious casualties. After theses landings it formed a temporary composite battalion with the 1st Royal Dublin Fusiliers, which was known as the 'Dubsters'. After service in Egypt, it was sent to France where it joined the 16th (Irish) Division. It later absorbed the men from the disbanded 2nd, 8th and 9th Battalion. At the end of the war, it was serving with 57th Division near Lille.

2nd Battalion
The regiment's second regular battalion was based in Aldershot on the outbreak of the war and was initially attached to the Guards Brigade of the 1st Division. It was sent to France as part of the BEF in August 1914 and later served with the 1st, 16th (Irish), 31st and 50th Divisions. All of its wartime service was on the Western Front, where it served in numerous actions from the opening stages of the war in 1914.

3rd (Reserve) Battalion
This reserve battalion was activated at Tralee on 4 August 1914. It served on garrison duties in Ireland until 1917 when it was sent to England. In May 1918 it absorbed the men from the 4th and 5th Battalions and was part of the Plymouth Garrison at the end of the war.

4th (Extra Reserve) Battalion
This battalion was activated at Kinsale on the outbreak of war. It carried out garrison duties at various locations around Ireland, England and Scotland until 1918 when it was absorbed by the 3rd Battalion.

5th (Extra Reserve) Battalion
This battalion was activated in Limerick on 4 August 1914. It served on garrison duties in Ireland, Scotland and England before being absorbed by the 3rd Battalion in 1918.

6th (Service) Battalion
This K1 battalion was formed at Tralee in August 1914. After training at the Curragh and in England, it was sent to Gallipoli with the 10th (Irish) Division, where it took part in the Suvla landings. In 1916 it absorbed the personnel from the 7th Battalion. The 6th battalion also served in Salonika and Egypt before being sent to France in 1918 where it was absorbed by the 2nd Battalion.

7th (Service) Battalion
This battalion was also a K1 unit and was raised at Tralee in August 1914. It served with the 10th (Irish) Division in Gallipoli, Salonika and Egypt. In 1916, its remaining men were absorbed into the 6th Battalion.

8th (Service) Battalion
This K2 battalion was formed in Fermoy in September or October 1914. Attached to the 16th (Irish) Division, it served on garrison duties in Ireland until

being moved to England in late 1915. The battalion was sent to France in December 1915 and absorbed the men from the 9th Battalion in 1916. This battalion was disbanded in France in 1916, its men going to the 1st Battalion.

9th (Service) Battalion
This K2 battalion was formed in September or October 1914 and it was attached to the 16th (Irish) Division. After duties in Ireland and England, it was sent to France in December 1915. It was disbanded in France in May 1916, its remaining men going to other battalions of the regiment.

1st (Garrison) Battalion
This battalion was formed in Cork in April 1917 as a home service battalion. Its original draft was from the disbanded 1st Garrison Battalion of the Durham Light Infantry. It served on garrison duties in England. In November 1917, three companies of this battalion were sent to Italy as part of the allied expedition in support of the Italian army. This detachment remained in Italy until the end of the war.

2nd (Home Service) Garrison Battalion
This battalion was formed at Prees Heath in England in November 1917 from the remaining men of the 1st Garrison Battalion. At the end of the war it formed part of the Plymouth Garrison.

At the end of the war, the wartime battalions of the Royal Munster Fusiliers were gradually disbanded. The two remaining regular battalions served on garrison duties abroad. In 1922, the 1st Battalion was in Silesia while the 2nd Battalion was based at Alexandria in Egypt. Both battalions were returned to England and the regiment was disbanded in 1922.

Colonels (from 1881)

1881	General Corbet Cotton (1st Battalion)
1881	Field-Marshal Sir Frederick P. Haines (2nd Battalion)
1890	General William R. Preston
1892	General Henry Meade Hamilton
1895	Lieutenant-General Robert Stuart Baines
1899	Lieutenant-General William Rickman
1900	Lieutenant-General John Wimburn Laurie
1912	Lieutenant-General Sir Herbert S.G. Miles (to disbandment)

Battle honours
Plassey, Condore, Masulipatam, Badara, Buxar, Rohilcand 1774, Rohilcand 1794, Carnatic, Sholinghur, Guzerat, Deig, Bhurtpore, Afghanistan, Ghuznee, Ferozeshuhur, Sobraon, Punjaub, Chillianwallah, Goojerat, Pegu, Delhi, Lucknow, Burmah, South Africa 1899–1902, Retreat from Mons, Marne 1914, Aisne 1914, Ypres 1914, Ypres 1917, Langemarck 1914, Langemarck 1917, Gheluvelt, Nonne

Bosschen, Givenchy 1914, Aubers, Loos, Somme 1916, Somme 1918, Albert 1916, Bazentin, Pozières, Guillemont, Ginchy, Flers-Courcelette, Morval, Messines 1917, Passchendaele, St Quentin, Bapaume 1918, Rosières, Avre, Arras 1918, Scarpe 1918, Drocourt-Quéant, Hindenburg Line, Canal du Nord, St Quentin Canal, Beaurevoir, Cambrai 1918, Selle, Sambre, France and Flanders 1914–18, Italy 1917–18, Kosturino, Struma, Macedonia 1915–17, Helles, Landing at Helles, Krithia, Suvla, Landing at Suvla, Scimitar Hill, Gallipoli 1915–16, Egypt 1916, Gaza, Jerusalem, Tell 'Asur, Palestine 1917–18.

The honour 'Mediterranean 1901' was awarded to the 5th Battalion (Royal Limerick County Militia).

Motto
The motto associated with the 101st Royal Bengal Fusiliers was 'Heaven's Light Our Guide'. This sounds like an unlikely motto for a regiment of hard-bitten East India Company soldiers. One suspects that it was inflicted on the regiment by some evangelically-minded officer.

Regimental music
Marches associated with the Royal Munster Fusiliers include 'St Patrick's Day', 'The British Grenadiers' and 'Won't you come home to Bombay'.

Mascot
Between 1915 and disbandment in 1922, the regiment owned an Irish Wolfhound named 'Garry'.

Nicknames
Due to their tattered appearance during the Indian Mutiny, soldiers of the regiment became known as the 'Dirty Shirts'.

THE PRINCE OF WALES'S LEINSTER REGIMENT (ROYAL CANADIANS), 1881–1922

Formerly the 100th Foot or Prince of Wales's Royal Canadian Regiment and the 109th Bombay Infantry, 1804–1922

This regiment traced its origins back to two earlier regiments, which in themselves had complex early histories. The first was the 100th Prince of Wales Royal Canadians which traced its origins to an earlier regiment designated as the 100th Foot that had been formed in Ireland and had served, and been disbanded in Canada.

The second regiment was the 109th Foot, formerly an East India Company regiment. These two regiments were amalgamated in 1881 to form the Prince of Wales's Leinster Regiment (Royal Canadians).

100th FOOT OR PRINCE OF WALES'S ROYAL CANADIAN REGIMENT, LATER THE 1st BATTALION OF THE PRINCE OF WALES'S LEINSTER REGIMENT (ROYAL CANADIANS)

Formation

This regiment was originally designated as the 100th Foot, a designation previously borne by several different regiments. In 1760 the 100th (Highland) Regiment of Foot was raised but was disbanded in 1763 after service in Martinique.

The second regiment to bear this designation was the 100th Foot, raised in 1780 and disbanded in 1785 after service in India. The 100th (Gordon Highland) Regiment of Foot was raised in 1794 but following a reduction in the size of the army was redesignated as the 92nd Highlanders, becoming the second battalion of the Gordon Highlanders in 1881.

The Irish connection with this regimental number began in 1804 when Frederick John Falkiner was authorized to raise an infantry regiment. By the end of the year this regiment was almost at full strength and was designated as the 100th County of Dublin Regiment in 1805, Falkiner becoming its first colonel. This regiment saw service in Canada and, on 21 October 1805, 271 officers and men were drowned in a shipwreck off Newfoundland. The remainder of the regiment saw service during the British-American War of 1812–14, being garrisoned successively at Quebec, Montreal, Fort George, Three Rivers and again in Quebec. In 1812 its title was changed to 100th Prince Regent's County of Dublin Regiment of Foot. The regiment served as marines and distinguished itself at the capture of Fort Niagara. After Waterloo it was renumbered as the 99th Regiment of Foot (Prince Regent's County of Dublin). It was disbanded at Chatham, England in July 1818. Its colours bore the single battle honour 'Niagara'. It is interesting to note that many of its disbanded soldiers had left the regiment in Quebec and moved to the Richmond area of Ontario to occupy lands that had been granted to them. Some of their descendents would later serve in the revived 100th Foot from 1858 onwards.

Due to the post-Napoleonic reductions and re-numbering of regiments, the 102nd Foot was re-designated as the 100th Foot until it too was disbanded in 1818. This regiment had no Irish connections. Between 1816 and 1818 the number was borne by the Duke of York's Irish Regiment. After service in the West Indies and Canada, this regiment was also disbanded at Chatham in 1818.

The sixth regiment to have this designation went on to become the 1st Battalion of the Leinster Regiment. It was raised in Quebec in 1858 and it was originally intended that it should see service in the Indian Mutiny. The new battalion was designated as the 100th (or Prince of Wales's Royal Canadian) Regiment of Foot. Ultimately the mutiny was over by the time the battalion was up to full strength and they were posted overseas. Before leaving England, they were presented with the colours of the disbanded 100th (Prince Regent's County of Dublin) Regiment, which fittingly bore the battle honour 'Niagara'.

Operational history

1859–63 The regiment first served abroad in Gibraltar.
1863–6 Stationed in Malta.
1866–8 Based in Canada
1869–74 Stationed in Scotland and England.
1874–6 Stationed in Ireland. HQ in Richmond Barracks, Dublin. Detachments in Sligo, Mullingar, Trim, Boyle and Navan. In 1875, detachments in the Curragh, Kilkenny, Waterford, Duncannon Fort, Carrick-on-Suir and Dungarven. In 1876 detachments in Waterford, Dungarven, Clonmel and Carrick-on-Suir.
1876 Based at Aldershot.
1877 The regiment moved to India where it was initially stationed at Jullundur. It would remain in India until 1894.
1881 In 1881, under the new Territorial legislation, it was redesignated as the 1st Battalion of the Prince of Wales's Leinster Regiment (Royal Canadians). Under the new system, Birr in Co. Offaly, was stipulated as being the HQ of the 100th recruiting district and would henceforth be the regimental depot of the regiment. The regimental recruiting district took in counties Westmeath, Meath, Offaly and Laois.[22]

109th BOMBAY INFANTRY, LATER THE 2nd BATTALION OF THE PRINCE OF WALES'S LEINSTER REGIMENT (ROYAL CANADIANS)

Formation

Two previous regiments had previously borne the number 109: the short-lived 109th Foot of 1761–3 and the 109th (Aberdeenshire) Regiment of Foot raised in 1794 and soon afterwards amalgamated into the 53rd Foot.

The third regiment to bear this designation would later become the 2nd Battalion of the Leinster Regiment. It was raised at Poona, India, in 1853 from recruits from the 1st Bombay Fusiliers and the 2nd Bombay Light Infantry and also a draft of new recruits. The new regiment was originally designated as the 3rd Bombay European Regiment of the Honourable East India Company's army.

Operational history

1857–9 During the Indian Mutiny the regiment was attached to the Central India Field Force under General Sir Hugh Rose. It saw action at the capture of Ratghur fort, the battle of Baroda, the relief of Saugor and the storming of the strong fortress of Garracota. It was also present at the forcing of the Muddenpur Pass and the battles of Betwa, Koouch, Calpee and Morar and

---

22 By WW1, Co. Louth was included in the regimental recruiting area.

	the storming of Jhansi, among other engagements. Finally, they were present at the recapture of Gwalior. For these actions they received the single battle honour of 'Central India'. In 1858 the regiment transferred from the control of the EIC to the Crown.
1860	Due to depleted numbers, the regiment was reinforced by 500 men of the Jager Corps of the British German Legion, a unit of German volunteers originally raised to serve in the Crimea. The regiment retained a large German contingent until the 1880s.
1862	The regiment re-designated as the 109th Foot on the amalgamation of H.E.I.C. regiments into the British Army.
1865–6	The regiment was stationed in Aden and took part in two inland expeditions against the forces of the Sultan Abdullah. During this campaign it was present at the battles of Bir Said and Ahmodia while also taking part in the capture of El Khor, Shugra and Ussulla.
1867–77	The regiment was stationed in India.
1878	Returned to England on home service.
1881	Under the new territorial legislation of 1881, it was re-designated as the 2nd Battalion of the Prince of Wales's Leinster Regiment (Royal Canadians).

THE PRINCE OF WALES'S LEINSTER REGIMENT (ROYAL CANADIANS)

On the amalgamation of these two battalions in 1881, the regiment was originally titled as the Prince of Wales's Royal Canadian Regiment. Shortly afterwards this was changed to The Prince of Wales's Leinster Regiment (Royal Canadians).

Apart from the two regular army battalions, there were also three reserve battalions that formed part of the Irish Militia. These were:

3rd Battalion (King's County Royal Rifles Regiment of Militia)
4th Battalion (Royal Queen's County Rifles Regiment of Militia)
5th Battalion (Royal Meath Regiment of Militia)

Operational history
1st Battalion

1894	In December the battalion was ordered to leave India and return to Ireland.
1895	The battalion arrived at Queenstown (Cobh) on 13th January. Stationed at Tipperary and later Birr and Dublin.
1898	It was posted to Halifax, Nova Scotia.

2nd Anglo-Boer War, 1899–1902

1900	The 1st Battalion returned to Aldershot before being dispatched to the Cape. It was attached to the 16th Brigade of the 8th Division, commanded by General Sir Leslie Rundle.

1901	Formed the garrison at Vrede.
1902	In April they took part in the action at Bethlehem. The battalion returned to Ireland in October and was based at Fermoy.
1904	Move to England and based at Shorncliffe.
1905	To Aldershot.
1908	The battalion moved to Devonport.
1911	The battalion was ordered to India and arrived at the Bareilly cantonments in October.
1912	Based at Chaubatia.
1913	Based at Bareilly. In November the battalion moved to Fyzabad.
1914	Stationed at Fyzabad at the outbreak of the First World War.

2nd Battalion

1882	The 2nd Battalion returned to Ireland and was stationed at the Richmond Barracks in Dublin, later being moved to the Curragh before moving to the regimental depot at Birr.
1885	The battalion transferred to Fermoy and in November it began to move to Limerick.
1886	Based at Limerick.
1887	At Limerick. Ordered to England in late 1887.
1888	Based at Shorncliffe
1891	Moved to Aldershot.
1894	The battalion went on service at Malta.
1895	Based in Bermuda.
1897	The battalion moved to Halifax, Nova Scotia.
1898	At Jamaica.
1898	Based at Barbados.

2nd Anglo-Boer War, 1899–1902

1901	At the outbreak of the Boer War the 2nd Battalion was still based in Barbados. It did not receive orders to move to South Africa until late in 1901.
1902	The battalion arrived at Cape Town on 16 January. They provided garrisons for various blockhouses on the Heilbron and Wilge River lines. It later served in Pretoria and the Transvaal. The 2nd Battalion remained in South Africa as part of the British garrison until 1905.
1905	The battalion was moved to Mauritius.
1907	Returned to India and initially stationed at Calcutta.
1911	The battalion returned to Ireland and was based at Cork. It was still stationed there at the outbreak of the First World War.

The Militia Battalions in the 2nd Anglo-Boer War

3rd Battalion

This battalion became active in 1900 and initially formed the garrison at Woolwich. In February 1900 the men of the battalion volunteered for active service and it arrived at Cape Town in March 1900. They then formed the garrison at Queenstown (SA) before moving to Stromberg and Aliwal North in the Cape Colony. In 1901 the battalion moved to Kimberely. It returned to Ireland in May 1902.

4th Battalion
This battalion was activated during the war but saw no service in South Africa being based at Salisbury and Dover.

5th Battalion
This battalion was also activated during the war and was based at Aldershot.

The First World War, 1914–18

Alongside the two regular battalions and the three militia battalions, the regiment raised two further service battalions during the course of the war. These battalions saw service not only in France and Flanders but also in Gallipoli, Macedonia and Palestine. On the outbreak of war, the regimental depot was at Birr, Co. Offaly.

1st Battalion
This battalion was at Fyzabad in India on the outbreak of the war. It sailed from Bombay on 16 October 1914, arrived at Plymouth on 16 November. Stationed at Morne Hill, Winchester as part of 82nd Brigade of the 27th Division. On 20 December 1914 landed at Havre. 26 November 1915 embarked at Marseilles for Salonika. Landed Salonika on 11 December 1915. On 2 November 1916 assigned to 29th Brigade of the 10th (Irish) Division. On 14 September 1917 sailed from Salonika for Alexandria, Egypt. On 31 October 1918, it was stationed in Palestine, near Nablus. During the course of the war, the 1st Battalion took part in numerous actions, including the battles of St Eloi, 2nd Ypres, 3rd Gaza and Deir Ibzia.

2nd Battalion
This battalion was in Cork at the outbreak of war and was later stationed at Cambridge and Newmarket before landing at St Nazaire on 14 September 1914, as part of 17th Brigade of the 6th Divison. On 14 October 1915 it was assigned to the 17th Brigade of the 24th Division at Reninghelst. On the 19 October 1915 it was reassigned to the 73rd Brigade of the 24th Division.

On 1 February 1918 it joined the 47th Brigade of the 16th (Irish) Division at Tincourt and absorbed the personnel from the disbanded 7th Battalion.

On 13 April 1918, it absorbed 5 officers and 281 men from the 6th Battalion of the Connaught Rangers, that battalion being reduced to cadre.

It joined the 88th Brigade of the 29th Division at Hondeghem on 23 April 1918. At the Armistice stationed west of Lessines in Belgium. During the war it took part in various battles including the Aisne, Meteren, Armentieres, Hooge, St. Eloi, the Somme, Guillemont, Vimy Ridge, 3rd Ypres, Messines, 4th Ypres and Courtrai.

3rd (Reserve) Battalion
Raised at Birr on 4 August 1914 and moved to Cork a few days later. It was active during the Easter Rebellion in Ireland in 1916, guarding key points in its area. In November 1917 moved to England and stationed at Portsmouth. In May 1918 absorbed the personnel from the 4th and 5th (Extra Reserve) Battalions. Still at Portsmouth at the end of the war.

4th (Extra Reserve) Battalion
Raised at Maryborough, Co. Laois on 4 August 1914. Later stationed at Crosshaven, Cork Harbour and Passage West, before moving to England in May 1915, where it was stationed at Devonport. In September 1915 the battalion returned to Ireland and was subsequently stationed at the Curragh Camp, Limerick and Tralee. Put on full alert during Easter Rebellion of 1916. In November 1917, it moved to England and was based at Dover. In May 1918 its personnel was absorbed into the 3rd (Reserve) Battalion.

5th (Extra Reserve) Battalion
Raised at Drogheda, Co. Louth, on 4 August 1914. Later stationed at Queenstown (Cobh) and Passage West. In May 1915 this battalion moved to England and was stationed at Plymouth. In September 1915 it returned to Ireland and was based at Mullingar before moving to the Curragh Camp in April 1916 as part of the 25th Reserve Brigade. During the 1916 Easter Rebellion, detachments of the battalion took part in the fighting around Dublin Castle, Parliament Street and Dame Street. They also were in action around Trinity College, Westmoreland Street and Tara Street. One member of the battalion, Private C. Moore was killed in the fighting and buried in Trinity College. In June 1917 the battalion moved to Laytown, near Drogheda and in August it was stationed at Boyle. It moved to Birr in September 1917 before moving to Scotland in November, where it was based at Glencorse, near Edinburgh. In May 1918 its personnel absorbed into the 3rd (Reserve) Battalion at Plymouth.

6th (Service) Battalion
Raised in Dublin in August 1914 as a 'K1' battalion, i.e. a battalion in Kitchener's First New Army. In September 1914 it was moved to Fermoy where it joined the 29th Brigade of the 10th (Irish) Division. It was later stationed at Birr and the Curragh Camp before moving to England in May 1915 where it was stationed at Basingstoke. On 9 July 1915 it sailed from Liverpool and arrived at Mudros on 26 July 1915. The battalion was attached to the ANZAC Corps and landed at Anzac Cove on 5 August 1915. On 29 September 1915 the battalion was evacuated to Mudros, re-embarking for the Salonika Expedition in October 1915. On 14 September 1917 it sailed from Salonika for Alexandria, Egypt, where it arrived on 19 September. In May 1918 it sailed from Port Said for France, arriving Marseilles on 1 June 1918. In early June it was temporarily assigned to both the 14th and 34th Divisions and on 20 July 1918 it was transferred to the 198th Brigade of the 66th Division. The battalion was disbanded at Abancourt on 12 September 1918.

7th (Service) Battalion
Raised in Fermoy in October 1914 as a K2 (Kitchener's Second New Army) battalion. Assigned to the 47th Brigade of the 16th (Irish) Division. In January 1915 moved to England and stationed at Kilworth. In September 1915 stationed at Blackdown. The battalion moved to France in December 1915. It was disbanded at Tincourt on 14 February 1918, the personnel going to the 2nd Battalion and the 19th Entrenching Battalion. It took part in several major battles including the Somme, Guillemont, Ginchy, Messines, 3rd Ypres and Cambrai.

At the end of the war, the regiment's service battalions were disbanded while the militia battalions were returned to reserve status. The 1st Battalion returned to India after the war and was stationed at Malabar and then Madras.

The 2nd Battalion joined the army of occupation in Germany and in June 1921 was stationed at Oppeln in Upper Silesia. The regular battalions returned to England in 1922 to be disbanded.

Battle honours
The regiment maintained the traditions of the earlier 100th and 109th Regiments and therefore included battle honours for service in Canada and India.

The majority of the regiment's battle honours date from the First World War and reflect its service in various theatres of the war including France and Flanders, Macedonia, Galliopli and Palestine. The regimental battle honours were:

Niagara, Central India, South Africa, 1900–2, Armentières, 1914, Ypres, 1915, Ypres 1917, Ypres 1918, Gravenstafel, St Julien, Frezenberg, Somme, 1916, Somme 1918, Delville Wood, Guillemont, Ginchy, Arras, 1917, Vimy, 1917, Messines, 1917, Pilckem, Langemarck 1917, St Quentin, Rosières, Courtrai, France and Flanders, 1914–18, Kosturino, Struma, Macedonia, 1915–17, Suvla, Sari Bair, Gallipoli, 1915, Gaza, Jerusalem, Tell Asur, Megiddo, Nablus, Palestine, 1917–18.

Colonels-in-chief
1919   King Edward VII

Colonels of the 100th or Prince of Wales's Royal Canadian Regiment of Foot, later 1st Battalion of the Leinster Regiment
1805   Brigadier-General Sir Frederick John Falkiner (until 1818 disbandment)
1858   General Henry Dundas, 3rd Viscount Melville
1862   Lieutenant-General Sir Edward Macarthur
1872   Major-General Charles Rochfort Scott
1872   General the Hon. Sir Alexander Hamilton-Gordon

Colonels of the 109th Bombay Infantry, later the 2nd Battalion of the Leinster Regiment
1862   General Sir William Wyllie
1873   General Mark Kerr Atherley
1880   General Sir Richard Denis Kelly

Colonels of the Prince of Wales's Leinster Regiment (Royal Canadians)

1881	General Sir Alexander Hamilton-Gordon (1st Battalion)
1881	General Sir Richard Denis Kelly (2nd Battalion)
1890	General Henry Meade Hamilton
1891	General Sir Patrick Leonard MacDoughall
1894	Lieutenant-General Alastair McIan Macdonald
1910	Major-General George Upton Prior
1919	Major-General Sir Gerald Farrell Boyd (until disbandment)

Regimental music

Various tunes are associated with the Leinster Regiment including 'The Royal Canadian', 'Come back to Erin', 'The Maple Leaf Forever' and 'God Bless the Prince of Wales'.

Nicknames

The 100th Regiment had several nicknames: 'the Crusaders', 'the Centipedes', 'the Beavers' and 'the Colonials'. The 3rd Bombay European Regiment, later the 2nd Battalion of the Leinster Regiment, was initially made up of a large number of Irish recruits. In India they came to be known for their strong physique and also a seeming immunity to exposure to the sun. It was due to this that they were given the nickname 'The Brass Heads' or 'The Steel Heads'. They were also known as the 'Poonah Pets'. Following the reinforcement of this battalion in 1860 by men from the Jager Corps, this battalion was also referred to as the 'German Mob' or the 'Jagers'.

THE LONDON IRISH RIFLES

1860–2006

Formation

Like the Liverpool Irish, this unit can trace its history back to the beginnings of the Volunteer Rifle movement in 1860. In March 1860, prominent members of London's large Irish community organized the formation of an Irish volunteer unit.

On its formation, this was designated as the **28th Middlesex (London Irish) Rifle Volunteer Corps**. There were some prominent figures among its early members including the Marquis of Donegal and William Howard Russell, the famous war correspondent. On its formation, the battalion had twelve companies based at Burlington House in London.

Operational history

1880	The unit was re-designated as a volunteer battalion of the Rifle Brigade, and was re-numbered as the **16th Middlesex (London Irish) Volunteer Corps**.
1881	Re-designated as the **4th Volunteer Battalion, the Rifle Brigade**.
1882	Again re-titled as the **3rd Volunteer Battalion, the Rifle Brigade**.

2nd Anglo-Boer War, 1899–1902

A contingent of eight officers and 200 men volunteered for service with the 2nd Royal Irish Rifles during the war. The London Irish Rifles battalion was later awarded its first battle honour, 'South Africa, 1900–02'.

1906   A battalion pipe band was formed.

1908   The battalion transferred to the newly formed Territorial Force and was absorbed into the London Regiment as the **18th (County of London) Battalion, the London Regiment (London Irish Rifles)**.

The First World War, 1914–18

During the course of the war, the 18th (County of London) Battalion raised three battalions. The original battalion was re-designated as 1/18th (County of London) Battalion (London Irish Rifles) and mobilised for active service on the outbreak of the war.

In March 1915 it was sent to France as part of the 141st Brigade of the 47th (2nd London) Division. It took part in its first battle at Festubert in May and then fought in the battle of Loos in September 1915. During this latter action, Sgt Edwards of the London Irish Rifles encouraged his men in the attack by kicking a football towards the German lines. This event is still commemorated by the London Irish on 'Loos Sunday' each year. The battalion remained on the Western Front for the rest of the war and fought in numerous actions including the Somme, Messines (1917), Cambrai (1917), Ancre (1918), Albert (1918).

The second battalion of the London Irish, the 2/18th (County of London) Battalion (London Irish Rifles) was raised in London in August 1914.

Attached to the 60th Division, it went to France in June 1916. Transferred to the Salonika front in late 1916, it later served in Palestine, where it fought in numerous actions, including Khubert Adesah (1917), where it suffered heavy casualties. This battalion was disbanded in Palestine in 1918 and its remaining personnel were attached to other Irish battalions then serving in the Middle East.

The 3/18th (County of London) Battalion (London Irish Rifles) was raised in May 1915 but remained in England as a reserve battalion.

The London Irish lost 1,016 men killed and 2,644 wounded during the war.

1919   The battalions of the London Irish Rifles were reduced to cadre, which were in turn disbanded.

1922   The London Irish Rifles re-formed as part of the Territorial Army as the **18th (County of London) Battalion, the London Regiment (London Irish Rifles)**. Based at the Duke of York's HQ in Chelsea.

1937   On the disbandment of the London Regiment, the battalion was re-designated as the **London Irish Rifles, the Royal Ulster Rifles**, becoming a territorial battalion of the Royal Ulster Rifles. The unit adopted the caubeen as its head-dress.

The Second World War, 1939–45

1939   The London Irish Rifles were organized into two battalions, personnel of the original battalion being used to form the training cadre of a second wartime battalion.

The 1st London Irish Rifles underwent a prolonged period of training before being sent to join the 10th Army in Iraq in 1942, being attached to the 168th Brigade of the 56th Infantry Division. This battalion took part in the invasion of Sicily in September 1943 and served throughout the Italian campaign, taking part in the battles of Monte Camino and Anzio.[23]

The 2nd London Irish Rifles landed in North Africa in 1942 and the battalion was attached to the 6th Armoured Division of the 1st Army and operated as lorried infantry. It was later attached to the 38th (Irish) Infantry Brigade of the 78th Division. With this brigade, it fought in numerous actions including Two Tree Hill, Bou Arada, Djebel Bel Mahdi and Djebel Tannougcha. It remained attached to this brigade for the rest of the war.

In 1943 the 2nd London Irish Rifles took part in the landings in Sicily and took part in the capture of Centuripe in August. During the Italian campaign, it fought in numerous actions including Termoli, San Salvo, Monte Cassino ('Cassino II), Spaduro, and during the Liri Valley and Argenta Gap campaigns. At the end of the war, it joined the army of occupation in Austria.

Despite the fact that both battalions of the London Irish Rifles were in the Italian campaign, they only established contact once while at the River Reno.

At the end of the war both battalions were disbanded.

1947   The London Irish Rifles was reformed as a single battalion unit and remained as the Territorial battalion of the Royal Ulster Rifles with its HQ at Duke of York's HQ, Chelsea.

1967   The battalion was reduced to company strength, officially attached to the North Irish Militia.

1968   On the amalgamation of the Royal Irish Fusiliers, Royal Inniskilling Fusiliers and the Royal Ulster Rifles in the Royal Irish Rangers, the unit was re-designated once again, becoming **D Company (London Irish Rifles) 4th Battalion, Royal Irish Rangers, North Irish Militia**.

1992   Following the 'Options for Change', the Royal Irish Rangers were absorbed into the new Royal Irish Regiment, which became the parent regiment to the London Irish Rifles.

1993   On the re-formation of the London Regiment, the London Irish Rifles transferred to this regiment being re-designated as **D (London Irish Rifles) Company, the London Regiment**. The unit remains as part of the Territorial Army and has its HQ at Camberwell.

Battle honours

South Africa, 1900–2, Festubert 1915, Loos 1915, Somme 1916, Somme 1918, Flers-

---

[23] Monte Camino was a battle on the Gothic line in Nov.–Dec. 1943, not to be confused with Monte Cassino, where the regiment also served.

Courcelette, Morval, Messines 1917, Ypres 1917, Langemarck 1917, Cambrai 1917, St Quentin, Bapaume 1918, Ancre 1918, Albert 1918, Pursuit to Mons, France and Flanders 1915–18, Dorian 1917, Macedonia 1916–17, Gaza, El Mughar, Nebi Samwil, Jerusalem, Jericho, Jordan, Palestine 1917–18, Bou Arada, El Hadjeba, Stuka Farm, Heidous, North Africa 1942–43, Lentini, Simeto Bridgehead, Adrano, Centuripe, Salso Crossing, Simeto Crossing, Malleto, Pursuit to Messina, Sicily 1943, Termoli, Trigno, Sangro, Anzio, Carroceto, Cassino II, Casa Sinagogga, Liri Valley, Trasimene Line, Santfatucchio, Coriano, Croce, Senio Floodbank, Rimini Line, Ceriano Ridge, Monte Spaduro, Monte Grande, Valli di Commacchio, Argenta Gap, Italy 1943–45.

Motto
'Quis separabit?' (Who shall separate us?)

Regimental music
The regimental quick march is the 'Garryowen'.

Regimental mascot
Since 1916, the regiment has had a succession of Irish Wolfhound mascots.

64th LANCASHIRE (LIVERPOOL IRISH) RIFLE VOLUNTEERS CORPS

Later the 8th (Irish) Battalion, the King's (Liverpool) Regiment. 'The Liverpool Irish', 1860 to the present

Formation
The Liverpool Irish can trace its lineage back to 1860 and it was originally one of the many volunteer rifle units that were created as a reaction to French re-armament. As early as December 1859, an advertisement was placed in the *Liverpool Echo* calling on members of the city's large Irish population to attend a meeting to discuss the formation of a 'Irish Volunteer Rifle Corps'. There was a huge response and the first training session of this new unit took place at the Concert Hall in Lord Nelson Street on 25 January 1860.

The unit's fist commanding officer was Lieutenant J.G. Plunkett, previously of the 5th Lancashire Militia and it was initially designated as the **64th Lancashire (Liverpool Irish) Rifle Volunteers Corps**. As this was a rifle unit, the original uniform was in rifle green and followed the pattern of that of the 60th Rifles (King's Royal Rifle Corps). During its relatively short history, this unit has had its title changed on numerous occasions.

Operational history
1880   Following the renumbering of the rifle volunteer units, the unit was re-designated as the **18th Lancashire (Liverpool Irish) Rifle Volunteers**.

1881   A further re-designation took place following the army reforms of 1881 and the unit became the volunteer battalion of the King's (Liverpool Regiment).

1888   In March, the battalion was re-designated as the **5th (Irish) Volunteer Battalion, the King's (Liverpool Regiment)**.

2nd Anglo-Boer War, 1899–1902

While the battalion itself did not serve in the war, 224 officers and men volunteered to serve in South Africa. They served with the 1st Battalion of the King's (Liverpool) Regiment, the 1st Battalion of the Royal Irish Regiment and with the Imperial Yeomanry. In 1900 two new companies, the 7th and 8th Companies, were raised. Due to the service of members of the Liverpool Irish in the war, the battalion was awarded the battle honour 'South Africa, 1899–1902'.

1905   One company was converted into a cyclist unit.

1908   Following the reorganization of the Militia and Volunteer units into the new Territorial Force, the battalion was re-titles as the **8th Battalion, the King's (Liverpool Regiment)**.

1909   The battalion's title was changed once again to the **8th (Irish) Battalion, the King's (Liverpool Regiment)**.

First World War, 1914–18

In 1914, the regiment's recruiting area took in all of Liverpool. Its regimental depot was in Seaforth Barracks.

1/8th (Irish) Battalion, the King's (Liverpool Regiment)

The existing battalion was mobilized on the outbreak of war and designated as above on the raising of a second battalion in October 1914. It was initially assigned to the Liverpool Brigade of the West Lancashire Division. In February 1915 it transferred to the North Lancashire Brigade (later 3rd Highland Brigade) and was assigned to the 51st Highland Division. In May 1915 it landed at Boulogne and later served with both the 55th (West Lancashire) Division and the 57th (2nd West Lancashire) Division. During the course of the war it took part in numerous battles including the Somme, Passchendale, Cambrai and the German offensive of March 1918; the 'Kaiserslacht'.

2/8th (Irish) Battalion, the King's (Liverpool Regiment)

This second service battalion was raised in October 1914 and was composed of volunteers from among the Liverpool Irish community.

It was attached to the 57th (2nd West Lancashire) Division and went to France in February 1917, taking part in several battles including Passchendale, Cambrai and the Hindenburg Line offensive. Due to casualties in both of the service battalions it was amalgamated with the 1/8th Battalion in January 1918.

3/8th (Irish) Battalion, the King's (Liverpool Regiment)

The third battalion was raised in May 1915 and was used to provide reinforcements for the two battalions in France. It remained in England and was disbanded at the end of the war.

In total, 912 members of the Liverpool Irish battalion were killed in the war.

1919   The amalgamated battalion of the regiment returned from Europe and was reconstituted as a Territorial battalion in 1920.
1922   On 31 March the regiment was deactivated, only the band continuing to exist.
1939   In March, with war looming, a decision was made to enlarge the Territorial Force and the battalion was re-formed as the **8th (Irish) Battalion, the King's (Liverpool) Regiment**.

Second World War, 1939–45

During the early years of the war, the regiment underwent training before serving as a garrison unit in England. In preparation for the Normandy invasion it was re-trained as beach unit. Under the command of Lieutenant-Colonel W.J. Humphrey, it was attached to the 7th Beach Group and assigned to the 3rd Canadian Division.

On D-Day, 6 June 1944, it landed with the first wave of Canadian troops at Mike Sector on Juno Beach. Fighting alongside Canadian units such as the Royal Winnipeg Rifles, the Regina Rifle Regiment and the 1st Canadian Scottish, it took part in a series of hard-fought actions around Courseulles-sur-Mer and Graye-sur-Mer, suffering heavy casualties.

1947   The regiment was converted into an artillery unit, being re-designated as **626th Heavy Anti-Aircraft Regiment, RA (Liverpool Irish)**.
1955   The unit was re-designated as **Q (Liverpool Irish) Battery, 470th (3rd West Lancashire) Light Anti-Aircraft Regiment, RA**.
1967   Following the amalgamation of the Territorial Army and the Volunteer Reserve, the unit was re-titled as **A (Liverpool Irish) Troop 208th (3rd West Lancashire) Battery, 103rd RA (The Lancashire Artillery Volunteers)**.
2001   The unit was converted into a field artillery battery, retaining the above title. It remains as a unit of the Territorial Army and is based in Liverpool. Among its uniform distinctions, it wears the dark green caubeen.

Battle honours

This unit has been awarded just one battle honour in its own right – 'South Afica, 1900–1902'. However, as a battalion of the King's (Liverpool Regiment) it shares some of that regiment's numerous battle honours.

Motto

'Erin go Bragh' (Ireland for Ever).

THE IMPERIAL YEOMANRY, 1900-2

Formation

The early phases of the **2nd Anglo-Boer War** (1899-1902) highlighted numerous shortcomings within the British Army in terms of organization, equipment, training and leadership and these led to a series of disastrous defeats at the hands of the Boer commandos. In the winter of 1899-1900, there were a series of defeats at battles such as Colenso and Spion Kop. A call was made for volunteers to make up the losses and there was a good response across the British Isles and many of these men joined the newly-established Imperial Yeomanry.

In the area of light cavalry/mounted infantry, British shortcomings had been particularly apparent and it was decided to form new units of Imperial Yeomanry composed of good horsemen and skilled marksmen to maximize both mobility and firepower in the hope of meeting the Boers on equal terms.

Three contingents of Imperial Yeomanry were sent to South Africa between 1900 and December 1901.[24] The force was organized as battalion-sized units and these were initially further subdivided into four companies and a machine gun section and consisted of 526 men, all ranks. In total 39 battalions and some independent companies were raised during the war.[25] The recruits were all volunteers and in England, Scotland and Wales they were raised from existing yeomanry regiments. Ireland was at something of a disadvantage as it had no regiments of yeomanry in its reserve establishment. Nevertheless, a call was made for volunteers and many men responded to this appeal. Many ex-soldiers or members of the militia volunteered to serve in the Irish yeomanry companies. Others enlisted directly from civilian life and there was a large contingent associated with various hunts from around Ireland. Volunteers enlisted for a period of twelve months. During the course of the war, Ireland raised two full battalions of Imperial Yeomanry and also some other companies that served in composite battalions. The Irish Imperial Yeomanry units were as follows:

8th Battalion
74th Dublin Company (transferred from 16th Battalion in 1902)
99th Irish Company

13th Battalion
45th Dublin Company
46th Belfast Company (transferred from 12th Battalion in 1902)
47th Duke of Connaught's Own or Lord Donoughmore's Company
54th Belfast Company

---

[24] 1st contingent, 1900 – 10,242 men. 2nd contingent, 1901 – 16,597 men. 3rd contingent, December 1901 – 7239 men. [25] This force should not be confused with the Mounted Infantry; 28 Battalions of Mounted Infantry served in the war and these were composed of men from regular army battalions. The Irish regiments provided men for several companies of Mounted Infantry.

17th Battalion
60th North Irish Horse Company   61st South Irish Horse Company[26]

29th (Irish Horse) Battalion[27]

131st Company	134th Company
132nd Company	175th Company
133rd Company	176th Company

Operational history
There is essentially no literature on the history of the Irish Imperial Yeomanry units in the 2nd Anglo-Boer War. From various published histories, it can be shown that these units saw extensive service and operated against Boer forces until the end of the war. In doing so they served in all theatres of operations in South Africa and served in the guerrilla and 'blockhouse' phases of the war.

The most memorable action of the Irish Imperial Yeomanry took place at Lindley on 31 May 1900 and it was memorable for all the wrong reasons. This action involved the 13th Battalion of the Imperial Yeomanry, which was composed of Irish companies and was led by the hapless Lt.-Col. Basil Spragge, a British regular. Spragge contrived to get his battalion surrounded, despite the fact that he could have withdrawn it from the engagement during its opening phases. After a fierce fire-fight in which over 80 members of the battalion were killed or wounded, the remainder of the unit surrendered to Boer forces commanded by Piet de Wet.[28] The battalion had included Lord Donoughmore's Company which had attracted many members of Irish foxhunts and was informally known as the 'Irish Hunt Company'. Among the dead was Sir John Power of the Irish whiskey family. Among the captured were lords Longford, Ennismore, Leitrim and Donoughmore.

The battalions of the Imperial Yeomanry were later awarded just the single battle honour 'South Africa'. There are various memorials to members of the Irish companies in locations around Ireland. One of the most prominent is in the grounds of the former St Andrew's Church, in Suffolk Street in Dublin.[29] After the end of the war, many men of these units joined the North Irish Horse and the South Irish Horse (see separate entries on those units).[30]

THE IRISH GUARDS, 1900–2006

Formation
Due to the distinguished service of the Irish regiments in South Africa during the early phase of the 2nd Anglo-Boer War, it was decided to form a new Irish regiment

---

[26] There were also companies of Hampshire and Leicestershire Yeomanry in this battalion.   [27] This oversize battalion consisted of 695 men, all ranks.   [28] Piet de Wet was the brother of General Christiaan de Wet.   [29] This church is now used as a tourist information office.   [30] Erskine Childers also mentioned an 'Irish Hospital' in his memoirs of the Boer War: *In the ranks of the C.I.V.* (London, 1901).

within the Household Brigade. This new regiment, the Irish Guards, was raised on 1 April 1900 under the provisions of Army Order No. 77 and was formed as a single battalion regiment.

The initial nucleus of the regiment was made up of 200 Irishmen who transferred from the 1st Battalion of the Grenadier Guards. Other soldiers later transferred into to the new regiment from Irish regiments such as the the Royal Munster Fusiliers and the Connaught Rangers. On 1 May 1900, the regiment's first commanding officer was appointed; Major R.J. Cooper from the 1st Battalion of the Grenadier Guards. In October 1900, Field-Marshal Lord Roberts was appointed as the regiment's first colonel-in-chief. He served in this capacity until his death in 1914. The regiment has not undergone any changes in title since its formation.

Operational history

2nd Anglo-Boer War, 1899–1902

1901   In November, a contingent of the Irish Guards was posted to South Africa where they served in the Guards Mounted Infantry Company.

The First World War, 1914–18

Alongside the regular, 1st Battalion, of the Irish Guards, two new battalions were raised during the war. The regiment's 1st and 2nd Battalions saw extensive service on the Western Front while it 3rd (Reserve) Battalion was based in England throughout the war.

1914   On the outbreak of the war, the 1st Battalion, stationed at Wellington Barracks was mobilized. It was inspected by Lord Roberts on 11 August and, attached to 4th (Guards) Brigade, 2nd Division, it landed in France on 13 August 1914. During the opening months of the war it took part in the battle of Mons, the Retreat from Mons (known within the regiment as the 'Retirement') and the battles of the Aisne, the Marne and 1st Ypres.

         The regiment's 3rd (Reserve) Battalion was raised in 1914 and was originally designated as the 2nd (Reserve) Battalion. (In July 1915, it was re-designated as the 3rd (Reserve) Battalion on the formation of the 2nd Battalion and it remained at Warley Barracks for the rest of the war).

1915   The 1st Battalion of the Irish Guards fought in the battles of Festubert and Loos and, in August, transferred to 1st Guards Brigade of the newly-formed Guards Division.

         In July, the regiment's 2nd Battalion was formed at Warley Barracks. It landed in France on 17 August and was attached to the 2nd Brigade of the Guards Division, later fighting in the battle of Loos.

1916   During September the battalions of the Irish Guards joined other battalions of the Guards Division in the area of Ginchy. They then took part in the battle of Flers-Courcelette and Lesboeufs.

1917   The Irish Guards battalions fought in the battles of Cambrai and 3rd Ypres (Passchendaele).

1918   During this last year of the war, the Irish Guards opposed the German March offensive (the 'Kaiserslacht') and took part in the battles of Arras, Bapaume and the actions on the Canal du Nord, among others. At the Armistice, the 1st Battalion was based at Maubeuge, near Mons, where it had first seen action in 1914. The 2nd Battalion was stationed at Criel Plage, near Le Treport.

During the course of the war, over 9,600 men served with the three battalions of the Irish Guards. The regiment suffered fatal casualties of 115 officers and 2,235 other ranks.

The 1st and 2nd Battalions remained in Cologne as part of the army of occupation until 1919.

1919   The 2nd and 3rd Battalions of the Irish Guards were disbanded. The 1st Battalion was stationed at Inkerman Barracks in Woking.

1922   Posted in Constantinople (Istanbul) as part of an allied force that was stationed there is the hope of deterring war between Turkey and Greece.

1923   Stationed in Gibraltar.

1924   The regiment returned to England.

1936   The Irish Guards were posted to Egypt and stationed at Cairo. The regiment also saw service in Palestine before returning to England.

The Second World War, 1939–45

1939   In April, the regiment's 2nd Battalion was re-formed as war became increasingly inevitable. On the outbreak of the war, both battalions of the Irish Guards were based at Wellington Barracks in London.

1940   A 'Holding Battalion' was raised and this was later re-designated as the 3rd Battalion, Irish Guards.

In April, the 1st Battalion, Irish Guards was attached to the 24th Guards Brigade and served throughout the Norwegian campaign. The battalion suffered serious losses, including its commanding officer, when its transport ship, the *Chobry*, was bombed. It returned to England at the end of this unsuccessful campaign.

The 2nd Battalion, Irish Guards, was attached to 'Harpoon Force' in May 1940 and took part in the operations in the Hook of Holland that covered the evacuation of the Dutch royal family and government. On its return from Holland, it was sent to Boulogne on 22 May as part of an operation to relieve the pressure on the forces evacuating from Dunkirk and Calais. During this operation, the battalion lost over 200 men killed, wounded and missing.

1941   The 1st Battalion was based in London and then Scotland, undergoing two years of training and re-equipping before being sent to North Africa in 1943.

The 2nd Battalion, Irish Guards, was equipped with Covenanter Tanks and was attached to the 5th Guards Armoured Brigade in the newly-formed Guards Armoured Division. It would remain in England until 1944, undergoing years of training as it prepared to fight in its new role as a tank battalion.

1943 The 3rd Battalion, Irish Guards, was attached to the Guards Armoured Division. It was trained to operate as lorried infantry in co-operation with the regiment's 2nd Battalion.

The 1st Battalion was sent to North Africa and arrived in Algiers in March.

During the North African campaign it took part in numerous actions including Medjez and Djebel Bou.

1944 The 1st Battalion took part in the Anzio landings in January 1944 and took part in several actions in that beach-head campaign including Aprilia and Carroceto. In March, reduced to 267 men, the battalion was taken out of the line. The 1st Battalion was returned to England where it remained for the rest of the war.

Before the D-Day landings, the 2nd (Armoured) Battalion, Irish Guards, was attached to the 5th Guards Armoured Brigade while the 3rd Battalion, Irish Guards, was attached to the 32nd Guards Brigade. Operating within the Guards Armoured Division, these battalions landed in France after the D-Day landings and took part in 'Operation Goodwood', which entailed an offensive towards Falaise. They then took part in 'Operation Bluecoat' in the bocage country around Caumont. During these campaigns they took part in several actions including Cagny, Montchamp, Maisoncelles, Estry, Le Busq and Estry.

In August, the 2nd (Armoured) Battalion and the 3rd Battalion, Irish Guards, took part in the push towards Brussels. Operating as the Irish Guards Battle Group under the command of Lt. Col. J.O.E. ('Joe') Vandeleur, on 10 September it captured a bridge over the Meuse-Escaut Canal at the De Groote Barrier. The bridge was later re-christened as 'Joe's Bridge'.

During 'Operation Market Garden', the Irish Guards Battle Group acted as the spearhead of XXX Corps, reaching Eindhoven on 18 September, after experiencing stiff German resistance.

1945 The Irish Guards Battle Group took part in 'Operation Veritable' and crossed the Rhine on 30 March. The 2nd (Armoured) Battalion and the 3rd Battalion, Irish Guards, remained in action with this battle group until the unconditional surrender of German forces in May 1945. In June the 2nd (Armoured) Battalion, Irish Guards was converted back into an infantry battalion. During the Second World War, the three Irish Guards battalions lost 845 officers and men killed in action, while almost 1,600 men, all ranks, had been wounded.

1946 The 2nd Battalion remained in Germany as part of the army of occupation. The 3rd Battalion returned to England where it was disbanded.

1947 The 2nd Battalion was returned to England and disbanded. The regiment was re-established as a single battalion regiment and was sent to Palestine.

1948	The Irish Guards were stationed in Tripoli.
1949	Based in England.
1951	Posted to Hubbelrath, Germany, as part of 4th Guards Brigade, BAOR.
1953	The Irish Guards were moved to Egypt and stationed in the Suez canal Zone.
1956	The regiment returned to England.
1958	Posted to Cyprus and attached to 1st Guards Brigade. In November the regiment returned to England and was stationed at Windsor.
1961	Posted to Hubbelrath, Germany and attached to 4th Guards Brigade.
1963	The regiment returned to England.
1966	Posted to Aden and attached to 24th Infantry Brigade.
1967	Stationed in England.
1970	The regiment was stationed in Hong Kong.
1972	Based in England.
1973	Belize.
1974	The Irish Guards returned to England and were then stationed in Münster, Germany, and attached to 4th Guards Armoured brigade, BAOR.
1977	Stationed in England.
1979	Based in Belize.
1980	The regiment was sent to Rhodesia as part of the Commonwealth monitoring group.
1981	The regiment was based in England. In September, a bus full of guardsmen was the target of an IRA bomb attack and many soldiers were injured.
1982	The Irish Guards were posted to Münster, Germany, and attached to 4th Armoured Brigade.
1983	Members of the regiment took part in two field exercises in Canada.
1984	Attached to BAOR in Germany.
1986	The regiment returned to England and was based at Chelsea.
1988	Stationed in Belize.
1990	The regiment was stationed in Berlin.
1992	Stationed in England.
1993	The Irish Guards undertook a tour of duty in Northern Ireland.
1994	Based in England.
1995	The regiment undertook a second tour of duty in Northern Ireland.
1997	Based in England but detachments went on exercises in Kenya, Oman and the Falkland Islands.
1998	The Irish Guards were based in Münster in Germany.
1999	The regiment served on peacekeeping duties in Kosovo.

Iraq 2003

The regiment was attached to 7th Armoured Brigade (the 'Desert Rats') and after desert warfare training in Kuwait, was deployed in Iraq in March 2003. During March and April, the Irish Guards took part in operations around Basra. Following these operations, the regiment was returned to England. It was later awarded the battle honour 'Basra', the first awarded to the regiment since the end of the Second World War.

2006 At the time of writing, the regiment is based at Wellington Barracks, London.

Colonels-in-chief

1901	HM King Edward VII	1936	HM King George VI
1910	HM King George V	1952	HM Queen Elizabeth II
1936	HM King Edward VIII		

Colonels

1900	Field-Marshal Lord Roberts
1914	Field-Marshal Lord Kitchener
1916	Field-Marshal Lord French
1925	Field-Marshal the Earl of Cavan
1946	Field-Marshal Lord Alexander
1969	General Sir Basil O.P. Eugster
1984	HRH Jean, Grand Duke of Luxembourg
2000	The Duke of Abercorn

Colours

The Queen's Colour of the regiment has crimson gules and a central motif that incorporates the royal cipher and the insignia of the Order of St. Patrick.

The Regimental Colour consists of a Union flag with a central design that incorporates a company badge. This badge features the crest of Ireland within the collar of the Order of St Patrick, the whole surmounted by the crown and with a scroll bearing the numeral IX.

The badges of the regiment's different companies are used on the colours in rotation. The Queen's and Regimental Colours both contain a selection of the regiment's battle honours and these are also borne on the regimental drums.

Battle honours

Mons, Retreat from Mons, Marne 1914, Aisne 1914, Ypres 1914, Ypres 1917, Langemarck 1914, Gheluvelt, Nonne Bosschen, Festubert 1915, Loos, Somme 1916, Somme 1918, Fleurs Courcelette, Morval, Pilckem, Poelcappelle, Passchendaele, Cambrai 1917, Cambrai 1918, St Quentin, Lys, Hazebrouck, Albert 1918, Bapaume 1918, Arras 1918, Scarpe 1918, Drocourt-Queant, Hindenburg Line, Canal du Nord, Selle, Sambre, France and Flanders, 1914–18, Pothus, Norway 1940, Boulougne 1940, Cagny, Mont Pincon, Neerpelt, Nijmegen, Aalst, Rhineland, Hochwald, Rhine, Bentheim, North-West Europe 1944–45, Medjez Plain, Djebel Bou Aoukaz 1943, North Africa 1943, Anzio, Aprilia, Carroceto, Italy 1943–44, Basra 2003.[31]

---

[31] Not all of these battle honours are carried on the regimental colours as they are far too numerous. A selection of the most significant battle honours appears on the regimental colours.

Motto
'Quis Separabit' (Who shall separate us)

Regimental music
Regimental Quick March 'St Patrick's Day'. Regimental Slow March 'Let Erin Remember'. There are also marches associated with the different companies of the Irish Guards:

Number 1 Company: 'The Holy Ground'. Number 2 Company: 'Boys of Wexford'. Number 4 Company: 'The South Down Militia'.[32]

Regimental mascot
In August 1902 the Irish Wolfhound Club offered to present the regiment with a prize wolfhound to use as a regimental mascot. A pedigree wolfhound, which was named on his Kennel Club papers as the 'Rajah of Kidnal' was chosen but this title was shortened by the men to 'Paddy' and then changed again to the more dignified title of 'Brian Boru'.

The Irish Guards have owned a succession of Irish Wolfhounds since then, all of which had distinctively Irish names such as 'Leitrim Boy', 'Cruachan', 'Fionn' and 'Connor'. Until 1961, the regimental mascot was known as the 'regimental pet'. The Irish Guards is the only regiment of the Household Division that has a live mascot.

Nicknames
The Irish Guards are usually referred to as 'the Micks'. In the regiment's early years, its members were also known as 'Bobs Own' due to the regimental association with Lord Roberts.

THE SOUTH IRISH HORSE, 1902–22

Formation
The South Irish Horse was raised in January 1902 in the aftermath of the 2nd Anglo-Boer War. Like the North Irish Horse, it recruited veterans from the Irish companies of the Imperial Yeomanry that had served in South Africa. The units initial recruits included men who had seen service with the 45th, 74th and 61st (South Irish Horse) Companies of the Imperial Yeomanry.

The unit was initially titled the **South of Ireland Imperial Yeomanry** and had its HQ in Limerick. It maintained four squadrons, one in Cork, one in Limerick and two in Dublin and the unit's HQ was later moved to Beggar's Bush Barracks in Dublin. On the foundation of the Territorial Force in 1908, the regiment became a unit of the Special Reserve Force and was re-titled the **South Irish Horse**.

---

32 There is no company designated as 'Number 3 Company' in the Irish Guards. The regimental Support Company has no specific march associated with it.

Operational history
The First World War, 1914–18

The South Irish Horse was mobilized for active service on the outbreak of the war. The regimental depot was in Clonmel while it was authorized to recruit in all of southern Ireland. The regiment's B Squadron was sent to France with the BEF and formed a composite regiment with squadrons of the North Irish Horse. Operating as GHQ troops it was involved in the opening phase of the war and the retreat from Mons.

During the war the squadrons of the regiment were initially detached and employed as divisional cavalry. Squadrons of the regiment were later reformed as regiments and served as corps cavalry. In 1917, the South Irish Horse was dismounted and served as infantry for the remainder of the war. The war service of the regiment's squadrons are as follows:

> A Squadron was attached to the 21st Division at Aldershot in 1915 and landed in France in September. It later served as part of the cavalry regiment of XV, IX and XVIII Corps.
> B Squadron formed part of the original BEF and serving as GHQ cavalry, it landed in France in August 1914. It later served with 2nd Division and as an element of I Corps' cavalry regiment, where it was re-titled as S Squadron.
> C Squadron was attached to the 16th (Irish) Division at Aldershot in 1915 and landed in France in December. It was later attached to I Corps' cavalry regiment.
> E Squadron landed in France in March 1916 and was attached to the 39th Division. In May 1916 it joined I Corps' cavalry regiment.
> F Squadron landed in France in May 1917 and was initially attached to XVIII Corps' cavalry regiment.
> S Squadron was attached to the 32nd Division in Salisbury in 1915 and landed in France in November. In May 1916 it was attached to XV Corps' cavalry regiment and was re-named as B Squadron, changing its designation with the B Squadron mentioned above. As B Squadron it later served with the cavalry regiments of IX and XVIII Corps.

As mentioned above, the various squadrons of the South Irish Horse were later used as corps cavalry. In May 1916, C, E and S Squadrons were unified to form the 1st South Irish Horse Regiment and served as the cavalry regiment of I Corps. In August 1917 the 1st South Irish Horse Regiment was dismounted and sent to Etaples where it was amalgamated with the 2nd South Irish Horse to form the 7th (South Irish Horse) Battalion, Royal Irish Regiment.

A, B and later F Squadrons were unified as the 2nd South Irish Horse Regiment and served as the corps cavalry to XVIII Corps,. In August 1917, the regiment was dismounted and amalgamated into the 7th (South Irish Horse) Battalion, the Royal Irish Regiment.

The 7th (South Irish Horse) Battalion, the Royal Irish Regiment was attached to the 49th Brigade of the 16th (Irish) Division. Following its losses during the German offensive of March 1918, it was reduced to cadre. It was later reformed using replacements from the Royal Munster Fusiliers and the Royal Dublin Fusiliers. It served with the 21st Brigade of the 30th Division until the end of the war and was Ellezelles in Belgium at the Armistice.

The South Irish Horse's HQ unit was based at Cahir in Tipperary and was designated as 3rd South Irish Horse Regiment.

1919 The 7th (South Irish Horse) Battalion, the Royal Irish Regiment was disbanded, the South Irish Horse being reformed as a reserve cavalry regiment.

1922 The regiment was disbanded on the formation of the Irish Free State.

Regimental colours
Following the disbandment of the regiment, its colours were laid up in St Patrick's Cathedral. These were later destroyed by vandals. Replacement colours were subsequently laid up in the cathedral.

Battle honours
Loos, Somme 1916, Somme 1918, Albert 1916, St Quentin, Rosières, Avre, Ypres 1918, Courtrai; France and Flanders 1914–18

THE NORTH IRISH HORSE, 1902–2006

Formation
During the 2nd Anglo-Boer War a number of Irish companies served with the Imperial Yeomanry in South Africa. These included the 45th Company (Dublin) and the 60th North Irish Company. Due to the fine performance of these Irish companies in South Africa, it was decided to raise two new units in Ireland under the terms of the Militia and Yeomanry Act of 1901. These units became the North Irish Horse and the South Irish Horse.

The North Irish Horse was initially designated as the North of Ireland Imperial Yeomanry and was raised on 7 January 1902 as a two squadron unit. Two further squadrons were added to the establishment and recruiting began in 1903. The regiment maintained its HQ in Belfast with squadrons in Enniskillen, Londonderry and Dundalk. 1908 On the creation of the Territorial Force, the unit was transferred to the Special Reserve and re-designated the **North Irish Horse**.

Operational history
The First World War, 1914–18

1914 On the outbreak of way, the regiment's depot was in Belfast and its recruiting area took in counties Down, Antrim, Tyrone, Cavan, Derry, Donegal, Armagh, Monghan and the city of Belfast.

   The North Irish Horse were mobilized for service on the outbreak of war and A and C Squadrons went to France with the BEF, landing at Le

Havre in August. With the South Irish Horse, they were the first Irish non-regular soldiers to serve in the war and were attached as GHQ troops. During 1914, they took part in the retreat from Mons and fought in the battles of Le Cateau, the Marne, the Aisne and Armentières. All of this regiment's service was on the Western Front during the war and a depot unit was maintained in Antrim.

The war service of the regiment's squadrons was as follows:

A Squadron was attached to GHQ in August 1914 but was attached to the 55th Division in January 1916 and served as divisional cavalry. In may 1916, the squadron was to VII Corps and served as the corps cavalry regiment.

B Squadron was attached to the 59th Division and was based in Hertfordshire from August 1915 to April 1916. In May 1916, F Squadron was re-designated as B Squadron.

C Squadron landed in France in August 1914 and served as GHQ troops. In April 1915 it transferred to the 3rd Division and served as divisional cavalry. In May 1916 it was attached to X Corps, becoming that corps cavalry regiment.

D Squadron was attached to the 51st Division as divisional cavalry and landed in France in May 1915. In May 1916 it became VII Corps' cavalry regiment.

E Squadron was attached to the 34th Division in 1915 and arrived in France in January 1916. In May 1916 it transferred to VII Corps as corps cavalry.

F Squadron was attached to the 33rd Division and landed in France in November 1915. In 1916 it spent periods on attachment with the 1st Cavalry Division, the 49th Division and the 32nd Division. In May 1916 it was re-designated as B Squadron and was attached to X Corps' cavalry regiment.

In May 1916, A, D and E Squadrons were formed the 1st North Irish Horse and served as VII Corps' cavalry regiment until July 1917, when it transferred to XIX Corps. In September 1917 it transferred to V Corps and was then dismounted, serving as a cyclist unit until the end of the war.

In June 1916, B and C Squadrons with the service squadron of the 6th Inniskilling Dragoons formed the 2nd North Irish Horse. This regiment initially served as the cavalry regiment to X Corps but in August 1917 it was broken up. The regiment's personnel were sent for infantry training and the men from the two North Irish Horse squadrons were later absorbed by the 9th Battalion of the Royal Irish Fusiliers. This battalion then took the title 9th (North Irish Horse) Battalion, the Royal Irish Fusiliers, and was attached to 108th Brigade, 36th (Ulster) Division.

During the course of the war, squadrons of the regiment took part in numerous battles including the Somme, Albert, Messines, 3rd Ypres and Bapaume.

1919	At the end of the war, the regiment was disembodied.
1922	The regiment was reformed as a cadre unit.
1939	As war became increasingly inevitable, the regiment was re-formed as an armoured car unit in the Supplementary Reserve. In September, it was transferred to the Royal Armoured Corps.

The Second World War, 1939–45

1939–42	The North Irish Horse was initially equipped with ancient Rolls Royce armoured cars but, designated as an 'Infantry Tank Unit' in 1941, training began on Valentine tanks. It moved to England where it was equipped with Churchill tanks and underwent further training as an infantry support unit.
1943	In January the regiment was sent to North Africa as part of the 25th Tank Brigade. Following its arrival in Algiers, the North Irish Horse was attached to the First Army and was almost immediately in action in the battle at Hunt's Gap. During the North African campaign, the regiment acted as armoured support for four different infantry divisions and took part in numerous actions including Sedjenane and Longstop Hill and was the first tank regiment to enter Tunis on 8 May 1943.
1944	The regiment was transferred to the Italian front where it joined the Eight Army and supported the 1st Canadian Division in its attack on the Hitler Line. In this action the North Irish Horse lost 32 tanks and 36 men killed. The regiment remained in Italy for the remainder of the war, taking part in several other actions, including the assault on the Gothic Line in August.
1945	At the ceasefire in 1945 the regiment was at Rovigo, north of Ferrara.
1946	The regiment was demobilized.
1947	The North Irish was reconstituted as an armoured car unit in the Territorial Army.
1967	In a series of TA reforms, D (North Irish Horse) Squadron became a unit of the Royal Yeomanry Regiment. The remainder of the North Irish Horse (Territorials) was attached to 5th Battalion, Royal Inniskilling Fusiliers, TA.
1969	The regiment re-organized as two units: D (North Irish Horse) Squadron, the Royal Yeomanry Regiment and 69 (North Irish Horse) Squadron, 32nd (Scottish) Signal Regiment.
1993	The North Irish Horse squadron of the Royal Yeomanry was reorganized as an independent reconnaissance unit, attached to 107 (Ulster) Brigade.
1995	69 Signal Squadron transferred to 40th (Ulster) Signal Regiment, Royal Signals.

Following the strategic review of 1998, the North Irish Horse was reorganized as:

B (NIH) Squadron, the Queen's Own Yeomanry.
69 (NIH) Squadron, 40 (Ulster) Signal Regiment.

Battle honours
Retreat from Mons, Marne 1914, Aisne 1914, Armentières 1914, Somme 1916, Somme 1918, Albert 1916, Messines 1917, Ypres 1917, Pilckem, St Quentin, Bapaume 1918, Hindenburg Line, Ephéy, St Quentin Canal, Cambrai 1918, Selle, Sambre, France and Flanders 1914–18, Hunt's Gap, Sedjenane I, Tamera, Mergueb Chaouach, Djebel Rmel, Longstop Hill 1943, Tunis, North Africa 1943, Liri Valley, Hitler Line, Advance to Florence, Gothic Line, Monte Farneto, Monte Cavallo, Casa Fortis, Casa Bettini, Lamone Crossing, Valli di Commacchio, Senio, Italy 1944–45.

Regimental music
The Garryowen

THE TYNESIDE IRISH BRIGADE, 1914–18

Formation
Due to large-scale migration during the nineteenth century, there was a significant Irish community living in the Tyneside area at the outbreak of the First World War. Inspired by the recruiting initiatives in other areas, the Irish lord mayor of Newcastle and members of the city's Irish Club proposed the formation of a 'Tyneside Irish Force'.

This idea was quashed by the War Office but faced with increasing pressure from the Irish Tyneside community, it was eventually decided that Irish service battalions could be formed for the local regiment, the Royal Northumberland Fusiliers. The response of the Irish community was huge, by the end of September the Newcastle Irish Club alone had recruited 1,000 men. By January 1915, over 5,500 men had joined the newly formed Irish battalions.

The regiment's recruiting area took in the Newcastle area while its depot was based at Alnwick Camp.

Operational history
The Irish volunteers of the Tyneside were used to form four service and two reserve battalions of the Northumberland Fusiliers:

> 24th (Service) Battalion (1st Tyneside Irish), Northumberland Fusiliers
> 25th (Service) Battalion (2nd Tyneside Irish), Northumberland Fusiliers
> 26th (Service) Battalion (3rd Tyneside Irish), Northumberland Fusiliers
> 27th (Service) Battalion (4th Tyneside Irish), Northumberland Fusiliers
> 30th (Reserve) Battalion (Tyneside Irish), Northumberland Fusiliers (formed July 1915)
> 34th (Reserve) Battalion (Tyneside Irish), Northumberland Fusiliers (formed June 1916)

1915   The four service battalions were used to form the Tyneside Irish Brigade; the 103rd Brigade of the 34th Division, and underwent initial training on Salisbury Plain.

1916   The service battalions went to France in January 1916 and, after an initial phase of front-line training were moved to the Somme sector in preparation for the major offensive of 1916. Here the Tyneside Irish Brigade took up positions which they christened as the 'Tara-Usna Line'
   On the first day of the battle of the Somme offensive, 1 July 1916, the Tyneside Irish Brigade suffered disastrous casualties as it attacked in the direction of La Boiselle in an effort to reach the Bapaume Road. The remains of the brigade reached its objective of Contalmaison but was pushed back by a German counter-attack. The survivors of the Tyneside Irish Brigade fought in later actions of the Somme offensive.

1917   The Tyneside Irish fought in the battle of Arras in 1917 but due to heavy losses the 24th and 27th Battalions were amalgamated to form the 24th/27th Battalion of the 103rd Brigade, 34th Division.

1918   In February 24th/27th Battalion was disbanded while the 25th and 26th Battalions were amalgamated with battalions of the 102nd Tyneside Scottish Brigade. The remaining Tyneside Irish fought in the defence against the German March offensive – the 'Kaiserslacht', but were reduced to cadre strength later in the year.

The colours of the Tyneside Irish Brigade were later laid up in Newcastle's two cathedrals. During the course of the war, the Tyneside Irish suffered over 80 per cent casualties and this illustrated the inherent dangers of raising 'Pals' battalions as the Irish community in the area was decimated.

RESERVE CAVALRY REGIMENTS, 1914–18

During the course of the First World War, a number of reserve cavalry regiments were raised in Ireland. These were tasked with recruiting and training cavalry soldiers for the regiments stationed in Belgium, France and elsewhere. Some members of these regiments became involved in the fighting during the 1916 Rising. Details of these reserve cavalry regiments are given below and these include details of the parent regiments that they recruited and trained men for. Drafts of recruits were sent to both regular cavalry regiments and also regiments of the Yeomanry that had been activated for war service. Many of these Yeomanry regiments saw service in the Middle East. It should also noted that there had been previous 1st and 2nd Reserve Cavalry Regiments raised in England but that these were re-designated in 1917 and new regiments bearing these designations were raised in Ireland.

1st Reserve Cavalry Regiment
This regiment was raised at the Curragh in 1917 using personnel from the 6th, 7th and 8th Reserve Cavalry Regiments. It was attached to the 3rd Reserve Cavalry Brigade and remained at the Curragh for the rest of the war. It raised and trained

recruits for the 5th Royal Irish Lancers and also the 9th, 12th, 16th, 17th and 21st Lancers. It also supplied recruits to service squadrons of the Bedford, Lincoln, Surrey and East Riding and the City of London Yeomanry regiments.

2nd Reserve Cavalry Regiment
This regiment was also raised at the Curragh in 1917 using personnel from the 9th and 10th Reserve Cavalry Regiments. It was attached to the 3rd Reserve Cavalry Brigade and remained at the Curragh until the end of the war. It sent drafts of recuits to the 8th Royal Irish Hussars and also the 3rd, 4th and 7th Hussars. Further recruits were sent to the 1st and 2nd County of London Yeomanry and the Westmoreland and Cumberland Yeomanry, among others.

6th Reserve Cavalry Regiment
This regiment was formed in Dublin on the outbreak of war in 1914. It was initially affiliated with the 5th Royal Irish Lancers and the 12th Lancers and from 1916 was attached to the 3rd Resrve Cavalry Brigade.
It also recruited for Yeomanry regiments and these included the City of London Yeomanry and the 1st County of London Yeomanry. In 1917 it was absorbed into the newly formed 1st Reserve Cavalry Regiment.

8th Reserve Cavalry Regiment
The 8th Reserve Cavalry Regiment was formed at the Curragh on the outbreak of war in August 1914.
It initally recruited and trained men for the 16th and 17th Lancers and was also affiliated with Yeomanry regiments which included the Dorset and Oxford Yeomanry. It was absorbed into the 1st Reserve Cavalry Regiment in 1917.

10th Reserve Cavalry Regiment
This regiment was formed on the outbreak of war and originally recruited for the 4th Hussars and the 8th Royal Irish Hussars. In April 1916, the regiment was attached to the 3rd Reserve Cavalry Brigade. Its affilated Yeomanry regiments were the Duke of Lancaster's, the Lancashire Hussars and the Westmoreland and Cumberland Yeomanry. In 1917 it was aborbed into the new 2nd Reserve Cavalry Regiment at the Curragh.

The **9th Reserve Cavalry Regiment** was raised in England (Shorncliffe) in 1914 but was moved to Ireland in 1915, initially being based in Newbridge, Co. Kildare. It was later stationed in the Curragh and was affiliated with the 3rd and 7th Hussars and the 2nd and 3rd County of London Yeomanry.

The **14th Reserve Cavalry Regiment** was likewise raised in England (Longmoor) in 1914 but moved to Ireland 1916 where it remained until early 1917.

THE ROYAL IRISH RANGERS, 1968–92

Formation
This regiment was formed on 1 July 1968 through the amalgamation of the Royal Inniskilling Fusiliers, the Royal Ulster Rifles and the Royal Irish Fusiliers. Through this amalgamation, the new regiment's full official title actually was **Royal Irish Rangers (27th (Inniskilling) 83rd and 87th)**. The new Royal Irish Rangers were therefore the heirs to the traditions of three regiments that could trace their lineage as far back as the seventeenth century. The ranks of private and rifleman were changed within the regiment, being replaced with the rank of 'ranger'. On formation the regiment consisted of three battalions:

> 1st Battalion, based at Worcester, which was composed of the former Royal Inniskilling Fusiliers.
> 2nd Battalion, based at Gibraltar, which was composed of the former Royal Ulster Rifles.
> 3rd Battalion, based at Catterick, which was composed of the former Royal Irish Fusiliers.

In December 1968, the 3rd Battalion was amalgamated into the 1st and 2nd Battalions as the army was reduced in size following the withdrawal from the Suez zone in Egypt. The traditions of the three founding regiments were therefore maintained within the two surviving regular battalions and their associated Territorial Army battalions.

Operational history
During its relatively short history, the battalions of the Royal Irish Rangers saw extensive service at home and abroad, including service with UN forces. This included tours in Northern Ireland, England and with the BAOR in Germany. The regiment also saw service in Cyprus, Gibraltar and Bahrain and took part in training exercises in Libya, Denmark, Canada, Texas and Oman, among other locations. In 1992 the Royal Irish Rangers were amalgamated with the Ulster Defence Regiment to form the new Royal Irish Regiment.

From its foundation, a series of Territorial Army battalions within the North Irish Militia were associated with the Royal Irish Rangers. These included:

> 5th Battalion, Royal Inniskilling Fusiliers (TA)
> 6th Battalion, Royal Ulster Rifles (TA)
> 5th Battalion, Royal Irish Fusiliers (TA)

The current Royal Irish Regiment retains a Ranger TA battalion.

Colonels-in-chief
1968   Field-Marshal, HRH Henry William Frederick Albert, 1st Duke of Gloucester

1975   HRH Princes Alice, Duchess of Gloucester
1989   HRH Brigitte, Duchess of Gloucester

Colonels

1968   Lieutenant-General Sir Ian Cecil Harris
1972   Major-General James H.S. Majury
1977   Major-General David N.C. O'Morchoe, 'The O'Morchoe'
1979   Major-General Humphey E.N. ('Bala') Bredin
1985   Brigadier-General Mervyn N.S. McCord
1990   General Sir Roger Neil Wheeler[33]

Motto

Faugh a Ballagh (Clear the Way)

Mascot

The Royal Irish Rangers adopted the Irish Wolfhound as its mascot. Traditionally these wolfhounds were named 'Brian Boru'. Between 1968 and 1992, the regiment had owned Brian Boru I to V in succession.

THE ULSTER DEFENCE REGIMENT, 1970–92

Formation

The Ulster Defence Regiment was formed due to the severe rioting and sectarian violence in Northern Ireland during the late 1960s. The 1969 report of Lord Hunt's advisory committee recommended the disbandment of the RUC Special Constabulary and the establishment of an RUC reserve. The report also recommended that a locally recruited military force be established and this became the Ulster Defence Regiment. It was authorized by act of parliament in January 1970 and became operational on 1 April, carrying out its first operational patrols on the same day.

At its establishment, the regiment was the largest infantry regiment in the British Army. It consisted of seven battalions; one in each of the six counties of Northern Ireland with a further battalion based in Belfast. Further battalions were later added to the establishment and by 1972 the organization of the UDR was as follows:

> 1st Battalion (Co. Antrim), St Patrick's Barracks, Ballymena
> 2nd Battalion (Co. Armagh), Armagh Barracks
> 3rd Battalion (Co. Down), Anderson Centre, Ballykinler
> 4th Battalion (Co. Fermanagh), Coleshill Centre, Enniskillen
> 5th Battalion (Co. Londonderry), Shackleton Barracks, Ballykelly
> 6th Battalion (Co. Tyrone), St Lucia Barracks, Armagh
> 7th Battalion (City of Belfast), Palace Barracks, Holywood, Co. Down
> 8th Battalion (Co. Tyrone), Killymeal House, Dungannon

[33] There was also a series of deputy colonels associated with the regiment.

9th Battalion (Co. Antrim), Steeple Road, Antrim
10th Battalion (City of Belfast), Malone Road, Belfast
11th Battalion (Craigavon), Mahon Road, Portadown, Co. Armagh
Regimental HQ at Lisburn.

In 1973, the UDR admitted its first women soldiers who came to be known as 'Greenfinches'. A permanent regimental cadre was established in 1976. There were further re-organizations of the regiment in 1984 and 1991, some of the regiment's battalions being amalgamated. It reached a maximum strength of 9,200, all ranks.

Operational history
During its relatively short history, the Ulster Defence Regiment was almost constantly on active service during one of the darkest periods in Irish history. Many of its members were called out for long periods of full-time service as they served on anti-terrorist and security duties. By 1980, the majority of the regiment was composed of soldiers on full-time service. The operations in which the UDR served are too numerous to mention. For a complete history of the regiment see John Potter's *A testimony to courage: the regimental history of the Ulster Defence Regiment* (London, 2002).

From its formation in 1970, the men and women of the UDR were often the target of terrorist attacks. In total, 197 soldiers were killed, many of them being targeted while off-duty. A further 60 ex-UDR men and women were killed after they had left the regiment. Over 450 men and women were wounded in attacks. In 1992 the Ulster Defence Regiment was amalgamated with the Royal Irish Rangers to form the new Royal Irish Regiment.

Colonels

1970	General Sir John D'Arcy Anderson
1977	Brigadier-General Henry J.P. Baxter
1982	Brigadier-General Peter W. Graham
1986	Colonel James D.C. Faulkner
1986	Lieutenant-General Sir David T. Young
1991	General Sir Charles Huxtable (continued as colonel of Royal Irish Regiment)

Music
Quick marches associated with the regiment include the 'Garrowen' and 'Sprig of Shilleagh'. The regimental slow march was 'Oft in the stilly night'.

THE ROYAL IRISH REGIMENT, 1992–2006

Formation
This regiment was formed on 1 July 1992 through the amalgamation of the Royal Irish Rangers and the Ulster Defence regiment. The Royal Irish Rangers had been formed in 1968 through the amalgamation on the Royal Inniskilling Fusiliers, the

Royal Irish Fusiliers and the Royal Ulster Rifles. The traditions of these earlier regiments are maintained by the modern Royal Irish Regiment. The battalions of the Ulster Defence Regiment had been formed in 1970.[34] The full official title of this new regiment was **The Royal Irish Regiment (27th (Inniskilling) 83rd and 87th) and The Ulster Defence Regiment)**. The modern Royal Irish Regiment has no connection with the former Royal Irish Regiment that was formed in 1684 and disbanded in 1922 (see separate entry on that regiment).

On its formation, the regiment immediately became the biggest infantry regiment in the British Army and initially consisted of two general service battalions, which were liable for overseas service, seven home service battalions and two Territorial Army battalions. The regiment was originally organized as follows:

General Service Battalions
    1st Battalion (formerly 1st Bn, Royal Irish Rangers)
    2nd Battalion (formerly 2nd Bn, Royal Irish Rangers)

Home Service Battalions
    3rd (County Down) Battalion (formerly 3rd Bn, Ulster Defence Regiment)
    4th (Country Fermanagh and County Tyrone) Battalion (4th/6th Bn UDR)
    5th (County Londonderry) Battalion (5th Bn UDR)
    6th (County Armagh) Battalion (2nd/11th Bn UDR)
    7th (City of Belfast) Battalion (7th/10th Bn UDR)
    8th (County Tyrone) Battalion (8th Bn UDR)
    9th (County Antrim) Battalion (1st/9th Bn UDR)

Territorial Army Battalions
    4th Battalion, Royal Irish Rangers (Volunteers)
    5th Battalion, Royal Irish Rangers (Volunteers)

Since 1993, there have been further re-organizations and amalgamations. At the time of writing the Royal Irish Regiment is composed of one active service battalion, three home service battalions and one Territorial Army battalion. The home service battalions of the regiment are scheduled for disbandment in 2007. The regiment is organized as follows:

    1st Battalion, Fort George, Inverness, Scotland. Attached to 16th Air Assault Brigade
    2nd Battalion, Holywood, Co. Down
    3rd Battalion, Armagh
    4th Battalion, Omagh, Co. Tyrone

The regiment also has a Territorial Army battalion, the Royal Irish Rangers, with its HQ in Portadown and training centres in Armagh, Ballymena, Enniskillen, Newtownards and Belfast.

---

[34] See earlier entries on the Ulster Defence Regiment, the Royal Irish Rangers and also the regiments that formed the RI Rangers.

Operational history

The home service battalions of the Royal Irish Regiment have served on security duties within Northern Ireland since the regiment's foundation in 1992. Since 1993, there has only been one general or active service battalion, designated as the regiment's 1st Battalion.

The 1st Battalion has seen service in Bosnia, Kosovo, Cyprus, while also serving in England and Germany. To date, it has also completed three tours of Northern Ireland, operating alongside the home service battalions. The 1st Battalion has also seen recent active service in Iraq, taking part in Operation Talic 1 in 2003 and Operation Talic 7 in 2005. The battalion is now based in Inverness and is attached to the 16th Air Assault Brigade. At the time of writing, a detachment of the regiment is on active service in Afghanistan.

Colonel-in-chief
1992   HRH, Prince Andrew, the Duke of York

Colonels
1992   General Sir Charles Huxtable
1996   General Sir Roger Neil Wheeler
2001   Lieutenant-General Philip Charles C. Trousdell[35]

Battle honours
The Royal Irish Regiment has inherited the battle honours of the Royal Irish Rangers, which itself had inherited the honours of three historic Irish regiments; the Royal Inniskilling Fusiliers, the Royal Irish Fusiliers and the Royal Ulster Rifles. (see entries on these regiments). Its most recent battle honour was 'Iraq 2003'.

Regimental music
The regimental quick march is 'Killaloe'

Mascot
The Royal Irish Regiment has adopted the Irish Wolfhound as its official mascot.

The regiment maintains the practice of the Royal Irish Rangers and names its wolfhound as 'Brian Boru'. In 1992, the Royal Irish Regiment adopted Brian Boru V, previously the mascot of the Royal Irish Rangers, as its mascot.

RESERVE, MILITIA AND VOLUNTEER UNITS 1744–2006 (BRITISH ARMY)

THE FENCIBLE REGIMENTS, 1756–1803

The first Fencible regiments were raised in 1756 on the outbreak of the Seven Years War and these were disbanded with the peace of 1763. Further Fencible regiment were

---

[35] A number of deputy-colonels have also been associated with the regiment.

raised on the outbreak of the American Revolutionary War. In Ireland, the main phase of Fencible service followed the declaration of war between Britain and France in 1793.

The Fencible regiments were of both infantry and cavalry and were initially destined only for home service. Irish Fencible regiments included:

> Lord Roden's or the 1st Irish Fencible Regiment
> Lord Glenworth's or the 2nd Irish Fencible Regiment
> The Loyal Irish Fencibles
> The Ancient Irish Fencibles or Ancient Irish Fencible Infantry
> The Tarbert Fencibles[36]

Many of the Fencible regiments volunteered for overseas service. The Ancient Irish Fencibles served in the Egyptian campaign of 1801 while the Tarbert Fencibles served in England and the Channel Island. The majority of the regiments were disbanded in 1801 and peace with France seemed imminent but some remained in service until 1803.

THE VOLUNTEERS, 1744–93

The origins of the Irish Volunteer movement were rooted in a tradition of independent military action on the part of the island's Protestant community.

During the various wars of the eighteenth century, volunteer units were raised from among Ireland's population; often as a response to the military incapacity of the government. Some of these units dated back to the 1740s and were founded because of fears of further Jacobite rebellions and French invasion.

The main phase of Volunteer activity dated from the 1770s, however, with the majority of units being raised in 1778 and 1779. Following the outbreak of the Revolutionary War in America, the Protestant community realized that it would be unlikely that the financially hard-pressed government would be unable to defend the country. This fears were not unjustified; in April 1778 the American privateer, Paul Jones, made a raid into Belfast Lough and captured a British ship. It was against a backdrop of invasion fears that renewed energy went into founding Volunteer units across the country. The Volunteer movement took on a deeper political significance and was used by leaders of the Protestant ascendancy class to pressurize the government for parliamentary and trade reforms.

The units of the Volunteers are listed below and where possible, the date of the unit's foundation is included. The Volunteer units included infantry, cavalry and even artillery. Some of these units survived until the foundation of the Irish Militia in 1793.[37]

---

36 This regiment was originally thought to have been formed in Scotland but was actually raised in 1799 by Sir Edward Leslie of Tarbert, Co. Kerry. 37 The main source on Volunteer units is still Thomas McNevin's *The history of the Volunteers, 1782*. The foundation and the history of these units would benefit from further research and it would also be interesting to explore the links between Volunteer and later Militia units.

VOLUNTEER CAVALRY UNITS

County Cork
True Blue Cavalry (1745)
Mitchelstown Light Dragoons (1744)
Black Pool Horse (1776)
Youghal Cavalry (1776)
Brandon Cavalry (1778)
Muskerry Blue Light Dragoons (1778)
Duhallow Rangers (1778)
Imokilly Horse (1778)
Imokilly Blue Horse (1779)
Kilworth Light Dragoons (1779)
Doneraile Rangers Light Dragoons (1779)
Glanmire Union Cavalry (1779)
Cork Cavalry
Mallow Cavalry (1782)
Great Island Cavalry (1782)

County Clare
County Clare Horse (1779)
Sixmilebridge Independents

County Kerry
Kerry Legion Cavalry (1779)
Woodford Rangers

County Limerick
Kilfinnan Light Dragoons (1777)
County Limerick Horse (1779)
Connaught Rangers (1779)
County Limerick Royal Horse
Small County Union Light Dragoons
True Blue Horse
Connell's Light Horse
Riddlestown Hussars

County Tipperary
Tipperary Light Dragoons (1776)
Templemore Light Dragoons (1776)
Sleiverdagh Light Dragoons (1778)
Clanwilliam Union Cavalry (1779)
Lora Rangers (1779)
Munster Corps Cavalry
Clogheen Union Cavalry (1781)
Ormond Union Cavalry (1779, later amalgamated with the Ormond Union Infantry; see below).
Newport Cavalry (later amalgamated with Newport Volunteers: see below).

County Waterford
Lismore Blues (1778)
Curraghmore Rangers (1779)
Waterford Union Cavalry

VOLUNTEER INFANTRY AND ARTILLERY UNITS

County Cork
Cork Artillery
Imokilly Blue Artillery
True Blue (1745)
Cork Boyne (1776)
Mallow Boyne (1776)
Bandon Boyne (1777)
Carbery Independents (1777)
Aughrim of Cork (1777)
Hawke Union of Cove (1778)
Blackwater Rangers
Blarney Volunteers
Newmarket Rangers
Curriglass Volunteers (1779)
Castlemartyr Society (1779)
Inchigeelagh Volunteers (1779)
Muskerry Volunteers (1779)

Loyal Newberry Musqueteers (1777)
Cork Union (1776)
Culloden Volunteers of Cork (1778)
Ross Carbery Volunteers
Passage Union (1778)
Bandon Independents (1778)
Youghal Independent Blues (1778)
Youghal Rangers (1778)
Kinsale Volunteers (1778)
Hanover Society, Cloughnakilty (1778)
Kanturk Volunteers (1778)

Doneraile Rangers (1779)
Bantry Volunteers (1779)
Kilworth Volunteers (1779)
Mallow Independents (1779)
Youghal Union Fusiliers (1779)
Duhallow Volunteers (1779)
Kinnelea and Kerrach Union (1779)
Charleville Volunteers
Imokilly Blue Infantry
Castle Lyons Volunteers

County Clare
Ennis Volunteers (1778)
Inchiquin Fusiliers (1779)

Kilrush Union (1780)

County Kerry
Royal Tralee Volunteers (1779)
Kerry Legion (1779)
Killarney Foresters (1779)
Gunsborough Union (1779)

Miltown Fusiliers
Laune Rangers
Dromore Volunteers

County Limerick
Royal Glin Artillery (1779)
Kilfinnan Foot (1776)
County Limerick Fencible Volunteers
Loyal Limerick Volunteers (1776)
Castleconnel Rangers (1778)

Adare Volunteers
Rathkeale Volunteers (1779)
The German Fusiliers
True Blue Foot
The Limerick Independents (1781)

County Tipperary
Tipperary Volunteers (1776)
Roscrea Blues
Ormond Union (1779, later amalgamated with the Ormond Union Cavalry. See above).
Borrisokane Volunteers (1779)
Ormond Independents (1779)
Clonmel Independents (1779)
Castle Otway Volunteers
Cashel Volunteers (1779)

Fethard Independents (1779)
Nenagh Volunteers (1779)
Thurles Union (1779)
Drum Division of Thurles Union (1779)
Kilcooly True Blues (1779)
Newport Volunteers (This unit was later amalgamated with the Newport Volunteer Cavalry).
Carrick Union (1779)
Caher Union (1781)

County Waterford
The Waterford Artillery

In all seven Waterford companies were raised between 1778 and 1782, taking the various titles of 'Waterford Independents', 'Royal Oaks or Waterford Independent Blues' and 'Waterford Grenadiers'. Within this distinctive titled arrangement, they also numbered their companies from 1 to 7.

The Waterford Independents
    No. 1 Company was raised in March 1778 by Captain Henry Alcock.
    No. 2 Company was raised by Captain Robert Shapland in March 1778.
    No. 3 Company was raised in May 1778 by Captain Hannibal William Dobbyn.
    No. 6 Company was raised in September 1781 by Lieutenant Henry Hayden.
    The Royal Oaks or Waterford Independent Blues. Two companies, numbered 4 and 5, were raised in September 1779 by Colonel Cornelius Bolton.
    The Waterford Grenadiers, No. 7. Raised in June 1782 by Captain David Wilson as a single company unit.

Other County Waterford units
    Tallow Independent Blues (1778)   Cappoquin Volunteers (1779)
    Dungarvan Volunteers (1779)   Waterford Volunteers No. 7 (1782)

VOLUNTEER UNITS IN ULSTER, LEINSTER AND CONNAUGHT

Aghavoie Loyals (1782)
Aldborough Legion (1777)
Arlington Light Cavalry (1779)
Arran Phalanx
Athy Independents (1779)
Athy Volunteers (1779)
Aughnacloy Battalion
Ashfield Volunteers
Aughrim Light Horse
Ballintemple Forresters (1779)
Barony Rangers (1778)
Barony of Forth Corps (1779)
Ballyleek Rangers (1779)
Ballina and Ardnaree Loyal Volunteers (1779)
Belfast Union (1778)
Belfast Light Dragoons (1781)
Belfast Battalion (1779)
Belfast Volunteer Company (April 1778)
Belfast First Volunteer Company (March 1778)
Burros Volunteers (1779)
Burros in Ossory Rangers (1779)
Builders' Corps (1781)
Castlebar Independents (1770)
Castle Mount Garret Volunteers (1778)
Callan Union (1779)
Carlow Association (1779)
Carrickfergus Company (1779)
Castledurrow Light Horse (1778)
Castledurrow Volunteers (1779)
Carlow (County) Legion (1779)
Clanricarde Brigade (1782)
Clane Rangers (1779)
Constitution Regiment (Co. Down)
Down First Regiment
Drogheda Association (1777)
Dublin Volunteers (1778)
Dublin (County) Light Dragoons (1779)
Dublin Independent Volunteers (1780)
Duleek Light Company (1778)
Dunkerrin Volunteers (1779)
Dunlavin Light Dragoons (1777)
Dunmore Rangers (1779)
Dundalk Horse
Dungiven Battalion (1778)
Echlin Vale Volunteers (1778)
Edenderry Union (1777)
Edgeworthstown Battalion (1779)
English Rangers (1779)
Eyrecourt Buffs (1779)
Independent Enniskilliners

Fartullagh Rangers (1779)
Finea Independents (1779)
Fingal Light Dragoons (1783)
French Park Light Horse (1779)
Glenboy and Killemat Regiment (1779)
Glin Royal Artillery (1776)
Glorious Memory Battalion (1780)
Goldsmith's Corps (1779)
Graigue Volunteers (1779)
Granard Infantry Union Brigade (1782)
First Volunteers of Ireland (1766)
Irish Brigade (1782)
Kell's Association (1779)
Kile Volunteers (1779)
Kilcullen Rangers (1779)
Kilkenny Rangers (1770)
Kilkenny Volunteers (1779)
Lawyers' Corps (1779)
Larne Independents (1782)
Leap Independents (1780)
Liberty Volunteers (1779)
Limavady Battalion (1777)
Liney Volunteers (1778)
Lisburne Fusiliers
Londonderry Fuzileers [sic] (1778)
Longford Light Horse (1779)
Lowtherstown Independent Volunteers (1779)
Magherafelt (First) Volunteers (1773)
Maryborough Volunteers (1776)
Merchants' Corps (1779)
Monaghan Rangers (1780)
Monastereven Volunteers (1778)
Mote Light Cavalry (1778)
Mountain Rangers (1779)
Nass Rangers (1779)[38]
New Ross Independents (1777)
Offerlane Blues (1773)
Orior Grenadiers (1779)
Ossory True Blues (1773)
Parsonstown Loyal Independents (1776)

Portarlington Infantry (1779)
Raford Brigade (Light Cavalry) (1779)
Ralphsdale Light Dragoons
Raphoe Battalion (1778)
Rathdown Light Dragoons (1779)
Rathdowny Volunteers (1776)
Rathangan Union (1782)
Rockingham Volunteers (1779)
Rosanallis Volunteers (1774)
Roscommon Independent Forresters (1779)
Ross Union Rangers (1779)
Ross Volunteer Guards (1779)
Roxborough Volunteers (1777)
Royal 1st Regiment (Co. Antrim)
Sligo Loyal Volunteers (1779)
Society Volunteers of Derry (1782)
Stradbally Volunteers (1779)
Strokestown Light Horse (1779)
Talbotstown Invincible (1780)
Trim Infantry (1779)
Tullamore True Blue Rangers (1778)
Tullow Rangers (1778)
Tully Ash Real Volunteers (1783)
Tyrrel's Pass Volunteers (1776)
Tyrone First Regiment (1780)
Ulster Volunteer True Blue Battalion (1779)
Ulster First Regiment
Ulster Fourth Regiment
Ulster Regiment Artillery
Union Light Dragoons (Meath)
Union Light Dragoons (Dublin City)
Upper Cross and Coolock Independent Volunteers (1779)
Waterford Royal Battalion (1779)
Wexford Independent Light Dragoons (1775)
Wexford Independent Volunteers (1779)
Wicklow Forresters (1779)
Wicklow Association Artillery
Willsborough Volunteers (1779)

[38] Presumably the Naas Rangers.

REGIMENTS OF THE IRISH MILITIA

The Irish militia regiments were formed in 1793 and some regiments claimed descent from earlier volunteer regiments. The militia was organized on a county basis while the larger towns and cities also had regiments of their own.

The Militia Act of 1793 allowed Catholics to carry arms and they provided the rank and file of the new units while members of the Protestant community served as officers.

During the course of the next two centuries, the regiments of the Irish militia were activated or 'embodied' on several occasions. They saw service in the 1798 Rebellion and were embodied again on various occasions up to 1815.

Drafts from the militia regiments were used to bring regular army regiments up to strength and as a result detachments of Irish militia regiments saw service overseas during the Napoleonic wars. At the battle of Waterloo in 1815, for example, the 28th and 32nd Regiments had been reinforced with drafts from the Tyrone Militia while the Coldstream Guards had been reinforced with a draft from the North Mayo Militia.[39]

In 1855 the militia was embodied again after the outbreak of the Crimean War and due to the Indian Mutiny, many regiments remained embodied until 1860. In 1900 these reserve battalions were activated and provided garrisons in England, Gibraltar, the Maltese Islands and also in South Africa and remained in service until the end of the 2nd Anglo-Boer War.

The regiments of the Irish militia were also effected by various re-organizations of the army during the nineteenth century. In 1881 under the terms of the Cardwell reforms, the Irish militia units were re-designated as the reserve battalions of regular Irish regiments. For example, the South Mayo Rifles Regiment of Militia, became the 3rd Battalion of the Connaught Rangers. Several battalions were disbanded in 1908 following a series of army reforms. During the First World War, these reserve battalions again served on garrison duties in Ireland and England.

Within the Irish militia units there were also regiments raised specifically as artillery in 1855. In 1881 they transferred to a separate militia artillery system and in 1902 they were re-organized as militia regiments within the Royal Garrison Artillery. In 1908 the majority were disbanded and only the Antrim Artillery Militia and the Cork Artillery Militia remained.

The reserve battalions based in the south of Ireland were disbanded in 1922. Those based in Northern Ireland went into suspended animation in 1921 and were finally disbanded in 1953. Having been founded in 1793, the last descendents of the Irish militia regiments did not disappear until 1953, by which time Northern Ireland had been brought fully into the Territorial Army organization.

There has been relatively little research carried out on the Irish militia. The main source for this subject remains Sir Henry McNally's *The Irish Militia, 1793–1816: a social and military study* published in 1949, while A.S. White's *Bibliography of regi-*

---

[39] The full title of the Tyrone regiment was the 'Royal Tyrone Regiment of Fusiliers (Militia)'.

mental histories of the British Army includes several references to contemporary published histories of the Irish militia regiments. A history of the Irish militia during the period 1793 to 1802 is forthcoming and a new publication on this subject can only be welcomed.[40] Further research is required on both the organization and deployment of the Irish militia from its foundation until its final disappearance in the 1950s.

The regiments of the Militia also co-existed with the units of the Irish Yeomanry, which were formed in 1793. Despite the title, these units were not exclusively cavalry and also included some infantry yeomanry units. As was the case with the Militia, many of these new units claimed descent from earlier units of the Volunteers. The units of the Irish Yeomanry were active in the suppression of the 1798 Rebellion but the majority were disbanded soon afterwards. New units were raised in 1803 but the majority of them disappeared after the end of the Napoleonic wars in 1815, although some units remained until 1834.[41]

THE REGIMENTS OF THE IRISH MILITIA BY COUNTY:

Antrim
Formed in 1793. Active during 1798 Rebellion. Re-embodied in 1855 as the Antrim Militia (The Queen's Royal Rifles). In 1860 its HQ was in Bristol, England. Re-designated as the 4th Battalion of the Royal Irish Rifles in 1881. Re-designated as 3rd Battalion Militia in 1921.

Royal Antrim Artillery
Formed in 1855. In 1860 based in Shorncliffe, England. In 1902 re-designated as a militia regiment of the Royal Garrison Artillery. In 1908 re-designated as a special reserve regiment of the Royal Garrison Artillery. HQ in Carrickfergus.

Armagh
Formed in 1793. Active in the 1798 Rebellion. Present at the battle of Ballinamuck where it captured the colour of the French 70th Demi-Brigade, becoming the only militia regiment to capture an enemy colour. Re-embodied in 1855 as the Armagh Light Infantry and it supplied a large draft for the regular army during the Crimean war. HQ In Armagh. In 1881 it was re-designated as the 3rd Battalion of the Royal Irish Fusiliers.

Carlow
Formed in 1793. Re-embodied in 1855 as the Carlow Rifles with HQ in Carlow. In 1881 re-designated as the 8th Battalion of the King's Royal Rifle Corps. Disbanded in 1908.

Cavan
Formed in 1793 with HQ in Cavan. Re-embodied in 1855 as the Cavan Militia with HQ in Cavan. In 1881 re-designated as the 4th Battalion of the Royal Irish Fusiliers. Disbanded in 1922.

---

40 This volume by Ivan F. Nelson was published by Four Courts Press in 2007.   41 For a comprehensive study of the Irish Yeomanry, see Allan F. Blackstock's *An Ascendancy army: the Irish Yeomanry, 1796–1834* (Dublin, 1998).

Clare

Formed in 1793. In 1817 HQ at Clare Castle, Enniskillen. In 1855 re-embodied as the Clare Militia with HQ in Ennis. Re-designated in 1881 as the 7th Clare Brigade, South Irish Division Artillery. In 1902 re-designated as a militia regiment of the Royal Garrison Artillery. Disbanded in 1908.

Cork

North Cork

Formed in 1793 and achieved a dubious notoriety during the 1798 Rebellion. In 1855 re-embodied as the North Cork Rifles. In 1881 re-designated as the 9th Battalion King's Royal Rifle Corps. Disbanded in 1908.

South Cork

Formed in 1793 with HQ at Rathcormack. Re-embodied in 1855 as the 87th or South Cork Light Infantry. In 1881 re-designated as the 3rd Battalion of the Royal Munster Fusiliers. In 1908 became the 4th Battalion (Extra Reserve) of the Royal Munster Fusiliers. Disbanded in 1922.

Cork City

Formed in 1793. Re-embodied in 1855 as the Cork City Regiment. In 1856 re-titled as the Royal Cork City Artillery. In 1860 its HQ in Ballincollig. In 1881 re-designated as the 3rd Royal Cork City Brigade, South Irish Division Artillery. In 1902 re-designated as a militia regiment of the Royal Garrison Artillery. In 1908 amalgamated into the special reserve of the Royal Garrison Artillery. HQ at Fort Westmorland on Spike Island in Cobh Harbour.

West Cork Artillery

Formed in 1855. In 1860 its HQ in Macroom. In 1902 re-designated as an element of the Cork regiment of the Royal Garrison Artillery militia regiments. In 1908 amalgamated with the Cork City Artillery into the special reserve of the Royal Garrison Artillery.

Donegal

Formed in 1793. In 1855 re-embodied as the 102nd or Prince of Wales's Own Donegal Militia. In 1860 its HQ in Colchester. In 1881 re-designated as the 3rd Brigade North Irish Division Artillery.

Donegal Artillery

Formed in 1855. In 1860 its HQ at Charlemont. In 1902? Re-designated as a militia regiment in the Royal Garrison Artillery. Disbanded in 1908.

Down

North Down

Formed in 1793. In 1796 took part in the expedition against the French landing in Bantry Bay. Re-embodied in 1855 as the Royal North Down Militia (Rifles). In 1860 its HQ in Newtownards. In 1881 re-designated as the 3rd Battalion of the Royal Irish Rifles.

South Down
Formed in 1793. In 1855 re-embodied as the Royal South Down Light Infantry. In 1860 its HQ in Hillsborough. Re-designated as the 5th Battalion Royal Irish Rifles in 1881.

Dublin
Dublin City
Formed in 1793. Re-embodied in 1855 as the Royal Dublin City Militia (Queen's Own Royal Regiment). In 1860 its HQ in Plymouth, England. In 1881 re-designated as the 4th Battalion of the Royal Dublin Fusiliers. Disbanded in 1922.

Dublin City Artillery
Formed in 1855. In 1860 based in Colchester, England. In 1902 re-designated as the Dublin City militia regiment of the Royal Garrison Artillery. Disbanded in 1908.

Dublin County
Formed in 1793 with its HQ in Lucan. In 1855 re-embodied as the Dublin County Light Infantry. In 1881 re-designated as the 5th Battalion Royal Dublin Fusiliers. Disbanded in 1922.

Fermanagh
Formed in 1793 with its HQ in Enniskillen, Re-embodied in 1855 as the Fermanagh Light Infantry, In 1860 its HQ in Chester, England, In 1881 re-designated as the 3rd Battalion Royal Inniskilling Fusiliers, Re-designated as the 4th Battalion (Extra Reserve) in 1921, Disbanded in 1953.

Galway
Formed in 1793 with HQ at Ballinasloe. Re-embodied in 1855 as the Galway Militia with HQ at Loughrea. In 1881 re-designated as the 4th Battalion Connaught Rangers. In 1908 re-designated as the 3rd Battalion Connaught Rangers. Disbanded in 1922.

Galway Artillery
Formed and disbanded in 1855.

Kerry
Formed in 1793 with HQ in Tralee. Re-embodied as the Kerry Militia in 1855. In 1860 its HQ at the Curragh. In 1881 re-designated as the 4th Battalion Royal Munster Fusiliers. In 1908 re-designated as the 3rd Battalion Royal Munster Fusiliers. Disbanded in 1922.

Kildare
Formed in 1793 with HQ in Naas. Re-embodied as the Kildare Rifles in 1855 with HQ in Naas. In 1881 re-designated as the 3rd Battalion Royal Dublin Fusiliers. Disbanded in 1922.

Kilkenny
Formed in 1793 with HQ in Kilkenny. Re-embodied in 1855 as the Kilkenny Fusiliers with HQ in Kilkenny. In 1881 re-designated as the 5th Battalion Royal Irish

Regiment. Re-designated in 1908 as the 4th Battalion (Extra Reserve). Disbanded in 1922.

King's County (Co. Offaly)
Formed in 1776 as the Parsonstown Loyal Independent Volunteer Corps. Taken on militia establishment in 1793 as the King's County Militia, with HQ at Parsonstown (Birr, Co. Offaly). Re-embodied in 1855 as the King's County Royal Rifles with HQ at Parsonstown. In 1881 re-designated as the 3rd Battalion of the Leinster Regiment. Disbanded in 1922.

Leitrim
Formed in 1793 with HQ in Carrick-on-Shannon. Re-embodied in 1855 as the Leitrim Rifles with HQ in Mohill. In 1881 re-designated as the 8th Battalion of the Rifle Brigade. Disbanded in 1922.

Limerick
Limerick County
Formed in 1793 as the Royal Limerick County Militia with HQ in St Francis' Abbey. Re-embodied in 1855. In 1860 its HQ in Portsmouth, England. In 1874 re-designated as the Royal Limerick County Militia (Fusiliers). In 1881 re-designated as 5th Battalion Royal Munster Fusiliers. Embodied during 2nd Anglo-Boer War, stationed on Gozo in the Maltese Islands. Disbanded in 1922.

Limerick City Artillery
Formed in 1793 with HQ in Limerick City. Re-embodied in 1855 as Limerick Artillery. In 1881 re-designated as the 4th Brigade North Irish Division Artillery. In 1902 re-designated as the Limerick City militia regiment of the Royal Garrison Artillery. Disbanded in 1908.

Londonderry Artillery
Formed in 1855 as the Londonderry Artillery Company. In 1881 re-designated as the 9th Brigade North Irish Division Artillery. In 1902 re-designated as the Londonderry militia regiment of the Royal Garrison Artillery. Disbanded in 1908.

Londonderry
Formed in 1793 with HQ in Londonderry. Re-embodied in 1855 as Londonderry Light Infantry with HQ in Londonderry. In 1881 re-designated as the 9th Brigade North Irish Division Artillery.

Longford
Formed in 1793 as the Prince of Wales's Royal Longford Militia with HQ in Newtown Forbes. Re-embodied in 1855 as the Longford Rifles Militia with HQ in Longford town. In 1881 re-designated as the 6th Battalion of the Rifle Brigade. Disbanded in 1922.

Louth
Formed in 1793 with HQ at Colton. In 1797 it absorbed the Drogheda Militia. Re-

embodied as the Louth Rifles in 1855. In 1860 its HQ in Kinsale. In 1881 re-designated as the 6th Battalion Royal Irish Rifles. Disbanded in 1908.

North Mayo
Formed in 1793 with HQ in Castlebar. In 1855 re-embodied as North Mayo Militia with HQ in Ballina. Re-designated as the 6th Battalion of the Connaught Rangers in 1881. Disbanded in 1922.

South Mayo
Formed in 1793 with HQ in Westport. Re-embodied in 1855 as the South Mayo Rifles with HQ in Westport. In 1881 re-designated as the 3rd Battalion Connaught Rangers. In 1889 amalgamated with 6th Battalion to form new 3rd Battalion. Disbanded in 1908

Meath
Formed in 1793 as the Royal Meath Militia with HQ in Kells. Re-embodied in 1855 as the Royal Meath Militia. In 1860 its HQ in Trim. In 1881 re-designated as the 5th Battalion of the Leinster Regiment. Disbanded in 1922.

Monaghan
Formed as the Monaghan Militia in 1793 with HQ in Monaghan town. In 1855 re-embodied with HQ in Monaghan town. In 1881 re-designated as the 5th Battalion of the Royal Irish Fusiliers. Disbanded in 1922.

Queen's County (Co. Laois)
Formed as Queen's County Militia in 1793 with HQ in Maryborough. In 1855 re-embodied at the Queen's County Militia (Royal Rifles) with HQ in Maryborough. In 1881 re-designated as the 4th Battalion Leinster Regiment. Disbanded in 1922

Roscommon
Formed in 1793 with HQ in Boyle. Re-embodied in 1855 with HQ in Boyle. In 1881 re-designated as the 5th Battalion of the Connaught Rangers. Disbanded in 1922

Sligo
Formed in 1793 with HQ in Sligo town. Re-embodied in 1855 as the Sligo Rifles with HQ in Sligo town. In 1881 re-designated as the 8th Brigade North Irish Division Artillery. In 1902 re-designated as the Sligo militia regiment of the Royal Garrison Artillery. Disbanded in 1908.

Tipperary Artillery
Formed in 1793 as the Duke of Clarence's Munster Artillery or South Tipperary Militia with HQ in Clonmel. In 1855 re-embodied as the Duke of Clarence's Munster Artillery or 1st South Tipperary Militia. In 1860 its HQ in Gosport, England. In 1881 transferred to artillery militia. In 1902 re-designated as the Tipperary militia regiment of the Royal Garrison Artillery. Disbanded in 1908.

Tipperary Light Infantry
In 1855 the 2nd or North Tipperary Light Infantry embodied with HQ in Cashel.

This regiment mutinied in Nenagh in July 1856 and was disbanded. In 1881 re-designated as the 4th Battalion the Royal Irish Regiment. Disbanded in 1922.

Tyrone
Formed as Tyrone Militia in 1793 with HQ in Caldeon. Re-embodied in 1855 as the Royal Tyrone Fusiliers. In 1860 its HQ in Omagh. In 1881 re-designated as the 4th Battalion Royal Inniskilling Fusiliers. Became an extra reserve battalion in 1921. Disbanded in 1953.

Tyrone Artillery
Tyrone Artillery Militia formed in 1855 with HQ in Moy. Transferred to Artillery Militia in 1855.

Waterford
Formed in 1793 as the Waterford Militia with HQ in Waterford City. In 1855 re-embodied as the Waterford Artillery. In 1860 its HQ in Gosport, England. In 1881 re-designated as the 6th Brigade South Irish Division Artillery. In 1902 re-designated as the Waterford militia company of the Royal Garrison Artillery. Disbanded in 1908.

Westmeath
Formed in 1793 with HQ in Mullingar. In 1855 re-embodied as the Westmeath Rifles. In 1860 its HQ in Castelton-Delvin. In 1881 re-designated as the 9th Battalion of the Rifle Brigade. Disbanded in 1922.

Wexford
Formed in 1793 with HQ in Wexford town. Re-embodied in 1855 with HQ in Wexford. In 1881 re-designated as the 3rd Battalion of the Royal Irish Regiment. Disbanded in 1922.

Wicklow
Formed in 1793 as the Wicklow Militia with HQ in Wicklow. Re-embodied in 1855 as the Wicklow Rifles Militia with HQ in Wicklow. In 1881 re-designated as the 7th Brigade North Irish Division Artillery. In 1902 it is re-designated as the Wicklow militia regiment of the Royal Garrison Artillery. Disbanded in 1908.

THE TERRITORIAL ARMY OF NORTHERN IRELAND

The regiments of the Irish Militia formed the bulk of reserve forces in Ireland from 1793 to 1922. Ireland was not included in the acts that formed the Territorial Force in 1908 and the Territorial Army in 1920 as, from 1881 the battalions of the Militia served as the reserve battalions of the Irish regiments. In 1902 the South Irish Horse and the North Irish Horse served as the cavalry element of the Irish reserves.

The organization of the reserves in Northern Ireland after 1922 requires further research. In the decades that followed, many units were raised or activated and served as militia battalions of regular Irish regiments, reserve and special reserve units and also training units. After WWII, Northern Ireland was brought fully into the Territorial Army organization and today maintains a large TA force consisting of units of all branches and corps. These units are organized into the 107th (Ulster) Brigade (TA).[42] The units of the TA in Northern Ireland are:

206 (Ulster) Battery, Royal Artillery	Coleraine and Newtownards
69 (NIH) Signal Squadron	Limavady
23 Intelligence Company	Newtownabbey
Northern Ireland TA Band	Holywood
85 Signal Squadron	Bangor
The North Irish Horse	Belfast
40 (Ulster) Signal Regiment	Belfast
152 (Ulster) Ambulance Regiment	Belfast
204 (NI) Field Hospital	Armagh, Belfast and Ballymena
211 Ambulance Squadron	Coleraine and Derry
253 (NI) Field Hospital	Belfast and Derry
Queen's University OTC	Belfast
Royal Irish Rangers[43]	HQ in Portadown, also Armagh, Ballymena, Enniskillen, Newtownards and Belfast.

---

[42] This 107th Brigade designation perpetuates one of the brigade titles of the 36th Ulster Division in WW1. [43] This battalion is the TA element of the Royal Irish Rangers.

CHAPTER 8

South African Irish regiments, 1885–2006

The earliest Irish unit in South Africa was the Cape Town Irish Rifles which was raised in April 1885 following a public meeting organized by Michael Doyle, a member of the Irish community in Cape Town. At this inaugural meeting 26 men enlisted and a further 200 more had joined the unit within a fortnight. It was designated as the Cape Town Irish Volunteer Rifles and was commanded by a Major O'Reilly. It was absorbed in 1891 into the Duke of Edinburgh's Own Volunteer Rifles as H (Irish) Company.

During the 2nd Boer War a second Irish unit was formed by Captain Daniel Patrick Driscoll in March 1900 and it became known as 'Driscoll's Scouts'. This second Irish unit took part in the siege of Wepener and operations around Lindley and Fouriesburg and finished the war in the Western Transvaal. There were also other volunteer units, such as 'Geoghegan's Horse' which were formed by Irish settlers or men of Irish descent. The modern South African Irish Regiment was formed at the outbreak of the First World War. The regiment has had a varied history and at different times has served as both an infantry and artillery unit.

Formation

In August 1914 three army officers met at the Irish Club in Johannesburg and decided to form an Irish regiment from among the Irish community of that city. They were Major George Twomey, Captain J. Jeoffreys and a Captain MacDonald. It was initially intended to call this new unit the 'Imperial Irish Horse'.

Their proposal was officially sanctioned and on 9 September 1914, six companies formed up at Booysens Camp, Johannesburg. According to archival sources the regiment officially came into being on 1 December 1914 but this date continues to be disputed by members of the South African Irish Regiment who maintain that the date of formation was in September 1914, thus making the regiment more senior in the list of regiments in the South African Citizen Force.

The first honorary colonel of the SAIR was Mrs Louis Botha, who was of Irish descent and whose maiden name was Emmet. The regiment's first commanding officer was Lt.-Col. F.H. Brennan.

Operational history

The First World War, 1914–18

1914   The SAIR was put into action almost immediately after its formation and took part in the suppression of the Afrikaner Rebellion of 1914. It was then

	assigned to the Northern Force commanded by General Louis Botha and landed at Walvis Bay in German South West Africa (modern-day Namibia) on 25 December 1914.
1915–21	At the end of the campaign in German South West Africa, the regiment returned to Cape Town where it was demobilized on 23 July 1915. While there was an Irish company in the 5th South African Infantry during the campaign in East Africa, the South Irish Regiment was not re-formed during the war. It remained in suspended animation until 31 December 1920 when it was officially disbanded and removed from the army establishment. In January 1921 the Duke of Connaught presented a colour to the regimental association in recognition of its wartime service.

The Second World War, 1939–45

1939	In November 1939 the regiment was reformed as the 1st South African Irish Regiment. A second battalion was raised in December 1939 but was soon disbanded, its personnel being assigned to the first battalion. The regiment was then simply re-designated the South African Irish Regiment. At the same time a regimental pipe band was formed and pipes and sheet music were obtained from Ireland.
1940	In April the regiment was moved to the camp at Premier Mine. It was mobilized in June and brigaded with the 2nd Botha Regiment and the 3rd Transvaal Scottish to form the 5th South African Infantry Brigade. This brigade was moved to Kenya in late 1940.
1941	The regiment took part in the invasion of Southern Abyssinia in February and distinguished itself in actions at El Gumu, Hobok, Banno and at the capture of Mega. In May the regiment was moved to Suez and took up positions at Mersa Matruh on 23 May. During attempts to relieve Tobruk in November, the regiment and the other units of the 5th SA Brigade were decimated at Sidi Rezagh. Casualties were heavy and only 140 members emerged from the Sidi Rezagh battle.
1942	Due to its casualties at Sidi Rezagh, in February, the regiment ceased to exist as an independent unit. The majority of its survivors were re-trained as artillery and formed 11th Battery of the 4th Field Regiment, SA Artillery. This battery fought at the battle of El Alamein in September 1942.
1943–5	The battery returned to South Africa and was reformed as the 4th Battery, 22nd Field Regiment, SA Artillery. It formed part of the 6th South African Armoured Division and later served in Africa and Italy. The regiment was awarded the battle honours 'East Africa, 1940–41', 'Mega', 'Western Desert, 1941–43' and 'Sidi Rezagh'.
1946	Following the end of the Second World War, members of the regiment campaigned to have the unit retained as part of the Citizen Force (the South African reserve). It was also hoped that it would be re-converted into

an infantry unit. In 1946 the unit became a permanent part of the Citizen Force but it remained an artillery unit, being designated as the 22nd Field Regiment (South African Irish) South African Artillery.

1960   The regiment was returned to its infantry role and regained its original title as the South African Irish Regiment. It was involved in controlling civil disturbances in 1960 and 1961. It performed similar duties on various occasions over the next thirty years.

1968   Comdt van Kerckhoven of the SAIR formed the Hunter Group, dedicated to providing training in anti-insurgency methods to members of the volunteer Citizen Force. The cadre was provided by the SAIR and men were also drafted in who had seen service in Rhodesia, Angola and South-West Africa (Namibia). The Hunter Group was a resounding success, training over 700 members of the Citizen Force in reconnaissance techniques, anti-insurgency and guerrilla warfare tactics.

1976   The Hunter Group was re-organized into the Reconnaissance Commando (Reserve) and the 2nd Airborne Reconnaissance Company. Both units saw active service in South-West Africa and Angola.

1987   The SAIR was converted to a mechanised infantry unit.

1991   The regiment was converted to motorized infantry.

2006   At the time of writing, the South African Irish Regiment ranks as 16th in order of precedence among the infantry battalions of the South African Citizen Force. It is based at Johannesburg and maintains a pipe and drum band.

Honorary colonels

1914	Mrs Louis Botha	1966	Colonel W.J. Busschau
1945	Colonel T.W. Cullinan	1977	Colonel C.A. Twomey

Commanding officers up to 1982

1914	Lt.-Col. F.H. Brennan	1965	Cmdt. G. van Kerckhoven
1939	Lt.-Col. J.A.M. Moreland	1970	Cmdt. E.M. Kristal
1940	Lt.-Col. D.I. Somerset	1972	Maj. C.I. Steyn
1940	Lt.-Col. J.F.K. Dobbs	1975	Cmdt. S.W.J. Kotze
1942	Lt.-Col. C. McN. Cochran	1975	Cmdt. J.C. Bosch
1945	Lt.-Col. F.H.G. Cochran	1980	Cmdt. J.H. Swanepoel
1951	Lt.-Col. J. Geber	1982	Cmdt. S.H. Moir
1956	Cmdt. C.A. Twomey		

Regimental colour and battle honours

The colour of the SAIR is a green field with harp emblem and the motto 'Faugh-a-ballagh'. The staff of the colour incorporates a springbok and also an artillery badge and includes the following battle honours:

South West Africa, 1914–15, East Africa 1940–1, Mega, Western Desert 1941–43, Sidi Rezagh.

Regimental marches
Originally the regimental march was 'The County Down Militia'. This was later changed to 'Killaloe'. 'The wearing of the green' is also associated with the SAIR.

Motto
On the formation of the regiment in 1914 this was 'Quis Separabit' (Who will separate us). During the Second World War this was changed to 'Faugh a Ballagh' (Clear the Way).

Mascot
During the Second World War, the regimental mascot was an Irish terrier.
In 1946 an Irish wolfhound named 'Paddy' was obtained as a regimental mascot and there have been further wolfhound mascots since then.

IRISH COMMANDOS IN THE 2nd ANGLO-BOER WAR, 1899–1902

During the 1st Anglo-Boer War of 1880–1, Irishmen served with the Boer forces. The most prominent of these was Alfred Aylward, a noted Fenian. There was, however, no actual Irish pro-Boer unit. By the outbreak of the 2nd Boer War in 1899, there was a significant Irish community in South Africa and many of them made common cause with the Boers in their efforts to resist British invasion. During the course of the war two Irish units, or 'commandos', were raised and these were designated as the 1st and 2nd Irish Transvaal Brigades.

1st IRISH TRANSVAAL BRIGADE

Formation
This unit was the raised by the Irish 'Uitlander' community in the Transvaal. The initial overtures were made to the Transvaal government by prominent members of the Irish community such as Thomas Madden, Daniel O'Hare, Dick McDonagh and Soloman Gillingham. The corps was authorized by the Transvaal government on 13 September 1899, four weeks before the outbreak of the war.

The initial recruits were raised from among the Irish in the Transvaal and a large contingent came from Johannesburg. The brigade was organized in accordance with the Boer commando system. Further volunteers travelled from Ireland to join the commando and various estimates have been given of the commando's strength. It is now generally accepted that it never exceeded 300. It is known that at least 75 of these men travelled from Ireland. A further 42 had addresses in South Africa while others travelled from England, America and France. The origins of many other members of the brigade are unknown but the majority were either Irish or of Irish descent.

On some official documents the unit was referred to as the 'Irsche Corps'. The brigade was initially commanded by Colonel John Blake, a veteran of the U.S. cavalry. Blake was later wounded outside Ladysmith and the commando was led by Major John MacBride, who commanded on the occasions during which Blake was absent. In the Irish press the brigade was often referred to as the 'Irish Brigade' or 'Blake's Brigade'. Most often it was referred to as 'MacBride's Brigade' or 'MacBride's Commando'. Due to the fact that so many Irish regiments were present with the British Army in South Africa, members of the brigade fought against these Irish regiments in several engagements.

Operational history

1899   The Irish brigade took part in several early engagements in the war and was present at the battle of Dundee/Talana Hill on 20 October where it was in action against detachment of the Royal Dublin Fusiliers and the Royal Irish Fusiliers. On 28 October the brigade arrived outside Ladysmith and took up positions at Pepworth Hill. It would serve throughout the siege of Ladysmith. It took part in the battle of Modderspruit on 30 October, resisting British attempts to relieve the town. On 15 November the Irish brigade took part in the battle of Colenso, opposing the advance of the 5th (Irish) Infantry Brigade across the Tugela River.

1900   A small detachment of the unit took part in the battle of Spion Kop on 24 January 1900. On 24 February, the Irish brigade took part in the fighting around Hart's Hill. During the Boer retreat from Ladysmith, the Irish slowed the British advance by fighting a rearguard action at Lombard's Kop on the 28 February. In April the brigade was reinforced by over 50 men of the Irish-American Ambulance Corps. These men were Irish-Americans and Irishmen who had travelled to the Transvaal to serve in a field ambulance unit. On arriving at Middelburg, they took off their Red Cross insignia and joined the brigade for active service. On 3 May they fought a delaying action at Brandfort and subsequently fought similar actions at the Sand and Klip rivers. During the campaign in the Transvaal, the brigade formed a demolition squad or 'Wreckers Corps', which destroyed several railway bridges. In late May the brigade took part in some last-ditch efforts to stop the British forces entering Johannesburg. This was the home-town of some of the unit, and when it fell to Lord Roberts, many were captured. In early June, the unit was among the last of the Boer forces to evacuate Pretoria. Major MacBride took command of the brigade due to the absence of Blake. A detachment of the unit who had no horses were sent to join the Boer garrison at the POW camp in Nooitgedacht. On 11–12 June the brigade took part in the battle at Diamond Hill. Thereafter they formed part of the rearguard and took part in a long and demoralizing retreat to Balmoral and from there to Middelburg and Belfast (Transvaal). On 27 August the Irish brigade fought its last action at Bergendal Farm. The unit then moved to the border of Portuguese East Africa (modern-day Mozambique). Major MacBride and around 20 survivors of the brigade crossed into Portuguese territory on 23 September 1900.

1900–2 While the departure of MacBride signalled the end of the 1st Irish Transvaal Irish Brigade, some of the members of the unit remained in South Africa and served with other commandos. These Irish 'bitterenders' continued to fight a guerrilla campaign until the final Boer defeat in 1902.

Colours of the 1st Irish Transvaal Brigade
This unit had a series of colours during the course of the war. On its formation in 1899 it carried a colour with the inscription 'Remember Mitchelstown'. This colour was a relic of the 1867 Fenian rising and was carried to South Africa by John MacBride.

In December 1899 a second colour was sent out by the Irish Transvaal Committee on the initiative of Maud Gonne. It was made of green poplin and had a gilt braid border and fringe. It bore an Irish harp motif and carried the inscriptions 'Irish Transvaal Brigade' and 'Ar dTir, Ar Muinteár, Ar dTeanga' – (Our country, our people, our language). This colour became a treasured possession of the brigade and, in particular, McBride himself. He left it with state secretary F.W. Reitz for safekeeping who returned it to him in Paris. This colour is now in the National Museum of Ireland.

Mascot
The men of the brigade would appear to have treated various horses as mascots. A horse named 'Irish Willie' was an early mascot but went missing after the fight on the Sand River.

MacBride's 'Fenian Boy' was also held in much affection and may have travelled with the survivors of the brigade into Portuguese East Africa in September 1900.

2nd IRISH TRANSVAAL BRIGADE

Formation
A second Irish commando was formed in January 1900 and was it was the brainchild of Arthur Lynch, an Irish-Australian, and Soloman Gillingham. This second unit never numbered more than 150 men and included not only Irish but Americans, French, Italians, Australians and Boers, among others. Significantly, there were also some men who had previously served with the 1st Irish Transvaal Brigade.

Operational history
On 13–14 May 1900, the unit took played an important role at the battle of Biggarsberg. After this action, the unit seems to have rapidly disintegrated. Some

members were present at the defence of Johannesburg in late May. Lynch himself later appeared at various junctures in the subsequent campaign.

Casualties of the Irish Brigades
Due to the fluid nature of the Irish units' campaigns, official records were not always forwarded to the Boer government.

Thirty-one members of the Irish units are known to have died – all from the 1st Brigade; 23 were wounded while 37 became prisoners of war. It is likely that the number of casualties was actually higher.

CHAPTER 9

New South Wales Irish Rifles, 1896–1930

In November 1895 a meeting of prominent members of the Irish community was held in the town hall in Sydney. Among those present was Cardinal Moran, who had been born in Carlow. As a result of this meeting a deputation was sent to both the Australian premier, Sir George Gibbs, and the officer commanding NSW forces, Major-General Sir Eric Hutton. It was agreed that an Irish unit be formed as part of the NSW militia and this unit came into being in 1896 as the New South Wales Irish Rifles.[1]

Operational history

1896   The new unit was raised in March 1896 and was originally of two companies. It was designated as the New South Wales Irish Rifles. With the NSW Scottish Rifles and the St George's Rifles, it formed the 5th (Union Volunteer) Infantry Regiment.

1897   The St George's Rifles became an independent unit and the NSW Irish Rifles and the NSW Scottish Rifles joined with companies from the Illawara district to form the 8th (Union Volunteer) Infantry Regiment. The NSW Irish Rifles provided five companies for this regiment, based at Sydney and Newcastle.

1899   Militia legislation prevented the unit from serving overseas in the 2nd Anglo-Boer War of 1899–1902 but twenty-three members of the NSW Irish Rifles volunteered to serve with Australian units in South Africa.

1903   Under the terms of the military reforms and the establishment of the Commonwealth Force, the five companies of the NSW Irish Rifles were established as a separate unit, breaking the connection with the NSW Scottish Rifles. Based at Sydney, the unit was re-designated the NSW Irish Rifle Regiment.

1908   The regiment was awarded the battle honour 'South Africa, 1899–1902' due to the fact that members of the unit served in the 2nd Anglo-Boer War.

1912   Under the terms of further army re-organization, named units were abolished. The regiment was re-designated the 33rd Infantry Regiment.

1913   Four companies of the 33rd Infantry Regiment formed the 34th Infantry Regiment. During WWI, these units could not serve overseas due to the terms of the militia legislation, yet many members of the original regiments served with other units in the Australian Imperial Force.

1918   Companies of the 33rd and the 36th Infantry Regiments amalgamated to

---

1 It should also be noted the Company F, Adelaide Rifles, raised in 1901, was an Irish company but was augmented and effectively disappeared in 1908.

	form the 5th Battalion, 4th Infantry Regiment. The remainder of the 33rd and 34th Infantry Regiments were amalgamated into the 2nd Battalion, 55th Infantry Regiment.
1921	Following a further series of amalgamations, these battalions were formed into the 55th Battalion. They were authorized to perpetuate the traditions of the 55th Battalion, Australian Imperial Force, a distinguished unit that had seen service in Egypt, France and Flanders during WWI.
1927	The regiment was authorized to bear the WWI battle honours of the 55th Battalion, AIF. It also was allowed revive its territorial title and was re-designated as the 55th Battalion (New South Wales Irish Rifle Regiment). The regimental motto, 'Faugh a ballagh' was also re-adopted.
1929	Linked with the 53rd Battalion.
1930	The word 'Irish' dropped from the regimental title, the unit changing its title to 55th Battalion (New South Wales Rifle Regiment).
1937	The regimental motto changed to 'Animo et Fide' ('By courage and faith').

The Second World War, 1939–45

The 55th Battalion saw distinguished service during WWII and served in campaigns in New Guinea, Bougainville and New Britain. While soldiers of Irish descent served with the regiment, it effectively ceased to be an Irish regiment in 1930. The 55th Battalion was disbanded in 1946.

It is interesting to note that the Irish units in Australia had such a short history, when one considers that it was, and remains, a country with a large population of Irish descent.

Battle honours

The single battle honour of the New South Wales Irish Rifles was 'South Africa, 1899–1902'. When it was absorbed into the 55th Battalion, it then perpetuated the WWI honours of the 55th Battalion AIF. During WWII the 55th Battalion was awarded further battle honours. The full list of battle honours of the 55th Battalion reads:

South Africa 1899–1902, Somme 1916–1918, Bullecourt, Ypres 1917, Menin Road, Polygon Wood, Poelcappelle, Passchendale, Ancre 1918, Villers-Bretonneux, Amiens, Albert 1918, Mont St. Quentin, Hindenburg Line, St Quentin Canal, France and Flanders 1916–1918, Egypt 1916, South West Pacific 1942–45, Buna-Gona, Sanananda Road, Liberation of Australian New Guinea

Motto

Following its formation in 1896, the companies of the New South Wales Irish Regiment adopted the motto 'Ready'. They kept this motto while serving as companies of the 7th and 8th (Union Volunteers) Regiments.

On becoming a separate regiment in 1903, the unit adopted a more traditional Irish motto: 'Faugh a ballagh' (Clear the Way). This motto was re-adopted in 1927 when territorial titles were re-introduced. A new motto, 'Animo et Fide' was approved for the 55th Battalion in 1930 but did not appear in orders until 1937.

CHAPTER 10

Canadian Irish regiments, 1859–2006

The earliest Irish regiments in Canada owe their origins to the Rifle Volunteer movement on the mid-nineteenth century. Several independent Irish companies were established and one of the earliest of these was the Halifax Rifles, raised in Nova Scotia in December 1859. This was also referred to as the Nova Scotia Irish Company. A second Irish company was named '1st Company, Irish Volunteers' and was also raised in December 1859. Both of these companies were amalgamated into the Halifax Volunteer Battalion and a series of later amalgamations effectively destroyed their Irish identity. Other independent Irish volunteer companies suffered a similar fate.

These independent Irish companies were, however, the ancestors of three 20th century Canadian Irish regiments, which trace their origins to the outbreak of the First World War. On the outbreak of war, the Irish communities of Montreal, Vancouver and Toronto obtained permission to raise regiments from the Canadian Department of the Militia and proceeded to recruit men for service in France and Flanders. While it was originally hoped that these regiments would serve in the Canadian Expeditionary Force, permission was not granted for them to do so. Instead they were used to provide drafts of reinforcements for Canadian battalions on the Western Front and also served as the parent or sponsoring units for several overseas battalions.

THE IRISH CANADIAN RANGERS, 1914–18

Formation
This regiment was raised in Montreal in 1914 by prominent members of the Irish community in that city. The organization and recruiting committee was led by H.J. Trihey and many of the its members later held commissions in the regiment. In November 1914, the regiment held its first public parade and this led to a rise in recruitment.

Operational history
The First World War, 1914–18
1915   On 14 April, the Irish Canadian Rangers were reviewed by the Duke of Connaught. The battalion was 400 strong at this time. In June, a detachment of around 400 men were drafted into the 60th Overseas Battalion of the Canadian Expeditionary Force. This battalion served with the Canadian 3rd Division in France.

1916 In February, the regiment was re-designated as the 199th Battalion of the CEF. On being presented with regimental colours by the Duchess of Connaught, the battalion was thenceforth known as the 199th Duchess of Connaught's Own Irish Canadian Rangers. From December 1916 to February 1917, a party of the regiment went on a recruiting tour of Ireland, where they were guests at various civic receptions in Cork, Limerick, Dublin and Belfast.

1917 In February, the battalion was attached to the 15th Canadian Infantry Brigade of the 5th Division. The battalion was then amalgamated with the 22nd and 23rd Canadian Reserve Battalions. This amalgamation effectively destroyed the battalion's separate Irish identity.

THE CANADIAN IRISH FUSILIERS, 1913–1945

Formation

This regiment was actually formed before the outbreak of the First World War and was Canada's first Irish regiment. It was formed due to the efforts of members of Vancouver's Irish community and was initially designated as the 11th Regiment by the Department of the Militia.

Operational history

The First World War, 1914–18

1914 A regimental depot was established in British Columbia but the regiment was never designated as an overseas battalion. Drafts from the Canadian Irish Fusiliers joined the 121st Battalion (New Westminster) CEF, which came to be known as the 'Western Irish Battalion'.

1915 The 7th Irish Fusiliers were drafted into the 7th Canadian Infantry Battalion (British Columbia). This battalion served with the 1st Division in France and Flanders from February 1915 to the Armistice.

1916 While the regimental depot was maintained in Canada, the Western Irish Battalion mobilized for overseas service in August 1916 but they in turn were amalgamated into the 16th Reserve Infantry Battalion. This battalion was absorbed by the 2nd Reserve Battalion and provided reinforcements for the Canadian battalions in France and Flanders.

1917–18 Later drafts from the regiment served with the 29th Canadian Infantry Battalion. After the Armistice, the Irish Fusiliers survived as a regiment in Canada's non-permanent militia.

1936 The regiment was amalgamated with the Vancouver Regiment to form the Irish Fusiliers of Canada (Vancouver Regiment).

The Second World War, 1939–45

On being mobilized for overseas service, the regiment was posted to Jamaica where it formed part of the garrison. It was disbanded at the end of the war.

Motto
'Faugh a Ballagh' (Clear the Way)

THE IRISH REGIMENT OF CANADA, 1915–2006

Formation
This regiment was formed due to the efforts of members of the Irish Club and the Irish Rifle Club in Toronto. It was activated on 15 October 1915 and was originally designated as the 110th Irish Regiment.

Operational history
The First World War, 1914–18
During the course of the war, the regiment raised a series of battalions for overseas service. The first was the 110th Canadian Overseas Battalion which proceeded overseas in 1916 but was broken up to provide reinforcements for other Canadian battalions. The colours of the regiment were deposited in Belfast Cathedral and were collected by a party at the end of the war.

The regiment also sponsored the 108th (Sportsmen's) Battalion and the 208th Canadian Irish Battalion. These battalions served in France and Flanders until the Armistice and suffered over 60 per cent casualties. They were awarded the following battle honours:

> Arras 1917–1918, Ypres, Hindenburg Line,
> Scarpe 1918, Canal Du Nord, Hill 70,
> Amiens, Pursuit to Mons, Dracourt-Queant,
> France and Flanders 1918

1919	After the war the regiment became part of the non-permanent militia and was stationed at the Fort York Armoury in Toronto.
1920	The regiment dropped its numerical designation and was renamed as the Irish Regiment.
1932	Re-titled as the Irish Regiment of Canada. At the same time the regiment adopted a more distinctive style of dress which included a dark green bonnet or caubeen and a saffron kilt. This was for all members, not just members of the regimental band.
1936	On the disbandment of the First Canadian Machine Gun Battalion, elements of this unit were amalgamated with the Irish Regiment of Canada. Therefore it was re-designated as the Irish Regiment of Canada (MG) and operated as a machine-gun battalion.

The Second World War, 1939–45

1939	On the outbreak of the Second World War, elements of the regiment formed the garrisons at the airfields at Borden and Malton. The regiment was reorganized into two battalions, one active and one reserve.

1940	The 'MG' suffix was dropped and the regiment reverted to the infantry role.
1942	After a period spent in coastal defence, the 1st Battalion was posted overseas. They spent a year on training and manoeuvres and also a period as the garrison of the royal estate at Sandringham.
1943	In November the battalion landed in Italy as part of Operation Timberwold and joined with the Perth Regiment and the Cape Breton Highlanders to form the 11th Brigade, 5th Canadian Armoured Division, where they operated as lorried infantry. They spent the winter of 1943–4 in positions near Orsogna and Armelli.
1944	In April the battalion took up positions at Aquafondata, near Monte Cassino, before moving into the front line at Sante Elia. Here they were subjected to shelling and also attacked by German patrols.
	As part of Operation Chesterfield, the battalion took part in the Melfa River crossing and the advance on the 'Hitler Line' of defences in May and then spent the month of June in a training camp at Caiazzo.
	In the assault on the 'Gothic Line' in August 1944, the battalion took part in a successful brigade attack on the village of Montecchio, breaching the German defences. In September they were took part in actions at Tomba de Pesaro and Coriano. A company of the battalion was captured at San Mauro. The battalion then went into quarters at San Giovanni.
1945	The battalion was moved to the Belgium and Holland in March where they took part in Operation Goldflake. On 27th March 1945 they moved into positions at Nijmegan Island, south of Arnhem.
	On 16 April the allied line was infiltrated by night near Oterloo and the battalion took part in a desperate but eventually successful defence.
	In the closing months of the war, they captured the town of Delfzijl, before moving to Friesland where they took the surrender of many German troops.
	On 2 May 1945 the battalion suffered its last casualties, less than a week from the end of the war in Holland.
	Following the end of the war, the battalion returned to Canada where it became a reserve unit once again.
1965	As part of a drastic reduction in the size of the Canadian reserves, on 31 March 1965 the regiment was reduced and transferred to the supplementary order of battle. On the same date, however, the 58th Field Regiment, Royal Canadian Artillery was converted to infantry and re-designated as the 2nd Battalion, Irish Regiment of Canada. This meant that the regiment would survive but it created an unusual situation in which a 2nd Battalion continued to operate as part of the reserve forces without a 1st Battalion being in existence. The 2nd Battalion, Irish Regiment of Canada continues to serve as part of the Canadian army reserves and is based at Sudbury, Ontario. Several college cadet forces are also associated with the regiment.

Battle honours
The battle honours that are authorized for the regiment's colours are:

Arras, 1917–1918, Amiens, Drocourt-Quent, Canal Du Nord, France-Flanders 1918, Scarpe 1918, Hindenburg Line, Pursuit to Mons, Melfa Crossing, Montecchio, Lamone Crossing, Hill 70, Liri Valley, Gothic Line, Coriano, Italy 1943–1945, Delfzijl Pocket, Northwest Europe 1945

Motto
'Fíor go Bás' (Faithful unto Death)

Mascot
During WWII, the regiment had an Irish wolfhound named 'Captain Kilkenny'.

CHAPTER 11

The Irish Defence Forces

The modern Irish army, or Defence Forces, traces its history back to the Irish Volunteers, which were formed in November 1913. The Irish Volunteers fought in the 1916 Rising and then the War of Independence of 1919–21. Following the foundation of the Irish Free State in 1922, a new National Army was formed and operated against anti-Treaty forces during the Irish Civil War of 1922–23. In terms of lineage, therefore, the modern Defence Forces trace a lineage back to 1913 and this includes both the Irish Volunteers and the National Army of 1922.

In the context of this gazetteer, a number of points should be made at the start of this section. Firstly, while the Irish Volunteers were organized in a formal military structure, in practice they employed a great deal of flexibility while on operations. This was especially true during the War of Independence. Therefore, while Volunteer forces maintained a formal command, brigade and battalion structure, while on operations they formed into 'Flying Columns' and 'Active Service Units'. In the guerrilla warfare of 1919–21, this proved to be the best way of engaging British forces. The organizational structure of the Volunteers in 1921 is listed below but the reader can assume that there was a great deal of flexibility in this and that personnel from different units formed local flying columns for operations.

Secondly, the post–1922 National Army was organized along conventional lines and its organization during different periods is outlined below. After the end of the Civil War, it was re-organized and reduced in size on a number of occasions before being expanded again during WWII or 'the Emergency'.

After 1945, further reductions took place. During the course of these reforms of the army, it was not unusual for battalion designations to be re-used. Therefore, in the table of Civil War army organization one will find a 41st Infantry Battalion. During the Emergency, there was a 41st Battalion in the Local Defence Forces (LDF). Finally, in 1965, a 41st Irish Battalion served with the UN in Cyprus. None of these three 41st Battalions shared a common lineage and their histories were totally unconnected. This practice of re-using battalion designations can lead to a certain amount of confusion but there are no units now in existence that use titles of the 1922 National Army.

In the context of this gazetteer, this has major implications. The simple fact is that, since 1922, the Irish Defence Forces has not adopted a regimental system. In the army's organizational philosophy, military units have been viewed in a utilitarian fashion; they are something that can be raised, disbanded or re-named as occasion demands. For the majority of Irish soldiers, their loyalties are bound up with the idea of their corps or branch of service. To the modern Irish soldier, what is important is the branch of the army in which they serve, but modern Irish soldiers also display fierce loyalty to their parent regiment or battalion.

The Irish Defence Forces have established an enviable record of service on United Nations missions. These Irish UN units are dealt with in another separate section. In 1980, women were admitted into the PDF for the first time, initially only as officer cadets. Women now serve as both officers and enlisted ranks in all branches of the PDF and serve on overseas missions.

The organization of the Defence Forces at various stages is outlined below. These tables of organization also include material on the Irish Volunteers.

There were also contingents of the short-lived Irish Citizen Army active in 1916 and details of these are provided below. It should also be pointed out that each Volunteer unit had an associated unit of Cumann na mBan.

IRISH VOLUNTEER FORCES IN DUBLIN, APRIL 1916

P.H. Pearse	Commandant General and Commander in Chief of Irish Volunteers
J. Connolly	Commandant General and Commander Dublin Division Irish Volunteers
J.M. Plunkett	Commandant General

Composite Headquarters Battalion
Muster Point   Liberty Hall (Beresford Place) then General Post Office, Sackville Street (150 men, then reports of increases up to 350 men including late arrivals and stragglers).

1st (Dublin City) Battalion Irish Volunteers (less D Company)
E. Daly   Commandant.
P. Beaslai   Vice-Commandant.
Muster Point   Blackhall Street (250 men)

1st (Dublin City) Battalion Irish Volunteers (detachment)
S. Heuston   Captain, D Company, 1st (Dublin City) Battalion, Irish Volunteers.
Muster Point   Mountjoy Square (12 men)

2nd (Dublin City) Battalion Irish Volunteers
T. MacDonagh   Commandant and Commander Dublin Brigade, Irish Volunteers.
J. MacBride   Major and de-facto Vice-Commandant.
Muster Point   Fr Mathew Park (200 men)

3rd (Dublin City) Battalion Irish Volunteers
E. de Valera   Commandant and Adjutant Dublin Brigade Irish Volunteers.
Muster Point   Brunswick Street, also Earlsfort Terrace and Oakley Road (130 men)

4th (Dublin City) Battalion Irish Volunteers
E. Céannt   Commandant.
C. Brugha   Vice-Commandant
Muster Point   Emerald Square (near Dolphin's Barn, 100 men)

5th (North Dublin) Battalion Irish Volunteers
T. Ashe   Commandant
Muster Point   Knocksedan (near Swords, 60 men)

Irish Citizen Army
M. Mallin   Commandant (Vice-Connolly)
Countess Markievicz   Deputy to Michael Mallin.
Muster Point   Liberty Hall (Beresford Place, 100 men)

Irish Citizen Army (detachment)
S. Connolly   Captain.
Muster Point   Liberty Hall (Beresford Place, 30 men)

Kimmage Garrison
G. Plunkett   Captain
Muster Point   Kimmage (Plunkett family estate, 56 men)[1]

IRISH REPUBLICAN ARMY ORGANIZATION ON 11 JULY 1921[2]

Dublin Brigade

1st Battalion	4th Battalion	7th Battalion
2nd Battalion	5th Battalion	Irish Citizen Army Battalion
3rd Battalion	6th Battalion	

FIRST SOUTHERN DIVISION

Cork No. 1 Brigade

1st Battalion	5th Battalion	9th Battalion
2nd Battalion	6th Battalion	10th Battalion
3rd Battalion	7th Battalion	
4th Battalion	8th Battalion	

Cork No. 2 Brigade

1st Battalion (Fermoy)	Glenworth Battalion
Castletown Roche Battalion	Lismore Battalion (see 2Bn, Waterford, 2 Brigade)

1 It is estimated that on 24 April 1916, the combined IV and ICA strength in the Dublin area was around 1,100 men, all ranks. This would rise to around 1,500 during the days that followed. There were also contingents of the Fianna and Cumann na mBan not included in this total. I am grateful to Mike McNally for this table of the Volunteers organization.   2 This table or organization outlines the IRA organization at the end of the War of Independence.

Cork No. 3 Brigade
1st Battalion	4th Battalion	7th Battalion
2nd Battalion	5th Battalion	
3rd Battalion	6th Battalion	

Cork No. 4 Brigade
1st Battalion	3rd Battalion	5th Battalion
2nd Battalion	4th Battalion	

Cork No 5 Brigade was formed after Truce and before 1 July 1922.

Waterford No. 1 Brigade
1st Battalion	2nd Battalion	3rd Battalion

Waterford No. 2 Brigade
1st Battalion	3rd Battalion	4th Battalion
2nd Battalion		

(1st and 2nd Brigades amalgamated, 6 July 1921)

Kerry No. 1 Brigade
1st Battalion	6th Battalion
2nd Battalion	7th Battalion
3rd Battalion	8th Battalion (these companies transferred to 3rd and
4th Battalion	6th Battalion on 11 July 1921)
5th Battalion	9th Battalion (formed after Truce and pre-1 July 1922)

Kerry No. 2 Brigade
1st Battalion	4th Battalion	Dunmore East Battalion
2nd Battalion	5th Battalion	
3rd Battalion	6th Battalion	

Kerry No. 3 Brigade
1st Battalion	3rd Battalion	4th Battalion
2nd Battalion		

West Limerick Brigade
1st Battalion	3rd Battalion	5th Battalion
2nd Battalion	4th Battalion	

SECOND SOUTHERN DIVISION

Mid-Tipperary Brigade
1st Battalion	2nd Battalion	3rd Battalion

South Tipperary Brigade
1st Battalion	4th Battalion	7th Battalion
2nd Battalion	5th Battalion	8th Battalion
3rd Battalion	6th Battalion	9th Battalion

Kilkenny Brigade
1st Battalion   4th Battalion   7th Battalion
2nd Battalion   5th Battalion   8th Battalion
3rd Battalion   6th Battalion   9th Battalion

Mid-Limerick Brigade
1st Battalion (Limerick City)   3rd Battalion (Adare)
2nd Battalion (Castleconnell)   4th Battalion (Caherconlish)

East Limerick Brigade
1st Battalion   2nd Battalion   3rd Battalion
4th Battalion   5th Battalion   6th Battalion

THIRD SOUTHERN DIVISION

Laois Brigade
1st Battalion   2nd Battalion   3rd Battalion
4th Battalion   5th Battalion   6th Battalion

Offaly No. 1 Brigade
1st Battalion   2nd Battalion   3rd Battalion   4th Battalion

Offaly No. 2 Brigade
1st Battalion   2nd Battalion   3rd Battalion   4th Battalion

North Tipperary No. 1 Brigade
1st Battalion (Nenagh)   5th Battalion (Templederry)
2nd Battalion (Toomevara)   6th Battalion (Newport)
3rd Battalion (Portroe)   7th Battalion (Roscrea)
4th Battalion (Borrisokane)

1ST WESTERN DIVISION

East Clare Brigade
1st Battalion   2nd Battalion   3rd Battalion
4th Battalion   5th Battalion   6th Battalion

Mid-Clare Brigade
1st Battalion   2nd Battalion   3rd Battalion
4th Battalion   5th Battalion   6th Battalion

West Clare Brigade
1st Battalion   3rd Battalion   5th Battalion
2nd Battalion   4th Battalion

South-East Galway Brigade
Loughrea Battalion   Ballinasloe Battalion   Portumna Battalion

East Galway Brigade
Consisted of Ballinasloe and Mountbellew Battalions but disbanded in May 1921

South-West Galway Brigade
1st Battalion (Gort)
2nd Battalion (Ardrahan)
3rd Battalion (Athenry)

South Mayo Brigade
1st Battalion (Cross)
2nd Battalion (Ballinarobe)
3rd Battalion (Claremorris)
4th Battalion (Balla)

North Galway Brigade
1st Battalion (Tuam)
2nd Battalion (Dunmore)

South Roscommon Brigade
1st Battalion 2nd Battalion 3rd Battalion 4th Battalion

Mid-Galway No. 1 Brigade
1st Battalion 2nd Battalion 3rd Battalion 4th Battalion

Sligo Brigade
1st Battalion 4th Battalion 7th Battalion 10th Battalion
2nd Battalion 5th Battalion 8th Battalion
3rd Battalion 6th Battalion 9th Battalion

North Roscommon Brigade
1st Battalion 3rd Battalion 5th Battalion
2nd Battalion (Elphin) 4th Battalion

East Mayo Brigade
1st Battalion 2nd Battalion 3rd Battalion 4th Battalion

THIRD WESTERN DIVISION

West Mayo Brigade
1st Battalion 2nd Battalion 3rd Battalion 4th Battalion

North Mayo Brigade
1st Battalion (Ballina)
2nd Battalion (Foxford)
3rd Battalion (Ballycastle)
4th Battalion (Crossmolina)
5th Battalion (Corballa)
6th Battalion (Bangor)
7th Battalion (Belmullet)

West Connemara Brigade
1st Battalion (Leenane)
2nd Battalion (Rossmuck)
3rd Battalion (Roundstone)
4th Battalion (Clifden)

East Connemara Brigade
1st Battalion (Spiddal)
2nd Battalion (Inverin)
3rd Battalion (Moycullen)

(A North West Mayo Brigade was formed after the Truce.)

1st NORTHERN DIVISION

1st Brigade (Donegal area)
1st Battalion   2nd Battalion   3rd Battalion[2a]

2nd Brigade
1st Battalion   3rd Battalion   5th Battalion
2nd Battalion   4th Battalion

3rd Brigade
1st Battalion   2nd Battalion   3rd Battalion   4th Battalion

4th Brigade
1st Battalion (formerly South   2nd Battalion
  Donegal Brigade)   3rd Battalion

Derry City Battalion

2nd NORTHERN DIVISION

1st Brigade (Tyrone)
1st Battalion (Coalisland & Stewartstown)   3rd Battalion (Carrickmore)
2nd Battalion (Dungannon)

2nd Brigade (Tyrone)
1st Battalion (Omagh)   3rd Battalion (Fintona)
2nd Battalion (Dromore)

3rd Brigade
1st Battalion   3rd Battalion (Bellaghy)
2nd Battalion (Cookstown)

4th (Maghera) Brigade
1st Battalion (Gortin)   3rd Battalion (Dungiven)
2nd Battalion (Maghera)

3rd NORTHERN DIVISION

1st Belfast Brigade
1st Battalion   3rd and 4th Battalions no longer existed in July 1921
2nd Battalion

2nd Brigade (Antrim)
1st Battalion   2nd Battalion   3rd Battalion   4th Battalion

3rd Brigade (East Down)
1st Battalion   2nd Battalion   3rd Battalion

2a This battalion was the antecedant of the current 3rd Infantry Battalion

4th NORTHERN DIVISION

1st Brigade (South Armagh)
North Louth Battalion
Carnlough Battalion
Newtownhamilton Battalion

2nd Brigade (South West Down)
1st Battalion 2nd Battalion 3rd Battalion

3rd Brigade (North Armagh)
1st and 2nd Battalions formed after Truce
3rd Battalion (Lurgan)
Armagh Independent Battalion

5th NORTHERN DIVISION (MONAGHAN)

1st Brigade
B Battalion (Scotstown) C Battalion

2nd Brigade (Monaghan Town)
Monaghan Battalion Ballybay Battalion Carrickmacross Battalion

3rd Brigade
Cootehill Battalion Cavan Battalion Crosserlough Battalion
Carrickallen Battalion

FIRST EASTERN DIVISION

1st Meath Brigade
1st Battalion 2nd Battalion 3rd Battalion 4th Battalion

2nd Meath Brigade
1st Battalion 2nd Battalion 3rd Battalion 4th Battalion

3rd Meath Brigade
1st Battalion 2nd Battalion 3rd Battalion 4th Battalion

4th Meath Brigade
1st Battalion 2nd Battalion 3rd Battalion

5th Mullingar Brigade
1st Battalion 2nd Battalion 3rd Battalion 4th Battalion

Fingal Brigade
1st Battalion 2nd Battalion 3rd Battalion 4th Battalion

South Louth Brigade
1st Battalion (Drogheda)
2nd Battalion (Dunleer)
3rd Battalion (Ardee)

North Kildare Independent Brigade

South Wexford Brigade

| 1st Battalion | 2nd Battalion | 3rd Battalion | 4th Battalion |

North Wexford Brigade

| 1st Battalion | 2nd Battalion | 3rd Battalion | 4th Battalion |

Carlow Brigade

| 1st Battalion | 3rd Battalion | 5th Battalion |
| 2nd Battalion | 4th Battalion | 6th Battalion |

1st MIDLAND DIVISION (FORMED AUTUMN OF 1921)

Athlone Brigade

1st Battalion	Belturbet Independent Battalion
2nd Battalion	Corlough Independent Battalion
3rd Battalion	Ballinagh Battalion, West Cavan Brigade

South Leitrim Brigade

| 1st Battalion | 2nd Battalion | 3rd Battalion | 4th Battalion |

Fermanagh Brigade

| 1st Battalion (Enniskillen) | 3rd Battalion (Derrylinn and Arney) |
| 2nd Battalion (Belcoo) | 4th Battalion (Tempo) |

Longford Brigade

| 1st Battalion | 3rd Battalion | 5th Battalion |
| 2nd Battalion | 4th Battalion | 6th Battalion |

Scottish Brigade

1st Battalion (Glasgow)	4th Battalion (Fife)
2nd Battalion (Motherwell)	5th Battalion (Dumbarton)
3rd Battalion (Edinburgh)	

Also battalions in Liverpool, London, Manchester and Newcastle-on-Tyne.[3]

NATIONAL ARMY ORGANIZATION, JULY 1923

The National Army that served in the Civil War was the result of a huge expansion and re-organization of the new state's army. In March 1923, the National Army reached its highest strength with 48,176 men, all ranks.

Army GHQ Parkgate Street, Dublin
Dublin Command HQ Collins Barracks, Dublin
Athlone Command HQ Custume Barracks, Athlone
Cork Command HQ Collins Barracks, Cork

[3] Military Archives, Bureau of Military History file, CD 322.

The Irish Defence Forces

Curragh Command HQ   Curragh Camp
Claremorris Command HQ   Claremorris
Donegal Command HQ   Rock Barracks, Ballyshannon
Kerry Command HQ   Ballymullen Barracks, Tralee
Limerick Command HQ   Limerick Barracks (now Sarsfield Barracks)
Waterford Command HQ   Clonmel

The Special Infantry, Salvage Corps, Armoured Car Corps, Pay Corps, Signal Corps and Coastal Marine Services all had their HQs in Portobello Barracks, Dublin.
    The Army Medical Corps HQ at St Brichin's Hospital, Dublin.
    The Mechanised Transport Corps HQ at Gormanston Aerodrome.
    The Works Corps HQ at Beggar's Bush Barracks, Dublin.
    The Railway Protection Corps HQ at Griffith Barracks, Dublin.

Location of Infantry Battalions

1st Infantry Battalion	Keogh Barracks	(Dublin Command)
2nd Infantry Battalion	Birr	(Athlone Command)
3rd Infantry Battalion	Drumboe	(Donegal Command)
4th Infantry Battalion	Galway	(Claremorris Command)
5th Infantry Battalion	Athlone	(Athlone Command)
6th Infantry Battalion	Killarney	(Kerry Command)
7th Infantry Battalion	Limerick	(Limerick Command)
8th Infantry Battalion	Portobello Barracks	(Dublin Command)
9th Infantry Battalion	Cahirciveen	(Kerry Command)
10th Infantry Battalion	Cork City	(Cork Command)
11th Infantry Battalion	Nenagh	(Limerick Command)
12th Infantry Battalion	Ennis	(Limerick Command)
13th Infantry Battalion	Collins Barracks	(Dublin Command)
14th Infantry Battalion	Waterford City	(Waterford Command)
15th Infantry Battalion	Bandon	(Cork Command)
16th Infantry Battalion	Mountjoy Prison	(Dublin Command)
17th Infantry Battalion	Kenmare	(Kerry Command)
18th Infantry Battalion	Tipperary	(Limerick Command)
19th Infantry Battalion	Castleisland	(Kerry Command)
20th Infantry Battalion	Carlow	(Dublin Command)
21st Infantry Battalion	Clones	(Dublin Command)
22nd Infantry Battalion	Boyle	(Athlone Command)
23rd Infantry Battalion	Longford	(Athlone Command)
24th Infantry Battalion	Tallaght	(Dublin Command)
25th Infantry Battalion	Clonmel	(Waterford Command)
26th Infantry Battalion	Ballina	(Claremorris Command)
27th Infantry Battalion	Tralee	(Kerry Command)
28th Infantry Battalion	Gort	(Limerick Command)
29th Infantry Battalion	Curragh Camp	(Curragh Command)

30th Infantry Battalion	Bantry	(Cork Command)
31st Infantry Battalion	Newcastle West	(Limerick Command)
32nd Infantry Battalion	Macroom	(Cork Command)
33rd Infantry Battalion	Naas	(Dublin Command)
34th Infantry Battalion	Tuam	(Claremorris Command)
35th Infantry Battalion	Sligo	(Donegal Command)
36th Infantry Battalion	Templemore	(Waterford Command)
37th Infantry Battalion	Gormanston	(Dublin Command)
38th Infantry Battalion	Kanturk	(Cork Command)
39th Infantry Battalion	Charleville	(Limerick Command)
40th Infantry Battalion	Fermoy	(Cork Command)
41st Infantry Battalion	Wexford	(Waterford Command)
42nd Infantry Battalion	Youghal	(Cork Command)
43rd Infantry Battalion	Curragh Camp	(Curragh Command)
44th infantry Battalion	Westport	(Claremorris Command)
45th Infantry Battalion	Mullingar	(Dublin Command)
46th Infantry Battalion	Donegal	(Donegal Command)
47th Infantry Battalion	Killarney	(Waterford Command)
48th Infantry Battalion	Navan	(Dublin Command)
49th Infantry Battalion	Dundalk	(Dublin Command)
50th Infantry Battalion	Gorey	(Dublin Command)
51st Infantry Battalion	Maryboro	(Athlone Command)
52nd Infantry Battalion	Claremorris	(Claremorris Command)
53rd Infantry Battalion	Cavan	(Dublin Command)
54th Infantry Battalion	Curragh Camp	(Curragh Command)
55th Infantry Battalion	Keogh Barracks	(Dublin Command)
56th Infantry Battalion	Portobello Barracks	(Dublin Command)
57th Infantry Battalion	Collins Barracks	(Dublin Command)
58th Infantry Battalion	Dundalk	(Dublin Command)
59th Infantry Battalion	Kinsale	(Cork Command)
60th Infantry Battalion	Limerick	(Limerick Command)
61st Infantry Battalion	Curragh Camp	(Curragh Command)
62nd Infantry Battalion	Curragh Camp	(Curragh Command)
63rd Infantry Battalion	Curragh Camp	(Curragh Command)
64th Infantry Battalion	Curragh Camp	(Curragh Command)
65th Infantry Battalion	Curragh Camp	(Curragh Command)[4]

DEFENCE FORCES ORGANIZATION, 1926

By March 1926, the strength of the re-organized National Army, now re-titled as the Defence Forces, stood at 15,522, all ranks. In the intervening years it had undergone

---

4 *Army Gazette*, 1923.

a huge reduction in size, which had created much discontent and had resulted in an army mutiny in March 1924, which was confined to a small group of officers who later resigned.

Army GHQ	Parkgate Street, Dublin
No.1 Brigade HQ	Finner Camp, Ballyshannon
No. 2 Brigade HQ	Custume Barracks, Athlone
No. 3 Brigade HQ	Collins Barracks, Cork
No.4 Brigade HQ	Limerick Barracks[5]
No. 5 Brigade HQ	Kilkenny Barracks[6]
No.6 Brigade HQ	Collins Barracks, Dublin
No. 7 Brigade HQ	Portobello Barracks, Dublin
No. 8 Brigade – disbanded	
No. 9 Brigade HQ	Stewart Barracks, Curragh Camp

Brigade Companies

No.1 Brigade Company	Gormanston
No. 2 Brigade Company	Kilkenny Barracks
No. 3 Brigade Company	Collins Barracks, Dublin
No. 4 Brigade Company	Portobello Barracks, Dublin
No. 5 Brigade Company	Finner Camp, Ballyshannon
No. 6 Brigade Company	Custume Barracks, Athlone
No. 7 Brigade Company	Collins Barracks, Cork
No. 8 Brigade Company	New Barracks, Limerick
No. 9 Brigade Company	Gormanston

Infantry

1st (Irish Speaking) Infantry Battalion	Renmore Barracks, Galway
2nd Infantry Battalion	Finner Camp, Donegal
3rd Infantry Battalion	Boyle, Co. Roscommon
4th Infantry Battalion	Cavalry Barracks, Castlebar, Co. Mayo
5th Infantry Battalion	'K Lines Encampment', Curragh Camp
6th Infantry Battalion	Disbanded
7th Infantry Battalion	Naas, Co. Kildare
8th Infantry Battalion	Stewart Barracks, Curragh Camp
9th Infantry Battalion	Military Camp, Buncrana, Co. Donegal
10th Infantry Battalion	Balllymullen Barracks, Tralee, Co. Kerry
11th Infantry Battalion	Disbanded
12th Infantry Battalion	McCann Barracks, Templemore
13th Infantry Battalion	Disbanded
14th Infantry Battalion	New Barracks, Limerick
15th Infantry Battalion	Ponsonby Barracks, Curragh Camp
16th Infantry Battalion	Collins Barracks, Cork
17th Infantry Battalion	Columb Barracks, Mullingar

[5] Now Sarsfield Barracks.   [6] Then described as 'Military Barracks, Kilkenny'. Now Stephens' Barracks.

18th Infantry Battalion	Collins Barracks, Cork
19th Infantry Battalion	Collins Barracks, Dublin
20th Infantry Battalion	Kilkenny Barracks
21st Infantry Battalion	Collins Barracks, Dublin
22nd Infantry Battalion	Portobello Barracks, Dublin
23rd Infantry Battalion	Portobello Barracks, Dublin
24th Infantry Battalion	Dundalk Barracks
25th Infantry Battalion	Custume Barracks, Athlone
26th Infantry Battalion	Disbanded
27th Infantry Battalion	Portobello Barracks, Dublin

Artillery

Corps HQ	Artillery Barracks, Kildare
No. 1 Battery	Artillery Barracks, Kildare
No. 2 Battery	Artillery Barracks, Kildare

Armoured Car Corps

Corps HQ	'Tintown', the Curragh Camp
No.1 Coy	'Tintown', Curragh Camp.
No. 2 Coy	Collins Barracks, Dublin
No. 3 Coy	Collins Barracks, Cork
No. 4 Coy	Custume Barracks, Athlone

Corps of Engineers

Corps HQ	Griffith Barracks, Dublin
Western Command HQ	Custume Barracks, Athlone
Eastern Command HQ	Collins Barracks, Dublin
Southern Command HQ	Collins Barracks, Cork
Curragh Camp Coy	Curragh Training Camp
Engineer Training Depot	Engineer Barracks, Curragh Camp

Army Medical Service

Corps HQ	GHQ, Parkgate Street
Training Depot	St Bricin's Hospital, Dublin
Eastern Command HQ	Military Hospital, Portobello Barracks, Dublin
Southern Command HQ	Military Hospital, Collins Barracks, Cork
Western Command HQ	Military Hospital, Custume Barracks, Athlone

Army Signal Corps

Corps HQ	Red House, Infirmary Road, Dublin
GHQ Coy	Parkgate Street, Dublin
Eastern Command Coy	Collins Barracks, Dublin
Southern Command Coy	Collins Barracks, Cork
Western Command Coy	Custume Barracks, Athlone
Curragh Command Coy	Beresford Barracks, Curragh Camp

Army Transport Corps

Corps HQ	GHQ, Parkgate Street, Dublin
HQ Coy	Portobello Barracks, Dublin
Mechanised Transport Department	Gormanston Camp, Co. Meath[7]
Horse Transport Department	McKee Barracks, Dublin
Remount Depot	
No. 1 Command Coy	Collins Barracks, Dublin
No. 2 Command Coy	Custume Barracks, Athlone
No. 3 Command Coy	Collins Barracks, Cork
Training Depot Coy	Curragh Camp

Military Police

Corps HQ	McKee Barracks, Dublin
Depot Coy	McKee Barracks, Dublin
Eastern Command Coy	Collins Barracks, Dublin (HQ in Military Barracks, Kilkenny)
Southern Command Coy	Collins Barracks, Cork (HQ in New Barracks, Limerick)
Western Command Coy	Adamson Castle, Athlone (HQ at Finner Camp)
Curragh Camp Coy	Curragh Camp

MP detachments also at the detention barracks in Arbour Hill, the Curragh Camp and Athlone.

Army School of Instruction	Keane Barracks, Curragh Camp
School of Music	Beggar's Bush Barracks, Dublin[8]

After 1926, the Defence Forces were reduced still further. By 1930, the army numbered 4,925. On the outbreak of the Second World War in 1939, the army numbered just 7,493 with a further 10,578 reservists available on mobilisation. By April 1940 this had risen to 14,454, all ranks.[9] Thereafter the army strength varied but after 1941 it numbered over 30,000. The figures below provide an indication of army strength between 1940 and 1945:

June 1940	20,902
June 1941	40,174
May 1945	31,415[10]

---

7 In 1926, this depot's phone number was 'Balbriggan 6'. 8 *Army List and Directory*, 1926. 9 All above come from SRIs in Military Archives, 1923–1990. 10 Military archives, EDP 13/1 'Total army strengths by commands, 15/6/40 to 1/5/45'.

DEFENCE FORCES ORGANIZATION ON 1 DECEMBER 1940

Army HQ Staff at Parkgate Street
The army was organized into four commands: Curragh Command, Eastern Command, Southern Command and Western Command. Operationally, the army was designed to operate on a four brigade structure.
There was a separate Air Defence Command.

Infantry Corps
The Infantry Corps consisted of infantry and rifle battalions. The structure also incorporated battalions of the Volunteer Force, which made up the 7th to 13th Battalions. The Infantry Corps alone consisted of 24,306 men, all ranks.

1st Infantry Battalion	15th Infantry Battalion
2nd Infantry Battalion	16th Infantry Battalion
3rd Infantry Battalion	17th Infantry Battalion
4th Infantry Battalion	18th Infantry Battalion
5th Infantry Battalion	19th Infantry Battalion
6th Infantry Battalion	20th Infantry Battalion
7th (Dublin) Infantry Battalion	21st Infantry Battalion
8th (Thomand) Infantry Battalion	22nd Rifle Battalion
9th (Desmond) Infantry Battalion	23rd Infantry Battalion
10th (Uisneach) Infantry Battalion	24th Rifle Battalion
11th (Dublin) Infantry Battalion	25th Rifle Battalion
12th (Desmond) Infantry Battalion	31st Infantry Battalion
13th (Connaught) Infantry Battalion	(26th to 30th Battalions did not exist.)
14th Infantry Battalion	

Corps of Artillery

1st Field Artillery Battalion	Southern Coastal Defence Artillery
2nd Field Artillery Battalion	Western Coastal Defence Artillery
3rd Field Artillery Battalion	1st Anti-Aircraft and Anti-Tank Battery
4th Field Artillery Battalion	2nd Anti-Aircraft and Anti-Tank Battery
3.7' Howitzer Battery	3rd Anti-Aircraft and Anti-Tank Battery
Anti-Aircraft Battalion	4th Anti-Aircraft and Anti-Tank Battery[11]

Cavalry Corps

1st Motor Squadron	2nd Cyclist Squadron
2nd Motor Squadron	3rd Cyclist Squadron
3rd Motor Squadron	4th Cyclist Squadron
4th Motor Squadron	5th Cyclist Squadron
1st Armoured Squadron	6th Cyclist Squadron

[11] 3,232 men were serving in Artillery Corps in December 1940. [12] There were 2,003 men serving in the Cavalry Corps.

The Irish Defence Forces

2nd Armoured Squadron
Carrier Squadron
1st Cyclist Squadron

7th Cyclist Squadron
8th Cyclist Squadron[12]

Corps of Engineers
1st Field Engineer Coy
2nd Field Engineer Coy
3rd Field Engineer Coy
4th Field Engineer Coy
1st Coastal Defence Engineer Coy

Survey company
1st Maintenance Coy
2nd Maintenance Coy
3rd Maintenance Coy
4th Maintenance Coy[13]

Corps of Signals
1st Field Signals Coy
2nd Field Signals Coy
3rd Field Signals Coy
4th Field Signals Coy
Field Forces Coy

Air Corps Coy
1st Garrison Signals Coy
2nd Garrison Signals Coy
3rd Garrison Signals Coy
4th Garrison Signals Coy[14]

Ordnance Corps
1st Garrison Ordnance Coy
2nd Garrison Ordnance Coy

3rd Garrison Ordnance Coy
4th Garrison Ordnance Coy[15]

Supply and Transport Corps
1st Field S&T Coy
2nd Field S&T Coy
3rd Field S&T Coy
4th Field S&T Coy

1st Garrison S&T Coy
2nd Garrison S&T Coy
3rd Garrison S&T Coy
4th Garrison S&T Coy[16]

Army Medical Service
1st Field Ambulance Coy
2nd Field Ambulance Coy
3rd Field Ambulance Coy
4th Field Ambulance Coy

1st Field Hospital Coy
2nd Field Hospital Coy
3rd Field Hospital Coy
4th Field Hospital Coy

Corps of Military Police
1st Field MP Coy
2nd Field MP Coy
3rd Field MP Coy
4th Field MP Coy
1st Garrison MP Coy

2nd Garrison MP Coy
3rd Garrison MP Coy
4th Garrison MP Coy
No. 2 Detention Barrack Staff
No. 1 Internment Camp Staff[17]

1st Battalion Construction Corps (517 men)

---

13 In December 1940, there were 1,359 men in the Corps of Engineers. 14 There were 747 men serving in the Corps of Signals. 15 In the Ordanance Corps, there were 612 men serving. 16 1,504 men served in the S&T Corps. 17 There were 779 men serving in the Military Police in December 1940.

In December 1940, there was a total of 38,978 men, all ranks, serving in the Irish army. There was also a further 2,691 men in the 2nd Line Reserve. Apart from the establishments of the units above, each corps had its own depot and school while there were also staffs at military hospitals, the Military College, the Army School of Music and the Army School of Physical Culture. These men would be included in the overall total.

DEFENCE FORCES ORGANIZATION ON 31 DECEMBER 1944

Army HQ staff
2 divisional staffs   8 Brigade staffs
4 command staffs

Infantry Corps (14,775 men)
1st to 25th Infantry Battalions   31st Infantry Battalion

Corps of Artillery (3,252 men)
1st Field Artillery Regiment, consisting of:
1st Field Battery   21st Field Battery
2nd Field Battery   1st Anti-tank Battery

2nd Field Artillery Regiment, consisting of:
10th Field Battery   19th Field Battery
14th Field Battery   2nd Anti-Tank Battery

3rd Field Artillery Regiment, consisting of:
9th Field Battery   16th Field Battery
12th Field Battery   3rd Anti-Tank Battery

4th Field Artillery Regiment, consisting of:
8th Field Battery   20th Field Battery
15th Field Battery   4th Anti-Tank Battery

5th Field Artillery Regiment
4th Field Battery   13th Field Battery
7th Field Battery   5th Anti-tank Battery

6th Field Artillery Regiment
5th Field Battery   11th Field Battery
6th Field Battery   6th Anti-Tank Battery

7th Field Artillery Regiment
3rd Field Battery   18th Field Battery
17th Field Battery   7th Anti-Tank Battery

22nd Field Battery (attached 1st Infantry Battalion)
Anti-Aircraft Battalion   West Coast Defence Artillery
South Coast Defence Artillery

Cavalry Corps (2,337)
1st to 8th Motor Squadrons
1st to 4th Armoured Squadrons
1st to 16th Cyclist Squadrons

Corps of Engineers (2,106 men)
1st to 4th Field Engineer Companies
6th to 9th Field Engineer Companies[18]
Survey Company
Coast Defence Company
1st to 4th Maintenance Companies
Civil Defence Fire-fighting Coy

Corps of Signals (1,445 men)
1st to 8th Field Signals Companies
Field Forces Company
Air Corps Company
1st to 4th Garrison Signals Companies

Ordnance Corps (923 men)
Ordnance Depot Company (417 men)
1st to 4th Garrison Companies
Ammunition Depot Unit
Optical Workshop Unit

Supplies and Transport Corps (2,123 men)
1st to 7th Field Companies
1st and 2nd Supply Companies
Field Forces company
1st to 4th Garrison Companies
Horse Transport Company (288 men)

Army Medical Service (1,724 personnel)
1st to 8th Field Ambulance Companies
1st to 5th Hospital Companies

Corps of Military Police (1,121 men)
1st to 8th Field MP Companies
1st to 4th Garrison MP Companies
No. 2 Detention Barracks Staff
No. 1 Internment Camp Staff
No. 2 Internment Camp Staff
No. 4 Internment Camp Staff
POW Camp Staff

Construction Corps
No. 1 and No. 2 Construction Corps Depot Companies
1st to 10th Working Companies

2nd Line Volunteers (3,201 personnel)
26th Rifle Battalion
5th Field Engineer Coy
Electricity Supply Board Company of Engineers
Bus Companies Supply and Transport Corps, 1st to 4th Companies
6th to 16th Hospital Companies
1st to 12th Mobile Surgical Teams
1st to 4th Motor Ambulance Convoys
10 reserve officers on 'special duties'

Total strength, 31 December 1945: 19,088

18 5th Field Engineer Coy was part of the 2nd Line Reserve.

DEFENCE FORCES ORGANIZATION ON 31 DECEMBER 1970

In 1959, the Permanent Defence Forces were integrated with the FCA (reserves) and therefore, in 1970 some units had a large number of FCA personnel. Apart from the army's HQ staff, there were also four command staffs and six brigade staffs.
The PDF establishment in 1970 was 13,094 but actual strength was 8,497.

The 1st Line Reserve consisted of 1,716, all ranks. The FCA (2nd Line Reserve) establishment was 22,646 but actual strength was 19,748. The organizational table of units is outlined below. Where the numbering sequence is interrupted, it simply means that a certain PDF unit was followed by an FCA unit in the sequence. FCA units are dealt with in a separate section.

Infantry
'Border groups in aid of the Civil Power'
1st Infantry Company Group   3rd Infantry Company Group
2nd Infantry Company Group   4th Infantry Company Group
(316 men, all ranks)

1st Infantry Battalion   5th Infantry Battalion
2nd Infantry Battalion   6th Infantry Battalion
3rd Infantry Battalion   12th Infantry Battalion[19]
4th Infantry Battalion   27th, 28th, 29th Infantry Battalions[19a]

Artillery
1st FAR (includes 226 FCA personnel)   5th FAR (excluding cadre, all FCA)
2nd FAR (277 FCA)   6th FAR (excluding cadre, all FCA)
3rd FAR (excluding cadre, all FCA)   1st Anti Aircraft Regiment (395 FCA)
4th FAR (299 FCA)   Coastal Defence Artillery (71 PDF plus
                                           81 FCA)

Cavalry
1st Tank Squadron   2nd Motor Squadron
1st Armoured Car Squadron   4th Motor Squadron
1st Motor Squadron

Engineers
1st Field Engineer Company (118 PDF, 66 FCA)
2nd Field Engineer Company (119 PDF, 43 FCA)
4th Field Engineer Company (70PDF, 80FCA)
1st Maintenance Company   4th Maintenance Company
2nd Maintenance Company   Survey Company
3rd Maintenance Company   Depot Company

19 The 7th to 11th Battlaions were all FCA (reserve). All infantry battalions above the 12th were FCA.
19a Three battalions of the Eastern Command Infantry force created in 1978, for Border duty.

Signals
1st Field Signal Company
2nd Field Signals Company
4th Field Signals Company

Air Squadron Detachment
HQ Signal Detachment

Ordnance
1st Garrison Company
2nd Garrison Company
3rd Garrison Company

4th Garrison Company
Depot Company (106 men)

Supplies and Transport
1st Field S&T Company (39 PDF, 41 FCA)
2nd Field S&T Company (54 PDF, 43 FCA)
4th Field S&T Company
2nd Garrison S&T Company

3rd Garrison S&T Company
4th Garrision S&T Company

Service
1st Hospital Company
2nd Hospital Company

3rd Hospital Company
4th Hospital Company

Military Police
2nd Garrison Company
3rd Garrison Company

4th Garrison Company

Observer Corps
20 men in various headquarter locations.
Provision for many more on establishment but not on strength (includes provision for 3,772 FCA personnel)

DEFENCE FORCES ORGANIZATION, 2004

After 1970, the Irish Defence Forces have undergone further re-organization. It is now based on a three brigade system. Current army establishment stands at around 8,500 men and women. These Irish soldiers serve in the units listed below and also serve for overseas duty with UN and other operations.

1st Southern Brigade

1st Southern Brigade HQ	Cork
3rd Infantry Battalion	Kilkenny
4th Infantry Battalion	Cork
12th Infantry Battalion	Limerick/Clonmel
1st Field Artillery Regiment	Cork
1st Cavalry Squadron	Cork
1st Logistics Support Battalion	Cork

1st Field Engineer Coy   Cork
1st Field CIS Coy   Cork
1st Southern Brigade MP Coy   Cork
1st Southern Brigade Training Centre   Cork

2nd Eastern Brigade
2nd Eastern Brigade HQ   Dublin
2nd Infantry Battalion   Dublin
5th Infantry Battalion   Dublin
27th Infantry Battalion   Dundalk
2nd Field Artillery Regiment   Dublin
2nd Cavalry Squadron   Dublin
2nd Logistics Support Battalion   Dublin
2nd Field Engineer Coy   Dublin
2nd Field CIS Coy   Dublin
2nd Eastern Brigade MP Coy   Dublin
2nd Eastern Brigade Training Centre   Dublin

4th Western Brigade
4th Western Brigade HQ   Athlone
1st Infantry Battalion   Galway
6th Infantry Battalion   Athlone/Cavan
28th Infantry Battalion   Ballyshannon/Letterkenny/Lifford
4th Field Artillery Regiment   Mullingar
4th Cavalry Squadron   Longford
4th Logistics Support Battalion   Athlone
4th Field Engineer Coy   Athlone
4th Field CIS Coy   Athlone
4th Western Brigade MP Coy   Athlone
4th Western Brigade Training Centre   Athlone

Defence Forces Training Centre
DFTC HQ Curragh
Army Ranger Wing   Curragh
1st Air Defence Regiment   Curragh (army asset)
1st Armoured Cavalry Squadron   Curragh (army asset)
DFTC Military Police Coy   Curragh
DFTC Supply & Services Unit   Curragh
Logistics Base Staff   Curragh
Military College Staff[20]   Curragh

[20] The Military College consists of the Command and Staff School, Infantry School, UN-Training School and Cadet School. There are also staffs for the Combat Service Support College and the Combat Support College in the Curragh.

Special Establishments
These include the personnel of:
- the Equitation School
- the Defence Forces School of Music
- the No. 1 Band and the Band of the 4th Brigade
- No. 1 Security Coy
- Gormanston Camp Coy
- the training staffs at Kilbride Camp, Coolmoney and Galway

IRISH UNITED MISSIONS, 1958–2006

Ireland joined the United Nations in 1955 and since 1958, members of the Irish Defence Forces have served with UN missions across the world. The first Irish UN mission was in 1958 when Irish officers served as observers with the UNOGIL mission in Lebanon. In same year Irish officers were attached for the first time to UNTSO, the United Nations Truce Supervision organisation and Irish personnel have been served with this force ever since in various locations. The UNTSO mission has been the longest UN commitment by Irish personnel. To date, Irish soldiers have served in numerous truce supervision operations such as OGG-T (Observer Group Golan-Tiberias) and well as serving as UNTSO liaison officers in Cairo, Beirut and Gaza.

Since 1958, Irish soldiers have completed over 55,000 tours of duty with UN missions across the world, the majority of these tours lasting for six months.

The most high profile of these missions were the ONUC (Congo), UNIFICYP (Cyprus) and UNIFIL (Lebanon) missions. By the time that the 89th Infantry Battalion withdrew from the UNIFIL mission, Irish servicemen and women had completed over 31,000 tours of duty with this mission alone. While the activities of Irish soldiers have often been overlooked by the Irish media, they have played a major role in bringing some form of stability to areas of conflict across the word. Renowned for both their professionalism and people skills, at the same time Irish troops have never been anything less then firm when dealing with difficult situations. This long-term involvement has not been without cost, over 100 Irish soldiers having lost their lives on UN service since 1958.[21]

The Defence Forces currently has troops serving with different missions abroad, the biggest contingent being in Liberia. In 2005 alone, over 2,200 Irish personnel served on foreign missions.

Organization de Nations Unies au Congo
ONUC, July 1960 to June 1964
In total 6,191 Irish servicemen served with this United Nations mission to the Congo, the various Irish battalions suffering 26 fatal casualties. After gaining independence, the Congo had descended into civil war as factions led by Patrice Lumumba and

---

[21] *Irish Sword*, 20:79 (Summer 1996) was a special issue on Irish UN missions.

Moise Tshombe battled for control of the former Belgian colony. The various Irish units served in locations in Kivu and Katanga provinces.

In November 1960, nine men were killed in an ambush at Niemba and further Irish soldiers later lost their lives in action around Elizabethville.

> 32nd Infantry Battalion, July 1960 to January 1961
> 33rd Battalion, August 1960 to January 1961
> 34th Infantry Battalion, January to June 1961
> 1st Infantry Group, May to November 1961
> 35th Infantry Battalion, June to December 1961
> 36th Infantry Battalion, December 1961 to May 1962
> 37th Infantry Battalion, May 1962 to November 1962
> 2nd Armoured Car Squadron, Oct 1962 to April 1963
> 38th Infantry Battalion, November 1962 to May 1963
> 3rd Armoured Car Squadron, April 1963 to October 1963
> 39th Infantry Battalion, April to October 1963
> 2nd Infantry Group, October 1963 to May 1964

UN Forces in Cyprus
UNFICYP, April 1964 to December 1973

In 1960, Cyprus was granted independence by Britain and in the years that followed hostility between the island's Greek and Turkish populations increased. Irish soldiers served on this mission in a situation that was always tense and was punctuated by sudden episodes of kidnapping and murder. In total, Irish troops completed over 9,600 tours of duty on Cyprus.

> 40th Infantry Battalion, April to October 1964
> 3rd Infantry Group, 1964 to January 1965
> 41st Infantry Battalion, October 1964 to April 1965
> 4th Infantry Group, January to July 1965
> 42nd Infantry Battalion, April 1965 to October 1965
> 5th Infantry Group, October 1965 to April 1966
> 6th Infantry Group, April 1966 to October 1966
> 7th Infantry Group, October 1966 to April 1967
> 8th Infantry Group, April 1967 to September 1967
> 9th Infantry Group, September 1967 to March 1968
> 10th Infantry Group, March 1968 to September 1968
> 11th Infantry Group, August 1968 to March 1969
> 12th Infantry Group, March 1969 to September 1969
> 13th Infantry Group, September 1969 to March 1970[22]
> 18th Infantry Group, March to October 1970

---

[22] There were also Infantry Groups formed numbered 14th, 15th, 16th and 17th but, because of the security situation in Ireland, they were used for duty on the border.

19th Infantry Group, September 1970 to April 1971
20th Infantry Group, April to October 1971
21st Infantry Group, October 1971 to April 1972
22nd Infantry Group, April to October 1972
23rd Infantry Group, October 1972 to April 1973
24th Infantry Group, April to October 1973
25th Infantry Group, October 1973 to May 1974
26th Infantry Group, April to May 1974 (personnel from both the 25th and 26th Infantry Groups also served on an emergency mission to Sinai as part of the UNEF II contingent)

UNIFIL: United Nations Interim Force in Lebanon, 1978 to present
Irish soldiers have served on monitoring missions in Lebanon since 1958 but the crisis of 1978 saw a larger involvement on the part of the Irish army. Following a PLO attack on Israel in March 1978, the Israeli Defence Forces (IDF) had invaded south Lebanon as far as the Litani River. Irish troops formed part of the UN force (UNIFIL) that was sent to Lebanon in the hope of restoring order.

The intervention of this 'interim' force was ultimately to last over twenty years and by the time the last Irish battalion withdrew in 2001, Irish servicemen and women had completed over 31,000 tours of duty in Lebanon. It was never anything less than a difficult mission. The HQ of the 'Irishbatt' area was at Camp Shamrock at Tibnin with further Irish posts at Brashit, Sultaniyah and Shaqra, among other locations. The various Irish battalions in south Lebanon found themselves quite literally sandwiched between the Israeli army and also 19 other different 'armed elements' which included Fatah, the Christian militia (known as DFF or 'De Facto Forces') and later Hezbollah.

In general, the UNIFIL mission was an extremely dangerous throughout its duration. There were also periods of increased military activity with further associated dangers for Irish troops, such as during the At-Tiri incursions in 1980. Also, the various opposed factions were constantly firing into the Irish area of operations. During the 64th Infantry Battalion's tour for instance (1988–9), there were 181 firing incidents in the Irish area in November alone. During the 73rd Infantry Battalion's tour (1993), 896 x 155mm shells, 75 x tank rounds, and 6 x Katyusha rockets fell in the Irish area during one phase of heightened activity. The most dangerous periods coincided with the Israeli operations 'Accountability' (1993) and 'Grapes of Wrath' (1996).

By the end of the Irish battalion-sized missions in 2001, 46 Irish soldiers had lost their lives in Lebanon. The Defence Forces maintains a presence with UNIFIL HQ and had personnel serving with the mission during the Israeli incursions in 2006. It has since been suggested that DF personnel will return to Lebanon as part of the increased UN presence in area.

43rd Infantry Battalion, May to November 1978
44th Infantry Battalion, November 1978 to April 1979
45th Infantry Battalion, April to October 1979
46th Infantry Battalion, October 1979 to April 1980

47th Infantry Battalion, April to October 1980
48th Infantry Battalion, October 1980 to April 1981
49th Infantry Battalion, April to October 1981
50th Infantry Battalion, October 1981 to May 1982
51st Infantry Battalion, April to October 1982
52nd Infantry Battalion, October 1982 to April 1983
53rd Infantry Battalion, April 1983 to October 1983
54th Infantry Battalion,, October 1983 to May 1984
55th Infantry Battalion, April to November 1984
56th Infantry Battalion, October 1984 to May 1985
57th Infantry Battalion, April to November 1985
58th Infantry Battalion, October 1985 to April 1986
59th Infantry Battalion, April to November 1986
60th Infantry Battalion, October 1986 to May 1987
61st Infantry Battalion, April to November 1987
62nd Infantry Battalion, October 1987 to May 1988
63rd Infantry Battalion, April to November 1988
64th Infantry Battalion, October 1988 to April 1989
65th Infantry Battalion, April to November 1989
66th Infantry Battalion, October 1989 to April 1990
67th Infantry Battalion, April to November 1990
68th Infantry Battalion, October 1990 to April 1991
69th Infantry Battalion, April to November 1991
70th Infantry Battalion, October 1991 to April 1992
71st Infantry Battalion, April to November 1992
72nd Infantry Battalion, October 1992 to April 1993
73rd Infantry Battalion, April to November 1993
74th Infantry Battalion, October 1993 to April 1994
75th Infantry Battalion, April to November 1994
76th Infantry Battalion, October 1994 to April 1995
77th Infantry Battalion, April to October 1995
78th Infantry Battalion, October 1995 to May 1996
79th Infantry Battalion, April to November 1996
80th Infantry Battalion, October 1996 to April 1997
81st Infantry Battalion, April to November 1997
82nd Infantry Battalion, October 1997 to April 1998
83rd Infantry Battalion, April to November 1998
84th Infantry Battalion, October1998 to May 1999
85th Infantry Battalion, April to November 1999
86th Infantry Battalion, October 1999 to May 2000
87th Infantry Battalion, April to November 2000
88th Infantry Battalion, October 2000 to April 2001
89th Infantry Battalion, April to November 2001

Alongside the major UN missions outlined above, since 1962 Defence Forces personnel have served on numerous other UN missions. In some cases this has been as part of observer or monitoring missions while in other cases it has been as part of larger emergency interventions, such as was the case in Somalia (1993–5) and East Timor (2000–2). Since 1978 there have also been Irish officers posted to the UN headquarters in New York.

Irish personnel have undertaken ceasefire monitoring duties and have also overseen the decommissioning of weapons. In some cases, as with the UNHCR mission in the former Yugoslavia, they have also assisted in the distribution of humanitarian relief. For some of these missions, the Irish contribution has been quite small. For example, with the UNRWA mission to the Middle East, only two Irish officers served over the course of four years. In other cases the Irish contribution has been more significant. To date over 130 Irish personnel have served with the MINURSO mission in the Western Sahara while over 300 have served with the various missions to East Timor between 1999 and 2004. In many of these missions, Irish officers have held senior appointments.[23]

A listing of missions that have involved Irish personnel is provided below:

United Nations Truce Supervision Organization (UNTSO), Middle East[24]	1958–2006
United Nations Observer Group in Lebanon (UNOGIL)	1958
Organisation des Nations Unies au Congo (ONUC)	1960–4
UN Temporary Executive Authority (UNTEA), New Guinea	1962
UN Peace Keeping Force in Cyprus (UNFICYP)	1964–73
UN India-Pakistan Observer Mission (UNIPOM)	1965–6
UN Emergency Force (UNEF II), Sinai	1973–7
UN Headquarters New York (UNNY)	1978–2006
UN Interim Force in Lebanon (UNIFIL)	1978–2006
UN Inspection Teams (UNIT), Iran and Iraq	1984–8
UN Military Observer Group in India and Pakistan (UNMOGIP)	1987–92
UN Relief and Works Agency (UNRWA), Middle East	1988–92
UN Good Offices Mission in Afghanistan & Pakistan (UNGOMAP)	1988–90
UN Iran–Iraq Military Observer Group (UNIIMOG)	1988–91
UN Observer Group in Central America (ONUCA)	1988–92
UN Transition Assistance Group Namibia (UNTAG)	1989–90
Office of the Secretary General in Afghanistan and Pakistan (OSGA(P))	1990–4
Office of the Secretary General in Afghanistan (OSGA)	1994–6
UN Special Mission in Afghanistan (UNSMA)	1996–9
UN Iraq-Kuwait Observation Mission (UNIKOM)	1991–2003
Second UN Angola Verification Mission (UNAVEM II)	1991–3
UN Mission for the Referendum in Western Sahara (MINURSO)	1991–2006
UN Advance Mission in Cambodia (UNAMIC)	1991–3

23 For further details of Defence Forces overseas missions, see the UN special edition of *An Cosantóir*, published in 2005. 24 During service with UNTSO Irish personnel have completed over 470 tours of duty on different truce monitoring missions.

UN Transitional Authority in Cambodia (UNTAC)	1991–3
UN Observer Mission in El Salvador (ONUSAL)	1992–4
UN Military Liaison Office in Yugoslavia (UNMLO(Y))	1992–6
UN Protection Force (UNPROFOR), former Yugoslavia	1992–6
UN High Commission for Refugees, Yugoslavia (UNHCR(Y))	1992–3
Second UN Operation in Somalia (UNOSOM II)[25]	1993–5
UN Mission to Haiti (UNMIH)	1994–6
UN Observer Mission Prevlaka (UNMOP), Yugoslavia	1996–9
UN Preventative Deployment Force (UNPREDEP), Yugoslavia	1996–9
UN Transitional Authority in Eastern Slavonia (UNTAES), Croatia	1996–8
UN Special Commission (UNSCOM), Iraq	1996–2003
UN Monitoring Verification and Inspection Commission (UNMOVIC), Iraq	1996–2003
UN Disengagement Observer Force (UNDOF), Golan Heights	1997–8
UN Mission in East Timor (UNAMET)	1999–2004
Intervention Force in East Timor (INTERFET)	1999–2004
UN Transitional Administration in East Timor (UNTAET)	1999–2004
UN Mission of Support in East Timor (UNMISET)	1999–2004
UN Interim Administration in Kosovo (UNMIK)	1999–2006
UN Mission in Ethopia and Eritrea (UNMEE)	2000–3
UN Observer Mission in Congo (MONUC)	2001–6
International Emergency Multinational Force in the Congo, ('Operation Artemis)	2003
International Security Assistance Force (ISAF), Afghanistan	2001–6
UN Mission in Côte d'Ivoire (MINUCI), Ivory Coast	2003–6
UN Operation in Côte d'Ivoire (UNOCI), Ivory Coast	2003–6
UN Mission in Liberia (UNMIL)	2003–6

Since 1997, Irish troops have also served with NATO-led and EU-led missions in the Balkans. These have included the SFOR, EUFOR, and KFOR missions in Bosnia and Kosovo. In 1984, Irish officers began to serve with the Organisation for Security and Co-operation in Europe (OSCE) and this service has seen the secondment of Irish officers to the OSCE mission to Georgia in 1994. Since 1991, Irish officers have also served with European Community/Union missions.[25a] These missions have included:

EC Monitor Mission (ECMM), Yugoslavia	1991–2006
EC Task Force in Russia (ECTF(R))	1992
EC Task Force in Yugoslavia (ECTF(Y))	1993–2006
EU Mission to South Africa (EUNELSA)	1994

Irish officers have also served with several international aid agencies including GOAL, CONCERN, the Red Cross, the Irish Honduran Support Group and the Irish Rwandan

---

[25] The period in which Irish Defence Forces personnel served with UNOSOM II in Somalia witnessed the killing of 24 Pakistani UN troops in June 1993 and the October 1993 'Black Hawk Down' incident that resulted in the deaths of US Army Rangers. [25a] Irish officers and a senior NCO have served with European Union Military Staff (EUMS) in Brussels since 2000.

Support Group. At the time of writing, the Defence Forces' largest overseas contingent is as part of the UN mission in Liberia (UNMIL). In 2003, the first Irish troops travelled to this troubled African country, which has been torn apart by civil war since 1989. The first Irish contingent consisted of the 90th Infantry Battalion and also elements of the Army Ranger Wing. With the rotation of the 94th Infantry Battalion in November 2005, Irish troops had completed over 2,000 tours of duty in Liberia.

ARMY RESERVES IN THE IRISH DEFENCE FORCES, 1923–2006

The issue of the organization of reserve forces has been the focus of much debate within the Defence Forces since the re-organization of the army in 1923. As the amount spent by the government on national defence has been relatively small when compared to other European countries, it was predictable that there would always be a level of competition for resources between regular Permanent Defence Forces (PDF) and any reserve forces.

Alongside this problem, for a long period there was a lack of consensus within the Defence Forces as to the role and organization of the reserve forces. What emerged was often a confused approach as the Department of Defence experimented with different types of organization while at the same time trying to define the actual role of Ireland's defence forces. In the late 1920s and early 1930s, various different types of reserve forces existed concurrently, competing for recruits as the government struggled to define its policy on reserve forces.

While there were numerous successful European models that could have been adopted, the government preferred to adopt a trial by experimentation approach. One of the main problems of this approach has been the multiple re-organizations of the whole reserve force. From the perspective of this gazetteer, it can only be stated that there are no reserve regiments now in existence that were founded in the early years of the state. The history of Ireland's reserve forces is outlined below:

1923	The Defence Forces Act made provision for reserve forces but none were actually established.
1927	The A Line Reserve was established, composed of men who had completed their military service.
1928	A B Line Reserve was established of men recruited directly into the reserve. In total, the A and B Line Reserves formed nine infantry battalions numbered 6th to 14th and also other corps units, with the exception of Military Police and Ordnance.
1929	A Volunteer Reserve was established to recruit civilians directly into the reserve forces. This force co-existed with the previous A and B Line Reserve. The Volunteer Reserve consisted of an Officer Training Corps (OTC) and the 1st City of Dublin Battalion.
	By 1930 the OTC had units in University College, Dublin, Trinity College, Dublin, University College, Cork, and Royal College of Surgeons In Ireland. A further Volunteer Reserve unit was later formed in Cork: the 1st Cork Field Battery.

1931 A report of this year outlined the reserves as consisting of:
   a reserve of officers, composed of ex-regular officers
   the A and B Reserve
   the Volunteer Reserve and the OTC.

1932 The strength of the army consisted of 14,632 men in total, of which only 5,793 officers and men were serving in the regular army. The reserve actually made up the majority of Ireland's army but both the OTC and the Volunteer Reserve continued to recruit badly.

1934 In March recruiting began for the newly-formed Volunteer Force. This was an initiative of de Valera's Fianna Fail government and the force was envisaged as a counter-balance to Cumann na nGael elements within both the army and the existing reserves. Despite the fact that it introduced yet another reserve force into the army structure, it was highly successful, recruiting over 11,000 men by March 1935.

The Volunteer Force is also interesting as it represented perhaps the only occasion in the history of the Irish Defence Forces when a conscious effort was made to establish a system of titled regiments in an effort at creating an ethos of lineage, history and *espirit de corps*.

The force was organized on a three-line basis, the first-line members joining for a higher level of annual training. The second line enlisted for a lesser annual commitment while the third line was made up of civilians whose specializations would be called upon in wartime; i.e. doctors and engineers.

The regiments of the Volunteer Force and their respective recruiting districts, are outlined below:

   the Regiment of Oriel (Louth, Meath and Monaghan)
   the Regiment of Leinster (Kildare, West Wicklow, Wexford and Carlow)
   the Regiment of Dublin (County and Borough of Dublin and East Wicklow)
   the Regiment of Ormond (Kilkenny, Waterfod and Tipperary)[26]
   the Regiment of Thomond (Limerick and Clare)
   the Regiment of Connaught (Galway, Mayo and Roscommon)
   the Regiment of Breffni (Cavan, Longford, Leitrim and Sligo)
   the Regiment of Tírconnail (Donegal)
   the Regiment of Uisneach (Laois, Offaly and Westmeath)

1935 The OTC and the Volunteer Reserve were disbanded. A new regiment was established in the Volunteer Force, the Regiment of Pearse, which effectively operated as an OTC unit.

1939 On the outbreak of the Second World War, the army numbered 19,136 all ranks. Of these around 4,300 were A and B Reserve while a further 7,200 were from the Volunteer Force.

---

26 This regiment re-named as Regiment of Ossory in 1935.

1940 The reserves were totally re-organized for the Emergency period and in June the Local Defence Force was founded under the terms of the Emergency Powers Order. It was planned that this would be split into an A and B Group. A Group would serve as a military reserve while the B Group would serve as auxiliary police. Just under 45,000 men enlisted in the LDF in its first year.

1941 In January this new reserve force was re-organized. The A Group retained the title of Local Defence Forces while the B Group was re-named as the Local Security Force and tasked with operating in co-operation with An Garda Síochána.

1942 The strength of the LDF stood at 98,429 organized into local rifle platoons and companies which were further grouped into battalions and district groups.

1943 The strength of the LDF reached its wartime high at 103,530.

LOCAL DEFENCE FORCES (LDF) ORGANIZATION

EASTERN COMMAND

Area	Unit
Dublin North	41st Battalion
	42nd Battalion
	11th Cyclist
	11th Eningeers
	11th Communications
	41st Field Artillery
	Collinstown
	Coastal
	Liffey
	LDF Cyclist Regiment
	ARP Dublin
Dublin South	43rd Battalion
	44th Battalion
	45th Battalion
	11th Field Ambulance
	11th Supply & Transport
	Baldonnel
	Dun Laoghaire
	Rathfarnham
	ARP Dun Laoghaire
Oriel	Cavan
	Carrickmacross
	Bailieboro
	Dundalk
	Monaghan

Area	Unit
Boyne	Drogheda
	Gormanston
	Kells
	Trim
Wicklow	Bray
	Wicklow
	26th Battalion

CURRAGH COMMAND

Area	Unit
Kildare-Offaly	Athy
	Curragh
	Edenderry
	Naas
	Tullamore
Leix-Carlow	Abbeyleix
	Carlow
	Muinebeag
	Portlaoise
Waterford City	46th Battalion
Waterford-Kilkenny	Callan
	Carrick-on-Suir
	Castlecomber
	Kilkenny
	Kilmacthomas
	Thomastown
Wexford	Baltinglass
	Enniscorthy
	Gorey
	New Ross
	Wexford

WESTERN COMMAND

Area	Unit
Breffni	Arva
	Ballyconnell
	Carrick-on-Shannon
	Mohill
Galway (East)	Athenry
	Ballinasloe
	Gort

Area	Unit
	Loughrea
	Tuam
Shannon	Athlone
	Boyle
	Birr
	Castlerea
	Roscommon
	Strokestown
Galway (West)	Clifden
	Oughterard
Midlands	Castlepollard
	Granard
	Longford
	Mullingar
Mayo	Ballina
	Belmullet
	Castlebar
	Claremorris
	Swinford
	Westport
Sligo	Ballymote
	Enniscrone
	Manorhamilton
	Sligo
Donegal	Ballyshannon
	Buncrana
	Dungloe
	Killybegs
	Letterkenny
	Milford
	Inishowen
Galway City	50th Battalion

SOUTHERN COMMAND

Cork City	47th Battalion
	48th Battalion
Clare	Ennis
	Ennistymon

Area	Unit
	Killaloe
	Kilrush
	Lisdoonvarna
Cork (North)	Blarney
	Fermoy
	Kanturk
	Mallow
Cork (West)	Bandon
	Bantry
	Carrigaline
	Castletownbere
	Clonakilty
	Macroom
	Skibbereen
Kerry	Cahirciveen
	Dingle
	Listowel
	Killarney
	Killorglin
	Tralee
Limerick City	49th Battalion
Limerick	Abbeyfeale
	Adare
	Bruff
	Galtee
	Nenagh
	Newcastlewest
	Newport
	Pallas
Tipperary	Cahir
	Clonmel
	Dungarvan
	Lismore
	Middleton
	Templemore
	Thurles
	Tipperary

1946   As part of post-war reductions in the size of the army and reserve, the LDF was run down and brought to peacetime establishment.

1947   The reserves were re-organized once again, on this occasion into a First Line Reserve consisting of ex-servicemen and also a reformed volunteer reserve force. This new reserve took the Irish form of the 'Local Defence Force' title and was named as the Fórsa Cosanta Áitúil or FCA.

1950   The strength of the FCA stood at 21,784 men, all ranks.

1959   The units of the Permanent Defence Forces (PDF) were integrated with FCA personnel.

FORSA COSANTA ÁITUIL (FCA) ESTABLISHMENT 1970

In 1970, the Irish Defence Forces was organized into four command areas. On operations, the army was organized into six brigades. The FCA establishment is listed below but it should be pointed out that the FCA and Permanent Defence Forces (PDF) had been integrated since 1959. Therefore some units contained a mixed establishment of PDF, FCA and 1st Line Reserve personnel. These units have been indicated below. The table of FCA establishment is somewhat deceptive therefore as other units which were not designated as being FCA, contained FCA personnel. It was not until 1979 that this integration policy was ended.

Infantry FCA (with PDF cadres)

7th Infantry Battalion	17th Infantry Battalion
8th Infantry Battalion	18th Infantry Battalion
9th Infantry Battalion	19th Infantry Battalion
10th Infantry Battalion	20th Infantry Battalion
11th Infantry Battalion	21st Infantry Battalion
13th Infantry Battalion	22nd Infantry Battalion
14th Infantry Battalion	23rd Infantry Battalion
15th Infantry Battalion	24th Infantry Battalion
16th Infantry Battalion	

Artillery
1st Field Artillery Regiment (226 FCA)
2nd Field Artillery Regiment (277 FCA)
3rd Field Artillery Regiment (excluding cadre, all FCA)
4th Field Artillery Regiment (299 FCA)
5th Field Artillery Regiment (excluding cadre, all FCA)
6th Field Artillery Regiment (excluding cadre, all FCA)
1st Anti-Aircraft Regiment (395 FCA)
Coastal Defence Artillery, Southern command (71 PDF plus 81 FCA)

Cavalry
3rd Motor Squadron   11th Motor Squadron
5th Motor Squadron

Engineers
1st Field Engineer Coy (118 PDF, 66 FCA)
2nd Field Engineering Coy (119 PDF, 43 FCA)
3rd Field Engineering Coy
4th Field Engineering Coy (70PDF, 80FCA)
5th Field Engineering Coy
11th Field Engineering Coy

Signals
3rd Field Signals Coy   11th Field Signals Coy
5th Field Signals Coy

Supplies and Transport
1st Field S&T Coy (39PDF, 41FCA)   4th Field S&T Coy (55PDF, 10 1st
2nd Field S&T Coy (43PDF, 54 1st   Line Reserve, 50 FCA)
  Line Reserve, 43 FCA)   5th Field S&T Coy
3rd Field S&T Coy   11th Field S&T Coy

Army Medical Service
1st Field Medical Coy   4th Field Medical Coy (at cadre strength)
2nd Field Medical Coy   5th Field Medical Coy (at cadre strength)
3rd Field Medical Coy   11th Field Medical Coy

Military Police Corps
1st Field MP Coy   4th Field MP Coy
2nd Field MP Coy   5th Field MP Coy
3rd Field MP Coy   6th Field MP Coy

1976	The strength of the entire Defence Forces stood at 34,385, of which 18,850 were FCA.
1979	The Defence Forces were re-organized and the PDF and FCA were separated, ending the integration arrangement that dated back to 1959.
1981	The DF strength was 38,086 of which 22,214 were FCA.
1990	A report of this year showed that the strength of the army was 11,395 PDF personnel, 878 1st Line Reserve and 15,320 FCA.
2002	As part of a departmental White Paper, the structure of the Defence Forces was vastly re-organized. This re-organization also included the FCA, which was re-named as the Reserve Defence Forces. The reserves were totally re-structured and the pre-2005 establishment and post-2005 establishment are both outlined below.

PRE-2005 FCA ESTABLISHMENT

3rd Southern Brigade
    9th Infantry Battalion
    10th Infantry Battalion
    11th Infantry Battalion
    13th Infantry Battalion
    14th Infantry Battalion
    15th Infantry Battalion
    22nd Infantry Battalion
    23rd Infantry Battalion
    3rd Field Artillery Regiment
    8th Field Artillery Regiment
    3rd Field Engineer Coy
    3rd Field Signals Coy
    3rd Cavalry Squadron
    1st Field MP Coy
    3rd Field MP Coy
    3rd Field Transport Coy
    1st Field Medical Coy
    3rd Field Medical Coy

5th Western Brigade
    16th Infantry Battalion
    17th Infantry Battalion
    18th Infantry Battalion
    19th Infantry Battalion
    24th Infantry Battalion
    25th Infantry Battalion
    5th Field Artillery Regiment
    9th Field Artillery Regiment
    5th Field Engineer Coy
    5th Field Signals Coy
    4th Field MP Coy
    5th Field MP Coy
    5th Field Transport Coy
    5th Field Med Coy

6th Eastern Brigade
    20th Infantry Battalion
    21st Infantry Battalion
    7th Infantry Battalion
    8th Infantry Battalion
    7th Field Artillery Regiment
    6th Field Artillery Regiment
    11th Field Engineer Coy
    11th Field Signals
    11th Cavalry Squadron
    2nd Field MP Coy
    6th Field MP Coy
    11th Field Transport Coy
    27th Field Medical Coy

ESTABLISHMENT OF THE RESERVE DEFENCE FORCES FOLLOWING THE 2005 RE-STRUCTURING OF THE FCA

1st Southern Brigade
    RDF HQ
    32nd Reserve Infantry Battalion (Tralee)
    33rd Reserve Infantry Battalion (Wexford)
    34th Reserve Infantry Battalion (Fermoy)
    31st Reserve Artillery Regiment (Templemore)
    31st Reserve Cavalry Squadron (Clonmel)
    31st Reserve Engineering Coy (Limerick)

31st Reserve CIS Coy (Limerick)
31st Reserve MP Coy (Limerick)
31st Reserve LSB (Limerick)RDF 1st BTC

2nd Eastern Brigade
RDF HQ
62nd Reserve Infantry Battalion (Cathal Brugha Barracks, Dublin)
65th Reserve Infantry Battalion (McKee Barracks, Dublin)
67th Reserve Infantry Battalion (Aiken Barracks, Dundalk)
62nd Reserve Artillery Regiment (McKee Barracks)
62nd Reserve Cavalry Squadron (Cathal Brugha Barracks)
62nd Reserve Engineering Coy (McKee Barracks)
62nd Reserve CIS Coy (Cathal Brugha Barracks)
62nd Reserve MP Coy (Cathal Brugha Barracks)
62nd Reserve LSB Coy (Cathal Brugha Barracks)
RDF 2nd BTC

4th Western Brigade
RDF HQ
51st Reserve Infantry Battalion (Galway)
56th Reserve Infantry Battalion (Athlone)
58th Reserve Infantry Battalion (Finner)
54th Reserve Artillery Regiment (Mullingar)
54th Reserve Cavalry Squadron (Longford)
54th Reserve Engineering Coy (Galway)
54th Reserve CIS Coy (Athlone)
54th Reserve MP Coy (Athlone)
54th LSB (Galway)
RDF 4th BTC

The reserve component of the 1st Air Defence Regiment consists of:
2nd Air Defence Battery   4th Air Defence Battery
3rd Air Defence Battery

Archives

For a comprehensive listing of archival sources for Irish military history, the reader should consult Brian Hanley's *A guide to Irish military heritage* (Dublin, 2004), produced by the Military Heritage of Ireland Trust. This guide provides a wealth of information on archival sources in Ireland and also gives references to useful websites that deal with numerous aspects of Ireland's military history. The main repository of records for the modern Irish Defence Forces is the Military Archives in Cathal Brugha Barracks in Dublin.

Due to the fact that thousands of Irish soldiers served in foreign armies, there are also numerous collections with material of Irish relevance abroad. In England, there are official records in the National Archives in Kew and in the collections of personal papers in the Imperial War Museum and the National Army Museum. There are also regimental museums all over England that hold the personal papers of Irish officers and soldiers.

The main repository of records for all Irish regiments in the French service is the Service Historique de la Défense, based at Chateau Vincennes, outside Paris. Further material relating to Irish military pensioners is held at Les Invalides, Paris. Also in Paris, there are files relating to Irish officers and soldiers in the Bibliothèque Nationàle, the Archives Nationales and the Archives du Ministère des Affaires Étrangères.

In Italy, material relating to Irish units is held in the Vatican Archives and also in various branches of the Archivio di Stato, most notably the branches in Parma and Naples. The American National Archives in Washington holds much material relating to Irish regiments in the American Civil War while further material is held in the various state archives around the country. There is further material held in military and national archives in Spain, Austria, South Africa and Australia.

Museums

In October 2006, the National Museum of Ireland opened a major new military exhibition at its premises at Collins Barracks in Dublin. It is entitled 'Soldiers and Chiefs: the Irish at war at home and abroad since 1550'. This excellent exhibition covers all aspects of Ireland's long and distinguished military history and makes reference to the Irish soldiers who in numerous different armies, from the sixteenth century up to modern service with the UN. There is also a museum in Collins Barracks, Cork.

There are also further regimental museums in Ireland. These include the museums of the Connaught Rangers (Boyle House, Roscommon), the Royal Ulster Rifles (Belfast), the Royal Inniskilling Fusiliers (Enniskillen), the Royal Irish Fusiliers (Armagh) and the Royal Irish Regiment (Ballymena). Both the Imperial War Museum and the National Army Museum in London hold artefacts relating to the Irish regiments. Some other regimental museums in England also hold material of Irish interest. For a full listing of these museums, see the website of the Army Museums Ogilby Trust (http://www.armymuseums.co.uk).

Due to the extensive nature of Irish military service, it is also possible to find artefacts with Irish regimental connections in museums across Europe and the United States. Again, Brian Hanley's *A guide to Irish military heritage* provides a comprehensive list of museums with material relating to Irish regiments.

Select bibliography

Journals and magazines
An Cosantóir
Die Suid-Africaanse Krygshistoriese Vereeniging (Journal of the South African Military History Society)
History Ireland
Irish Guards Journal
Journal of the Army Records Society
Regiment
Rivista Historia Militar
Revue Historique des Armées
Revue de Société des Amis du Musée de l'Armée
Soldiers of the Queen
The Irish Sword
The War Correspondent

General histories
T. Bartlett and K. Jeffery, *A military history of Ireland* (Cambridge, 1996).
Desmond and Jean Bowen, *Heroic option: the Irish in the British army* (Barnsley, South Yorksire, 2005).
T. Bowman, *Irish regiments in the Great War: discipline and morale* (Manchester, 2003).
A.E.C. Bredin, *A history of the Irish soldier* (Belfast,1997).
D. Chandler and I. Beckett (eds), *The Oxford History of the British Army* (Oxford, 1996).
C. Messenger, *For love of regiment* (2 volumes, London, 1994–6).

Stuart army
J. D'Alton, *King James's Irish army list, 1689* (Limerick, 1997).
R. Doherty, *The Williamite War in Ireland, 1688–91* (Dublin, 1998).
F. Hogan, *Négotiations de Monsieur Le Comte d'Avaux en Irelande, 1689–90* (2 volumes, Irish Manuscripts Commission, Dublin, 1934–58).
S. Ede-Borrett, *The army of James II: uniforms and organisation* (Leeds, 1987).
J. Kinross, *The Boyne and Aughrim: the war of the two kings* (Moreton-in-Marsh, Gloucs., 1998).
W.A. Maguire (ed.), *Kings in conflict: the revolutionary war in Ireland and its aftermath, 1689–1750* (Belfast, 1990).
S. Mulloy (ed.), *Franco-Irish correspondence, 1688–1692* (3 vols, Irish Manuscripts Commission, Dublin, 1983).
M. McNally and G. Turner, *The battle of the Boyne: the Irish campaign for the English crown* (Oxford, 2005).
É. Ó Ciardha, *Ireland and the Jacobite cause, 1685–1766* (Dublin, 2002).

American and South American armies

J.G. Bilby, *The Irish Brigade in the Civil War* (2nd edition, Cambridge, MA, 1997).

T. Conolly, *An Irishman in Dixie: Thomas Conolly's diary of the fall of the Confederacy* (Columbia, SC, 1988).

D.P. Conyngham, *The Irish Brigade and its campaigns* (New York, 1867, reprinted New York, 1994).

F.H. Dyer, *A compendium of the war of the rebellion* (Morningside Press, 1994).

F. Forde, 'The Sixty-Ninth Regiment of New York' in *Irish Sword*, 17:68 (1989), 145–58.

J. P. Gannon, *Irish rebels: Confederate Tigers: a history of the 6th Louisiana Volunteers* (Mason City, IA, 1998)

J.L. Garland, 'Irish soldiers of the American Confederacy' in *Irish Sword*, 1:3 (1951–2), 174–80.

J.L. Garland, 'The Irish Dragoons in the American Civil War' in *Irish Sword*, 1:1 (1949–50), 37–9.

J.L. Garland, 'Michael Corcoran and the formation of his Irish Legion' in *Irish Sword*, 17:66 (Summer 1967), 26–40.

D. Gleeson, *The Irish in the South, 1815–1877* (Chapel Hill, NC, 2001).

E. Gleeson, *Rebel sons of Erin: a Civil War unit history of the Tenth Tennessee Infantry Regiment (Irish) Confederate States Volunteers* (Vincennes, IN, 1993).

T. Hooker & Ron Poulter, *The armies of Bolivar and San Martin* (Oxford, 1991).

M. Hogan, *The Irish soldiers of Mexico* (Guadalijara, Mexico, 1998).

M. Hogan, 'The Irish Soldiers of Mexico' in *Crisis Magazine* (March 2004), 31–6.

M.P. Joselyn (ed.), *A meteor shining brightly: essays on Maj.-Gen. Patrick R. Cleburne* (Macon, GA, 1998).

L. Kohl (ed.), *Irish green and blue: the Civil War letters of Peter Welsh, colour sergeant, 28th Massachusetts Volunteers* (New York, 1960).

E. Lonn, *Foreigners in the Union Army and Navy* (Baton Rouge, LA, 1951).

E. Lonn, *Foreigners in the Confederacy* (Gloucester, MA, 1965).

W. McCarter, *My life in the Irish Brigade*, ed. Kevin E. O'Brien (Campbell, CA, 1996).

R.B. McCormack, 'The San Patricio deserters in the Mexican War, 1847' in *Irish Sword*, 3:13 (Winter 1958), 246–55.

J.F. Maguire, *The Irish in America* (London, 1868).

D.B. Mahin, *The blessed place of freedom: Europeans in Civil War America* (Washington, DC, 2002).

St Clair A. Mulholland, *The story of the 116th Pennsylvania Volunteers in the War of the Rebellion* (New York, 1996).

T.J. Mullen, 'The Irish Brigades in the Union Army, 1861–65' in *Irish Sword*, 9:37 (Winter 1970), 318–29.

P.D. O'Flaherty, 'The 69th Regiment at Bull Run' in *Irish Sword*, 7:26 (Summer 1965), 2–4.

K. O'Grady, *Clear the Confederate way: The Irish in the army of Northern Virginia* (Mason City, IA and London, 2000).

C. Samito (ed.), *Commanding Boston's Irish Ninth: the Civil War letters of Colonel Patrick R. Guiney* (New York, 1997).

P.F. Stevens, *The Rogue's March: John Riley and the St Patrick's Battalion, 1846–48* (Washington, DC, 1999).

F. von Allendorfer, 'An Irish regiment in Brazil, 1826–1828' in *Irish Sword*, 3:10 (Summer 1957), 28–31.

F. von Allendorfer, 'The Western Irish Brigade' in *Irish Sword*, 2:7 (Winter 1955), 177–83.
The Irish Sword, 23:91 (Summer 2002) was a special issue devoted to the subject of Ireland and the American Civil War.

British army
For a comprehensive listing of regimental histories of Irish regiments in the British army, see A.S. White, *A bibliography of regimental histories of the British Army* (2nd edition, N&M Press, 1992).

Anon., *North Irish Horse battle report, North Africa and Italy* (Belfast, 1946).
Anon., *Memoirs and services of the Eighty-Third Regiment, County of Dublin, from 1793 to 1907* (London, 1908).
C. Blacker, *Change and challenge: the story of the 5th Royal Inniskilling Dragoon Guards 1928–1978 together with an account of their parent regiments, the 5th Princess Charlotte of Wales's Dragoon Guards and the 6th Inniskilling Dragoons* (London, 1978).
J.M. Brereton, *A history of the 4th/7th Royal Dragoon Guards and their predecessors* (Catterick, North Yorks., 1982).
J. Calder, *A year in the life of the London Regiment: an illustrated record* (London, 2001).
R. Cannon, *Historical record of the Sixth or Inniskilling Regiment of Dragoons, containing an account of the formation of the regiment in 1689 and its subsequent service to 1843* (London, 1843).
R. Cannon, *Historical record of the Fourth or Royal Irish Regiment of Dragoon Guards* (London, 1839).
M. Chappell, *Wellington's Peninsula regiments (1): the Irish* (Oxford, 2003).
B. Cooper, *The Tenth (Irish) Division in Gallipoli* (Dublin, 1993 ed.).
M.J. Corbally, *London Irish Rifles, 1859–1959: the regimental centenary* (Glasgow, 1959).
Major J.J. Crooks, *History of the Royal Irish Regiment of Artillery* (Dublin, 1914).
R. Doherty, *The North Irish Horse: a hundred years of service* (Staplehurst, Kent, 2002).
R. Doherty and D. Truesdale, *Irish winners of the Victoria Cross* (Dublin, 2000).
R. Doherty, *Clear the way: a history of the 38th (Irish) Brigade, 1941–47* (Dublin, 1993).
R. Doherty, *Irish Volunteers in the Second World War* (Dublin, 2001).
R. Doherty, *Irish generals in the Second World War* (Dublin, 2004).
C. Falls, *The history of the 36th (Ulster) Division* (Belfast and London, 1922).
John Filmer-Bennett, *The Royal Inniskilling Fusiliers, 1945–1968* (London, 1978).
Desmond J. Fitzgerald, *History of the Irish Guards in the Second World War* (Aldershot, 1949).
Sir Frank Fox, *The Royal Inniskilling Fusiliers in the World War* (London, 1928).
Sir Frank Fox, *The Inniskilling Fusiliers in the Second World War* (Aldershot, 1951).
H. Gibb, *Record of the 4th Royal Irish Dragoon Guards in the Great War, 1914–18* (London, 1925).
G. Le M. Gretton, *The campaigns and history of the Royal Irish Regiment, from 1684 to 1902* (Edinburgh and London, 1911).
H. Hanna, *The Pals at Suvla Bay* (Dublin, 1917).
H. Harris, *The Irish regiments in the First World War* (Cork, 1968).
R.G. Harris, *The Irish regiments, 1683–1999* (2nd ed., Staplehurst, Kent, 1999).
J.R. Harvey, *The history of the 5th (Royal Irish) Regiment of Dragoons from 1689 to 1799, afterwards the 5th Royal Irish Lancers from 1858 to 1921* (Aldershot, 1923).
F.C. Hitchcock, *Stand To: a diary of the trenches, 1915–18* (London, 1937).
P.R. Innes, *History of the Bengal European Regiment, now the Royal Munster Fusiliers* (London, 1885).

E.S. Jackson, *The Inniskilling Dragoons: the records of an old heavy cavalry regiment* (London, 1909).

E.A. James, *British Regiments, 1914–1918* (5th ed., Dallington, East Sussex, 1998).

T. Johnstone, *Orange, Green and Khaki: the story of the Irish regiments in the great war, 1914–18* (Dublin, 1992).

Rudyard Kipling, *The Irish Guards in the Great War* (2 volumes, London, 1923).

G.B. Laurie, *History of the Royal Irish Rifles* (London, 1914).

J. Lucy, *There's a devil in the drum* (London, 1938).

J.D. Lunt, *The scarlet lancers: the story of the 16th/5th Queen's Royal Lancers, 1689–1992* (London, 1993).

F. Luttman-Johnson, *Records of the services of the 3rd Battalion, the Prince of Wales's Leinster Regiment (Royal Canadians) in the South African War* (London, 1913).

H. Malet, *Memoirs of the 18th Hussars* (London, 1907).

Allan Mallinson, *Light Dragoons: the origins of a new regiment* (Barnsley, Yorks., 1993).

Major Arthur Mainwaring, *Crown and company: the historical records of the 2nd Battalion, Royal Dublin Fusiliers*, vol. 1 (London, 1911)

D. Murphy, *Ireland and the Crimean War* (Dublin, 2002).

D. Murphy, *Irish Regiments in the World Wars* (Oxford, 2007).

D. Orr and D. Truesdale, *'The Rifles are there': the story of the 1st and 2nd Battalions, the Royal Ulster Rifles in the Second World War* (Barnsley, Yorks., 2005).

J. Potter, *Testimony to courage: the regimental history of the Ulster Defence Regiment* (London, 2001).

N. Steevens, *The Crimean Campaign with the Connaught Rangers, 1854–56* (London, 1878).

JW. Taylor, *The 1st Royal Irish Rifles in the Great War* (Dublin, 2002).

J. W. Taylor, *The 2nd Royal Irish Rifles in the Great War* (Dublin, 2005).

W.C. Trimble, *The historical record of the 27th Inniskilling Regiment* (London and Enniskillen, 1876).

P. Verney, *The Micks: the story of the Irish Guards* (London, 1970).

Irish Guards: the first hundred years 1900–2000 (Staplehurst, Kent, 2000).

Y.J. Watkins, *With the Inniskilling Dragoons: the record of a cavalry regiment during the Boer War, 1899–1902* (London, 1904).

Frederick Ernest Whitton, *The annals of the Prince of Wales's Leinster Regiment (Royal Canadians)* (London, 1922).

Fredrick Ernest Whitton, *A history of the Prince of Wales's Leinster Regiment (Royal Canadians)* (2 volumes, London, 1924).

W.T. Willcox, *The historical records of the Fifth (Royal Irish) Lancers from their foundation as Wynne's Dragoons (in 1689) to the present day* (London, 1908).

Colonel H.C. Wylly, *Crown and company: the historical records of the 2nd Battalion, Royal Dublin Fusiliers*, vol. 2 (Aldershot, 1923).

Colonel H.C. Wylly, *Neill's Blue Caps* (3 volumes, Aldershot, 1924).

French army

M. Byrne, *Memoirs* (Paris 1863, Dublin 1972).

P. Carles, 'Le corps Irlandais au service de la France sous le Consulat et l'Empire' in *Revue Historique des Armées*, 2 (1972), 55–74.

R. Chartrand and P. Courcelle, *Émigré and foreign troops in British service (1), 1793–1802* (Oxford, 1999).

R. Chartrand and P. Courcelle, *Émigré and foreign troops in British service (2),1803–15* (Oxford, 1999).
B. Clark and F.G. Thompson, 'Napoleon's Irish Legion, 1803–15: the historical record' in *Irish Sword*, 12:48 (Summer 1976), 165–72.
A. Corvisier, *L'Armée Française de la fin du XVIIIe Siècle au Ministère de Choiseul* (Paris, 1964).
G.C. Dempsey, *Napoleon's mercenaries: foreign units in the French army under the Consulate and Empire, 1799–1814* (London, 2002).
E. Fieffe, *Histoire des Troupes Etrangeres au service de France* (Paris, 1854).
J. Fleetwood, 'An Irish field-ambulance in the Franco-Prussian War' in *Irish Sword*, 6:24 (Summer 1964), 137–48.
J.G. Gallagher, *Napoleon's Irish Legion* (Carbondale, IL, 1993).
N. Genet-Rouffiac, 'The Wild Geese: les regiments irlandais au service de Louis XIV (1688–1715) in *Revue Historique des Armées*, 222 (March 2001), 35–48.
R. Hayes, *Irish swordsmen of France* (Dublin, 1934).
G. Hayes-McCoy, 'The Irish Company in the Franco-Prussian War' in *Irish Sword*, 1:4 (1952–3), 275–83.
M. Hennessy, *The Wild Geese* (Greenwich, 1973).
M.W. Kirwan, *La Compaigne Irlandaise: reminiscences of the Franco-German War* (Dublin and London, 1873).
C. Malaguti, *Historique du 87e Régiment* (Saint-Quentin, 1892).
M.G. McLaughlin and Chris Warner, *The Wild Geese: the Irish Brigades of France and Spain* (London, 1980).
W.S. Murphy, 'The Irish Brigade of France at the siege of Savannah' in *Irish Sword*, 2:6, (Summer 1955), 95–102.
E. Ó Ciardha, *Ireland and the Jacobite cause, 1685–1766: a fatal attachment* (Dublin, 2002).
C. Petrie, 'The Irish Brigade at Fontenoy' in *Irish Sword*, 1:3 (1951–2),166–72.
Lieutenant Rethore, *Historique du 92e Régiment d'Infanterie* (Paris,1889).
J. Richard and M.C. Reinertsen (eds), *L'armée française: an illustrated history of the French Army, 1790–1885 by Edouard Detaille* (New York, 1992).
R.V. Steele, 'FitzJames Regiment of Horse of the Irish Brigade' in *Irish Sword*, 2:7 (Winter 1955), 188–94.
R.V. Steele, 'The Regiment of Dillon' in *Irish Sword*, 3:11 (Winter 1957), 93–7.

Spanish army
F. Barado y Font, *Historia del ejercito española* (Madrid, 1884).
K. Bradley and M. Chappell, *International brigades in Spain, 1936–39* (Oxford, 1994).
E.M. Brett, *The British Auxiliary Legion in the First Carlist War, 1835–38* (Dublin, 2005).
F. Diez-Plaja, *El ejercito imperial* (Barcelona, 1951).
F. Forde, 'The Ultonia Regiment of the Spanish Army' in *Irish Sword*, 12:46 (Summer 1975), 36–41.
E. Holt, *The Carlist wars in Spain* (London,1967).
B. Jennings, *Wild Geese in Spanish Flanders, 1528–1700* (Dublin, 1964).
F. McGarry, *Irish politics and the Spanish Civil War* (Cork, 1999).
M.G. McLaughlin and C. Warner, *The Wild Geese: the Irish Brigades of France and Spain* (London, 1980).
T. Mullen, 'The Hibernia Regiment of the Spanish Army' in *Irish Sword*, 8:32 (Summer 1968), 218–25.

M. O'Riordan, *Connolly Column* (Dublin, 1979).
F. Ryan, *The book of the XV Brigade* (1938, republished 1975).
A. Somerville, *History of the British Legion and war in Spain* (London, 1839).
R.A. Stradling, *The Irish and the Spanish Civil War, 1936–1939* (Manchester, 1999).

Italian armies
G. F-H. Berkeley, *The Irish Battalion in the Papal Army of 1860* (Dublin, 1929).
The Marquess McSwiney, 'Notes on some Irish regiments in the service of Spain and of Naples in the eighteenth century' in *Proceedings of the Royal Irish Academy*, Series C, vol. XXXVII (1924–7), 158–74.
R. Dudley Edwards (ed.), *Ireland and the Italian Risorgimento* (Dublin, 1960).
J. O'Brien, 'Irish public opinion and the Risorgimento' in *Irish Historical Studies*, 24:135 (May 2005), 289–305.
P.A. O'Sullivan, 'The Irish Company in the Duke of Parma's bodyguard', unpublished MA thesis, University College Dublin (1959).

South Africa
O.E.F. Baker, 'The South African Irish Regiment: an exemplar of the military traditions of the Irish in South Africa' in *Journal of the South African Military History Society/ Die Suid-Africaanse Krygshistoriese Vereeniging*, vol. 6, no.1.
S. Monick, *Shamrock and Springbok: the Irish impact on South African Military History, 1689–1914* (Johannesburg, 1989).
S. Monick, and O.E.F. Baker, *Clear the Way, 'Faugh-a-ballagh': the military heritage of the South African Irish, 1880–1990* (2 volumes, Johannesburg, 1993).
D.P. McCracken, *The Irish pro-Boers* (Johannesburg and Cape Town, 1989).
D.P. McCracken, *MacBride's Brigade: Irish commandos in the Anglo-Boer War* (Dublin, 1999).

Irish Volunteers and post-1922 army
N. Conway, *The Bloods: the first fifty years of the Third Infantry Battalion* (1972).
J. P. Duggan, *A history of the Irish army* (Dublin, 1991).
F. Hannon (ed.), *21 years of loyal and dedicated service: 3rd Field Artillery Regiment, 1959–1980* (Kilkenny, 1980).
J. Millar (ed.), *50 Bliain Órga D'en F.C.A. leis an 16ú Cathlán Coisithe, 1946–1996* (Offaly, 1996).
L. O'Brien, *A history of the Pearse Battalion, 1946–1959* (Dublin, 2005).
D. MacCarron, 'Step together: Ireland's Emergency army, 1939–46 as told by its veterans (Dublin, 1999).
D. MacCarron and B. Younghusband, *The Irish Defence Forces since 1922* (Oxford, 2004).
T. McCaughren, *The peacekeepers of Niemba* (Dublin, 1966).
C. Cruise O'Brien, *To Katanga and back: a UN case history* (London, 1962).
B. O'Shea (ed.), *In the service of peace: memories of Lebanon* (Dublin, 2001).
D. Power, *The siege of Jadotville* (Dublin, 2005).
R. Smith, *The fighting Irish in the Congo* (Dublin, 1962).
R. Smith, *Under the Blue Flag* (Naas, 1980).
G. White and B. O'Shea, *The Irish Volunteer soldier, 1913–1923* (Oxford, 2003).
Irish Sword, special UN edition, volume 20:79 (Summer 1996).
United Nations Publications, *The Blue Helmets: A review of UN peace-keeping* (New York, 1986).

Addendum

While this book was in press I discovered another entry to be added to the Irish regiments in the British army:

No. 12 (IRISH AND WELSH) COMMANDO, 1940–3

In the summer of 1940 it was decided to form a series of army commando units to undertake raids into territory occupied by Axis forces. Thousands of officers and men volunteered for this duty in the hope of playing a more active part in the war. In August 1940 a commando unit was raised in Northern Ireland using volunteers from Irish and Welsh regiments. It was designated as No. 12 (Irish and Welsh) Commando.

After intensive training, No. 12 Commando carried out a series of raids on targets in Norwegian territory in 1941 including raids on Spitsbergen and the Lofoten Islands. It later carried out raids on the French coast. These included the raid on the German radar facility at Bruneval in February 1942, where No. 12 Commando covered the extraction of airborne troops. Following a re-organisation of the commando force in 1943, this commando was disbanded and its remaining personnel transferred to other units.

***

The Military Heritage of Ireland Trust acknowledges the support of the Defence Forces in this project.